Economics of Development and Planning

History, Principles, Problems and Policies

Fourth Revised and Enlarged Edition

Volume I

K.R. GUPTA

ATLANTIC

PUBLISHERS & DISTRIBUTORS (P) LTD

Published by

ATLANTIC

PUBLISHERS & DISTRIBUTORS (P) LTD

7/22, Ansari Road, Darya Ganj,
New Delhi-110002
Phones : +91-11-23273880, 23275880, 23280451
Fax : +91-11-23285873
Web : www.atlanticbooks.com
E-mail : info@atlanticbooks.com

Branch Office
5, Nallathambi Street, Wallajah Road,
Chennai-600002
Phones : +91-44-64611085, 32413319
E-mail : chennai@atlanticbooks.com

ISBN 978-81-269-1010-6 (Vol. I)
ISBN 978-81-269-1012-0 (Set)

Printed in India at Nice Printing Press, A-33/3A, Site-IV, Industrial Area, Sahibabad, Ghaziabad, U.P.

Preface

During the last two decades or so, there has been a vast output of literature on economic development, which however, lies widely scattered in various journals, documents, reports and papers published by the official, semi-official and non-official bodies in different countries and by international organisations; and in specialized books, monographs, continuums, research studies and sample surveys. An attempt has been made in this book to bring the widely scattered material under one cover.

Economics of Development and Planning is a standard book on the subject. It has a wide coverage, and comprehensively treats all the essential topics on the subject including theory, problems and policies of development. The views of major schools of thought represented by leading economists like Adam Smith, Ricardo, Malthus, Mill, Karl Marx, Keynes, Joan Robinson and J.A. Schumpeter have been explained for a proper understanding of present problems and policies for economic development, enabling the reader to know what great thinkers of the past have contributed to the subject. Old ideas shorn of circumstantial support have been appraised impartially, and the basic difference in approaches to development have been brought to the fore equipping the policymakers for better policy judgements.

Various economic theories like those of Capital Accumulation, Economic Growth, Critical Minimum Effort, Big Push and Harrod-Domar Model, Mahalanobis Model and Lewis Model of Economic Development have been included. Key economic concepts like capital formation from domestic as well as foreign sources, capital-output ratio, deficit financing, inflation, vicious circle of poverty, credit control, increasing returns to scale, balance of payments and many others have been discussed in detail. Besides, several other aspects of economic development, e.g. factors inhibiting growth, occupation structure, production-function approach to growth, role of public enterprise, resource allocation, etc. have been explained giving references from India's current economic scenario.

The book has been thoroughly revised and enlarged into two volumes. While new chapters on topics as latest as Social Capital, Liberalisation and Globalisation of Indian Economy, and Special Economic Zones have been included, those on Fiscal Policy and Foreign Trade have been replaced with comprehensive new chapters on these topics. Besides, the chapter 'Planning in India' has been updated right upto the Eleventh Five-Year Plan (2007-12) giving major objectives of economic planning in India such as alleviating poverty, bringing social change and broad-based development.

The book in the present form is more complete in coverage and hence, more useful to the students and teachers of Economics. The first eleven chapters will be of great interest to the students of History of Economic Thought. It will immensely benefit those preparing for various competitive examinations and also help those concerned with the formulation and execution of economic policies.

K.R. Gupta

Contents

VOLUME 2

Classical School

1

For a proper understanding of the present problems and the policies for economic development, a study of the development of the theory of economic growth is very essential. Meier and Baldwin have this to say in this regard:

> Since we are all too much affected by the times in which we live and are too prone to generalise from transitory circumstances, we are not likely to gain a clear understanding of economic development if we simply start with existing conditions and attempt to disentangle the major factors currently at work. A better approach might be to examine what the great thinkers of the past have contributed to the subject. Then we can attempt to determine in what respects they were right or wrong in the light of subsequent history.
>
> In this manner, we can free ourselves, at least partially, from the confines of our own times. And by sharpening our long-run perspective we can better equip ourselves for an analysis of the diverse conditions of the present.[1]

According to Nag:

> Old ideas shorn of circumstantial support may be appraised with impartiality and the basic differences in approaches to development may be brought to the fore, thereby equipping ourselves better for making policy judgements.[2]

In a book of this nature covering a wide field, it is not possible to comprehensively examine the views on economic growth of all the economists. We shall, therefore, briefly survey the views of only the major schools of thought and of only a few leading economists, *viz.,* (1) Adam Smith, Ricardo, Malthus and Mill from the classical

---

1. Gerald M. Meier and Robert E. Baldwin, *Economic Development* (New York, 1959), p. 18.
2. D.S. Nag, *Problems of Underdeveloped Economy* (Agra, 1962), p. 345.

school, (2) Karl Marx, (3) the historical school, particularly List, (4) the neo-classical school, particularly Marshall, (5) Schumpeter, (6) Keynes, secular stagnationists, Domar, Harrod, Joan Robinson, Meade, Mahalanobis, Lewis, Leibenstein, Myrdal, and Rostow, among the modern theorists on economic growth.

The classical school is recognised to be the first among the economists which tried to discover the causes of long-run growth and to analyse the process of growth. They realised the importance of casual relations among different sectors of the economy and tried to show the effect of such relationship on economic development. Their approach to the components of an economy was, of course, narrow. They believed that national income consisted of wages, rents and profits only. Agriculture and manufacturing alone were the productive activities for them. Nevertheless, within their narrow perspective, they analysed the process of development, and formulated certain policies which could accelerate development. Adam Smith, Ricardo, Malthus and Mills are the important economists in the classical school. Let us briefly discuss their views.

ADAM SMITH

1. Introductory

Adam Smith is the most famous among the classical economists. His *An Enquiry into the Nature and Causes of Wealth of Nations (1776)* is considered a classic in economics. Adam Smith has tremendous influence on later writers. A major part of Ricardo's theory of economic growth is nothing, but a rigorous, reasoned and elaborated statement of Adam Smith's ideas. Adam Smith's work consists more of a rough summary of economic ideas than of a rigorous and well-reasoned analysis.

2. Laissez Faire

Adam Smith advocates a policy of *laissez faire*. This is the best means of promoting development. It is always safe to leave the economy to be propelled by an 'invisible hand,' *i.e.*, the forces of competition motivated by individual self-interest. In a well-known passage, he argues:

> But the annual revenue of every society is always precisely equal to the exchangeable value of the whole produce of its industry, or rather is precisely the same thing with that exchangeable value. As every individual, therefore,

> endeavours as much as he can both to employ his capital in the support of domestic industry, and so to direct that industry that its produce be of the greatest value; every individual necessarily labours to render the annual revenue of society as great as he can...he intends only his own gain, and he is in this, as in many other cases, led by an invisible hand to promote an end which was no part of his intention.
>
> The statesman, who should attempt to direct private people in what manner they ought to employ their capitals, would not only load himself with a most necessary attention, but assume an authority which could safely be trusted not only to one single person, but to no council or senate whatever, and which would nowhere be so dangerous as in the hands of a man who had the folly and presumption enough to fancy himself fit to exercise it.[3]

Adam Smith is immensely influenced by the eighteenth century doctrine of natural law which asserts that

> there is a set of rules of right or justice, and perhaps even of morality in general, which are, or may be, known by all men by the help either of 'reason' or by a moral sense, and which possess an authority superior to that of such commands of human sovereigns, and such customary legal and moral regulations, as may contravene them.[4]

He extends the philosophy of natural law to economics. Economic phenomena are manifestations of an underlying order in nature, governed by natural forces. Adam Smith strongly condemns government or private actions which tend to hinder free and atomistic competition. He believes in harmony between the interests of individuals and that of society.

> By pursuing his own interest he (the individual)[5] frequently promotes that of the society more effectively than when he really intends to promote it.[6]

---

3. Adam Smith, *The Wealth of Nations* (ed.) Edwin Cannon (New York, 1937), p. 423.
4. O.H. Taylor, *Economics and Liberalism, Collected Papers* (Cambridge, 1955), p. 73.
5. Words within parantheses added.
6. Smith, *n.* 3, p. 423.

> Every individual is continually exerting himself to find out the most advantageous employment for whatever capital he can command. It is his own advantage indeed, and not that of the society, which he has in view. But the study of his own advantage naturally, or rather necessarily leads him to prefer that employment which is most advantageous to the society.[7]

The legal system resulting from the operation of the natural forces is the best means of promoting development. Every individual should have the freedom to pursue his self-interest free from oppression by other members. Special advantage and restraints in the economic world are contrary to the natural law and tend to hinder economic growth.

Smith, though primarily a believer in *laissez faire*, recognises the need for reforms for creating environments conducive to economic development. He suggests four major programmes of reform: the removal of impediments to free choice of occupation, to free trade in land, to internal free trade and to free trade in foreign commerce. He recognises the need for government activity in fields like public education, and hygiene, public works, regulation of currency and coinage, progressive (in effect, proportional) taxation, patents, copyrights, and even moderate export and import taxes for the purposes of revenue and development. The government in Smith's time was corrupt, inefficient and incompetent. It is probably this which led Smith to condemn government activity beyond its fundamental duties of justice and security.

Adam Smith considers the ambition of the rising merchant class in the eighteenth century to be an important driving force for development. It played no less important role than that of the innovator during and after the industrial revolution. Many new operators of shops and of shipping, entrepreneurs in manufacturing, brokers and traders became engulfed in the ambition to acquire wealth, prestige, and power. In pursuit of these ambitions, they sacrificed their joys of life in order to save and invest.

> The poor man's son, whom haven in its anger has visited with ambition, when he begins to look around him, admires the condition of the rich. He finds the cottage of

7. *Ibid.*, p. 421.

> his father too small for his accommodation, and fancies he should be lodged more at his ease in a palace...It appears in his fancy like the life of some superior rank of being, and in order to arrive at it, he devotes himself for ever to the pursuit of wealth and greatness. To obtain the conveniences which these afford, he submits in the first year, to more fatigue of body and more uneasiness of mind, than he could have suffered through the whole of his life from the want of them.[8]

3. Division of Labour

In Smith's analysis of economic progress, division of labour plays an important role. It originates from a natural propensity among men "to truck, barter, and exchange one thing for another."[9] It is self-interest which leads to exchange and thus to the division of labour.

Differences in the degree of division of labour are an important factor responsible for international and intertemporal differences in productivity.

> This great increase of the quantity of work, which in consequence of the division of labour, the same number of people are capable of performing, is owing to three different circumstances; first, to the increase of dexterity in every particular workman; secondly, to the saving of the time which is commonly lost in passing from one species of work to another; and lastly, to the invention of a great number of machines which facilitate and abridge labour, and enable one man to do the work of many.[10]

While division of labour is technically feasible, its economic usefulness is limited by the extent of the market.

> When market is very small, no person can have any encouragement to dedicate himself entirely to one employment, for want of the power to exchange all that surplus part of the produce of his own labour, which is

---

8. Adam Smith, *The Theory of Moral Sentiments* (London, 1880), pp. 259-60.
9. Smith, n. 13, p. 1.
10. *Ibid.*, p. 53.

> over and above his own consumption, for such parts of the produce of other man's labour as he has occasion for.[11]

The size of the market, in turn, depends upon the amount of capital in existence and the institutional restrictions that are placed upon trade.

As the accumulation of stock must, in the nature of things, be previous to the division of labour, so labour can be more and more subdivided in proportion only as stock is previously more and more accumulated.[12]

Expansion of international trade is an important method of widening the market and of promoting the division of labour. Speaking of the discovery of America, Smith states:

> By opening a new and inexhaustible market to all the commodities of Europe, it gave occasion to new division of labour and improvement of art, which, in the narrow circle of the ancient commerce, could never have taken place for want of a market to take off the greater part of their produce. The productive powers of labour were improved and its produce increased in all the different countries of Europe, and together with it the real revenue and wealth of the inhabitants.[13]

Restrictions on international trade limit the size of the market. Trade restrictions diminish the scope for international specialisation and thereby lower domestic productivity.

> No regulation of commerce can increase the quantity of industry in any society beyond what its capital can maintain. It can only divert a part of it into a direction into which it might not otherwise have gone; and it is by no means certain that this artificial direction is likely to be more advantageous to the society than that into which it would have gone of its own accord.[14]

Adam Smith assumes that there is an automatic flow of innovation which permits the degree of division of labour to adjust itself to the

11. *Ibid.*, p. 321.
12. *Ibid.*, p. 260.
13. *Ibid.*, p. 416.
14. *Ibid.*, p. 421.

size of the capital stock. Changes in productivity, therefore, are not hindered by a lack of suitable technology. In contrast, the utilisation of the technological improvements is limited by the availability of sufficient capital.

> The person who employs his stock in maintaining labour, endeavours, therefore, both to make among his workmen the most proper distribution of employment, and to furnish them with the best machines which he can either invent or afford to purchase. His abilities in both these respects are generally in proportion to the extent of his stock, or to the number of people whom it can employ.[15]

4. Accumulation of Capital

The accumulation of capital plays an important role in the process of growth.

> Every increase or diminution of capital, therefore, mutually tends to increase or diminish the real quantity of industry, the number of productive hands, and consequently the exchangeable value of the annual produce of the land and labour of the country, the real wealth and revenue of all its inhabitants.[16]

> The annual produce of the land and labour of any nation can be increased in its value by no other means but by increasing either the number of its productive labourers, or the productive powers of those labourers who had before been employed. The number of its productive labourers, it is evident, can never be much increased, but in consequence of an increase of capital, or the funds destined for maintaining them. The productive powers of the same number of labourers cannot be increased, but in consequence either of some addition and improvement to those machines and instruments which facilitate and abridge labour; or of a more proper division and distribution of employment. In either case an additional capital is almost always required.... When we compare, therefore, the state of a nation at two different periods, and find, that the annual produce of its

15. *Ibid.*, p. 260.
16. *Ibid.*, p. 321.

> land and labour is evidently greater at the latter than the former, that its lands are better cultivated, its manufactures more extensive, we may be assured that its capital must have increased during the interval between those two periods.[17]

The rate of output expansion goes hand in hand with the rate of investment. The output expands only when investment is positive. A constant capital stock, however large it may be, means stagnation. A declining capital stock implies retrogression.

The rate of investment, according to Smith, is determined by the rate of saving. He writes, "Capitals are increased by parsimony and diminished by prodigality and misconduct."[18] He does not recognise the possibility of leakages between the flow of saving and the transformation of the flow into investment. He states:

> Whatever a person saves from his revenue he adds to his capital, and either employs it himself in maintaining an additional number of productive hands, or enables some other person to do so, by lending it to him for an interest, that is, for a share of profits. As the capital of an individual can be increased only by what he saves from his annual revenue or his annual gains, so the capital of society, which is the same with that of all the individuals who compose it, can be increased only in the same manner.[19]

He again writes: "That portion which he (a rich man) annually saves...for the sake of profit...is immediately employed as capital."[20] He further states:

> In all countries where there is tolerable security, every man of common understanding will endeavour to employ whatever stock he can command, in procuring either present employment or future profit. If it is employed in procuring present employment, it is a stock reserved for immediate consumption. If it is employed in procuring future profit, it must procure this profit, either by staying with him, or by going from him. In the one case it is fixed,

---

17. *Ibid.*, p. 326.
18. *Ibid.*, p. 321.
19. *Ibid.*
20. *Ibid.*

> in the other circulating capital. A man, must be perfectly crazy who, where there is tolerable security, does not employ all the stock which he commands, whether it be his own or borrowed of other people, in some one or other of these three ways.[21]

What governs the allocation of income as between consumption and saving (or investment, as Smith identifies saving with investment)? Smith states that the "consideration of his own private profit is the sole motive which determines the owner of any capital to employ it."[22] The ability to save and invest is, however, limited by income.

> The capital of all individuals of a nation is increased in the same manner as that of a single individual, by their continually accumulating and adding whatever they save out of their income. It is likely to increase the fastest, therefore, when it is employed in the way that affords the greatest revenue to all the inhabitants of the country, as they will thus be enabled to make the greatest savings.[23]

The desire to save and invest for profit is a normal one. "As soon as stock has accumulated in the hands of particular persons, some of them will naturally employ it in setting to work industrious people."[24] "Every individual is continually exerting himself to find the most advantageous employment for whatever capital he commands."[25] The result is that so long as there are any profits over and above compensation for risk to be made by investment, capital accumulation will continue.

In the process of economic development, as the stock of capital grows, the profits tend to decline. "As riches, improvement and population have increased, interest has declined."[26] The reason for this is the competition among capitalists. "When the stock of many rich merchants are turned into the same trade, their mutual competition naturally tends to lower its profits; and when there is a

21. *Ibid.*, p. 268.
22. *Ibid.*, p. 355.
23. *Ibid.*, p. 347.
24. *Ibid.*, p. 48.
25. *Ibid.*, p. 421.
26. *Ibid.*, p. 93.

like increase of stock in all the different trades carried on in the same society, the same competition must produce the same effect on them all."[27] With the growth of the stock of capital, the wage rates tend to rise as a result of the competition among entrepreneurs for the scarce labour.[28] Further, as more profitable investment opportunities are taken first, the increased capital can be employed only at lower profits.

The rate of profit is also influenced by the institutional environment—the degree of regulation of commerce, the degree of monopoly or competition, and the control of international trade.[29] In regard to these matters, the interest of profit receivers does not always coincide with that of society.

The actual rate of profit also includes a risk premium.[30] The minimum rate of profit is sufficient to compensate for this factor.[31] The height of the risk premium is also strongly affected by the institutional structure. Important are in this regard the security of property and the legality of lending operations.[32]

How does a decline in interest rate affect capital accumulation? Smith believed that a decline in interest rate would increase the supply of capital. He argued that the rentiers—who live on income from lending—when faced with a decline in interest rate will increase their lending activity in order to maintain a certain standard of living. If the interest rates are high, the only borrowers who can afford to pay are "prodigals and projectors"; only a small amount will, therefore, be lent. With a decline in the interest rate, entrepreneurs will enter the loanable funds market. "A great part of the capital of the country is thus thrown into the hands in which it is most likely to be employed with advantage."[33] At the same time, the decline in interest increases the supply of loanable funds. As the interest rates decline further, the rentiers will find that they can no

27. *Ibid.*, p. 37.
28. *Ibid.*, p. 336.
29. *Ibid.*, p. 250.
30. *Ibid.*, p. 111.
31. *Ibid.*, p. 96.
32. *Ibid.*, pp. 118-43.
33. *Ibid.*, pp. 339-40.

longer live on property income and will be forced to turn entrepreneurs themselves.

> As the ordinary rate of clear profit would be very small, so the usual market rate of interest which could be afforded out of it, would be so low as to render it impossible for any but the very wealthiest of people to live upon the interest of their money. All people of small or middling fortunes would be obliged to superintend themselves the employment of their own stocks. It would be necessary that almost every man should be a man of business, or engage in some sort of trade.[34]

By means of such social changes, capital accumulation will continue in spite of low rate of interest. In fact, according to Smith, "It is with industrious nations, who are advancing in the acquisition of riches, as with industrious individuals. A great stock, though with small profits, generally increases faster than a small stock with greater profits."[35] This happy state of affairs will continue until the country has acquired, "that full complement of riches which the nature of its soil and climate, and its situation with respect to other countries, allowed it to acquire." When the country possesses as much capital as it can profitably employ, and is "fully stocked in proportion to all the business it had to transact," the rates of interest would drop to a level at which the rate of profit is the minimum necessary to compensate for the risk premium. At this stage, additional investment will not lead to any profit, net of risk element, capital accumulation will stop, population will remain constant and the economy will enter the stationary state.

5. Cumulative Process

Smith believes that the development process is cumulative, that is, once started, it automatically gathers momentum. Given adequate market possibilities and the basis for capital formation, division of labour takes place and raises the level of productivity. The resultant increase in production and the probable growth of population associated with it increases the size of the market and makes possible larger savings out of the increased incomes. Further, with the increase in specialisation and the expansion of markets, the

34. *Ibid.*, p. 96.
35. *Ibid.*, pp. 94-95.

ability and incentive to introduce 'improvements of art' increase; these improvements lead to still further specialisation and productivity gains. Similarly any downward movement becomes cumulative in nature.

6. Stationary State

According to Smith the cumulative process of growth ultimately ends in a stationary state. This is the uppermost limit to growth. The stationary state is not a state of underdevelopment. In such an economy, the per capita output is stagnant, wages are at the subsistence level, profits are at the minimum consistent with risk, no net investment takes place, population remains unchanged and total income is constant.

> In a country which had acquired that full complement of riches which the nature of its soil and climate, and its situation with respect to other countries, allowed it to acquire; which could, therefore, advance no further, and which was not going backward, both the wages of labour and the profits of stock would probably be very low. In a country fully peopled in proportion to what either its territory could maintain or its stock employ, the competition for employment would necessarily be so great as to redue the wages of labour to what was barely sufficient to keep up the number of labourers, and the country being already fully peopled, the number could never be augmented. In a country fully stocked in proportion to all the business it had to transact, as great a quantity of stock would be employed in every particular branch as the nature and extent of trade would admit. The competition, therefore, would everywhere be as great and consequently the ordinary profit as low as possible.[36]

Whether the economy is to follow a path of growth or retrogression or is to be in a stationary state or a state of underdevelopment depends considerably on the nature of institutional setting. A poor legal system was responsible for the situation of China in Smith's time. Defective economic and political institutions were to be blamed for Bengal's plight.

---

36. *Ibid.*, pp. 94-95.

7. Sequence of Development

Smith believes that "according to the natural course of things"[37] as the economy moves towards the stationary state, the sequence of economic development is first agriculture, then manufactures, and finally, commerce. He believes that the production of an agricultural surplus to support the non-farm population is very essential for economic development. He describes the process of development like this: In the beginning, because of a highly favourable labour-resource ratio, clothing and housing are free goods. As population grows, these become scarce and yield a rent. This induces technical improvements which are applied to agriculture. With the application of technical improvements, it is possible to produce the required food with a smaller proportion of the labour force and thus the workers are relieved for other occupations.

> ...when by the improvement and cultivation of land, the labour of one family can provide food for two, the labour of half the society becomes sufficient to provide food for the whole. The other half, therefore, or at least the greater part of them, can be employed in providing other things, or in satisfying the other wants and fancies of mankind.[38]

Creation of agricultural surplus creates demand for the goods and services which can be bought with the surplus agricultural products. This induces the establishment of manufacturing industries. Interdependently, the increasing urban population requires more food and, therefore, has to increase the supply of manufactures to pay for it.

8. Conclusion

Adam Smith, though not very rigorous in his analysis, has a profound influence on the later economists. His emphasis on capital accumulation for economic development is a fundamental element in the later theories of development. His idea of the stationary state dominates the thinking of classical writers. His view that, during the course of development, real prices of manufactured commodities tend to fall and the real prices of some types of agricultural products tend to rise has considerable influence on the thinking of the classical writers. His policy of *laissez faire* aroused considerable

37. *Ibid.*, p. 360.
38. *Ibid.*, p. 163.

controversy among the later writers. His view of economic development as a gradual and self-perpetuating (of course, within limits) process is adopted by most of the later classical and neo-classical economists. Smith presents his views on economic growth in the form of general economic principles rather than in the form of a theory of economic growth. This is an important contribution towards the search for the most suitable approach to the study of economic development. Development is a very complex phenomenon and cannot be presented in a single clear-cut theory. Recent tendency towards theorising and towards model-building has done a great harm to economic analysis. The formulators of theories and the builders of models concentrate on a single or on a few variables to the utter neglect of all other variables which cannot be brought together in a single theory or a model.

DAVID RICARDO

1. Introduction

Ricardo is the first economist to present the classical doctrine into a consistent body of economic analysis. Drawing profusely on Adam Smith, he refines and extends the classical theory of economic development. But Ricardo is interested more in the theory of value and distribution than in the theory of economic development. Schumpeter goes to the extent of saying that Ricardo "all but identifies economics with the theory of distribution, implying that he had little or nothing to say about—to use his language—the laws which regulate total output."[39] Ricardo's views on economic development are not presented in a well-knit manner and are haphazardly scattered in his book, *The Principles of Political Economy and Taxation* (1817) and in his several letters written to other economists.

Ricardian model of economic development is based on two fundamental principles *viz.* (1) principle of diminishing returns and (2) principle of population growth. A thorough understanding of these two principles is very essential for understanding Ricardo's views on economic development. We describe below these two principles briefly.

39. Joseph A. Schumpeter, *History of Economic Analysis* (New York, 1954), pp. 568-69.

2. Diminishing Returns

When under the pressure of increasing population, cultivation is extended to less fertile land, the same doses of labour and capital yield a smaller increment of produce.

> Thus suppose land—No. 1, 2, 3,—to yield, with an equal employment of capital and labour, a net produce of 100, 90, and 80 quarters of corn. In a new country, where there is an abundance of fertile land compared with the population, and where therefore it is only necessary to cultivate No. 1, the whole net produce will belong to the cultivator, and will be the profits of stock which he advances. As soon as population has so far increased as to make it necessary to cultivate No. 2, increased rent would commence on No. 1.[40]

Similarly, if additional doses of labour and capital are applied to the same land, the successive increments in output will be smaller and smaller:

> It often, and indeed, commonly happens, that before No. 2, 3, 4, or 5, or the inferior lands are cultivated, capital can be employed more productively on those lands which are already in cultivation. It may perhaps be found that by doubling the original capital employed on No. 1, though the produce will not be doubled, will not be increased by 100 quarters, it may be increased by eighty-five quarters, and that this quantity exceeds what would be obtained by employing the same capital on land No. 3.[41]

Regardless of which course of action is followed, however, the marginal productivity of land, labour and capital declines. The rapidity of this decline is regulated by the rate at which innovations are introduced. In industry the effects of the technological progress outweigh the tendency towards diminishing returns and, therefore, there prevails the law of increasing returns.

> The actual price of all commodities, excepting raw produce and labour, has a tendency to fall in the progress of wealth and population; for though, on one hand, they are enhanced

---

40. David Ricardo, *The Principles of Political Economy and Taxation* (London: Dent and Son, 1937), p. 35.

41. *Ibid.*, p. 36.

> in real value, from the rise in the natural price of the raw material of which they are made, this is more than counterbalanced by the improvements in machinery, by the better division and distribution of labour, and by the increasing skill, both in science and art of the products.[42]

Ricardo appears to believe that the rate of innovations in agriculture would not be sufficient to offset the tendency for the diminishing returns to set in at either the intensive or the extensive margin of cultivation. The introduction of improvements in agricultural techniques, therefore, might sporadically check the tendency towards diminishing returns; but this would have only a temporary effect upon costs of agricultural production.

> With the progress of society the natural price of labour has always a tendency to rise, because one of the principal commodities by which its natural price is regulated (food) has a tendency to become dearer from the greater difficulty of producing it. As, however, the improvements in agriculture, the discovery of new markets whence provisions may be imported, may for a time counteract the tendency to a rise in the price of necessaries, and may even occasion their natural price to fall, so will the same causes produce the correspondent effects on the natural price of labour.[43]

Ricardo believes that secularly production of foods is subject to the law of diminishing returns. He postulates, in effect, that technological progress in agriculture is also subject to diminishing returns.

Secularly, manufacturing is subject to increasing returns, while agriculture is subject to diminishing returns. Which of these patterns, would prevail when the output of industry and agriculture is taken together? According to Ricardo, after all land has been brought under cultivation, the diminishing returns in agriculture outweigh the increasing returns in industry. As a result from a certain historical date onward, the rate of growth of output declines in expanding economies. By the same token, the rate of diminution of output diminishes in the receding economies.

> Although, then, it is probable that, under the most favourable circumstances, the power of production is still greater than

42. *Ibid.*, p. 52.
43. *Ibid.*

> that of population, it will not long continue so; for the land being limited in quantity, and differing in quality, with every increased portion of capital employed on it there will be a decreased rate of production, whilst the power of population continues always the same.[44]

While Adam Smith believes that the economy would grow at an accelerated rate, Ricardo's belief is that the growth would take place at a progressively declining rate.

3. Growth of Population

Ricardo defined land so as to include only the "original and indestructible powers of the soil."[45] Thus land, according to him, was fixed in supply.

In regard to the growth of population, Ricardo's views are similar to those of Adam Smith. Like Smith, he distinguishes between the market price of labour services and the "natural" wage rate. Ricardo's natural wage rate is the same as Smith's wage.

> The natural price of labour is that price which is necessary to enable the labourers, one with another, to subsist and to perpetuate their race, without either increase or diminution.[46]

If the market wages are above the natural wage, the growth of population would be encouraged and it would be discouraged in the reverse case.

> It is when the market price of labour exceeds its natural price that the condition of the labour is flourishing and happy, that he has it in his power to command a greater proportion of the necessaries and enjoyments of life, and therefore to rear a healthy and numerous family. When, however, by the encouragement which high wages give to the increase of population, the number of labourers is increased, wages again fall to their natural price, and indeed from a reaction sometimes fall below it. When the market price of labour is below its natural price, the condition of the labourers is most wretched; then poverty deprives them of those comforts which custom renders

44. *Ibid.*, p. 56.
45. *Ibid.*, p. 53.
46. *Ibid.*, p. 52.

> absolute necessaries. It is only after their privations have reduced their number, or the demand for labour has increased, that the market price of labour will rise to its natural price, and that the labourer will have to moderate comforts which the natural rate of wages will afford.[47]

The views of Ricardo and Smith in regard to the growth of population differ in some respects. In the first place, in Ricardo's analysis growth of labour is functionally related to (rather than, as in Smith's analysis, proportional to) the difference between the market and the natural wage rates. Secondly, Ricardo postulates an explicit upper limit to the rate of population growth while there is no such limit in Smith's analysis. Thirdly, while Ricardo's subsistence wage is historically variable, Smith's subsistence wage, which is physiologically determined, is (in the absence of diminishing returns) constant through time.

If the demand for labour is growing at a rate faster than that at which the population can increase, the money wages will have a tendency to rise. Such a situation is characteristic of the beginning stages of development of virgin territories. "The productive powers of labour are generally greatest when there is an abundance of fertile land; at such periods accumulation is often so rapid that labourers cannot be supplied with the same rapidity as capital."[48] Therefore, "in new settlements, where the arts and knowledge of countries far advanced in refinement are introduced, it is probable that capital has a tendency to increase faster than mankind."[49]

The natural wage has a tendency to rise because the operation of diminishing returns in agriculture raises both the money and real cost of the bundle of goods making up the subsistence level. "With the progress of society the natural price of labour has always a tendency to rise, because one of the principal commodities by which its natural price is regulated has a tendency to become dearer from the greater difficulty of producing it."[50] In addition, subsistence level is itself a socio-cultural phenomenon.

> It is not to be understood that the natural price of labour, estimated even in food and necessaries, is absolutely fixed

47. *Ibid.*, p. 55.
48. *Ibid.*, p. 53.
49. *Ibid.*, p. 55.
50. *Ibid.*, p. 52.

> and constant. It varies at different times in the same country, and very materially differs in different countries. It essentially depends on the habits and customs of the people. An English labourer would consider his wages under their natural rate, and too scanty to support a family, if they enabled him to purchase no other food than potatoes, and to live in no better habitation than a mud cabin; yet these moderate demands of nature are deemed sufficient in countries where "man's life is cheap" and his wants easily satisfied. Many of the conveniences now enjoyed in an English cottage would have been thought luxuries at an earlier period of our history.[51]

Natural wage rate, according to Ricardo, therefore, is a function of socio-cultural environment and the marginal productivity of land. The variations in the market rate of wages are caused by the forces of demand and supply. "The market price of labour is the price which is really paid for it, from the natural operation of the proportion of the supply to the demand."[52] The demand for labour varies in proportion to changes in the capital stock of the community. "For in proportion to the increase in capital will be the increase in the demand for labour; in proportion to the work to be done will be the demand for those who are to do it."[53]

The market rate of wages generally tends to conform to the natural rate. If demand for labour exceeds its supply, the market wage rises. High wages stimulate growth of population which tends to reduce money wages. Conversely, low wages discourage growth of population and thereby push up the wages towards their natural rate. "However much the market price of labour may deviate from its natural price, it has, like commodities, a tendency to conform to it."[54]

In the long run, the increases in labour force are strictly proportional to increases in capital. "If the increase of capital be gradual and constant, the demand for labour may give a continued

51. *Ibid.*, pp. 54-55.
52. *Ibid.*, p. 53.
53. *Ibid.*, p. 54.
54. *Ibid.*, p. 53.

stimulus to an increase of people."[55] If, however, there is a rise in the natural wage rate, the consequent increase in the supply of labour will fall short of the increase in demand, and the population will rise at a slower rate than capital. This would raise the market wage rate and lower the rate of profit on capital.[56] Equilibrium between the demand for and supply of labour will again be restored by a faster increase in supply and a slower rise in demand than before the rise in the subsistence wage.

To the extent the increase in the natural wage rate, measured either in money or in real cost, is due to diminishing returns in agriculture, the rise in the natural wage rate does not reflect a net gain in living standards of the working classes. It merely eats into entrepreneurial profits; and thereby slows down the future rate of capital accumulation and the rate of growth of the economy. Such a rise in the natural wage rate does not benefit anybody and harms some interests. It is, therefore, not in the interest of the society as a whole. For instance, this type of rise in the natural wage rate can be checked by improvements in agricultural technology[57] and by the importation of food.[58] This, however, cannot be checked for long. In the long run: "Every exertion of industry, unless accompanied by a diminished rate of increase in population, will add to the evil, for production cannot keep pace with it."[59] The rise in the natural wage rate owing to diminishing returns, though undesirable, creates its own antidote insofar as it tends to decrease the population pressure by lowering the rate of growth of population.

The welfare consequences for society are quite different when the rise in the natural wage rate is owing to the need of the working classes for higher universal standards of comforts and conveniences. In that case, the increase in natural wages leads to a real improvement in the living standards of the workers, who constitute "far the greatest part of every community.[60]

55. *Ibid.*, p. 53.
56. *Ibid.*, p. 71.
57. *Ibid.*, p. 56.
58. *Ibid.*, p. 80.
59. *Ibid.*, p. 56.
60. *Ibid.*, p. 61.

4. Capital Accumulation

Ricardo's definition of capital includes both the fixed and circulating varieties. "Capital is that part of the wealth of a country which is employed in production; and consists of food, clothing, tools, raw materials, machinery etc., necessary to give effect to labour."[61] The circulating capital constitutes the "wages fund." It grows in constant proportion to fixed capital, except when capital-deepening technological change takes place. Changes in the demand for labour, which are regulated by the wages fund, are, therefore, in proportion to changes in the economy's capital stock.

According to Ricardo, "There are two ways in which capital may be accumulated; it may be saved either in consequence of increased revenue or of diminished consumption."[62] All that is saved is invested and there is no hoarding or dishoarding. "For no one accumulates but with a view to make his accumulation productive."[63]

The rate of capital accumulation depends on two factors, *viz.*, (1) the ability to save and (2) the will to save. The first is determined by the size of the surplus over the total product necessary to maintain labour's subsistence level, or to put in Ricardo's words, the "net income" of the economy. The larger the amount of the surplus, the greater the power to save. For instance, "out of two loaves I may save one, out of four I may save three."[64] A portion of the "new income" is naturally utilised for the subsistence of the capitalists and landowners.[65] The size of this portion is determined by the intensity of their motive, that is by the rate of profit. "While the profits of stock are high, men will have a motive to accumulate." A decline in the rate of profit would encourage consumption. "Whilst a man has any wished-for gratification unsupplied, he will have a demand for more commodities; and it will be an effectual

61. *Ibid.*, p. 53.
62. *Ibid.*, p. 80.
63. *Ibid.*, p. 73.
64. Piero Sraffa (ed.), *David Ricardo: Works and Correspondence,* 10 Vols. (Cambridge, 1953), IX, p. 193.
65. Ricardo, n. 40, p. 73 and p. 266.

demand while he has any new value to offer in exchange for them."[66]

In Adam Smith's analysis, rate of saving was a negative function of the rate of profit. In contrast, Ricardo believed that the motive for capital accumulation "will diminish with every diminution of profit, and will cease altogether when profits are so low as not to afford them an adequate compensation for their trouble, and the risk which they must necessarily encounter in employing their capital productively."[67]

In Ricardo's analysis, two things can completely choke off the accumulation of capital, *viz.*, (1) disappearance of a surplus over subsistence and (2) decline in the rate of profit to the minimally acceptable rate. To study the dynamic course of capital accumulation in a Ricardian economy, we have to examine the behaviour through time of the system's "net income" and its rate of profits. Ricardo's use of the terms "profits" and "wages," (unless clearly believed as the rate of profits and the rate of wages) refers to the relative share of wages at the margin.[68] Since at the margin no rent is paid, profits depend only upon wages. Ricardo stated, "nothing can affect profits but a rise in wages."[69]

Ricardo emphasizes that the effect of capital accumulation would be different in different countries and will depend primarily on the fertility of land.

> However extensive a country may be where the land is of a poor quality, and where the importation of food is prohibited, the most moderate accumulation of capital will be attended with great reductions in the rate of profit, and a rapid rise in rent; and on the contrary a small but fertile country, particularly if it freely permits the importation of food, may accumulate a large stock of capital without any great diminution in the rate of profits, or any great increase in the rent of land.[70]

---

66. *Ibid.*, p. 193.
67. *Ibid.*, p. 73.
68. *Ibid.*, p. 281.
69. *Ibid.*, p. 70.
70. Sraffa (ed.), n. 64, Vol. I, p. 126.

Since Britain does not possess abundant fertile land, with the growth of population, inferior and inferior lands would have to be brought under cultivation; other things remaining unchanged, real prices of agricultural products would rise while those of manufactures would fall. Rent per unit of labour and capital on comparatively fertile land would rise. Money wages would also rise. Consequently, profits would fall leading to a decline in the rate of capital accumulation and hence in the rate of economic growth.

British economy can be saved only if it is reorganised in a manner that the rent per unit of labour and capital would not rise and profits would not fall. Doctrine of comparative advantage shows the way to achieve these objectives. It shows as to how an economy can most efficiently allocate its resources among industries developing at different rates of productivity growth. The doctrine of comparative advantage shows that, by adopting a policy of free trade, it is possible to keep agricultural prices, money wages and rents low, and real wages and profits high. Thus, it is possible to induce larger investments in the progressive manufacturing industries. There may also occur improvements in agricultural production. In this way, a country like England can experience a gradual increase in population and enjoy a lasting growth in real income.

Continuous growth is possible only if the distribution of income among landlords, labourers, and capitalists moves in favour of capital. Ricardo, therefore, opposes taxes on capital, wages, raw materials and necessities. He, also, opposes poor laws. All these levies raise money wages and lower profits. This redistributes income in favour of consumption and against investment leading to a decline in the rate of growth and thereby to a deterioration in the conditions of both the rich and the poor.

Barring the difficulties of providing food and necessities to additional labour, Ricardo believes that there are endless opportunities for investment in manufactures.

> ...there is no limit to demand—no limit to the employment of capital while it yields any profit, and that however abundant capital may become, there is no other adequate reason for a fall of profit but a rise of wages and further it may be added, that the only adequate and permanent cause for the rise of wages is the increasing difficulty of providing

> food and necessaries for the increasing number of workmen.[71]

In contrast to Adam Smith, he believes that even in the absence of foreign trade, there exist unlimited opportunities for investment.

Ricardo opposed tariffs. Factors of production being immobile between different countries, he shows that trading partners can increase their incomes by each specialising in those commodities in whose production it possesses a comparative cost advantage in real terms. Free trade increases the world income by a more efficient utilisation of world's productive resources.

Ricardo fully recognizes that for taking advantages of its potentialities, British economy requires fundamental reforms and readjustments, *viz.*, free trade, resource mobility, free competition and monetary stability. He realises that a high rate of capital accumulation is necessary for economic growth. He points out that for permanently improving the conditions of the poor, it is very necessary to keep their number under strict control. He further points out that for controlling the growth of population strenuous efforts by the labouring classes or by their legislature are essential. He is in favour of birth control to the extent permitted by the intellectual decencies of the times.

5. Behaviour of Wages, Profits and Rent

Ricardo studies the movement in the relative income shares of labour, capitalists and landlords during the process of economic growth. Ricardo holds that it is not possible to study the movement in *absolute* shares. "No law can be laid down respecting quantity, but a tolerably correct one can be laid down respecting proportions. Every day I am more satisfied that the former enquiry is vain and delusive, and the latter only the true objects of the science."[72]

As mentioned above, with the progress of the society, cultivation is extended to inferior and inferior lands, or labour and capital are used more intensively on the superior lands, leading to diminishing returns which raise rent. Thus with the progress of society, rent as a proportion of total output has a tendency to rise. With the rise in rents, prices of agricultural products will rise. On the other hand, in

71. *Ibid.*, p. 96.
72. Sraffa (ed.), n. 64, Vol. VIII, pp. 278-79.

manufacturing, the application of successive dozes of labour and capital does not result in diminishing returns in terms of output and hence the prices of manufactured goods do not rise. Thus with the progress of society and an increase in the production of all commodities, prices of agricultural commodities rise in terms of manufactured goods. Ricardo points out that improvements in agriculture can temporarily thwart the rise of rent in both money and commodity terms. He divides the agricultural improvements in two categories, *viz.*, (1) land-saving improvements, and (2) labour-saving improvements. Land-saving improvements decrease the required quantity of land for producing a certain amount of agricultural commodities. Labour-saving improvements, in contrast, decrease the required amount of labour, and not of land, for producing a certain amount of agricultural produce. These improvements increase the productivity of labour but the amount of land required for producing the previous amount of agricultural produce remains the same. The first kind of improvements lower rent in terms of both money and agricultural produce. The second type of improvements lower money rent but may not lower rent in terms of agricultural commodities. Ricardo, however, holds that, in the long run, rents and prices of agricultural commodities have a tendency to rise because agricultural improvements will not be sufficiently rapid to counteract the efforts of growth of population and the accumulation of capital.

In the course of the progress of society, real wages (*i.e.* wages in terms of goods) have a tendency to remain constant while money wages rise. During periods of rapid capital accumulation, real wages may rise above the subsistence level but this stimulates an expansion of population which, again, lowers the wages to the subsistence level. As seen above, with the progress of society, prices of agricultural goods have a tendency to rise. Consequently, more money will be required to attain the same standard of living (*i.e.* the subsistence level). As wages in terms of goods cannot fall below the subsistence level, wages in terms of money will rise with the progress of society.

With the progress of society, profits have a tendency to decline because, as seen above, the subsistence wage rate has a tendency to rise. Ricardo wrote, "natural tendency of profits is to fall; for, in the progress of society and wealth, the additional quantity of food required is obtained by the sacrifice of more and more labour." Periodically, the tendency towards diminishing returns is checked by the introduction of technological innovations. This leads to a decline in the share of subsistence wages in total output at the margin of cultivation. During such periods, profits go up. However, since technological progress is also subject to diminishing returns, the long run trend of profits will be downward.[73] In the beginning, the rate at which the profits decline, owing to diminishing returns, is sufficiently low to permit the share of profits in the total output to increase. In the early stages of growth, therefore, capital accumulation proceeds at an accelerated pace.[74] The downward pressure upon capital accumulation exerted by the falling rate of profits is outweighed by the upward pull of a larger net surplus over subsistence.

As society grows, however, the share of profits in total output begins to decline. As a result, the rate of capital accumulation slows down. Ultimately, as, under the pressure of increasing population, poorer and poorer lands are brought under cultivation, the portion of the product at the margin swallowed up by the subsistence wage becomes so great that the profit is reduced to the minimum. At this stage, the accumulation of capital comes to an end, population becomes constant, and the economy enters the stationary state.

6. Pattern of Development

The normal progress of the economy towards the stationary state is characterised by periods of temporary equilibrium, during which wages are at the subsistence level and population is stationary. During these periods, however, the economy's net income is positive and the rate of return on investment is above the minimum necessary. These temporary equilibria, therefore, cannot persist. New investment is taking place, which increases the demand for labour and raises wages above subsistence. This leads to an increase in population. Meanwhile, the temporary rise in wages lowers the rate of profits which leads to a decline in the rate of capital accumulation. When the supply of labour finally catches up the demand, a new equilibrium position is attained. Wages fall to subsistence which raises the rate of profit above the minimum

73. Ricardo, n. 40, pp. 71-75.

74. *Ibid.*, p. 55.

necessary. This leads to a new stimulus to capital accumulation and the process described above starts all over again. The successive equilibrium positions of the economy differ from each other in regard to the sizes of their population and capital stock. Moving from one equilibrium position to the other, the economy ultimately enters the stationary rate. The stationary economy has constant capital, maximum population, wages at subsistence level, profits at the minimum necessary for compensating the risk and a stationary total product.

All stationary states, however, are not equal. Ricardo considers subsistence level to be partly a socio-cultural phenomenon. Other things being equal, in a community with a comparatively higher subsistence level, capital accumulation and growth will be choked off earlier and the maximum population will be smaller. But, in such an economy, the standard of living of the workers will be higher. Ricardo considers such an economy superior to the one with larger population having a lower standard of living.

> The friends of humanity cannot but wish that in all countries the labouring classes should have a taste for comforts and enjoyments, and that they should be stimulated by all legal means in their exertions to procure them. There cannot be a better security against a superabundant population. In those countries where the labouring classes have fewer wants and are contented with the cheapest food the people are exposed to the greatest vicissitudes and miseries.[75]

Ricardo distinguishes between two types of underdeveloped economies. On the one hand, "those countries where there is abundance of fertile land, but where, from the ignorance, indolence, barbarism of the inhabitants, they are exposed to all the evils of want and famine, and where it has been said that population presess against the means of subsistence"[76]; on the other hand, "long settled countries, where, from the diminishing rate of supply of raw produce, all the evils of a crowded population are experienced."[77] The first type is a case of an underpopulated economy while

75. *Ibid.*, p. 57.
76. *Ibid.*, p. 56.
77. *Ibid.*

the second corresponds to an overpopulated underdeveloped community.

Ricardo suggests different policies for the two types of economies. A sparsely populated economy requires a more rapid rate of capital accumulation. This can be brought about by improvement in the technology and the socio-cultural setting.

> In the one case, the evil proceeds from bad government, from the insecurity of property, and from a want of education in all ranks of the people. To be made happier, they require only to be better governed and instructed, as the augmentation of capital, beyond the augmentation of people, would be the inevitable result.[78]

The case of a densely populated underdeveloped economy is a more hopeless one. In such an economy, an increase in capital only makes the matter worse since it encourages growth of population which merely increases pressure on scarce land resources. "Every exertion of industry, unless accompanied by a diminished rate of increase in the population, will add to the evil, for production cannot keep pace with it."[79] The only remedy for such an economy is control of population. This can be achieved by raising the economic aspirations of the lower classes of society.

7. Conclusion

History has falsified Ricardo's prediction of the advent of a stationary state. Both the fundamental principles in Ricardo's model of economic development—the principle of population and the principle of diminishing returns—have proved partially incorrect. Ricardo's predictions regarding the relative shares of labour, capitalists and landlords have not turned out to be true. Nevertheless, Ricardo makes significant contribution to the understanding of economic growth by emphasizing the importance of knowledge, responsible government, protection of private property, social capital, healthy agriculture, entrepreneurial ability, specialisation of labour, technological improvements, capital accumulation and free trade.

---

78. *Ibid.*

79. *Ibid.*, p. 56.

THOMAS ROBERT MALTHUS

1. Concept of Growth

Malthus is not interested in the long run development. He is primarily concerned with the progress of wealth in the short run. In the chapter 'On the Progress of Wealth' of his *Principles,* he analyses the causes which hinder growth rather than the causes which facilitate growth; his theory of growth is, thus, negative in character.

Malthus' concept of economic growth involves an increase in wealth as well as in value. What is required is an increase in the quantity of "material objects which are necessary, useful or agreeable to mankind."[80] It is no use producing goods which are not required by consumers and hence have no utility for them.

> ...wealth of a country depends partly upon the quantity of produce obtained by its labour, and partly upon such an adaptation of this quantity to the wants and powers of the existing population as is calculated to give it value. Nothing can be more certain than that it is not determined by either of them alone.[81]

Economic progress depends not only on the powers of production but also on the distribution of production. Quantity of goods and other material necessaries can be enlarged by increasing the power of production. But the value of these goods can be increased by a better distribution of these.

> Production and distribution are the two grand elements of wealth, which, combined in their due proportions, are capable of carrying the riches and population of the earth in no great length of time to the utmost limits of its possible resources; but which taken separately, or combined in undue proportions, produce only, after the lapse of many thousand years, the scanty population, which are at present scattered over the face of the globe.[82]

80. T.R. Malthus, *Principles of Political Economy* (Oxford, 1820), p. 28.
81. T.R. Malthus, *Principles of Political Economy* (Oxford, 1951), p. 301.
82. *Ibid.*, p. 371.

2. Accumulation of Capital

Accumulation of capital, fertility of soil and labour-saving inventions facilitate production. These reduce the cost of production and thus make possible the production of a large quantity of goods with the same amount of labour.

Malthus fully realises the role of capital accumulation in economic development. "It is certainly true that no permanent and continued increase of wealth can take place without a continued increase of capital."[83] Then he considers the conditions under which the capital accumulation will be most effective and lead to a further and continued increase of capital and wealth. Accumulation of capital increases the number of productive workers leading to an expansion of the production of goods. Accumulation of capital can continue only if the additional goods can find purchasers. Malthus, however, believes that accumulation of capital cannot continue because it will not be possible for the additional goods to find consumers.

> ...the consumption and demand occasioned by the workmen employed in productive labour can *alone*[84] furnish a motive to the accumulation and employment of capital; and with regard to the capitalists themselves, together with the landlords and other rich persons, they have, by the supposition, agreed to be parsimonious, and by depriving themselves of their usual conveniences and luxuries to save from their revenue and add to their capital. Under these circumstances, it is impossible that the increased quantity of commodities, obtained by the increased number of productive labourers, should find purchasers, without such a fall of price as would probably sink their value below that of the outlay, or, at least, so reduce profits as very greatly to diminish both the power and the will to save.[85]

J.B. Say held that supply creates its own demand and shortage of an overall effective demand cannot be a problem. Malthus, however, does not agree with Say's law and explodes it on a number of grounds. Say's law maintains that commodities are always exchanged

83. *Ibid.*, p. 314.
84. Italics in original.
85. Malthus, n. 81, p. 315.

for commodities. Malthus points out that commodities are exchanged not only for commodities but also for labour; consequently, a glut of commodities can occur leading to a fall in the price of these in terms of labour. Say's law considers commodities *vis-a-vis* commodities and neglects the problem of commodities *vis-a-vis* consumers. When we consider commodities *vis-a-vis* consumers, there arises the possibility of a glut in the market if the increase in the amount of the commodities is not followed by an increase in the demand of consumers for these because of stationary population or because of demand diminished by parsimony. Different commodities may still exchange for each other in the same ratio but the absolute price of these in terms of labour will fall leading to a decline in profits and hence in the rate of capital accumulation and economic growth.

Ricardo assumes that the supply of labour is completely elastic. Additional mouths will, therefore, be forthcoming to provide demand for the additional goods. Malthus, however, points out that the supply of capital can increase much faster than the growth of population and consequently there would occur a glut of the commodities.

> ...from the nature of population, an increase of labourers cannot be brought into the market, in consequence of a particular demand, till after the lapse of sixteen or eighteen years, and conversion of revenue into capital by saving, may take place much more rapidly.[86]

Believers in the automatic adjustment between demand and supply ignore the influence of indolence or love for ease in human nature. They assume that the demand for luxuries is unlimited. Actually this is not so and some people may prefer ease and leisure to additional consumption. Under such conditions there would appear a glut of commodities in the market. For example, if the agriculturists are disposed to consume luxuries produced by manufacturers and manufacturers those produced by agriculturists, the process of growth would go smoothly; but if one of the two parties prefer leisure to additional consumables, the other party would not find market for its products and there would occur a glut.

---

86. *Ibid.*, pp. 319-20.

Ricardians believe that the rich people who forego conveniences and luxuries will invest their savings and the accumulation of capital would generate effective demand. If the rich forego the consumption of conveniences and luxuries and invest their savings, more capital will go towards the production of necessities; this would increase the production of necessities still further and cause a glut leading to a fall in profits and consequently to a cessation of the accumulation process. As seen above, in the short period, accumulation of capital cannot increase demand through an increase in population.

3. Lack of Effective Demand

Ricardo, Say and James Mill consider money as nothing more than a medium of exchange and consequently assume that the value of money remains constant. Malthus recognises that money is more than a mere medium of exchange, and changes in the value of money can have significant effects on the economy.

> It is an abstract truth that we want commodities, not money. But, in reality no commodity for which it is possible to sell our goods at once, can be an adequate substitute for a circulating medium...The circulating medium bears so important a part in the distribution of wealth, and the encouragement of industry that it is hardly ever safe to set it aside in our reasoning....[87]

In contrast to Say's contention that savings are automatically invested, Malthus thinks that the idle purchasing power will sometimes be hoarded. Malthus, of course, is not very clear about this idea.

Excessive parsimony would thus diminish effective demand leading to widespread depression and unemployment. Growth of population alone cannot lead to a continuous increase in wealth. Mere desire or want for necessaries, conveniences and luxuries of the additional population would not constitute effective demand. Desire or want will become effective demand only when it is accompanied by something which will be acceptable in exchange for the desired or wanted goods. Additional population, whose possession is labour, will have effective demand only if the persons having disposable goods require labour and are ready to accept it in

87. *Ibid.*, p. 324 footnote.

return for goods. Additional labour will be in demand only if the value of its produce exceeds its wages. Thus increase in population can generate effective demand only if the demand and supply conditions of the commodities prior to the increase in population are such as warrant the employment of additional hands.

Increase in population will lower wages and hence cost of production and thus lead to an increase in profits; this would encourage production. But the extent to which production can be encouraged in this manner is strictly limited. There is a minimum level below which wages cannot fall without checking the increase in population or even decreasing it. But before this minimum level is reached, increase in production through the employment of additional labour will lower the value of goods and hence profits to such an extent that further employment will become unprofitable.

4. Methods of Increasing Effective Demand

Accumulation of capital, fertility of soil and the introduction of machinery can considerably increase production of goods but it will lead to economic progress only if sufficient effective demand is forthcoming. Increase in effective demand is as important as the increase in production. But there is no guarantee that an increase in production through accumulation of capital, fertility of soil, and the introduction of machinery will be automatically followed by an increase in effective demand for these goods. Effective demand can be increased through a more egalitarian distribution of wealth. Distribution of wealth can be favourably affected through three ways, *viz.*, (1) division of landed property, (2) internal and external commerce, and (3) the maintenance of unproductive consumers.

Division of landed property scatters wealth and money, and thereby leads to an increase in the volume of effective demand. A large number of moderately rich people would provide more effective-demand than a few rich living amidst a poverty-stricken multitude.

> Thirty or forty proprietors, with incomes answering to between one thousand and five thousand a year, would create a much more effectual demand for the necessaries, conveniences and luxuries of life, than a single proprietor possessing a hundred thousand a year.[88]

88. *Ibid.*, p. 374.

Though theoretically it is possible for a few rich to create a large demand, this has never happened in actual practice. "A large body of manufacturers and merchants can only find a market for their commodities among a numerous class of consumers below the rank of the great proprietors of land."[89] Malthus pointed out that a more egalitarian distribution of property would also increase production. "...Experience shows us that manufacturing wealth is at once the consequence of a better distribution of property."[90] But he fully realises that egalitarianism pushed to extremes would adversely affect the production of goods.

> With an excessive proportion of small proprietors both of land and of capital, all great improvements on the land, all great enterprises in commerce and manufactures, and most of the wonders described by Adam Smith, as resulting from the division of labour, would be at an end; and the progress of wealth would be checked by a failure in the powers of supply.[91]

Domestic as well foreign trade are useful. These enlarge the size of the market and thus facilitate the process of accumulation of capital and hence that of growth.

> No country with a very confined market, internal as well as external, has ever been able to accumulate large capital,, because such a market prevents the formation of those wants and tastes, and that desire to consume, which are absolutely necessary to keep up the market prices of commodities, and prevent the fall of profits.[92]

Domestic as well as external commerce increases the value of the products.

> Every exchange that takes place in a country, effects a distribution of its produce better adapted to the wants of the society. It is with regard to both parties concerned, an exchange of what is wanted less for what is wanted more, and must, therefore, raise the value of both the products.[93]

---

89. *Ibid.*, p. 375.
90. *Ibid.*
91. *Ibid.*, p. 376.
92. *Ibid.*, p. 388.
93. *Ibid.*, p. 383.

Ricardo views foreign trade as a means of obtaining cheaper commodities. Malthus points out that "this is only looking to one half of its advantages, and...not the larger half."[94] He views foreign trade as a means of increasing the value of goods by exchanging what is wanted less for what is wanted more.

A third method of maintaining or increasing the value of goods is the employment of individuals in personal services or the maintenance of a sufficiently large number of unproductive consumers. Unproductive consumers provide demand for the excessive production and thereby check a fall in the rate of profit. The ratio between productive workers and unproductive consumers, which would lead to the maximum rate of growth depends upon a number of factors, *viz.*, rate of accumulation of capital, fertility of the soil, progress of invention in machinery, consumption of the productive workers, etc.

5. Industrialisation

Malthus believes that after a certain limit people will not strive more and more for luxuries. He, therefore, advocates industrialisation. He states that the manufactures and commerce "infuse fresh life and activity into all classes of the state, afford opportunities for the inferior orders to rise by personal merit...stimulate the higher orders to depend on it for distinction.... They excite invention, encourage science and the useful arts, spread intelligence and spirit, inspire a taste for conveniences and comforts....[95] At the same time he warns against excessive proportion of manufacturing population because it "does not seem favourable to national quiet and happiness...variations in the channels of manufacturing industry and the facilities of obtaining a rent for its produce are perpetually recurring...the wages of manufacturing labour being subject to great fluctuations.... These fluctuations naturally tend to generate discontent and tumult and the evils which accompany them."[96] He concludes that a balanced growth of agriculture and industry is the best thing for any nation.

---

94. *Ibid.*, p. 396.
95. T.R. Malthus, *Observations on the Effect of Corn Law* (1814), pp. 24-25.
96. *Ibid.*, p. 24.

6. Non-economic Factors

Malthus, though does not discuss in detail, fully recognises the importance of non-economic factors in economic development.

> Among the primary and most important causes which influence the wealth of nations, must unquestionably be placed, those which come under the head of politics and morals. Security of property, without a certain degree of which, there can be no encouragement to individual industry, depends mainly upon the political constitution of a country, the excellence of its laws and the manner in which they are administered. And those habits which are the most favourable to regular exertions as well as to general rectitude of character, and are consequently most favourable to the production and maintenance of wealth, depend upon the same causes, combined with moral and religious instruction.[97]

7. Conclusion

Malthus makes an important contribution to the theory of economic growth by emphasizing the need for sufficient effective demand for continued growth. He anticipates some of the basic ideas of modern economists like Keynes and Kalecki.

JOHN STUART MILL

1. Role of Economic Factors

Mill believes that non-economic factors like beliefs, habits of thought, customs and institutions play an important role in economic development. Despotic and anti-progressive character of the customs, institutions and beliefs is an important cause of the backwardness of many countries. Economic progress depends upon two kinds of improvements, *viz.*, (1) extension of man's knowledge of the laws of nature and his capacity to remove barriers imposed by an unbeneficient nature, and (2) removal of the barriers imposed by men on themselves in the form of beliefs, customs, opinions and habits of thought. While trying to modify customs with a view to further development care should be taken that the growth and application of knowledge is not adversely affected.

---

97. Malthus, n. 81, pp. 309-10.

2. Developing and Non-developing Countries

Mill distinguishes between developing and non-developing countries. In the non-developing (Asian) countries, the surplus of food beyond the necessary consumption of the cultivators is "torn from the producers, either by the government,...or by individuals, who by superior force, or by availing themselves of religious or traditional feelings of subordination, have established themselves as lords of the soil."[98] The surplus is wasted by those who appropriate it and consequently no capital is formed. The miserable conditions in these countries are not the result of excessive population growth; numbers are "kept down by actual starvation.[99] In contrast, in developing (European) countries the appropriators of the surplus use it for capital formation. In certain regions the agriculture is so productive that half of the population, or even less than that can produce food for all and, therefore, the remaining population is, employed in the production of conveniences and luxuries, in transportation, in the supply of military requirements, in the construction of public works and so on. Given a favourable natural environment, economic progress in Asian countries is not impossible. Progress in these countries can be accelerated by strengthening the very weak principles of accumulation.

> The means are, first, a better government, more complete security of property, moderate taxes, and freedom from arbitrary exaction under the name of taxes, a more permanent and more advantageous tenure of land, securing to the cultivator as far as possible the undivided benefits of the industry, skill, and economy he may exert. Secondly, improvement of the public intelligence; the decay of usages or superstitions which interfere with the effective employment of the industry; and the growth of mental activity, making the people alive to new subjects of desire. Thirdly, the introduction of foreign arts, which raise the returns derivable from additional capital, to a rate corresponding to the low strength of the desire of accumulation: and the importation of foreign capital, which

98. J. S. Mill, *Principles of Political Economy,* (ed.), W.J. Ashley (London, 1940).

99. *Ibid.*, p. 159.

> renders the increase of production no longer exclusively dependent on the thrift or providence of the inhabitants themselves, while it places before them a stimulating example, and by instilling new ideas and breaking the chains of habits, if not by improving the actual condition of the population, tends to create in them new wants, increased ambition, and greater thought for the future.[100]

Increase in per capita income is possible only if the quantity and/or effectiveness of land and capital increase faster than labour and the forces causing improvements in these factors and in the manner of their use are sufficiently powerful.

3. Population

Population has a tendency to grow at a very fast rate. It is difficult to increase the means of production at a faster, or even at an equally fast rate. The result is the limitation of population either through positive or preventive checks. In backward countries, increase in population is checked by want and starvation. In advanced societies, the growth of population is checked by preventive measures with a view to avoid poverty and to improve the standard of living. Working classes, even in advanced countries, tend to multiply rapidly. For improving the economic conditions of the labour classes and for preventing the additional mouths from consuming the fruits of technical progress and capital accumulation, limitation of the growth of population is very essential. Growth of population should not be encouraged by governmental or other means. Relative numerical strength of the working classes should be decreased and their customs, habits and aspirations changed in a manner which restrains their rapid growth. It is, of course, not easy to change the habits and aspirations of the working classes. Emigration can temporarily relieve the pressures of rapid growth of population in older countries. It would also facilitate the exportation of excess capital and the development of underpeopled lands which in turn would enable the older countries to support a larger population through the free importation of cheap food.

4. Stationary State

Ultimately, every economy would reach a stable and stationary state. The advent of this state depends upon what happens within a

---

100. *Ibid.*, pp. 189-90.

country and upon its relations with the outside world. In the course of development, there is a tendency for the rent and money wages to rise and for profits to fall. Ultimately, profits reach the minimum at which the existing stock of capital is merely kept intact and not added to. In a closed economy the advent of the stationary state depends mainly upon the nature and the amount of the technological progress achieved, intensity of the desire to accumulate capital even at very low rates of return and the movement of the wage bill under the impact of the rising food costs and/or rising real wages. Since the advent of a stationary state is compatible for a time with both a stagnant and growing population, life in such a state might be pleasant or unpleasant. The things would be most pleasant if the advent of the stationary state is largely the result of the practice of prudential restraint. By opening the economy it is possible to temporarily postpone the advent of the stationary state. But ultimately an economy would reach a stationary state even if it is open.

5. Factors Limiting Production

Increase in production is limited by the deficiency of capital or of land. In Mill's system land is a more completely limiting factor. By limiting the capacity to increase agricultural produce, it limits capital accumulation which in turn limits the growth of population to the extent it depends on the growth of capital. The amount of land being limited, increase in the stock of capital results in a decline in the rate of return until it has descended to a level compatible merely with holding the stock of capital intact. Before the possibilities of an increase in agricultural produce are exhausted, cost of raw materials tends to rise because of the operation of the law of diminishing returns. The law of diminishing returns might "however be suspended, or temporarily controlled, by whatever adds to the general power of mankind over nature; and especially by an extension of their knowledge, and their consequent command, of the properties and powers of natural agents." The law operates more vigorously in agriculture. But to the extent raw materials enter into manufactured goods, growth of population is accompanied by an increase in the cost of manufactures. At the same time, however, operation of certain forces (*e.g.* extension of the division of labour, improvements etc.) tend to lower the cost of production of manufactures. As the cost of raw materials constitutes only a small portion of the total cost of the manufactures, and real cost and price of almost every manufacture have fallen and would probably continue to fall "beyond any limit which it would be safe to specify." It is by limiting food production and capital formation that the law of diminishing returns sets a limit to the growth of population and the expansion of output.

Deficiency of capital also sets a limit to the increase in production. The amount of "industry" or employment at any time depends upon the amount of available capital. Capital is the result of saving and is formed only when the conditions are sufficiently favourable. Even in the face of a growing population and labour force, a rapid rate of capital accumulation can lead to a rise in real wages and average output.

6. Accumulation of Capital

The rate of capital accumulation in a country depends upon two factors, *viz.*, (1) the magnitude of "the net produce of industry" or "the amount of the fund from which saving can be made" and (2) "the strength of the disposition to save." Since savings come out of a country's "net produce" consisting mainly of profits and rent, whatever increases "net produce" raises the rate of capital accumulation. The "strength of the disposition to save" depends upon two factors, one external and the other internal to the individual. It depends upon the rate of profit or return on savings and upon "the effective desire of accumulation" or the inclination to save at a given rate of return. Whatever increases the rate of return on savings or intensifies the inclination to accumulate raises the rate of capital formation and whatever causes an opposite effect lowers this rate. Emigration of capital to newer countries is important because of higher rate of return in these countries and also because, by increasing the scarcity of capital at home, it raises the domestic rate of return. Whatever other factors (*e.g.* improvements, new investment opportunities, war loans, misuse and waste of capital etc.) increase the domestic scarcity of capital and thereby raise the rate of return tend to increase both savings and savers.

Because of the operation of the law of diminishing returns in agriculture and the consequent limitation of population growth, profits tend to a minimum, *i.e.*, zero saving level. In the absence of improvements and where the population grows at a rate faster than the rate of capital accumulation, the decline in the rate of profits is accentuated. In old countries, in the absence of countervailing forces, the profits tend to decline at such a rapid rate that in a short time these would reach a minimum level, below which common people do not find sufficient motive to save. Once this minimum level is reached, capital accumulation, population and output become almost stationary and progress ceases. Cessation of capital accumulation would not result into unemployment and the full employment equilibrium would continue. Until even the working classes have reached the point of satiety, there cannot, as believed by Malthus, occurs a general oversupply of commodities or of capital. People do not save "from mere habit" and they consume whatever they save. Use of credit money divides the transaction into two operations—buying and selling—and thereby makes possible a temporary disequilibrium between money (commodity) demand and commodity (money) supply but any such disequilibrium is soon corrected.

7. Quality of Productive Factors

The principal forces which improve the quality of the requisites of production and increase the efficiency of their use include education, progress in science and the state of the arts, extension of specialisation, the improvement of the methods of economic organisation, enterprise and the contribution of the creative thinkers, changes in custom, habits and beliefs etc. Education plays the most important role in economic development. It generates or stimulates many forces making for socio-economic progress. It increases man's technical capacity to overcome the niggardliness of nature and contributes to his moral progress by changing the content of his mind. For economic development, technical progress is important, but moral progress is still more important. "All real amelioration in the lot of mankind depends on their intellectual and moral state."[101] "Successful production......depends more on the qualities of the human agents, than on the circumstances in which they work."[102]

8. Division of Labour

Division of labour is of two types, *viz.*, (1) simple co-operation or intra-occupational specialisation, and (2) complex co-operation or inter-occupational specialisation. Division of labour at the

---

101. J.S. Mill, *Autobiography*, (ed.), J.J. Coss (New York, 1924), p. 167.
102. *Ibid.*, p. 104.

national level has a number of benefits. It increases worker's dexterity, makes possible fuller utilisation of men and tools, stimulates inventions, permits individuals to be assigned to jobs in accordance with their particular capacities, and leads to an increase in the scale of production which yields important economies. Division of labour at the international level enables every country to specialise in the production of those commodities in which it possesses maximum relative advantage or minimum relative disadvantage. Thus it makes possible for a group of trading countries to obtain a larger aggregate output and thereby for each individual country to obtain a larger income. It enlarges the market for the trade commodities and thereby extends the division of labour, makes possible greater use of machinery and increases the likelihood of inventions and improvements in the process of production. Foreign trade stimulates effort, particularly in countries in the early stages of industrial development in which people are in a "quiescent, indolent, uncultivated state, with all their tastes either fully satisfied or entirely undeveloped and consequently are undisposed "to put forth the whole of their productive energies." It introduces new objects of desire, creates new wants and inculcates new tastes and in order to be able to obtain these things, people put forth greater effort and even save and accumulate capital for a still more complete satisfaction of these wants and desires. Similar is the effect of complex co-operation. It furthers economic development by increasing the elasticity of demand for income in terms of efforts. Inter-occupational specialisation leads to an increase in the variety of goods which increases desires and wants and for satisfying these additional wants men tend to put forth greater effort. It also enlarges the market and provides opportunities for the sale of the products.

Division of labour is limited by the extant of the market and the nature of the employment. In the absence of ample opportunities for export, extent of market is limited by a number of factors, *viz.*, too small a population, too scattered population, deficiency of roads and water carriage and poverty of population. Some industries, by their very nature, are not susceptible to a great division of occupations because different operations in these industries cannot be pursued simultaneously, *e.g.*, agriculture.

9. Role of State

Mill does not assign state an important role in economic development. Increase in the economic functions of the state destroys men's individuality and liberty. As compared with private bodies, governments are less flexible and less effective and progressive. There are few things which the government can do as well as the private individuals. Government is inferior in intelligence and knowledge. At the administrative level, it lacks delegation and decentralisation of responsibility for decision-making. As compared with state enterprise, private enterprise is more congenial to innovation. Regarding regulation of economic activities in general, competition is superior to all other alternatives. Though the proper functions of the state are much more extensive in backward countries than in advanced countries, the governments in the former countries might not be equipped to perform all these functions. As compared with Adam Smith, however, Mill assigns greater functions to the state. In principle, government may undertake any activity of importance to the general interest if the private enterprise fails to do it. The principal functions of the state include support of lower education, conduct of colonization, creation of environments favourable to private enterprise, establishment of an incentive-producing system of land ownership, construction of necessary public works *(e.g.,* irrigation, transport, etc.) where private enterprise is unable or unwilling to provide these etc.

The only exception, and that, too, with increasing reservation, Mill permits to the general principle of free trade is the infant-industry ease.

> The only case in which, on mere principles of political economy, protecting duties can be defensible, is when they are imposed temporarily (especially in a young and rising nation) in hopes of naturalizing a foreign industry, in itself perfectly suitable to the circumstances of the country. The superiority of one country over another in a branch of production often arises only from having begun it sooner. There may be no inherent advantage on one part, or disadvantage on the other, but only a present superiority of acquired skill and experience....A protecting duty, continued for a reasonable time, might sometimes be the least inconvenient mode in which the nation can tax itself for the

> support of such an experiment. But it is essential that the protection should be confined to cases in which there is good ground of assurance that the industry which it fosters will after time be able to dispense with it; nor should the domestic producers ever be allowed to expect that it will be continued to them beyond the time necessary for a fair trial of what they are capable of accomplishing.[103]

10. Conclusion

Mill's views on economic development are not very different from those of the modern writers. According to Mill, economic development depends upon the rate of capital accumulation, rate of population growth, rate of technical progress and the extent to which the shortages of arable land and raw materials can be overcome by improved methods or through importation. These factors of economic development are considerably influenced by the society's institutions, values, customs, habits, beliefs etc. In Mill's analysis, population is an endogenous and not an exogenous factor. Mill, of course, exaggerates the adverse influence of population growth on economic development. Similarly, he overemphasizes the retarding effect on development arising from the fact that land and natural resources are limited. He underestimates the improvability of agriculture.

103. Mill, n. 80, p. 922.

Karl Marx

2

1. Introduction

Karl Marx is a powerful and influential thinker. His thinking had and is having immense influence in shaping the history of the world. Followers of Marx support him with a tenacity akin to religious zeal. To an orthodox Marxist, an "opponent is not merely in error but in sin."[1] Marx is an "angry genius."[2] He predicts the inevitable downfall of capitalism and the advent of socialism.

Karl Marx makes a bold and sharp departure from the classical tradition of economic analysis. He agrees with classicists on the gloomy future of capitalism. But while classicists predict inevitable stagnation of a stationary state, he predicts a collapse of the capitalist system. He also differs with the classicists in regard to the course of this process. He does not believe in the wage-population link. Similarly, he does not consider diminishing returns to be a valid reason for the collapse of capitalism. He predicts the ultimate downfall of capitalism owing to sociological reasons, and only after it has reached a very high level of development.

Marx is not a pure economist. His analysis is a mixture of economics, sociology, political theory, history and philosophy. Because of the important role played by the ideas of Marx in shaping the policies in Russia, China and other Communist countries and in formulating the programmes of the Communist parties all over the world, we shall examine the Marxian theory of economic development in a little greater detail.

---

1. Schumpeter, *Capitalism, Socialism and Democracy* (New York, 1950), p. 5.
2. Robert Heilbroner, *The Worldly Philosophers* (New York, 1955), p. 130.

2. Materialistic Interpretation of History

An outstanding feature of the Marxian analysis is the materialistic interpretation of history which explains the foundations and evolution of all social life. Karl Marx believes that the relations of production determine the entire social, cultural, legal, and institutional structure of society. In the Preface to *The Critique of Political Economy,* he writes:

> In the social production of their means of existence men enter into definite, necessary relations which are independent of their will, productive relationships which correspond to a definite stage of development of their material productive forces. The aggregate of these productive relationships constitutes the economic structure of society, the real basis on which a juridical and political superstructure arises, and to which definite forms of social consciousness correspond. The mode of production of the material means of existence conditions the whole process of social, political and intellectual life. It is not the consciousness of men that determines their existence, but, on the contrary, it is their social existence that determines their consciousness.[3]

Engels also states:

> The materialistic conception of history starts from the principle that production, and with production the exchange of its products, is the basis of every social order; that in every society which has appeared in history the distribution of the products, and with it the division of society into classes or estates, is determined by what is produced and how it is produced, and how the product is exchanged. According to this conception, the ultimate cause of all social changes and political revolutions are to be sought, not in the minds of men, in their increasing insight into eternal truth and justice, but in changes in the mode of production and exchange; they are to be sought not in the philosophy but in the economics of the epoch concerned.[4]

---

3. Karl Marx, *A Critique of Political Economy,* translated by N.I. Stone (Chicago, Kerr & Co., 1904), p. 11.
4. Friederich Engels, *Anti-Duhring,* translated and reprinted in E. Burns, *A Handbook of Marxism* (London, Gollancaz, 1935), p. 279.

Marx rejects historical explanations which refer to metaphysics or psychological laws of human nature. History is not merely an aggregate of chance events. It follows certain discoverable laws which produce ever-changing and ever-new forms of social organizations.

Man is a social producer of his means of livelihood in the widest sense. Social production necessarily involves certain social relations, the quality of which will depend on the degree of development of the social productive powers. These social relations constitute the economic structure of society which in turn determines the political, legal and cultural patterns and thoughts and ideas. The mode of production determines even the nature of the class structure of the society. In every society, excepting the ultimate classless society under socialism, the class structure consists mainly of a dominant and directing class and a toiling and oppressed class. Marx does not deny that certain cultural expressions may arise independent of the mode of production and the relations of production. He, however, holds that such autonomous non-economic forces do not exert an important influence on historical development.

Change in society occurs because of the change in the material forces of production, that is, the elements that constitute the mode of production. Changes in these elements are the autonomous forces in the Marxian analysis. The economic circumstances change with the developments in techniques, inventions, discoveries etc. while the social relations created by these remain fixed and thus lag behind. The social relations become inappropriate to economic relations and, instead of facilitating, hamper the fullest utilization of the productive powers. Sooner or later, man will change social relationships to give free scope to the expanding productive powers. Social change involves a political revolution. The existing political structure based on property relations, which becomes incompatible with the changed economic circumstances, is replaced by one appropriate to the economic order. Marx states:

> At a certain stage of their development the material productive forces of society come into contradiction with the existing productive relationships, or what is but a legal expression for these, with the property relationships within which they had moved before. From forms of development of the productive forces these relationships are transformed

> into their fetters. Then an epoch of social revolution opens. With the change in the economic foundation the whole vast superstructure is more or less rapidly transformed.[5]

The class struggle is the mechanism which affects this change. Along with the development of the forces of production, the differences between the two classes widen. The oppressed class, which stands to gain from a change in the existing property relations that would give a free scope to the forces of production, asserts itself and attempts to secure the political control. Because this class is aligned with the all-powerful productive forces, it is sure to succeed. Out of revolution comes a new structure of property relations which is appropriate for the expansion of the new productive forces. The change in the property relations leads to a transformation of the social institutions and ideas. All history follows a cycle of revolution, progressive evolution, the rise of and need for resistance to institutional change as part of further progress, degeneration, and again, revolution.

3. Historical Evolution of Theory

Marx and Engels distinguish between four different stages through which the relations of production (and hence society) have passed: primitive communism, slavery, feudalism, and capitalism.

Under the primitive communism, all output is owned in common. There is classless society. The division of labour exists only between the sexes. In the words of Engels, "The man wages war, goes hunting and fishing, procures the raw material of food and the tools required for these. The woman looks after the house and the preparation of food and clothing, cooks, weaves and sews."[6] The discovery of the possibility of domesticating and breeding wild animals leads to a separation of pastoral tribes from other tribes. This is the first step towards specialisation and creates scope for exchange to take place. Horticulture, the forerunner of agriculture, also appears towards the end of this stage. Simultaneously the weaving loom and the smelting of ores are discovered.

These new production possibilities "gave human labour power, the capacity to produce a larger product than was necessary for its

5. Marx, n. 3, p. 11.

6. Friederich Engels, *The Origin of the Family, Private Property and the State,* translated and reprinted in Burns' *A Handbook of Marxism,* p. 315.

maintenance."[7] They also increase the demand for labour to such an extent as cannnot be fully met under the existing form of society. "In the general historical conditions then prevailing the first great social division of labour, with its increase of the productivity of labour and therefore of wealth, and its widening field of production, necessarily brought slavery in its train."[8] Thus primitive communism gives way to slavery.

In the second stage, slavery is the dominant relation of production. Labour becomes more specialised. Division of labour, particularly between town and country, increases. Exchange flourishes and there appears a class of merchants who acts as intermediaries between producers. The institution of metallic money, private ownership of land, interest, mortgages, and testamentary procedures come into existence. States appear out of the need to provide a system of checks and balances among the divergent interests of the classes of this more complex society.[9]

With the further development of productive forces, slavery gives place to feudalism. In the countryside, there prevails sefdom under which the serf is tied to land but has a certain amount of personal dignity. In the town and country, there appears agriculture and handicraft industries characterised by small-scale production and private ownership by the workers of their instruments and means of production. The guild system comes into existence. With the expansion of production and exchange, the feudal type of set up becomes a hindrance to the further growth of productive powers of the economy.

> In all their production the burghers had remained hemmed in by the feudal political forms of the Middle Ages, which this production—not only manufacture, but even handicraft industry—had long outgrown: they were still entangled in all the thousandfold guild privileges and local provincial customs barriers which had become mere irritants and fetters on production.[10]

---

7. *Ibid.*, p. 317.
8. *Ibid.*
9. *Ibid.*, p. 320 ff.
10. Engels, n. 4, p. 270.

Further, because of the private ownership of the instruments and objects of labour, the production is on a small and restricted scale. Feudalism cannot meet the challenge and is, therefore, replaced by capitalism.

> To concentrate and enlarge these scattered, limited means of production, to transform them into mighty levers of production of the present day, was precisely the historic role of the capitalistic mode of production and of its representative, the bourgeoisie....The mode of production peculiar to the bourgeoisie—called, since Marx, the capitalist mode of production—was incompatible with the local privileges and the privileges of birth as well as with the reciprocal personalities of the feudal system; [therefore] the bourgeoisie shattered the feudal system, and on its ruins established the bourgeois social order, the realm of free competition, freedom of movement, equal rights for commodity owners and all the other bourgeois glories. The capitalist mode of production could now develop freely.[11]

Under capitalism, the workers lose control and ownership of their instruments of production. There emerges a class of capitalists, who own the means of production, and a propertyless but free proletariat. In the words of Marx:

> The capitalist system presupposes the complete separation of the labourers from all property in the means by which they can realise their labours....The process, therefore, that clears the way for the capitalist system, can be none other than the process which takes away from the labourer the possession of his means of production; a process that transforms, on the one hand, the social means of subsistence and of production into capital, on the other, the immediate producers into wage-labourers.[12]

The technical conditions of production undergo a substantial transformation from handicraft cottage industries to manufacture and then to "machine-facture." The industry, with the help of

---

11. *Ibid.*, pp. 280-88.
12. Karl Marx, *Capital,* translated from third German edition by S. Moore and E. Aveling, revised according to the fourth German edition by E. Untermann (Chicago: Kerr & Co., 1906), Vol. I, pp. 785-86.

capital and paid labour, assumes the character of production for the market place. In manufacturing, "the spindles and looms, formerly scattered over the face of the country, are now crowded together in a few great labour-barracks, together with the labourers and the raw material."[13] There is a greater degree of division of labour and complete separation of manufacturing from agriculture.

Later, the industrial revolution introduces the machine and thereby improves large-scale production techniques. As a result, there is greater centralisation, more elaborate marketing and financial institutions, a predominance of industrial over financial capital, monopoly, increasing inequalities of income, and colonialism.

> Hand in hand with this centralisation, or this expropriation of many capitalists by few, develop on an ever expanding scale the co-operative form of the labour-process, the conscious technical application of science, the methodical cultivation of the soil, the transformation of the instruments of labour into, instruments of labour only usable in common, the economising of all means of production by their use as the means of production of combined, socialised labour, the entanglement of all peoples into the net of the world market, and this, the international character of the capitalistic regime.[14]

Gradually, this system also develops internal contradictions.

> The monopoly of capital becomes a fetter upon the mode of production, which has sprung up and flourished along with, and under it. Centralisation of the means of production and socialisation of labour at last reach a point where they become incompatible with their capitalistic integument. The integument bursts as under. The knell of capitalistic private property sounds. The expropriators are expropriated.[15]

For a proper understanding of Marx's theory of economic development, it is very essential to understand his concepts of surplus value and "reserve army."

---

13. *Ibid.*, p. 818.
14. *Ibid.*, p. 836.
15. *Ibid.*, p. 837.

4. Theory of Surplus Value

A clear understanding of the Marx's theory of surplus value is very essential because on it is based his analysis of economic development under capitalism. In a capitalistic society, the whole population is divided into two classes. One class consists of capitalists who own all means of production. The other class consists of labourers who possess only their own labour power. They earn their livelihood by the sale of their labour. Labour along with the means of production (the equipment and natural resources) owned by the capitalists can produce more than that needed for sustaining labour and maintaining the capital equipment intact. In other words, the economy is capable of producing a surplus over and above the value of subsistence needs of the workers and the value of raw materials and equipment used up in production. This is what Marx calls 'surplus value.' The surplus is appropriated by the capitalist class in the form of net profits, interest and rent.

The exchange value of labour power like that of any other commodity is determined by the amount of socially necessary labour time required for the production and reproduction of labour power. In other words, it is determined by the amount of socially necessary labour time embodied in the labourer's means of subsistence. The means of subsistence are historically determined by the conditions in which the labouring class has been formed in any country and custom. These should be sufficient for ensuring the perpetuation of the labour class by enabling the labourers to raise a family. After hiring the labourer, the capitalist sets him to work. The labourer embodies his labour into commodities whose exchange-value is determined by the amount of socially necessary labour contained in these. The produce belongs to the capitalist who hires the labourer and owns the means of production on which the labourer works. But labour is capable of working for a time longer than that necessary for producing its means of subsistence. The exchange value of the produce of the labourer obtained by the capitalist, therefore, is greater than the exchange value of the means of subsistence paid to labourer by him. Thus the capitalist gains a surplus from the employment of labour. The wage rates cannot rise above the subsistence level because of the existence of the "industrial reserve army." The amount of employment depends upon the available stock of capital and the given state of technology. Within the given state of technology, there is no possibility of the substitution of labour for capital. At any particular time, the supply of labour is greater than the maximum employment made possible by the existing stock of capital. The competition for employment from the redundant labour (*i.e.*, the industrial reserve army) does not permit the wages to rise above the subsistence level.

The value of any commodity produced under capitalistic conditions can be divided into three components, *viz.* (1) constant capital (c) which includes raw materials and the means of production; (2) the variable capital (v) which is the part spent on hiring labour; and (3) the surplus value (s). The first component is called constant capital because it does not alter its value in the process of production. The second component is called variable capital because it alters its own value in the process of production; it produces the equivalent of its own value and also a surplus value which may itself be a variable magnitude. The distinction is important because of its emphasis on the fact that surplus arises only from the utilisation of the variable capital. Algebraically, the value of a commodity can be written as

$$c + v + s = \text{total value.}$$

Marx describes three ratios with these components of the total value. The rate of surplus value (s) is defined as the ratio of surplus value (s) to variable capital (v). Symbolically speaking

$$\frac{s}{v} = s'$$

Rate of surplus expresses the degree of exploitation of labour by capital. Marx makes a distinction between the simple rate of surplus value $\frac{s}{v}$, and the annual rate of surplus value $\frac{sn}{v}$, where n stands for the number of turnovers of the variable capital during a year. The rate of profit (p) is the ratio of surplus value to total capital outlay (c+v). Symbolically speaking

$$\frac{s}{c+v} = p$$

The annual rate of profit can be expressed as $\frac{sn}{c+v}$, where n indicates the number of turnovers of the variable and constant capital during a year. The organic composition of capital *(q)* is the relation between the constant and the variable capital in the total capital used in production. Symbolically, it can be expressed as

$$q = \frac{c}{c+v}$$

Some writers express it as $\frac{c}{v}$. Rate of profit can be expressed in terms of the rate of surplus value and the organic composition of capital as follows:

$$p = \frac{s}{c+v} = \frac{sv}{v(c+v)} = \frac{sc+sv-sc}{v(c+v)} = \frac{s(c+v)-sc}{v(c+v)} = \frac{s(c+v)}{v(c+v)} - \frac{sc}{v(c+v)}$$

$$= \frac{s}{v} - \frac{s}{v} \cdot \frac{c}{c+v} = s'(l-q).$$

The magnitude of the rate of surplus value depends on three factors, *viz.* (1) the length of the working day, (2) the quantity of the commodities entering into the real wage, and (3) the productivity of labour. The capitalist aims at maximising the mass of surplus value. The rate of surplus value can be increased either by an extension of the working day, or by a lowering of the real wage rate, or by an increase in the productivity of labour, or by any combination of the three methods. Marx makes a distinction between absolute and relative surplus value. Increase in the length of the working day produces an absolute surplus value while lowering of the wage rate and/or increase in productivity produces a relative surplus value. The rate of surplus can be raised by lowering wages only temporarily because the minimum subsistence wages are essential for maintaining the supply of labour. Increase in the rate of surplus value by raising productivity involves a change in the state of technology. On balance, technological progress has a strong tendency to increase the quantity of capital associated with each labourer. Thus exploitation of better techniques requires a large stock of capital. The stock of capital can be increased only if the capitalists save the economic surplus and do not consume it. Raising the productivity of labour is the major way of increasing the surplus value. There are definite physical limits to which surplus value can be raised by lengthening the working day and/or by reducing real wages.

Another way in which an individual capitalist can increase his absolute profits is an expansion of his output under the existing state of techniques. This, of course, requires an increase in outlay for labour, raw materials and capital equipment. Thus, increase in profits requires an increase in the volume of capital through a re-investment of profits.

5. Concept of "Reserve Army"

As the capitalism advances, there occurs a secular rise in the organic composition of capital, and a secular decline in the variable capital relative to total capital and hence in the demand for labour.

> Since the demand for labour is determined not by the amount of capital as a whole, but by its variable constituent alone, that demand...falls relatively to the magnitude of the total capital, and at an accelerated rate, as this magnitude increases. With the growth of the total capital, its variable constituent or the labour incorporated in it also does increase, but in a constantly diminishing proportion.[16]

The supply of labour increases with the growth of population which, according to Marx, is determined exogenously.[17] In addition, the ranks of the "would-be employed" are also enlarged by the technical changes in production, which are labour-displacing in nature. The technological changes release

> not only the labourers immediately turned out by the machines, but also their future substitutes in the rising generation, and the additional contingent, that with the usual extension of trade on the old basis would be regularly absorbed...(Consequently,) the demand for labour is not identical with increase of capital, nor the supply of labour with increase of the working class.... Capital works on both sides at the same time. If its accumulation, on the one hand, increases the demand for labour, it increases on the other the supply of labourers by the setting free of them, whilst at the same time the pressure of the unemployed compels those that are employed to furnish more labour, and

16. *Ibid.*, p. 690.
17. *Ibid.*, p. 699.

> therefore makes the supply of labour, to a certain extent, independent of the supply of labourers.[18]

As a result of the above, normally, there is excessive supply of labour. The relative surplus population is essential for capitalism. It

> forms a disposable industrial reserve army, that belongs to capital quite as absolutely as if the latter had bred it at its own cost. Independently of the limits of the actual increase of population, it creates, for the changing needs of the self-expansion of capital, a mass of human material always ready for exploitation.[19]

The most important function of the reserve army is to facilitate a quick movement of capital among old branches of production and in new pursuits. It provides

> the possibility of throwing great masses of men suddenly on the decisive points without injury to the scale of production in other spheres...(it is, therefore,) a necessity of modern industry.... The course characteristic of modern industry, *viz.*, a decennial cycle (interrupted by smaller oscillations), of periods of average activity, production of high pressure, crisis and stagnation, depends on the constant formation, the greater or less absorption, and the reformation of the industrial reserve army of surplus population.[20]

The reserve army determines the money wage rates through its influence upon the bargaining power of labour.

> Taking them as a whole, the general movements of wages are exclusively regulated by the expansion and contraction of the industrial reserve army, and these again correspond to the periodic changes of the industrial cycle.[21]
>
> The industrial reserve army, during the periods of stagnation and average prosperity, weighs down the active labour-army; during the periods of over-production and paroxysm, it holds its pretensions in check. Relative surplus population is therefore the pivot upon which the law of demand and

---

18. *Ibid.*, pp. 701-02.
19. *Ibid.*, p. 693.
20. *Ibid.*, pp. 694-95.
21. *Ibid.*, p. 699.

> supply of labour works. It confines the field of action of this law within the limits absolutely convenient to the activity of exploitation and to the domination of capital.[22]

Wages, therefore, have a tendency to fluctuate cyclically around the level of subsistence, which is defined as "the value of the means of subsistence necessary for the maintenance of the labourer."[23]

The size of the reserve army expands with the increase in the stock of capital. The larger the amount of capital per worker, the greater the productivity of labour and hence the smaller the number of workers employed to produce a given level of output.

> The fact that the means of production, and the productiveness of labour, increases more rapidly than the productive population, expresses itself, therefore, capitalistically in the inverse form that the labouring population always increases more rapidly than the conditions under which capital can employ this increase for its own self-expansion.... The greater the social wealth...the greater is the industrial reserve army.[24]

As the economy advances, therefore, the reserve army expands and as a result the bargaining power of labour grows weaker and weaker.

> Accumulation of wealth at one pole, is, therefore, at the same time accumulation of misery, agony of toil, slavery, ignorance, brutality, mental degradation, at the opposite pole, *i.e.*, on the side of the class that produces its own product in the form of capital.[25]

Marx thus argues that with the advancement of capitalism, the condition of labourers grows progressively worse. In *The Communist Manifesto*, he states:

> The modern labourer, on the contrary, instead of rising with the progress of industry, sinks deeper and deeper below the conditions of existence of his own class. He

22. *Ibid.*, p. 701.
23. *Ibid.*, p. 190.
24. *Ibid.*, pp. 707-08.
25. *Ibid.*, p. 709.

> becomes a pauper, and pauperism develops more rapidly than population and wealth.[26]

He writes this more strongly in *Capital:*

> Within the capitalist system all methods for raising the social productiveness of labour are brought about at the cost of the individual labourer; all means for the development of production transform themselves into means of domination over, and exploitation of, the producers; they mutilate the labourer into a fragment of a man, degrade him to the level of an appendage of a machine, destroy every remnant of charm in his work and turn it into a hated toil; they estrange from him the intellectual potentialities of the labour-process in the same proportion as science is incorporated in it as an independent power; they distort the conditions under which he works, subject him during the labour-process to a despotism the more hateful for its meanness; they transform his life-time into working-time, and drag his wife and child beneath the wheels of the Juggernaut of capital. But all methods for the production of surplus value are at the same time methods of accumulation; and every extension of accumulation becomes again a means for the development of those methods. It follows therefore that in proportion as capital accumulates, the lot of the labourer, be his payment high or low, must grow worse.[27]

6. Economic Development under Capitalism

With the preceding background, we can, now, proceed with the statement of the Marxian theory of capitalistic development. In a forceful statement, Marx traces the path of capitalistic development like this:

> That which is now to be expropriated is no longer the labourer working for himself, but the capitalist exploiting many labourers. This expropriation is accomplished by the action of the immanent laws of capitalistic production

---

26. Karl Marx and Friederich Engels, *The Communist Manifesto*, (ed.), S.H. Beer (New York: Appleton-Century Crofts, 1953), p. 22.

27. Marx, n. 12, pp. 708-09.

> itself, by the centralisation of capital. One capitalist always kills many. Hand in hand with this centralisation or this expropriation of many capitalists by few, develop, on an ever-extending scale, the co-operative form of the labour-process, the conscious technical application of science, the methodical cultivation of the soil, the transformation of the instruments of labour into only usable in common, the economising of all means of production by their use as the means of production of combined, socialised labour, the entanglement of all people in the net of the world market, and this, the international character of the capitalistic regime. Along with the constantly diminishing number of the magnates of capital, who usurp and monopolise all advantages of this process of transformation, grows the mass of misery, oppression, slavery, degradation, exploitation; but with this too grows the revolt of the working class always increasing in numbers, and disciplined, united, organised by the very mechanism of the process of capitalist production itself. The monopoly of capital becomes a fetter upon the mode of production, which has sprung up and flourished along with, and under it. Centralisation of the means of production and socialisation of labour at least reach a point where they become incompatible with their capitalist integument. This integument is burst as under. The knell of capitalist private property sounds. The expropriators are expropriated.[28]

Marx's theory of capitalistic development consists of four major principles, *viz.,* (1) accumulation of capital, (2) the increasing misery of labour, (3) the concentration of capital, and (4) the falling rate of profit. Let us describe these principles in a little more detail. As these principles are interrelated, we shall consider these together.

Accumulation of capital is the fundamental condition of economic growth. What determines the rate of capital accumulation? According to Marx, the "magnitude of the capital accumulated clearly depends on the absolute magnitude of surplus value."[29] "Hence all the

---

28. Karl Marx, *Capital,* Friederich Engels (ed.) (Chicago, 1926), Vol. I, pp. 836-37.
29. Marx, n. 14, p. 656.

circumstances that determine the mass of surplus value, operate to determine the magnitude of the accumulation."[30]

The surplus value increases with the increase in the rate of exploitation of labour, the unit wage, or the number of labour units. Marx believes that the rate of exploitation of labour increases with the rise in productivity. "But hand in hand with the increasing productivity of labour, goes...a higher rate of surplus value, even when the real wages are rising. The latter never rise proportionally to the productive power of labour."[31] And the productivity increases with the enlargement of the size of capital stock. "The more... capital increases by means of successive accumulations, the more does the sum of the value increase that is divided into consumption-fund and accumulation fund."[32] In an advancing economy, therefore, the surplus value (or profit), and hence the possibility of accumulation, increases progressively.

All profit, of course, is not invested. A part of profit is used by the capitalists for consumption. "But it is by the owner of the surplus-value, by the capitalist alone, that the division is made."[33] What guides the capitalist in allocating his profit between consumption and investment? According to the classical economists, the guiding force was the rate of profit. But Marx believed that the inducement to invest was independent of the rate of profit or the rate of interest since the desire and necessity for investment were inherent in the psychological make-up of the capitalists and in the structure of society.

> Only as personified capital is the capitalist responsible. As such he shares with the miser the passion for wealth as wealth. But that which in miser is a mere idiosyncracy (sic) is, in the capitalist, the effect of the social mechanism, of which he is but one of the wheels....It compels him to keep constantly extending his capital, in order to preserve it, but extend he cannot, except by means of progressive accumulation....To accumulate, is to conquer the world of social wealth, to increase the mass of human being exploited

30. *Ibid.*, p. 657.
31. *Ibid.*, p. 662.
32. *Ibid.*, p. 667.
33. *Ibid.*, p. 648.

> by him, and thus to extend both the direct and indirect sway of the capitalist.[34]

The capitalist's motto must, therefore, be "Accumulate, accumulate! That is Moses and the Prophets."

While surplus value provides the funds for accumulating additional capital, the expanding population meets the need of additional labour force. Marx believes that in the long run wages are above the absolute subsistence level and, therefore, there is scope for a gradual increase in population. "Ordinary wages suffice, not only for its (the working class's)[35] maintenance, but for its increase."[36]

Labour stands to gain when the accumulation of capital occurs within a given state of technology. Under such conditions, accumulation of capital increases the demand for labour at a rate faster than the rate of population growth and thereby leads to a rise in the wage rates. But rise in wage rates would bring into operation forces which could check further increases in wage rates. Firstly, rise in wages diminishes the rate of profits and thereby discourages the accumulation of capital. Decline in the rate of accumulation of capital decreases the demand for labour and thus halts the rise in wage rates. Secondly, higher wages facilitate earlier marriages which lead to an increase in the supply of labour. This comes very close to the views held by Malthus. If this is all what Marx has to say about the process of accumulation, he cannot lament the unhappy condition of the working class. Marx, however, does not press the Malthusian principle of population too hard and maintains that in the absence of "an iron law of wages," wages are likely to rise above the subsistence level. Further, he says, "once given the general basis of the capitalistic system, then, in the course of accumulation, a point is reached at which the development of the productivity of social labour becomes, the most powerful lever of accumulation."[37] Thus he bases his dire forecasts for capitalism on the technological progress.

---

34. *Ibid.*, pp. 648-52.
35. Words within parenthesis added.
36. Marx, n. 28, p. 636.
37. *Ibid.*, p. 681.

Given the possibility of technological progress, the capitalists can increase the surplus value more by introducing labour-saving inventions which raise the productivity of specified amount of labour-time than by an accumulation through duplication of the old equipment. Replacement of labour by capital, or in other words, association of a larger amount of capital per labourer, raises the organic composition of capital. Introduction of inventions by all capitalists lowers the cost of production and hence prices. But the capitalist who introduces the improved methods of production before others increases his profits. He lowers his cost of production but price does not fall because his output constitutes only a small portion of the total output. Once a capitalist has introduced better techniques others follow; firstly to share higher profits and afterwards because of the price pressure from those who have already introduced improved techniques. Those who fail to introduce improved techniques are driven into the proletariat class by the competition of more efficient capitalists. In this way, through the process of elimination of those capitalists who fail to keep pace with the advances in technology, capital tends to concentrate in fewer and fewer hands.

Accumulation of constant capital through the introduction of improved equipment renders the labour surplus.

> The instrument of labour, when it takes the form of a machine, immediately becomes a competitor of the workman himself. The self-expansion of capital by means of machinery is thenceforward directly proportional to the number of the work-people, whose means of livelihood have been destroyed by that machinery.... The portion of the working class, thus by that machinery rendered superfluous, *i.e.*, no longer immediately necessary for the self-expansion of capital, either goes to the wall in the unequal contest of the handicrafts and manufacturers with machinery, or else floods all the more easily accessible branches of industry, swamps the labour market, and sinks the price of labour-power below its value.[38]

Capitalism is an unstable and explosive system because it discards workers at a rate faster than that at which it hires them. Labour-saving inventions which render labour unemployed are very rapid.

38. *Ibid.*, p. 470.

Industrial reserve army grows not only because of the labour-saving inventions but also because of the increase in population. The larger capitalists absorb the smaller ones, machines replace skilled labour and those who are lucky enough to retain their jobs are enslaved to a life of dull routine and monotony. Still worse, the competition of the unemployed for employment enables the capitalists to reduce wages to a near starvation level. Capitalists exact more surplus value from a given wage payment not only by reducing wages but also by extending the working day. In competitive struggle, the capitalists resort even to employing and over-working women and children at wages lower than those paid to men.

The matters are made worse by the tendency of the rate of profits to fall.[39] As shown earlier,

$$p = s'(1-q).$$

In the above equation, it is obvious that, if the rate of surplus (s') remains constant, the rate of profit (p) varies inversely with the organic composition of the capital (q). As shown earlier in the course of capitalistic development, because of technological progress q has a tendency to rise. Consequently p will have a tendency to fall. As p depends not only on the organic composition of capital but also on the rate of surplus, the rate of profit would not fall if the change in q is offset or even more than that by the change in s'. There are a number of factors which counteract the tendency of the rate of profits to decline either by keeping down the organic composition of capital or by raising the rate of surplus value, *viz.* (1) cheapening the elements of constant capital, (2) foreign trade, (3) increased degree of exploitation, (4) reduction of wages below the value of labour power, and (5) increase in the industrial reserve army. Technological progress which cheapens the materials entering into the constant capital tends to keep down the organic composition of capital. Foreign trade enables a country to obtain raw materials and the necessities of life at a cost cheaper than the domestic cost of production. "To the extent that foreign trade cheapens partly the elements of constant capital, partly the necessities of life for which the variable is exchanged, it tends to raise the rate of profit by

39. It may be mentioned that, though the rate of profits falls, the absolute mass value of the surplus increases because of the increase in aggregate production.

raising the rate of surplus value and lowering the value of the constant capital."[40] The last three factors counteract the tendency of the profit rates to decline by raising the rate of surplus value. All these factors however are not strong enough to completely offset the tendency of the profits to decline and, therefore, profits tend to decline. As the profits decline, the capitalists try to maintain their profits by increasing the degree of exploitation of labour and by intensifying the expropriation of their weaker fellow-capitalists resulting into a further concentration and centralisation of capital. This may bring some temporary relief but ultimately it raises the organic composition of capital and thus accelerate the decline in the rate of profits. Decline in profit rate lowers the rate of accumulation leading towards economic stagnation which threatens the very foundation of capitalism.

Cyclical fluctuations are an integral part of the Marxian theory of capitalistic development. Marx predicts that crises would become more and more severe putting the existence of the entire bourgeois society on trial, each time more threateningly. Crises are caused, primarily, by three factors, *viz.* (1) tendency of profits to decline, (2) imbalanced growth of the different sectors of production, and (3) under-consumption.

As seen earlier, in the course of capitalistic development, profit rate tends to decline because of a rise in the organic composition of capital. Another reason for the declining tendency of profit rate is the rise in the wages of labour. Capital accumulation increases the demand for labour. Once the reserve army is exhausted, wages start rising. Rise in wage rates leads to a decline in profit rates. Decline in profit rates promotes "over-production, speculation, crises, surplus capital along with surplus population."[41] Further, "the barrier of the capitalist mode of production becomes apparent...in the fact that the development of the productive power of labour creates in the falling rates of profit a law which turns into an antagonism of this mode of production at a certain point and requires for its defeat periodical crises.[42] Decline in the rate of profits slackens the rate of

40. Karl Marx, *Capital.* Friederich Engels (ed.) (Chicago, 1926), Vol. III, p. 278.
41. *Ibid.*, p. 283.
42. *Ibid.*, p. 303.

capital accumulation leading to a crisis. Depression leads to a depreciation and destruction of capital and, by rendering the labour unemployed, to an expansion of the reserve army which results in a decline in wage rates. Destruction of capital and the decline in wage rates restore the profitability of production and thus recreates the conditions favourable for accelerating the rate of capital accumulation.

Secondly, the crises result from an imbalanced growth of the different sectors of the economy. In a capitalistic economy, the production is unplanned. Capitalists do not possess complete knowledge of their markets. Rapidly changing conditions make it impossible for the capitalists to estimate their markets through a process of trial and error over time. The result is the occurrence of under-production and over-production in certain sectors leading to general crises.

Thirdly, periodic crises and economic stagnation result from a failure of the consumption to keep pace with production. Marx rejects Say's law of market, *viz.*, supply creates its own demand.

> Nothing can be more childish than the dogma, that because every sale is a purchase, and every purchase a sale, therefore the circulation of commodities necessarily implies an equilibrium of sales and purchases.... If the interval in time between the two complementary phases of complete metamorphosis of commodity becomes too great, if the split between the sale and the purchase becomes too pronounced, the immediate connection between them, their oneness, asserts itself by producing a crisis.[43]

The purpose of the capitalistic production is the creation of surplus. Once the surplus has been produced, it can be realised by the capitalists only by the sale of these commodities. If it is not possible to sell whole, or a part, of these commodities or if these can be sold only at reduced prices, the capitalists may realise no surplus value at all or realise only a part of the surplus value, or may even lose a part, or whole, of their capital. The conditions of the production and those of the realisation of surplus value are not identical. These are separated logically as well as by time and space. Production of surplus value depends on the productive powers of society while its

---

43. Marx, n. 28, pp. 127-28.

realization depends upon the consuming powers of society. The consuming power of the capitalist class is restricted "by the tendency to accumulate, the greed for an expansion of capital and a production of surplus value on an enlarged scale. This is the law of capitalistic production imposed by incessant revolutions in the methods of production themselves, the resulting depreciation of existing capital, the general competitive struggle and the necessity of improving the product and expanding the scale of production, for the sake of self-preservation and on penalty of failure."[44] The consuming power of the proletariat class is limited by their poverty. The inability of the capitalists to sell commodities at their values leads to an interruption of production resulting into a depression. Boom is the period during which more means of production are produced than can ultimately be utilised.

> The epochs in which capitalist production exerts all its forces are always periods of overproduction, because the forces of production can never be utilised beyond the point at which surplus value can be not only produced but also realised.[45]

7. An Appraisal

Marx has proved a false prophet. He predicts that because of its inherent contradictions, capitalism will ultimately give place to socialism. Contrary to his prediction, advanced capitalistic countries are living in the full swing of prosperity. On the other hand, socialism has occurred in societies which have not reached a very high degree of capitalistic development.

Marx grossly overemphasizes the role of economic factors. In Communist Manifesto he asserts that capitalism "left no other nexus between man and man than naked self-interest, than callous 'cash payment'." He holds that social, political and legal institutions and ideas are determined by economic factors. This, however, is not completely true. The actions of an individual are guided not only by the desire for economic advantage but also by the desire for power, leisure, advantage and security. Religious and family considerations also influence a person's actions. Further, social, political and legal

44. Marx, n. 40, pp. 286-87.
45. Karl Marx, *Capital,* Friederich Engels (ed.) (Chicago, 1926), Vol. II, p. 363.

institutions and ideas exert an important influence on economic forces. In fact, economic and non-economic factors act and react upon each other.

> ...cultural, social, and political forces, reflecting different facets of human beings, have their own authentic, independent impact on the performance of societies, including their own economic performance.[46]

Marx predicts centralisation of capital into fewer and fewer hands and the disappearance of the middle class. Actually the number of capitalists has increased and the smaller capitalists are prospering side by side the larger capitalists. Contrary to Marx's prediction, the middle class has grown stronger and stronger and in certain countries it dominates the society. Marx's prediction regarding concentration of capital (or enlargement of the scale of production), of course, has proved fairly true. Technological progress has considerably enlarged the scale of production. But concentration has not gone to the extent of Marx's prediction. Governments in advanced countries have taken measures to check attempts towards trusts, cartels and monopolisation. Tendency towards concentration has been particularly weak in the agricultural sector.

An important factor in the Marxian analysis leading to the downfall of capitalism is the declining tendency of the rate of profits. Classical economists, such as Ricardo and Mill, also predict a decline in the rate of profits but on grounds different from those on which Marx bases his prediction. Marx's prediction of a declining rate of profit is based not on shortage of effective demand—or in Marx's terminology on the difficulty of realising surplus value—but on the rising organic composition of capital irrespective of the state of aggregate effective demand. Marx assumes that the rate of exploitation remains constant. On this assumption, Marx's law of declining profits is nothing but a simple tautology.[47] Rate of exploitation remaining constant, association of a larger amount of capital per worker would necessarily lead to a decline in the rate of profit. Assumption of a constant rate of exploitation, however, invalidates an important doctrine of Marx,

---

46. W.W. Rostow, *The Stages of Economic Growth* (Cambridge, 1960), p. 150.
47. Joan Robinson, *An Essay on Marxian Economics* (London, 1960), p. 36.

that is, the real wages remain at the subsistence level. Association of a larger amount of capital per worker raises the productivity of labour. If the labour obtains a constant proportion of the increasing total product, wages would rise above the subsistence level. Further, if, because of the economies of large scale production, a certain increase in capital leads to a more than proportionate increase in output, wages and profit can rise simultaneously. Summarising her position, Mrs. Joan Robinson remarks that Marx's "explanation of the falling tendency of profits explains nothing at all."[48]

The empirical evidence does not support the theoretical predictions of Marx. The real wages of workers, for instance, have not declined to a miserably low level; on the contrary, these have consistently risen with the advancement of industrialisation. The share of wages in the total output has not declined. It has remained more or less constant. It is true that, as predicted by Marx, there has occurred some increase in the capital intensity of production, but the accumulation of capital has proceeded at such a rapid rate that the structural unemployment has not increased much. Most probably due to abundance of innovating activity, the capital-output ratio has declined slightly, implying a rise in the average productivity of capital. This rise has made possible both capital accumulation and an increase in real wages simultaneously. Contrary to Marx's prediction, industrial concentration has not increased much since the turn of the century. Inequalities in the distribution of income have not increased. Rather there has been a slight decrease in these. The amplitude of cyclical fluctuations has not increased secularly. "Current experience suggests that socialism is not a stage beyond capitalism but a substitute for it...This makes a drastic reconsideration of Marx's central hypothesis necessary."[49]

Marx's consideration of crises as an integral part of the capitalist development is an important step forward. Classical school does not give due consideration to the problem of crises. Marx's analysis of crises, however, is not very precise. According to Marx decline in profits causes a crisis by reducing the investible funds. He does not consider the effect of a decline in profits on the

---

48. *Ibid.*, p. 42.

49. Joan Robinson, "Marx, Marshall and Keynes," The Delhi School of Economics, Occasional Paper No. 9 (Delhi, 1955), p. 27.

inducement to invest. So long as aggregate demand—consumption plus investment outlay—remains unchanged, a decline in investible funds cannot explain a decline in total output which is the characteristic of a crisis. Second factor leading to crises is a disproportionate growth of the different sectors of the economy resulting from the unplanned nature of capitalistic economy. It is doubtful if overproduction or underproduction in particular lines can explain the overall crisis. Third factor leading to crises is the failure of consumption to keep pace with production. According to Marx the under-consumption arises because the consuming power of the workers is limited by their poverty and that of capitalists by their unlimited desire for accumulation. But if capitalists are willing to accumulate irrespective of the rate of profit, lack of consumption demand would be offset by the additional investment demand and would not result into a crisis. Marx does not consider as to how the lack of consumption demand affects the rate of profit which in turn affects the inducement to invest.

Some of the ideas introduced by Marx in the theory of economic development have been emphasised by modern writers on economic growth, *e.g.*, role of technological progress and capital accumulation in economic development, proper balance between consumption and investment for stable growth, relationship between saving-investment relation on the one hand and the distribution of income on the other hand.

8. Conclusion

Though Marx's analysis is weak, his views have created immense influence. Realising that pure and simple capitalism cannot stand the test of time, capitalist countries have started introducing more and more elements of socialism in their economies. Marx could not foresee active state participation in economic affairs which, to a considerable extent, has prevented the downfall of capitalism predicted by Marx. The state, through its monetary and fiscal policies, has considerably controlled business fluctuations. It has diminished the misery of workers by regulating wage rates and the conditions of work. It has diminished the inequalities of wealth by taxing the richer classes and spending the proceeds on the poorer classes.

Further, Marx could not foresee important measures which have been taken to improve the lot of the workers and to diminish their misery, *e.g.*, raising wages, reduction in the hours of work, security schemes, profit-sharing and co-partnership schemes, labour welfare activities, etc. These measures have decreased the discontentment of the working classes and thus dampened their revolutionary feelings.

In the absence of such developments, which Marx could not foresee, capitalism might have collapsed.

Historical School

3

1. Stage of Growth

Many economic historians distinguish between different stages through which a country passes in the course of its economic development. Adam Smith uses the sequence of hunting, pastoral, agricultural, commercial and manufacturing. The different stages in Marx's sequence of development are: (1) primitive communism, (2) the ancient slave state, (3) feudalism, (4) capitalism, (5) socialism, and (6) communism. The idea of the stages of development is particularly popular among the German economists of the nineteenth century. According to list every nation passes through five stages of economic growth, *viz.* (1) savagery, (2) pastoral life, (3) agriculture, (4) agriculture and manufactures, and (5) agriculture, manufacture and trades. Hildebrand concentrates on a particular sequence of exchange relations: (1) barter, (2) money economy, and (3) credit economy. Bucher takes the area of economic transactions as a criterion of the stage of economic development: *(a)* independent domestic or household economy (production solely for the household and absence of exchange), *(b)* town economy (custom production, direct exchange of products by producers), and *(c)* national economy (wholesale production wide circulation of goods).

All these classifications have been criticised on a number of grounds. A classification may conform to the historical experience of some countries but no single classification can hold true in case of all countries. The sequence of development is not identical in all countries. A country may skip certain stages of development, *i.e.* it may reach a 'later' stage without having gone through an 'earlier' stage. A feudal society, for instance, may reach the stage of socialism without passing through the stage of capitalism. Different stages of development are not mutually exclusive and there are hangovers from earlier stages. Anything after the stage of settled agriculture, or even that stage itself, is necessarily composite: agriculture-cum-trade or agriculture-cum-trade-cum-industry.

FRIEDERICH LIST

Because of lack of space, it is not possible to examine the views of all the members of the historical school. We shall, therefore, briefly examine the views only of Friederich List, the most outstanding among the members of the historical school.

2. Scope for Industrialisation

List distinguishes between five stages of economic growth, *viz.*, (1) the savage stage, (2) the pastoral stage, (3) the agricultural stage, (4) the agricultural and manufacturing stage, and finally, (5) the agricultural, manufacturing, and commercial stage. He is not much interested in the first three stages and most of his discussion relates to the transition from third stage to fourth and fifth stages. All countries are not suited for becoming manufacturing nations. Nature has not bestowed the torrid zone with gifts which make a country fit for manufacturing. They, nevertheless, possess a natural monopoly of many products greatly desired by the Northern countries. The best policy for these countries is to pursue a policy of free trade and to continuously exchange agricultural commodities for manufactured products.

> A country of the torrid zone would make a very fatal mistake, should it try to become a manufacturing country. Having received no invitation to that vocation from nature, it will progress more rapidly in riches and civilisation if it continues to exchange its agricultural production for the manufactured products of the temperate zone.[1]

A country in the temperate zone, once it has reached a fairly high level of agricultural development, and if it possesses, in addition, a relatively dense population and varied resources, can progress further only by introducing manufactures. This can be accomplished under free trade if all the countries engaged at the time in manufacturing are at the same level of progress and civilization. In case some countries are far ahead of others in manufactures, commerce, and navigation, this can be done only by protecting

---

1. Friederich List, *National System of Political Economy*, translated by G.A. Mantle, Stephen Colwell, (ed.) (Philadelphia, 1856), p. 75.

domestic industry from foreign competition. Protection should be afforded temporarily and only if the nation has natural basis for industry. It should be gradually withdrawn as the industries become stronger. Under no circumstances should agriculture be afforded protection. Agriculture greatly benefits from the existence of a powerful industry. Industry requires cheap food and raw materials. Moreover, differences in soil and climate afford agriculture a kind of natural protection. In List's analysis, protection is only a transitional measure aimed at bringing all suitable nations up to the level of the most developed nation (which at that time was England) and ultimately would be replaced by a system of universal free trade.

3. Industrialisation—A Great Dynamic Force

In List's analysis, manufacturing is a great dynamic force. It stimulates increase in productivity in agriculture by providing growing demands for its output by the non-farm (manufacturing) population and by the transfer of more rational and efficient methods of production developed in manufacturing. Establishment of manufacturing leads to a fuller utilisation of natural resources. It furthers accumulation of capital. It promotes commerce and navigation. Dynamism of manufacturing is not confined only to the economic field. It extends also to political, social and cultural fields.

> In a country devoted to mere raw agriculture, dullness of mind, awkwardness of body, obstinate adherence to old notions, customs, methods, and processes, want of culture, of prosperity, and of liberty, prevail. The spirit of striving for a steady increase in mental and bodily acquirements, emulation, and of liberty, characterise, on the contrary, a State devoted to manufactures and commerce.[2]

A high state of civilization cannot be attained without the development of manufacturing. Exclusively agricultural people are necessarily rude and barbarous.

4. Productive Powers

List emphasizes the importance of productive powers and immaterial capital *(e.g.,* education, skill etc.) "*The power of*

---

2. *Ibid.*, p. 159.

producing wealth is therefore infinitely more important than *wealth itself.*"[3]

> A person may possess wealth, *i.e.,* exchangeable value; if, however, he does not possess the power of producing, objects of more value than he consumes, he will become poorer. A person may be poor; if he, however, possesses the power of producing a larger amount of valuable articles than he consumes, he becomes rich.[4]

What is true of individuals also holds in case of nations. List sharply criticises Adam Smith for concentrating only on the value in exchange and neglecting non-material elements in the productive power. Immaterial elements like education, skill, culture, development of sciences and arts, liberty of thought and conscience, institutions, laws, religion, morality, security, domestic and public regulations etc. have immense influence on the productive powers of a nation.

5. Balanced Growth

List advocates a balanced and harmonious development of the economy. He emphasizes the importance of balance between material and mental occupations, between agriculture, manufacturing and commerce, and between different branches of manufacturing. He fully recognises the connection between development and complementaries both on technical side and on the demand side. He particularly emphasises the complementarity between transport and manufacturing and the mutual stimulation of correctly composed production and consumption. He warns against lop-sided development arising from specialisation in agriculture and dependence on imported manufactured goods.

List rejects *laissez faire.* He sharply criticizes Smith's idea of complete harmony between individual and national interests.

> Nor does the individual merely by understanding his own interests best, and by striving to further them, if left to his own devices, always further the interests of the community.... Robbers, thieves, smugglers, and cheats know their own local and personal circumstances and conditions extremely well, and pay the most active attention to their business;

---

3. *Ibid.,* p. 108. Italics in the original.
4. *Ibid.,* p. 108.

> but it by no means follows therefrom that society is in the best condition where such individuals are least restrained in the exercise of their private industry.[5]

It is necessary to maintain a number of favourable institutions including various social, political, and legal arrangements of democratic government. But the most important thing which government can do is to ensure the establishment of manufacturing industry.

6. An Appraisal

List comes very near to modern economists on economic growth. His theory of stages is very similar to the modern concept of primary, secondary and tertiary production formulated by A.G.B. Fisher and Colin Clark. Modern literature strongly emphasizes the role of industrialisation in economic development. In underdeveloped countries, protection is considered to be an important instrument of establishing industries. State is assigned an important role in economic development.

List, however, has been strongly criticized for advocating the same pattern of development for all countries. He does not appreciate the diverse conditions prevailing in different countries requiring different patterns of development. He simply makes a distinction between the countries of the temperate zone and those of the tropics but this is an additional error. The distinction is artificial and cannot be supported by history. List is wrong in maintaining that "the production of raw materials and commodities among the great nations of temperate climes has no real importance but in regard to internal trade."[6] Production of raw materials is very important for the foreign commerce of some countries in the temperate zone, *e.g.*, United States. Further, history shows a considerable growth of commerce even in the agricultural stage before the development of manufacturing.

---

5. *Ibid.*, p. 134.
6. *Ibid.*, pp. 76-77.

Neo-Classical School

4

1. Background

By the time the neo-classical economists came to the scene, significant developments had taken place. Spectacular technological and resource discoveries had occurred. These discoveries made possible the achievement of a rapid rate of economic development. The possibilities of continued growth based on these discoveries were fairly bright. Contrary to the belief of classical economists, real wages were high, and rents did not constitute an increasing share of the national income. The growing economic development had dispelled the fear of the advent of a stationary state characterised by subsistence wage rates, low profits and rising rents. These developments necessitated a restatement of the whole body of the classical economic thought. The most important impact of the new circumstances on the economic thought was that the problem of economic development, which engaged the prominent attention of the classical school, receded into the background.

The classical economists believe that it is legitimate to assume that the state of technology and natural resources remain constant and the changes in the size of population depend upon the level of per capita income. Thus they correlate capital accumulation with the growth of population and formulate principles with regard to the long-term behaviour of the rate of development. Later developments, however, show that changes in population are not related to changes in the per capita income in simple Malthusian manner. Further, capital accumulation is, to a considerable extent, stimulated by technological and resource discoveries which cannot be explained by any simple set of economic relations. It thus becomes apparent that changes in important economic variables (*i.e.*, population, capital stock, technology) on which depends the rate of growth of income, are determined primarily by forces generally considered outside the realm of economics. The recognition of the possibilities of important autonomous changes in the factor supplies considerably weakens the classical economic system.

2. Short-run Analysis

The neo-classical economists are primarily interested in the short-run problems. They study the distribution of income, valuation, or the theory of general equilibrium from a purely short-term point of view. Most of them are mainly interested in the interrelations between different parts of the economy at a particular moment of time rather than over a certain period of time. The type of development that one can find in the neo-classical school is to be achieved through a more efficient allocation of the given resources. The neo-classical economists hold that the allocation of resources is more efficient under competitive conditions than under monopolistic conditions. Consequently, from a given amount of productive resources, a greater national income can be obtained under competitive conditions than under monopolistic conditions. An important exception to the general practice of the neo-classical economists of concentrating on the short period is their study of the rate of interest—a price that establishes a relation between the present and the future. The discussion of the rate of interest opens up the subject of capital accumulation. It is in this field that the neo-classical economists make a significant contribution to the theory of development.

3. Capital Accumulation

The classical school assumes that under given technological conditions, production requires labour and capital in fixed proportions. The neo-classical economists discard this assumption and accept the possibility of substitution between labour and capital. The implication of this is that accumulation of capital is possible without an increase in population. Accumulation of capital, population remaining constant, leads to an increase in the national and per capita income. Technology remaining unchanged, accumulation of capital, of course, results in a decline in the marginal productivity of capital.

The rate of saving is determined by the rate of interest and the level of income. At a given level of income, savings can be increased by raising the rate of interest. Given the state of technique and the level of population, rate of interest also determines the rate of investment. Investment can be stimulated by lowering the rate of interest. Technological progress is an important factor stimulating the rate of investment.

Given the size of population, the process of capital accumulation envisaged by neo-classical school is like this. Imagine a sudden and once for all increase in investment opportunities created by some technological discoveries. The demand for investment goods rises. The rate of interest and consequently the rate of saving rises. Since the supply of factors specialised in the production of capital goods is limited, increase in the rate of investment raises the relative prices of the capital goods. Rise in the rate of interest and in the relative prices of capital goods acts as a rationing device and restricts investment to the projects yielding the highest rate of return. As these projects reach the stage of fruition, both the rate of interest and the relative prices of capital goods decline which makes possible the undertaking of projects yielding lower rates of return. The process of a decline in the rate of interest and in the relative prices of capital goods and the undertaking of projects with lower and lower rates of return continues. Ultimately, the rate of interest declines to such a low level that no incentive is left for saving. At this stage accumulation of capital ceases and the economy reaches a stationary state. Neo-classical economists assume that full employment is maintained during the entire process of capital accumulation. They also assume that the supply of money remains constant and consequently the expansion of output leads to a decline in the general level of prices.

Within a given state of technology, the process of capital accumulation is like this. Imagine a certain increase in the size of the population. Increase in the supply of labour lowers money wage rates. Assuming that the aggregate demand remains unchanged in spite of a decline in money wage rates, it becomes profitable for the producers to expand output by enjoying additional labour. Association of additional labour with the existing capital equipment raises the marginal productivity of capital and thus increases the demand for investment goods. The rate of interest and consequently the rate of saving rises and thus funds are provided for increased investment. Then the process of accumulation proceeds towards the stationary state in a manner exactly similar to that described in the previous case. At this stage, as in the previous case, expansion of output results into a decline in the general level of prices. The per capita income at the new stationary position may be higher than, lower than, or equal to that at the previous position. If the natural resources are abundant and the resultant percentage increase in capital stock is at least as large as the percentage increase in population, the per capita income may be higher at the new position. On the other hand, if the supply of natural resources is limited, growth of population may be accompanied by a decline in the per capita income.

Most of the neo-classical economists subscribe to three interrelated notions: (1) economic development is a gradual and continuous process; (2) the process of development is harmonious and cumulative; (3) future possibilities of continued economic growth are bright.

4. Gradual and Continuous Process

The notion that economic development is a gradual and continuous process is particularly evident in the writings of Marshall, the leader of the neo-classical school. It seems that Marshall is deeply influenced by the evolution theories of Darwin and Spencer which visualize the evolution of human life as a gradual and continuous process. "Progress' or 'evolution", industrial and social, is not mere increase and decrease. It is organic growth."[1] Marshal further states, "...the maxim that 'nature does not willingly make a jump' ...is specially applicable to economic development."[2] Unlike Schumpeter, the neo-classicals view the act of invention and the adoption of new techniques as a smooth, slow, time-consuming and continuous process.

> And though an inventor, or an organiser, or a financier of genius may seem to have modified the economic structure of a people almost at a stroke; yet that part of his influence, which has not been, merely superficial and transitory, is found on enquiry to have done little more than to bring to a head a broad constructive movement which had long been in preparation.[3]

1. A.C. Pigou (ed.), *Memorials of Alfred Marshall* (London, 1925), p. 317.
2. Alfred Marshall, *Industry and Trade* (London, 1919), p. 3.
3. Alfred Marshall, *Principles of Economics*, 8th ed. (London, 1930), p. xiii.

5. Harmonious and Cumulative Process

The neo-classical school believes that the process of growth is harmonious and cumulative. Contrary to the classical school and Marx, the neo-classicals believe that the economic development benefits all major income groups, and in particular the labour class. Unemployment may be temporarily caused by monetary factors, wars, introduction of improved techniques etc., but it is incompatible with the long-run equilibrium. The introduction of labour-saving techniques may reduce the demand for labour in the concerned industries but simultaneously

> the prices of the products are generally much reduced, so that the demand for them, and therefore also the demand for the relevant labour, is absolutely increased; which, of course, means a tendency to raise wages. On the other hand, the assumed technical progress brings about an increase of the total production of the community, and consequently an increase of its total income. From this we get a general increase of the demand for labour. When this demand is spread over all the different kinds of labour, working class as a whole derives an advantage from technical advances.[4]

Another aspect of the cumulative and harmonious nature of the growth process relates to the various internal and external economies. Internal economies are those which arise from an increase in the scale of an individual firm while external economies are those which arise from the general expansion of the firm's industry or other industries supplying its needs. Expansion in the scale of a firm makes possible the introduction of more complicated machinery, the better organisation of marketing and research activities, the greater specialisation of labour and management etc., which give rise to a number of economies. External economies "depend on the aggregate volume of production of the kind in the neighbourhood; while others again, especially those connected with the growth of knowledge and the progress of the arts, depend chiefly on the aggregate volume of production in the whole civilized world."[5] At

---

4. Gustav Cassel, *The Theory of Social Economy*, translated by J. McCabe and T. Fisher (London, 1923), I, p. 319.
5. Marshall, n. 3, pp. 365-66.

another place Marshall speaks of external economies resulting from "the growth of correlated branches of industry which mutually assist one another, perhaps being concentrated in the same localities, but anyhow availing themselves of the modern facilities for communication offered by steam transport, by the telegraph and by the printing press."[6] He emphasizes the interdependent and complementary nature of the economy. Expansion of an industry leads to an increase in industrial know-how. It enhances the rate of technological progress by providing better opportunities for the interchange of knowledge. It stimulates the growth of auxiliary and ancillary industries. It generates demand for the products of other industries. These repercussions improve the profit prospects for the firm within the industry and thereby stimulate additional growth which, in turn, has stimulating effects upon other sectors of the economy. Expansion of an industry not only lowers its own costs but also those in other industries. Growth in one sector of the economy stimulates growth in other sectors of the economy. Thus development tends to propagate itself in a cumulative manner.

6. Optimism

The above analysis gives a clear impression that the neo-classical school is optimistic about the future possibilities for continued growth. The neo-classical writers are not much bothered by the ghost of the 'stationary state.' "There seems to be no good reason for believing that we are anywhere near a stationary state...."[7] Ricardo believes that historically production is subject to the law of diminishing returns because the fertile lands are scarce. Neo-classicals have great faith in man's ability to overcome the limitations on growth imposed by nature through technological progress and improvements in the quality of labour. "...while the part which nature plays in production shows a tendency to diminishing return, the part which man plays shows a tendency to increasing return."[8] Further, "the tendencies to increasing and diminishing return appear well balanced, sometimes the one, sometimes the other being stronger."[9] Under these conditions, a

6. *Ibid.*, p. 317.
7. *Ibid.*, p. 323.
8. *Ibid.*, p. 318.
9. *Ibid.*, p. 670.

proportionate increase in labour and capital would leave their marginal productivity unchanged.

Technological limitations on the possibility of raising income are not very serious. Because of the internal and external economies, even with constant technology and labour supply, the possibilities of raising national income through capital accumulation are favourable enough. With the increase in the stock of capital over time, the marginal productivity of capital declines very slowly. A small decline in interest rate would "suffice, as a rule, to set free possibilities of the profitable use of durable goods to such an extent that the consequent demands for a disposal of capital completely exhaust the supply, and so prevent any further fall of the rate."[10] Further, technological knowledge and wants tend to grow gradually and monotonously; this continually opens up new possibilities for an increase in per capita income.

Savings are very essential for economic development. Technological possibilities cannot be exploited for raising per capita income without the availability of sufficient savings. The neo-classicals believe the habit of thrift to be growing. According to Marshall as compared with earlier periods, man "is more unselfish, and therefore more inclined to work and save in order to secure a future provision for his family; and there are already faint signs of a bright time to come, in which there will be a general willingness to work and save in order to increase the stores of public wealth and of public opportunities for leading a higher life."[11]

The neo-classical economists, of course, are not so optimistic about the distant future. The Malthusian ghost does bother them when they look far ahead. Knut Wicksell, a leading Swedish economist, states "The unprecedented growth of population recently witnessed in Europe, and still more in certain extra-European countries, will certainly, sooner or later—probably in the course of the present century—prepare the way for much slower progress and possibly for completely stationary conditions."[12] Marshall, also, remarks, "And yet, if the growth of population should continue for

10. Cassel, n. 4, p. 215.

11. Marshall, n. 3, p. 680.

12. Knut Wicksell, *Lectures on Political Economy*, translated by E. Classen. (London, 1934), p. 214.

very long even at a quarter of its present rate, the aggregate rental values of land for all its uses (assumed to be as free as now from restraint by public authority) may again exceed the aggregate of income derived from all other forms of material property."[13] When looking far ahead, nor are the neo-classical economists very optimist about the opportunities for continued growth through international trade. Marshall warns that when only "a few small areas" of the world do not possess the population and capital to produce their own manufactures, "those who have surplus raw products to sell will have the upper hand in all international bargains.... It is this contradiction, rather than the prospect of any immediate danger which makes me regard the future of England with grave anxiety.'"[14] In other words, the old industrial countries are likely to suffer a secular deterioration in their terms of trade. Further, as the new countries develop by introducing techniques developed in older countries, the latter would face increasing competition in their export markets.

7. Role of International Trade

Neo-classicals emphasize the importance of international trade. International trade leads to a more efficient allocation of world's productive resources and thereby to a larger volume of world output. By enlarging the size of the market, it enables a country to benefit from further specialization and the division of labour. A country can raise its national income by participating in world trade. Increase in income makes possible a larger volume of saving and thus a higher rate of domestic capital formation. Neo-classicals, of course, are not so ardent advocates of free trade as are the classicals. They accept the "infant industry" argument. "It may be admitted that there is some force in the claim that a protective tariff is needed to aid giant businesses in establishing a complete standardization on the most advanced modern model."[15] Another justification for tax offered by Marshall is that "the energy developed in a few high-class progressive industries may spread over a great

13. Marshall, n. 3, pp. XV-XVI.
14. Alfred Marshall, "Memorandum on the Fiscal Policy of International Trade" Official Papers (London, 1926), p. 402.
15. Alfred Marshall, *Money, Credit and Commerce* (London, 1929), p. 218.

part of the industrial system of the country."[16] Edgeworth recognises that a country can improve its terms of trade by a tax on imports or exports "...under conceivable circumstances advantage may result to the home country from a tax on exports or imports."[17] Though the neo-classicals recognise certain exceptions to the free trade, they favour a general policy of free trade. "Protection might procure economic advantage in certain cases, if there was a Government wise enough to discriminate those cases, and strong enough to confine itself to them; but this condition is very unlikely to be fulfilled."[18] According to Nicholson, "Free trade, like honesty, still remains the best policy."[19]

8. Appraisal of Neo-classical Analysis

The neo-classical theory of economic growth is inadequate and narrow. According to the neo-classicals, the rate of development depends primarily on changes in the size of population, capital stock, natural resources and technological improvements. They do not sufficiently recognise the importance for economic development of unmeasurable and non-economic elements like political, economic, social and legal institutions, attitude of the masses to seek material advancement, to work, to save etc. Marshall, of course, is an exception to this. He fully recognises the limited nature of his analysis and stresses the importance of unmeasurable and non-economic elements. Neo-classicals believe development to be gradual, continuous and harmonious process. Historically, however, development has been discontinuous. Further, it has created disharmony between different income-groups, at least, in the early stages. Neo-classical economists overemphasize the importance of interest rate, and minimise that of institutional factors, in determining savings and investment. Their assumption of full employment is not backed by an adequate analysis of the problem of maintaining an aggregate demand at a full employment level. Neo-classicals, like the classical economists, do not recognise the role of government in shaping institutions to promote economic development. They

16. *Ibid.*
17. F.Y. Edgworth, *Papers Relating to Political Economy* (London, 1925) II, pp. 16-17.
18. *Ibid.*, p. 18.
19. *Ibid.*, p. 17.

concentrate primarily on the analysis of relative values and permit the problem of economic development to recede into the background. This was probably because of their faith in the steady and harmonious economic growth.

Joseph A. Schumpeter

5

1. Introduction

The Schumpeterian theory of economic development was first presented in the book, *The Theory of Economic Development,* first published in German in 1911.[1] Later on, Schumpeter gave a more mature and complete version of his theory of economic growth in the book, *Business Cycles,* published in 1939.[2] A distinctive feature of the early theory of economic development of Schumpeter is its optimistic outlook. Economists before Schumpeter give a very pessimistic outlook about the progress of society. Classicals predicted the end of the development process in a stationary state while Marx believed in the ultimate downfall of capitalism. Schumpeter holds that capitalism can lead to ever-higher levels of real income at the cost of nothing more than temporary interruptions in economic activity. In Schumpeter's analysis, there is no place for the immutable law of diminishing returns and the Malthusian principle of population checking economic progress (Ricardo), there is no inherent tendency towards a maldistribution of income leading to successively more severe crises (Marx), nor is there a persistent tendency towards savings exceeding investment opportunities at the full employment level leading to chronic underemployment (stagnationists). Though Schumpeter starts with an optimistic outlook, he ends with a pessimistic view about the capitalistic system of society.

In contrast to neo-classicals who viewed development as a gradual and harmonious process. Schumpeter holds that development takes place by disharmonious leaps and spurts as entirely new investment horizons are exploited. Long-run development is accompanied by short-period booms and slumps.

---

1. Joseph A. Schumpeter, *Theory of Economic Development* (Cambridge, 1934).
2. Joseph A. Schumpeter, *Business Cycles* (New York, 1939).

In Schumpeter's analysis, the growth of output depends upon the rate of change of the productive factors, rate of change of technology, and the rate of change of socio-cultural set-up. All these factors, however, are not equally important contributors to the rate of growth of the economy. The changes in the supply of productive factors can bring about only a gradual evolution of the economic system. Schumpeter wrote, "Increase in productive resources might at first appear to be the obvious prime mover in the process of internal economic change. Physical environment being taken as constant... that increase resolves itself into increase of population and the increase in the stock of producers' goods."[3] However,

> the mere growth of the economy, as shown by the growth of population and wealth...calls forth no qualitatively new phenomena, but only processes of adaptation of the same kind as changes in the natural data...[In addition,] these changes are small per annum and therefore do not stand in the way of the applicability of the "static" method.[4]

In contrast, "Different methods of employment (of existing factor supplies), and not savings and increases in the available quantity of labour, have changed the face of the economic world in the last fifty years."[5]

2. Growth and Development—Distinguished

Schumpeter distinguishes between two classes of influences upon the dynamic evolution of an economy, *viz.*, (1) the effects of changes in factor availabilities, which he calls the "growth" component and (2) the effects of technological and social change which he refers to as "development" or "evolution."

Defining the first class of influences, Schumpeter writes:

> We shall designate by term (positive or negative) growth changes in population...and in the sum total of savings plus accumulations corrected for variation in the purchasing power...of the monetary unit. That term is to emphasize not only that variation in both these variables is continuous

3. *Ibid.*, p. 74.
4. Schumpeter, n. 1, p. 63 and footnote.
5. *Ibid.*, p. 68.

> in the mathematical sense...but also that it occurs at a rate which changes but slowly.[6]

He defines the second class of influences as below:

> Development in our sense is a distinct phenomenon, entirely foreign to what may be observed in the circular flow or in the tendency towards equilibrium. It is spontaneous and discontinuous change in the channels of the flow, disturbance of equilibrium, which for ever alters and displaces the equilibrium state previously existing. Our theory of development is nothing but a treatment of this phenomenon and the processes incident to it.[7]

Let us first analyse the growth component. As Schumpeter takes land to be constant, the growth component includes only the effects of changes in population and of increase in producer goods.

According to Schumpeter, population growth is exogenously determined. There does not exist a unique *a priori* relationship between changes in population and variations in the flow of goods and services.[8] Schumpeter considers population-induced increase in output to be a part of the "growth" component rather than that of "development" component. The growth of population is a slow process, which is not subject to violent independent fluctuations.[9] "On the whole it is much more correct to say that population grows slowly up to the possibilities of any economic environment than that it has any tendency to outgrow it and to become thereby an independent cause of change."[10]

The increases in producer goods, which normally result from a positive rate of net savings,[11] is also included in the "growth" portion of total output. "Long time changes in the rate of savings come about by truly infinitesimal steps.... Autonomously, abrupt changes in the rate of savings hardly ever occur."[12] Savings are rarely an independent cause of change.

---

6. Schumpeter, n. 2, p. 83.
7. *Ibid.*, p. 83.
8. *Ibid.*, p. 74.
9. Schumpeter, n. 1, p. 68.
10. *Ibid.*, p. 68.
11. Schumpeter, n. 2, p. 75.
12. *Ibid.*, p. 81.

> We start from competitive equilibrium, although extension to the imperfectly competitive case would not present any difficulties. Now, that equilibrium is incessantly disturbed by the flow of new savings which are being offered to the firm. If, however, the system is adapted to the actual rate of savings—an assumption which is not only reasonable under the circumstances of this model, but also much nearer the truth in reality than devotees of oversaving theories are in the habit of admitting—this disturbance will be currently absorbed; for, as long as saving goes on at all, each installment will depress the rate of interest to the extent required to create its own investment opportunity.[13]

Historically, the increase in the stock of producer goods is primarily the result of those dynamic elements which are largely absent in a smoothly expanding economy.

> Whatever definition of saving the reader adopts, it is clear that most of its sources, as well as most of the motives for it, would be absent in a stationary state. If we take up any of the familiar attempts at estimating statistically the amount of saving done in any country at any time, we see immediately that the bulk of it, whether done within the sphere of business or the sphere of households, flows from revenues or elements of revenues which would not exist at all in a stationary state, namely from profits, or from other incomes created or swelled by previous economic change. As to motives, it is equally obvious that most of them arise out of situations incident to economic change...its quantitative importance would be exceedingly small...if the economic process in any way approximated the equilibrium picture: Saving would be a "trickle."[14]

The savings and accumulation, therefore, primarily owe to profits. However, "without development there is no profit, without profit no development."[15] In a circular flow economy, there are no profits because the value of the means of production is precisely equal to the value of the means of production incorporated in it.

13. *Ibid.*, p. 79.
14. *Ibid.*, p. 83.
15. Schumpeter, n. 1, p. 154.

Profits arise when new techniques of production are employed to manufacture a certain product, or if a new product is introduced. Changes in the stock of producer goods, therefore, owe to changes in the fund of applied technical knowledge.

To turn to the "development" component, in regard to the socio-cultural factors, Schumpeter subscribes to Marx's materialistic interpretation of history. He states:

> Because of this fundamental dependence of the economic aspect of things on everything else, it is not possible to explain *economic* change by previous *economic* conditions alone. For the economic state of the people does not emerge simply from the preceding economic conditions, but only from the preceding total situation. The expository and analytical difficulties which arise from this are very much diminished, practically if not in principle, by the facts which form the basis of economic interpretation of history; without being compelled to take a stand for or against this view, we can state that the economic world is relatively autonomous because it takes up such a great part of a nation's life, and forms or conditions a great part of the remainder.[16]

In Schumpeter's analysis, economic development is more or less synonymous with discontinuous technological change.

> In so far as the "new combination" (of the productive factors) may in time grow out of the old by continuous adjustment in small steps, there is certainly change, possibly growth, but neither a new phenomenon nor development in our sense. In so far as this is not the case, and the new combinations appear discontinuously, then the phenomenon characterizing development emerges. For reasons of expository convenience, henceforth, we shall only mean the latter case when we speak of new combinations of productive means. Development in our sense is then defined by the carrying out of new combinations.[17]

Development in this sense covers the following five combinations: (1) The introduction of a new good—that is one with which

---

16. *Ibid.*, p. 58 (Italics in original).
17. *Ibid.*, pp. 65-66.

consumers are not yet familiar—or of a new quality of a good. (2) The introduction of a new method of production, that is one not yet tested by experience in the branch of manufacture concerned, which need by no means be founded upon a discovery scientifically new, and can also exist in a new way of handling a commodity commercially. (3) The opening of a new market, that is a market into which the particular branch of manufacture of the country in question has not previously entered, whether or not this market has existed before. (4) The conquest of a new source of supply of raw materials or half-manufactured goods, again irrespective of whether this source already exists or whether it has first to be created. (5) The carrying out of a new organisation of any industry, like the creation of a monopoly position (for example, through trustification) or the breaking of a monopoly position.[18]

3. Role of Entrepreneur

The development is not spontaneous. It must be actively promoted by some agency within the system. The agent who introduces new combinations of the factors of production is called by Schumpeter an "entrepreneur" and what he creates is termed as "enterprise" or "innovation." Entrepreneur is the central figure in Schumpeter's model of economic development. He revolutionises the pattern of production by exploiting inventions, by exploiting untried technological possibilities for producing new commodities, by producing old commodities in new ways, by opening up new sources of supply of materials, by opening new outlets for products, by reorganising an industry and so on. He considerably affects the consumer tastes and preferences.

> ...innovations in the economic system do not as a rule take place in such a way that first new wants arise spontaneously in consumers and then the productive apparatus swings round through their pressure....It is...the producer who as a rule initiates economic change, and consumers are educated by him if necessary; they are, as it were, taught to want new things, or things which differ in some respect or other from those which they have been in the habit of using.[19]

18. *Ibid.*, p. 66.
19. *Ibid.*, p. 64.

Schumpeter does not deny that sometimes spontaneous changes occur in the consumer's wants and preferences and producers cope with these. But such changes are not very important.

Entrepreneur is different from an ordinary manager. The manager runs the business on established lines while the entrepreneur introduces innovations. Entrepreneur is also different from a capitalist. The capitalist furnishes funds while the entrepreneur directs the use of these funds. "It is leadership rather than ownership that matters."[20] Entrepreneur need not necessarily be the inventor of the product or the process which he introduces. Entrepreneurship "does not essentially consist in either inventing or otherwise creating the conditions which the enterprise exploits. It consists in getting this done."[21] The distinctions mentioned above, of course, do not exclude the possibility of the same person being an entrepreneur, an inventor and a capitalist at the same time.

The entrepreneurs are not motivated solely by the desire for profit.

> First of all, there is the dream and the will to found a private kingdom, usually, though not necessarily, also a dynasty....Then there is the will to conquer; the impulse to fight, to prove oneself superior to others, to succeed for the sake, not of the fruits of success, but of success itself.... Finally, there is the joy of creating, of getting things done, or simply of exercising one's energy and ingenuity.[22]

Thus, like the Marxian capitalist, who accumulates for the sake of accumulation, the Schumpeterian innovator innovates, at least in part, for the sake of innovating.

The nature and activities of the entrepreneur are conditioned by the socio-cultural set up in which he operates. The capitalist rationality and bourgeois institutions are important prerequisites for the flourishing of entrepreneurial activity. "It is...quite wrong ...to say, as many economists do, that capitalist enterprise was one, and technological progress a second, distinct factor in the observed

20. Schumpeter, n. 2, p. 103.
21. Joseph A. Schumpeter, *Capitalism, Socialism and Democracy* (London, 1950), p. 61.
22. Schumpeter, n. 1, p. 93.

development of output; they were essentially one and the same thing or, as we may also put it, the former was the propelling force of the latter."[23]

To perform his functions the entrepreneur requires two things. In the first place, there must exist technical knowledge with which the entrepreneur can introduce new products or the new combinations of the factors of production. This, according to Schumpeter, poses no problem because there always exists a reservoir of unused technical inventions on which the would-be entrepreneur can bank. "It is no part of his function to 'find' or to 'create' new possibilities. They are always present, abundantly accumulated by all sorts of people."[24]

Secondly, since the introduction of innovations requires diversion of the means of production from existing channels into new processes, the entrepreneur must possess command over the factors of production. This is provided by monetary claims in the form of credit, which constitute "capital" in the Schumpeterian sense. "We shall define capital, then, as that sum of means of payment which is available at any moment for transference to entrepreneurs."[25]

For Schumpeter capital is not the stock of real assets of a community. It is a fund of liquid purchasing power. Further Schumpeterian capital is not a factor of production.

> The function of capital consists in procuring for the entrepreneur the means with which to produce. It stands as a third agent necessary to production in an exchange economy *between* the entrepreneur and the world of goods. It constitutes the bridge between them. It does not take part directly in production, it is not itself 'worked up'; on the contrary it performs a task which must be done before technical production can begin.[26]

4. Role of Credit

Savings out of current income played an important role in the classical models of economic development. In Schumpeter's model

23. Schumpeter, n. 21, p. 124.
24. Schumpeter, n. 1, p. 88.
25. *Ibid.*, p. 122.
26. *Ibid.*, p. 116.

of economic development, far more important role is played by the credit creation by banks. "The banker, therefore, is not so much primarily a middleman in the commodity 'purchasing power' as producer of his commodity."[27] Entrepreneurs carry out innovations with the help of finance obtained from banks. Successful completion of innovations yields funds out of which entrepreneurs pay back their loans to the banks.

> By far the greater part of it (saving)[28] does not come from thrift in the strict sense, that is from abstaining from the consumption of part of one's regular income, but it consists of funds which are themselves the result of successful innovation and in which we shall later recognise entrepreneurial profit.[29]

Credit enables entrepreneurs to obtain productive resources before they have acquired a normal claim to these.

> The essential function of credit in our sense consists in enabling the entrepreneur to withdraw the producers' goods which he needs from their previous employments, by exercising a demand for them, and thereby to force the economic system into new channels....By credit, entrepreneurs are given access to the social stream of goods before they have acquired the normal claim to it. It temporarily substitutes, as it were, a fiction of this claim for the claim itself. Granting credit in this sense operates as an order on the economic system to accommodate itself to the purposes of the entrepreneur, as an order on the goods which he needs: It means entrusting him with productive forces.[30]

Credit gives the entrepreneur a command over the factors of production before he has created a corresponding value in real goods and services. In the short run, therefore, the granting of credit is inflationary. But, when the fruits of successful innovation enter the market, the value added to the social product exceeds the value of the claims created by the amount of the entreprenurial-profit.

---

27. Schumpeter, n. 1, p. 74.
28. Words within parentheses added.
29. Schumpeter, n. 1, p. 72.
30. *Ibid.*, pp. 106-07.

> The equivalence between the money and commodity streams is more than restored, the credit inflation more than eliminated, the effect upon prices more than compensated for, so that it may be said that there is no credit inflation at all in this case—rather deflation—but only a non-synchronous appearance of purchasing power and of the commodities corresponding to it, which temporarily produce the semblance of inflation.[31]

5. Grouping of Entrepreneurial Activities

The entrepreneurial activities appear in a swarm-like fashion. "The new combinations are not, as one would expect, according to general principles of probability, evenly distributed through time... but appear, if at all, discontinuously in groups or swarms." This is because the "appearance of one or a few entrepreneurs facilitates the appearance of others, and these the appearance of more, in ever increasing numbers."[32]

First of all:

> Only a few people have these qualities of leadership and only a few in...a situation which is not itself already a boom can succeed in this direction. However, if one or a few have advanced with success many of the difficulties disappear. Others can follow these pioneers...Their success again makes it easier...for more people to follow suit, until finally the innovation becomes familiar and acceptance of it a matter of free choice.[33]

Secondly, as the entrepreneurial qualities are distributed according to a normal curve, "the number of individuals who satisfy progressively diminishing standards in this respect continually increase. Hence...with the progressive lightening of the task continually more people can and will become entrepreneurs."[34]

Thirdly:

> Reality also disclosed that every normal boom starts in one or a few branches of industry...and that it derives its

31. *Ibid.*, p. 110.
32. *Ibid.*, p. 228.
33. *Ibid.*
34. *Ibid.*, pp. 228-29.

> character from the innovations in the industry where it begins. But the pioneers remove the obstacles for the others not only in the branches of production in which they first appear, but...in other branches too.[35]

6. Economic Cycles

The swarm-like appearance of entrepreneurs is responsible for the cyclical nature of economic progress. The clustering of innovations causes a discontinuous disturbance which explains the features of a boom. It also requires a special process of adaptation of the economy in the form of periodic depressions, "which may therefore be defined from our standpoint as the economic system's struggling towards a new equilibrium position, its adaptation to the data as altered by the disturbance of the boom."[36]

The upper turning point arises because the credit-financed innovations bid up the production factor prices, while the goods resulting from innovations suddenly arrive in the market. Further, there occurs a credit deflation as a result of the repayment of loans by the entrepreneurs. At this stage there is no fresh demand for finance as the relationship between product prices and factor prices have rendered further innovations unprofitable. Losses occur and the depression persists until the cost price equilibrium stabilizes.[37] Then there appears a new swarm of innovations and whole cycle is repeated again.

7. Trend of Growth

Secularly, the capitalistic system is characterized by cyclically induced rising level of national income and output per head. Further, the long-run rise in average real income is accompanied by a redistribution of real output in favour of the lower income groups since productivity-raising innovations occur largely in the manufacture of mass-produced commodities which account for a larger share of a typical worker's budget. In this way, "the capitalist process, not by coincidence but by virtue of its mechanism, progressively raises the standard of life for the masses."[38]

---

35. *Ibid.*, p. 229.
36. *Ibid.*, p. 231.
37. *Ibid.*, pp. 242-43.
38. Schumpeter, n. 21, p. 68.

For Schumpeter, there was no limit to the increase in the rate of output per head. He did not subscribe to the idea that the economy has a tendency to ultimately reach the stationary state. As the expansion of output, in his analysis, is geared to the rate of innovation, a ceiling on per capita income would imply that technological progress is subject to historically diminishing returns. He could see no reason as to why it should be so.

> Technological possibilities are an uncharted sea....From the fact that some of them have been exploited before others, it cannot be inferred that the former were more productive than the latter. And those that are still in the lap of the gods may be more or less productive than any that have thus far come within our range of observation...There is no reason to expect slackening of the rate of output through exhaustion of technological possibilities.[39]

8. Operation of the Development Process

Schumpeter starts with a purely competitive economy in a stationary state characterized by a circular flow which regularly repeats itself. In a circular flow economy the economic system is in general 'equilibrium. All economic activity repeats in a routine manner. Every firm in the system is in perfect competitive equilibrium, with its costs, consisting of wages and rent, exactly equal to its receipts. Prices everywhere are equal to average costs; profits are zero; there are no savings; there is no net investment; interest rates are zero; population is constant; all the resources are fully employed. Every household, like every firm, is in full long-run equilibrium with receipts equal to expenditure; there is no scope for advantageous alteration in the budgetary pattern.

The essence of development is spontaneous and discontinuous change in the circular flow and disturbance of the existing equilibrium which gives place to a new equilibrium. The disturbance comes in the form of innovations. In a capitalistic society, there are always possibilities of new combinations of the means of production. Entrepreneurs recognise these profit opportunities and set out to exploit these. They borrow funds from the banks for obtaining productive resources to carry out the innovation. Once the initiative is taken by a few leaders, others follow in an increasing number and

39. *Ibid*., p. 118.

the path gets progressively smoothened for successors by an accumulation of experience and removal of obstacles.

The boom in entrepreneurial activity raises the demand for productive resources. There being no unemployed resources before the development process starts, competition among entrepreneurs for the existing productive resources will raise their prices. Consequently, money incomes will rise and a positive rate of interest emerge. Detachment of a part of productive resources of the existing firms by new entrepreneurs will lead to a diminution of the output of consumption goods. Demand for consumer goods remaining the same, their prices will rise leading to an increase in the revenue of the businessmen.

The innovational activity induces a second economic wave which is superimposed on the primary wave. Additional consumer spending encourages old firms to expand their production. Speculation develops as many people think that a rise in prices and income will continue indefinitely. New borrowing, then, finances not only entrepreneurs but also general expansion which is partly the result of speculative activity. Generally, in terms of quantity, the secondary wave is more important than the primary wave. The secondary wave covers a much wider surface and can be seen more easily. This is one reason why the element of innovation has been so much neglected in the traditional analysis of the business cycles. The primary process is free from cyclical clusters of errors, excesses of optimism and pessimism but these have an important place in the secondary wave. This leads to many unproductive loans and overindebtedness.

During the early stages, of the upswing, the composition of total output shifts from consumer to producer goods. But as the new plants start functioning, new commodities flow into the market. Here starts a process of 'creative destruction.' The new commodities cannot be smoothly absorbed into the economic system. There appears a disequilibrium and the process of adjustment begins to take place. The effect of the process of adjustment is not uniform on all 'old' firms.

> For some of the 'old' firms new opportunities for expansion open up: the new methods or commodities create New Economic Space. But for others the emergence of the new methods means economic death; for still others, contraction

> and drifting into the background. Finally, there are firms and industries which are forced to undergo a difficult and painful process of modernisation, rationalisation and reconstruction.[40]

The index of total output would not show these vital parts of the mechanism of the economic evolution; it would show merely an increase in aggregate output.

The expansion, however, would not continue indefinitely. In addition to several accidents and incidents, there are two important tendencies inherent in the process of economic expansion which cause a decline in economic activity. Firstly, entrepreneurial activity characteristically starts off in a definite direction and does not distribute itself equally over the whole economy. There are limits to which a particular industry can advance without a corresponding development of other industries. Secondly, innovations disturb the existing equilibrium leading to a constant revision of the values of different elements in the system with a view to adapt to changing temporary situations. It becomes very difficult to estimate costs and receipts. Uncertainty increases the risk of failure of the new enterprise. Before embarking on additional innovations, entrepreneurs tend to wait until the equilibrium is established again. This innovational activity ceases not because no more innovations are available but because the economic climate is unfavourable to further innovations. Further, as the innovations start yielding fruit, entrepreneurs repay the loans to banks. Repayment of loans causes deflationary effects. Decline in innovational activity and the repayment of loans by entrepreneurs lower prices and money income and thereby intensify the adjustment process. All this, however, is not sufficient to cause a full-fledged depression. It causes only a painful readjustment process or recession and, before long, the economic environments, again, become favourable for further entrepreneurial activity.

It is the cessation of innovational activity on the secondary investment wave which precipitates a full-fledged depression. As earlier a major portion of the investments in the secondary wave is of a speculative nature (*i.e.* investments are based on expected price rises) which would collapse at the slightest impairment of prices.

40. Schumpeter, n. 2, p. 134.

Further, in the secondary wave of prosperity, there develop reckless, fraudulent or otherwise unsuccessful enterprises which cannot stand the test of the adjustment during the recession. Consequently, as soon as the prices begin to fall, a part of the debt structure crumbles. This would not necessarily lead to a panic or crises. But when the prices begin to fall, there takes place a vicious spiral. Prices fall simply because they have fallen. Fall in prices enforces liquidation which in turn again leads to a further fall in prices. People begin to wonder as to how much there is to liquidate. They even go into hysterics about it. This pessimistic expectation may for a time acquire a causal role. Thus there occurs a vicious spiral of falling prices and contraction. Under the pressure of the breakdown of the secondary wave and of the bearish anticipation induced by it, the process outruns and misses the neighbourhood of the equilibruim to which it was moving and the abnormal liquidation leads to the conditions of depression.

When the depression has run its course, the system tends to work its way towards a new neighbourhood of equilibrium. This new neighbourhood of equilibrium is not the same which would have been reached in the absence of abnormal liquidation. Firstly, abnormal liquidation destroys many things which could and would have survived without it and thus produces a pattern different from that which would have evolved under a normal process. Secondly, depression may take considerable period of time. During this period economic data changes and what would have been a neighbourhood of equilibrium when the depression started is no longer one when all is over. The process from depression to new neighbourhood of equilibrium is known as Recovery.

It can be shown that depressive process has a tendency to stop itself. As seen earlier, the spiral process occurs because of a number of unfavourable individual events like bankruptcies, breaks in individual markets, shutdowns, etc. These induce similar events but each of them taken by itself loses momentum as its effects spread.

> The failure of a concern may cause the failures of other concerns, but part of its liabilities will be to firms which can stand the loss and which therefore act as buffers. Each addition to unemployment will cause further and further unemployment but, taken individually, at a decreasing rate. Individual contractions of output breed contraction all

> round, but the impact of each of them slackens and stops after having gone a certain way.[41]

Further, certain firms go bankrupt and close down creating possibilities for others to expand. Schumpeter calls it depression business. This spells not only actual and potential losses but also actual and potential gains. These tendencies lead to a petering out of spiral.

Thus, though it can be shown that a restrictive tendency will develop to counteract the spiral, it cannot be proved that it will invariably succeed in breaking it. "...we must recognise the possibility of a system so conditioned and of a spiral so violent that that tendency may fight a loosing battle at any given moment and that, theoretically, the system may never conquer the breathing space in which it would recover itself."[42] In such cases, help outside the economic system is necessary for bringing out recovery. Once the equilibrium is restored, the stage is set for a new wave of innovation and a repetition of the cycle.

The new equilibrium is higher than the old equilibrium from which the process of growth started. National and per capita income in real terms are higher in the new equilibrium. All major income groups benefit from an increase in national income. Labour, in particular, enjoys large gains because under capitalism a major portion of the innovational activity is directed towards mass-produced consumer commodities. Schumpeter, unlike Ricardo and Marx, does not emphasize a conflict between the owners of different factors of production during the process of growth.

To complete his model, Schumpeter considers the existence of investment financed from savings out of the current income, population growth and elements of imperfect competition. Further, he recognises that the process need not start from a stationary state; nor innovations be introduced merely in the neighbourhood of equilibrium. Introduction of these modifications does not change the essential characteristics of the model; they only blur the detailed operation of the pure model.

---

41. *Ibid.*, p. 153.
42. *Ibid.*, p. 154.

9. Pessimistic Trend

In his early writings, Schumpeter shows great faith in capitalism. He holds that it is capable of leading to ever-higher levels of real income at a small cost to society in the form of temporary interruptions in economic activity. Capitalism supports and extends rationality. It creates new social environments conducive to individual achievement in the economic field.

Later on, Schumpeter recognises that the economic and social foundations of capitalism are beginning to crumble.

> A more or less stationary state would ensue. Capitalism, being essentially an evolutionary process, would become atrophic. There would be nothing left for entrepreneurs to do....Profits and along with profits the rate of interest would converge toward zero....The management of industry and trade would become a matter of current administration, and the personnel would unavoidably acquire the characteristics of a bureaucracy. Socialism of a very sober type would almost automatically come into being.[43]

He bases his case for the downfall of capitalism on three principles, *viz.* (1) obsolescence of the entrepreneurial function, (2) the destruction of the institutional framework of capitalist society and (3) the destruction of the protecting political strata.

As seen earlier, the function of an entrepreneur is to revolutionise the pattern of production by introducing new things. Introduction of new things is a difficult task and cannot be done by the common men. But gradually obstacles are overcome and economic change results. The success of the early innovations smoothens the path and makes things easier. Innovations are reduced to routine. Technical progress becomes the business of teams of trained specialists who turn out what is required and make it work in predictable ways. Many things, which were previously visualized by entrepreneurs in a flash of genius, become strictly calculable and thus diminish the need for entrepreneurs. Consumers and producers become accustomed to new things and accept them as a matter of course. The diminution of resistance to economic change decreases the need

43. Schumpeter, n. 21, p. 131.

for the personality and will of entrepreneurs previously required for overcoming the resistance. Economic progress tends to become depersonalized and automatized. Bureau and Committee work tend to replace individual action. The entrepreneurs by their very success automatize progress and become superfluous. Entrepreneurs usurped of their functions are reduced to the position of routine managers receiving wages.

> The perfectly bureaucratized giant industrial unit not only ousts the small or medium-sized firm and 'expropriates' its owners, but in the end it also ousts the entrepreneurs and expropriates the bourgeoisie as a class which in the process stands to lose not only its income but also what is infinitely more important, its function.[44]

The entrepreneur, by his own success, tends to destroy not only his economic and social functions but also the institutional framework within which he works. The increase in the size of the unit of production destroys the vitality of basic capitalistic institutions like private property and freedom of contract. In big corporations "the figure of the proprietor and with it the specifically proprietory interest have vanished from the picture."[45] In such corporations there are three types of interests, *viz.*, (1) salaried executives, and all salaried managers and submanagers, (2) big stockholders, and (3) small stockholders. The first group tends to acquire an employee attitude and does not identify itself merely with the stockholding interests. The second group, though having vital and permanent connections with the concern, is divorced from both the functions and attitudes of an owner. The third group, having a minor interest, hardly bothers as to what is going on in the concern. Thus the usurpation of the functions of the property owners by the salaried managers weakens the institution of private property.

Similar has been the fate of the freedom of contract. In its full vitality, it means individual contracting regulated by individual choice between an indefinite number of possibilities. Today, it is associations of labourers and consumers, and not individual labourers and consumers, which make contracts with the giant concerns. The emergence of collective contracting has considerably restricted the

44. *Ibid.*, p. 134.
45. *Ibid.*, p. 141.

freedom of contract. New legal framework has been developed to facilitate collective contracting.

Entrepreneur, by his own success, destroys not only his functions and institutional framework of capitalism. During the sixteenth-eighteenth century, the rise of capitalism was accompanied by the rise of strong national states based on a monarchical type of government. Having subjugated the landed aristocracy, the royal power politically supported the rising royal power. But the very success of capitalism destroyed the royal power. As the economic power of the industrialists and merchants grew stronger and their rationalistic attitudes spread into every field, they entered the political field and secured power. They introduced wide political reforms based on their relationship attitudes. Capitalists and merchants, however, are not fit to rule. They do not possess any mystic glamour about them which considerably counts in the ruling of men. To the extent they are entrepreneurs, they are economic leaders. "But economic leadership of this type does not readily expand, like the medieval lord's military leadership, into the leadership of nations."[46]

Obsolescence of the entrepreneurial functions, the destruction of the international framework of capitalist society and the destruction of the protecting political strata are not enough to destroy capitalism. Active hostility against the social order is necessary. This need is fulfilled by the intellectuals who arouse and lead the anti-capitalist interests "...unlike any other type of society, capitalism inevitably and by virtue of the very logic of its civilisation creates, educates and subsidizes a vested interest in social work."[47] The capitalist process itself provides the intellectuals with greater freedom and larger means for practising their profession. This profession consists of criticism of persons, of current events, of classes and of institutions. By expanding educational facilities, capitalism increases the supply of educated and white-collar groups. Because of lack of employment opportunities, they find it difficult to secure jobs suiting their tastes and desires. This increases hostility towards the capitalistic system of society. Capitalism arouses a labour movement. In it the intellectuals find a class for which they

46. *Ibid.*, p. 137.

47. *Ibid.*, p. 146.

can provide intellectual leadership and thereby get an opportunity of securing anti-capitalist political reforms desired by them. This weakens the political framework on which capitalism rests and leads towards socialism.

Finally, capitalism has a tendency to lead to a disintegration of the bourgeois family. Rationalism extends even to family life. People start weighing the comparative pleasure from an additional child and an increase in leisure, freedom and real income. This weakens the family motive which provides an important drive for the accumulation of capital.

10. Conclusion

Schumpeter makes an important contribution to the theory of economic development. His analysis of economic development is very helpful in understanding the historical development of the capitalist economies. In the capitalist economies, entrepreneurs were the primary movers of the development process. Innovations played an important role in the process of development. Schumpeter fully recognises that in today's world entrepreneurial activity is not so important and the walls of capitalism are fast crumbling.

Schumpeter, of course, overemphasizes the role of credit creation in financing development projects. Development projects require long-term finance while banks grant loans mostly for short periods. Similarly, Schumpeter overemphasizes the importance of innovations in generating business cycles. In fact, innovations are only one among the many factors causing business cycles. Schumpeter's conclusion regarding the inevitable emergence of socialism is not based on sound analysis. What Schumpeter actually shows is that capitalism has changed and is undergoing further changes. He is not clear as to how socialism will emerge. "...we know nothing as yet about the precise way by which socialism may be expected to come except that there must be great many possibilities ranging from a gradual bureaucratization to the most picturesque revolution."[48]

48. *Ibid.*, pp. 162-63.

John Maynard Keynes

6

1. Introduction

It is widely accepted that no economist had a greater impact on economic analysis and policy than Lord Keynes. The basic ideas underlying Keynesian thought were a direct outcome of the state of the world economy during the thirties. Most of the Western capitalist countries were in the grip of a severe depression. The policy measures suggested by the economists of those days proved ineffective to cure the basic malaise afflicting these economies. It was against this background that Keynes suggested a completely different approach towards solving the unemployment problem. The Keynesian approach led to a complete revolution in the sphere of economic thinking and policy. In this chapter we assess as to how far the basic ideas forming the core of the Keynesian thought are relevant to the conditions prevailing in the underdeveloped economies.

2. Essence of the General Theory

Before we examine the relevance of the Keynesian Economics to underdeveloped countries, let us briefly state the essence of the General Theory. In the Keynesian system, the volume of employment in equilibrium depends upon *(i)* the aggregate supply function and *(ii)* the propensity to consume and the rate of investment. The aggregate supply function is simply the supply price of the total output measured in labour unit costs. The volume of employment is given by the point of intersection of the aggregate demand function and the aggregate supply function. At this point, the entrepreneurs' expected profits are maximised. The aggregate supply function is assumed to be stable or neutral up to the level of full employment. Thus changes in the volume of employment below the full employment level depend on changes in the aggregate demand function. Propensity to consume is a stable function of income. Any change in income leads to a change in consumption in the same direction; of course, the change in consumption is smaller than the change in income. Thus with every increase in income, the volume of savings goes on increasing. If the total effective demand and hence income and employment is to be maintained, investment will have to be increased corresponding to the increase in savings. The rate of investment depends upon the market rate of interest and the prospective marginal net yield of investment (marginal efficiency of capital). Rate of interest in turn depends upon the liquidity preference of the public and the total stock of money made available by the monetary authority.

3. Static Analysis

Thinking that the postulates of the classical theory are applicable only to a special case and not to the general case, Keynes claimed his theory to be a "general theory."[1] Actually, Keynes' theory is a static theory because it is mainly concerned with equilibrium positions. Arthur Smithies regards Keynesian analysis a special case of a general dynamic theory.[2] Keynes' analysis is concerned primarily with the short period. He takes "as given the existing skill and quantity of available labour, the existing quality and quantity of available equipment, the existing technique, the degree of competition, the tastes and habits of the consumer, the disutility of different intensities of labour and of the activities of supervision and organisation, as well as the social structure...which determine the distribution of the national income."[3] Growth, however, is concerned primarily with the long period and to a considerable extent depends on changes in the basic factors assumed by Keynes to be given. Keynesian analysis, thus, is not very relevant to the problems of growth.

4. Nature of Unemployment

The nature of the unemployment problem in an underdeveloped country is very different from that in an advanced capitalistic economy which Keynes had in mind while formulating his theory of employment. In advanced countries, unemployment results primarily

---

1. J.M. Keynes, *The General Theory of Employment, Interest and Money* (London, 1957), p. 3.
2. Arthur Smithies, "Effective Demand and Employment" in Semour E. Harris (ed.) *The New Economics* (London, 1949), p. 568.
3. Keynes, n. 1, p. 245.

from a lack of effective demand caused by oversaving. Unemployed labour exists side by side with idle equipment. This kind of unemployment is not very important in underdeveloped countries. A major portion of the population being at the subsistence level, the marginal propensity to consume is very high and oversaving is not a problem. On the contrary, the basic problem is that of a shortage of savings for investment. The main cause of unemployment is lack of equipment with which the labour is to work. Deficiency of demand, wherever it exists, is not because of oversaving but because of other reasons. It maybe because of lack of income or purchasing power. It may be because of structural maladjustments in production. That is, some industries grow out of balance with the rest of the economy and, therefore, experience a deficiency of demand for their products. Deficiency of demand for the products of cottage industries is mostly because of technological reasons.

Cyclical fluctuations in employment, an important characteristic of advanced economies, are not very important in underdeveloped countries because the aggregate demand is comparatively less unstable. Investment demand, which is the most unstable component, forms a smaller portion of the total demand. The consumption demand is comparatively stable because of a number of reasons. A major portion of the population being at the subsistence level, the consumption does not decrease with a decline in incomes of the people. The decline in income reflects primarily in dissaving and not in a decline in consumption. Because of the prevalence of a large degree of self-sufficiency, a major portion of the consumption of the workers consists of their own production. Durable and luxury goods, the demand for which is comparatively more unstable, are a small part of the total consumption. In many underdeveloped countries, the foreign trade forms only a small part of the total national output and, therefore, the fluctuations in foreign demand do not affect the aggregate demand considerably.

In underdeveloped countries, the recession affects mostly the money incomes and not the real incomes or output. The most important factor responsible for the comparative stability of real income during the business cycle is the predominance of agriculture in these economies. Production in agriculture is comparatively stable not only in underdeveloped but also in developed countries. A major part of the total costs in agriculture consists of fixed costs and variable costs are small. Variable costs being small, prices during the recession, generally, do not fall below the marginal cost and consequently the restriction of production is unprofitable. Because of the competitive nature of agriculture, it is not possible to raise prices by restricting production. In agriculture, the time-lag between inputs and outputs is very long and, consequently, the limits within which production can profitably be restricted in the short period are comparatively narrower. On the contrary, there is some evidence to show that the supply curve in agriculture is backward sloping, *i.e.*, supply increases during the recession and falls during the boom. In developed countries, the number of wage earners is very large. Further, wages are very inflexible because of contracts, legislation, trade union pressure etc. Business fluctuations, therefore, manifest themselves, mainly, in variations in employment and not in incomes. The incomes of those who are lucky enough to retain their employment remain almost unchanged. In underdeveloped countries, in contrast, a predominant part of the population is self-employed. Business fluctuations in such economies, therefore, reflect themselves primarily in changes in money incomes and not in employment. Most of those who are employed on wages in factories, plantations and mines continue their contacts back in their villages and during a recession can go back to their homes and share agricultural employment along with their other family members. Cyclical unemployment, thus, is not very important in underdeveloped economies.

5. Productivity of Employment

In underdeveloped countries, the qualitative aspect of the employment problem is as important as the quantitative aspect. The problem is not only of increasing the volume of employment but also of improving its income content. Income content of employment can be increased by combining a larger quantity of capital with labour and/or by improving technology. In advanced countries, possessing a sufficient amount of capital and up-to-date technology, qualitative aspect of employment is not very important. Keynes, therefore, concentrated on only the quantitative aspect.

In underdeveloped countries characterised by a large population, backward technology and shortage of capital equipment, the marginal productivity of labour is very low and, therefore, becomes equal to the marginal disutility of labour at a point where there exists considerable unemployment in the physical sense but not in the 'involuntary' sense. With every increase in the amount of capital and every improvement in technology, the marginal productivity of labour rises and, disutility curve of labour remaining unchanged, full employment equilibrium shifts upward. Thus in underdeveloped countries, we have a situation of an ascending level of "full employment" equilibrium.

> Apart from the level of full employment visualised by Keynes, there are as many levels of full employment as there are different stages of economic development. Indeed it is the transition from the level of full employment appropriate to a lower stage to another appropriate to a higher stage which constitutes the process of development. The economic process consists of two distinct categories, one, where given the level of economic development, you move from low employment to full employment, and the other, where you move from full employment at a given level of economic development to full employment at the next level of economic development.[4]

In underdeveloped countries, marginal productivity is lower not only of labour but also of capital. Comparatively lower marginal productivity of capital in an economy marked by a shortage of capital seems somewhat surprising. Keynes envisaged that the marginal efficiency of capital would fall with an increase in the stock of accumulated capital. In an underdeveloped country, the situation is quite the reverse. Up to certain point, the marginal efficiency of capital increases with the increase in the stock of capital. This is primarily because every investment creates some external economies which raise the marginal productivity of other investments. The doctrine of balanced growth proposes a simultaneous investment in a number of industries as a method of raising the marginal efficiency of capital.

6. Supply of Labour

In Keynes' model, the supply of labour is perfectly elastic at the ruling money wage-rate. In advanced countries, which Keynes had

---

4. V.K.R.V. Rao, "Investment, Income and the Multiplier in an Underdeveloped Economy," *Indian Economic Review* (February, 1952), pp. 66-67.

in mind while formulating his theory, the current money wage rate provides a standard of living higher than the subsistence level and consequently, there is scope for a cut in the real wage rate. Supply of labour, therefore, won't decrease much with a cut in the real wage rate, money wage rate remaining unchanged. In underdeveloped countries, in contrast, the prevailing money wage rate provides a bare subsistence level. Physical existence of labour is not possible at a lower real wage rate. Supply of labour, therefore, will be perfectly elastic not at the prevailing money wage rate but at the prevailing real wage rate. It is not possible to permit the price level to rise so long as the money wage rate remains unchanged.

7. Rate of Interest

According to Keynesian analysis, the rate of interest is determined by the demand for and supply of money. Demand for money arises out of three motives, *viz., (i)* transactive-motive, *(ii)* precautionary-motive and *(iii)* speculative-motive. Demand for money owing to transactive-motive and precautionary-motive is a relatively stable function of income and changes in this part of the total demand for money evoke quick response in the supply of money; this part of the total demand for money, therefore, does not exert an important influence on the rate of interest. It is the demand for money for speculative-motive which exerts the most important influence on the rate of interest. In underdeveloped countries, the speculative activity is not very important. Rate of interest in these countries is influenced more by customs, traditions and institutional factors than by the demand for money for speculative motive. Demand for money for investment also exerts an important influence on the rate of interest.

According to Keynes, rate of interest, along with the marginal efficiency of capital, is an important determinant of the rate of investment. The influence of the rate of interest on the rate of investment, however, has been doubted even in advanced countries. The inquiry conducted by the Oxford Economists Research Group revealed that the investment decisions of the businessmen are not significantly affected by the rate of interest.[5] Interest-elasticity of

5. J.E. Meade and P.W.S. Andrews, "Summary of Replies to Questions on Effects of Interest Rates," T. Wilson and P.W.S. Andrews (ed.), *Oxford Studies in Price Mechanism* (Oxford, 1952), pp. 28-30.

investment is likely to be lower in underdeveloped countries because of a number of factors. Firstly, the risk factor is more important in an economy passing through a transitional stage than in an advanced economy which is comparatively stable and in which the path of growth can be predicted much more safely. The more important the risk factor, the smaller will be the influence of the interest rate. Secondly, the interest rate is more important in case of long-term investments than in case of short-term investments. In underdeveloped countries, the long-term projects like railways, roads, irrigation, electricity etc. are, generally, undertaken by the state which is guided more by the welfare considerations than by the profit and loss calculations based on interest rate. Thirdly, in underdeveloped countries, the investors lack rationality. They prefer to invest their funds in the established lines even if the rate of return is higher in new lines. Fourthly, the rate of interest is more important in case of investments undertaken with borrowed funds than in case of those financed through internal resources. In underdeveloped countries, investment through borrowed funds is relatively less important.

8. Working of Multiplier

The notion of multiplier means that a certain amount of additional investment leads to an increase in income which is multiple of the initial investment. Additional investment raises incomes and thereby increases the demand for consumption goods. Increase in the demand for consumption goods further increases income and thereby leads to a further increase in the demand for consumption goods. In the absence of leakages, this process of increase in income and increase in the demand for consumption goods would continue till full employment is reached. Actually, because of a number of leakages, whole of the increased income is not spent, *i.e.,* marginal propensity to consume is less than unity. The process, therefore, stops much before the level of full employment is reached. It stops at the point savings become equal to investment. In the new equilibrium position, increase in income is a multiple of the initial additional investment.

The working of the multiplier assumes a sufficient degree of elasticity of production. Production, however, is comparatively inelastic in underdeveloped countries because of lack of capital, skill and other complementary factors. The vast amount of surplus manpower existing in underdeveloped countries cannot be used for increased production because of lack of complementary factors. Multiplier, therefore, works only in terms of money income and not in terms of real income and employment. In developed countries, in contrast, production is sufficiently elastic. During the recession period, there exists unemployment not only of labour but also of other complementary factors. Increase in demand caused by additional investment leads to an increase in production through the utilisation of unemployed resources. Thus, increase in money income is followed by an increase in real income. Of course, the increase between the two may not be identical and the rise in money income may be more than that in real income. The disparity between money income and real income goes on widening as the economy moves towards full employment. When the full employment is reached, the operation of the multiplier becomes very similar to that of the multiplier in underdeveloped countries.

9. Conclusion

The Keynesian conclusions and policies are not very relevant to the conditions prevailing in the underdeveloped countries. But this does not mean that the Keynesian economics is useless for these countries. The tools of analysis developed by Keynes are indispensable for analysing the problems of the underdeveloped countries.

Secular Stagnation

7

1. Introduction

The theory of secular stagnation is also known as 'economic maturity', 'growing underemployment', and 'secular underemployment equilibrium'. Almost all economists have recognised that unregulated and uncontrolled capitalistic system cannot lead to endless growth. The classical school believes that ultimately every economy would reach a stationary state in which growth will cease. Marx and Schumpeter predict an ultimate downfall of the capitalistic system. Harrod-Domar model shows that as the economy grows, it becomes more and more difficult to maintain full employment. Hansen believes that in mature economies, in the absence of state intervention, at the full employment level, net savings have a tendency to exceed net investment which would result into chronic underemployment equilibrium or secular stagnation. Stable growth can be maintained in mature economies only if the state continuously pursues appropriate monetary and fiscal policies. Let us examine the secular stagnation thesis in a little more detail.

2. Statement of the Doctrine

There is no better short statement of the stagnation thesis than that given by Keynes himself. "The richer the community, the wider will tend to be the gap between its actual and its potential production, and, therefore, the more obvious and outrageous the defects of the economic system. Not only is the marginal propensity to consume weaker in a wealthy community but, owing to its accumulation of capital being already larger, the opportunities for further investment are less attractive." When there had been no occurrence of secular stagnation in the past, say in the 19th century, the question may be raised as to why it should occur in future? To this Keynes replied:

> During the 19th century, the growth of population and of inventions, the opening up of new lands, the state of confidence and the frequency of war over the average (say) each decade, seem to have been sufficient, taken in conjunction with the propensity to consume, to establish a schedule of the marginal efficiency of capital which allowed a reasonable satisfactory average level of employment to be compatible with a rate of interest high enough to be psychologically acceptable to wealth owners.... Today and presumably for the future the schedule of the marginal efficiency of capital is for a variety of reasons, much lower than it was in the 19th century.[1]

In a mature economy, there is a log-run tendency towards a contraction in economic activity. Depressions are more intense and prolonged than booms. The essence of secular stagnation is "sick recoveries which die in their infancy and depressions which feed on themselves and leave a hard and seemingly immovable core of unemployment."[2]

Secular stagnation is not inconsistent with a rising trend of actual per capita income, and even with a rising trend of actual gross investment. It refers simply to a growing gap between the trend of full employment income (without inflation) and trend of actual income or between potential employment and actual employment. Secular stagnation may refer to a growing economy in which the rate of growth, though positive, is declining. It may refer to an economy in which actual employment is increasing if at the same time the gap between the attainable and actual employment is also increasing. Thus secular stagnation is compatible with a decline in per capita income, constant per capita income, or slowing down of the increase in per capita income. Secular stagnation originates from savings exceeding investment at the full employment level. The gap between savings and investment may be ascribed either to excessive savings (deficient consumption) or to deficient investment or to both. For explaining the tendency towards secular stagnation in mature economies, we have to analyse the causes responsible for

---

1 J.M. Keynes, *The General Theory of Employment, Interest and Money* (London, 1936), pp. 307-08.

2 A.H. Hansen, *Fiscal Policy and Business Cycles* (New York, 1941), p. 353.

excessive savings and insufficient investment opportunities. Let us first examine the factors which cause excessive savings.

3. Factors which Tend to Widen Savings Leakage

The aggregate private net savings consist of *(i)* undistributed corporate profits and *(ii)* personal savings. The secular tendency in advanced private enterprise countries has been to increase the size, measured in absolute amount and perhaps also as a percentage of the national income at full employment, of both these components. Let us first examine the secular tendency in respect of corporate undistributed profits.

The statistical evidence in advanced countries shows that the ratio, at full employment, of corporate undistributed profits to national income has risen over the secular long-term. This together with the rise in national income has meant a large increase, even when allowance is made for the rise in the price level, in the absolute amount of corporate undistributed profits.

The rising secular tendency in the ratio of corporate undistributed profits to national income, at full employment, appears mainly on account of two factors. The first is the rise in the ratio of corporate profits before tax to national income, presumably because of growing predominance of corporate enterprise and within it owing to imperfectly competitive market structures resulting in ever larger excess profits. The second is the rise in the ratio of corporate undistributed profits to total corporate profits after tax, presumably owing to the ambition of those who control corporations to expand their respective businesses and of share-holders to receive a large portion of their profits preferably in the form of tax-free bonus shares issued through capitalization of reserves rather than in the form of taxable dividends. The rise in the ratio of corporate tax liability to corporate profits before tax, of course, has been a factor working in the opposite direction. But this has not completely offset the favourable effect of the first two factors on corporate undistributed profits and, therefore, the net result has been rise in the ratio of such profits to national income. As such the absolute size of the leakage represented by corporate net saving has increased at a rate higher than that of the increase in national income.

To turn to the second component, the ratio of personal saving to national income depends upon *(i)* the ratio of disposable personal income to national income and *(ii)* the ratio of personal saving to disposable personal income (*i.e.*, the average propensity to save). The higher are these two factors at a given level of employment, the higher is the ratio of personal saving to national income.

The secular tendency in regard to the ratio of disposable personal income to national income is, undoubtedly, towards a decline. This is primarily because of two factors. Firstly, there has occurred a great increase in taxation, corporate and personal, because of the vast increase in government spending necessitated by the higher cost of defence and social services expected of modern welfare state. No doubt, there are also factors, operating in the opposite direction, *e.g.*, larger increase in government transfer payments relatively to private (personal and corporate) contributions for social insurance, and the vast increase in the net interest paid by government owing to the phenomenal increase in the size of public debt. But the factors working on the side of a decline in the ratio of disposable personal income to total national income have been more powerful than those operating on the side of a rise in it.

As regards the ratio of personal savings to disposal personal income, at full employment, economic development of present-day advanced private-enterprise countries has been characterised by the working of conflicting tendencies, some in favour of and others against the rise in the propensity to save. We examine below important of such tendencies.

Private enterprise countries, by definition, are characterised by private ownership of means of production. This implies unearned incomes. The amount of a person's unearned income depends, other things remaining unchanged, upon the amount of income-yielding assets, owned by him. This provides a powerful incentive for saving with a view to accumulate income-yielding assets. As such the increase in per capita real income, by enhancing the earner's capacity to save, has been an important factor tending towards a higher propensity to save. But there have also been factors tending to promote consumption *e.g.*, increasing urbanization of the population, progress of advertising, greater educational opportunities, progressive taxation, wider and fuller social security, better provision of social amenities, the rise in the habitual standards of living as a result of the increase in per capita income, and the fact that the capitalists, thanks to their greater wealth and more important social position, have become more aristocratic and are obliged to display their wealth somewhat more lavishly than was necessary for the "middle class of the nineteenth century."[3] But the factors unfavourable to personal saving (or favourable to personal consumption) have not completely offset the favourable effect on saving of the secular increase in per capita income.

The propensity to save also depends upon the extent of inequalities in the distribution of disposable personal income. The greater the inequalities, the higher would be the propensity to save. Though conceptual and statistical difficulties in the measurement of the degree of inequality of income-distribution bar a precise identification of the secular tendency in this regard, a few general conclusions can safely be stated. Large, and probably increasing, inequalities in the distribution of personal income before tax appear to be inherent in the private-enterprise system. The inequalities in the distribution of income arise firstly, because different workers earn different amounts depending upon the quality and quantity of work performed by each and secondly, because the ownership of income-yielding assets is very unequally distributed. The vast inequalities in the distribution of personal income before tax found in advanced private-enterprise countries are by and large on account of the second factor. And the inequality in the ownership of income-yielding assets has a tendency to widen with the process of economic growth. The groups getting larger incomes on account of ownership or control of income-yielding assets normally have a tendency to save a higher proportion of their income. The absolute amount saved by them per capita is, therefore, much larger than by the non-owning groups with smaller incomes. As such, at each round, the former tend to be richer.

The government transfer payments, which mainly go to the low-income classes, are one of the factors tending to reduce inequalities in the distribution of personal incomes. The amount of such payments has substantially increased in recent years as a result of wider coverage and higher rates of actual security benefits. But the equilibrium effect of this development is narrowly restricted by the fact that, at full employment, government transfer payments are likely to exceed private contributions for social insurance only by a moderate amount and that such contributions are likely to impinge,

---

3. Paul M. Sweezy, *The Theory of Capitalist Development*, 1946, p. 230.

directly or indirectly, on the relatively small incomes so that the net transfer of income from the rich to the poor is rather limited.

The tendency towards higher rate of tax on corporate profits and towards diversion of larger proportion of corporate net profits to reserves, through its adverse effect on dividend payments which mainly go to the relatively rich, is unfavourable to personal saving not only because it depresses the ratio of personal income of national income but also because it reduces the inequalities in personal incomes. The corporate taxation cannot be used as an instrument of reducing private saving beyond certain limits because of the resistance of the powerful owning classes to excessive corporate taxes, the difficulties involved in checking legal and illegal evasion, and the fears of adverse effects on investment. The higher rate of corporate saving, while undoubtedly unfavourable to personal saving, is worse than self-defeating from the point of the view of the matter under study because it, in fact, means a rise in the rate of total private saving including both corporate and personal saving.

The above discussion shows that high, and probably growing, inequalities in the distribution of personal income before tax with favourable effects on personal saving appear to be inherent in the private-enterprise economies.

Another factor which had led to the oversaving is the growth of joint stock and corporate form of business organisations. Corporate savings are becoming more and more important. These savings consist of depreciation reserves for replacement and are reflected in the amount of undistributed profits of corporations. They may, in fact, be much more than those required for financing replacement of capital equipment and new capital formation. The growth of life insurance and other institutions has also given a fillip to saving and thereby enhanced the chances of secular stagnation.

Insecurity is still another factor influencing the will to save. It strengthens the precautionary motive to saving. In this regard, modern private-enterprise economies have exhibited conflicting tendencies.

Such economies appear to be more unstable now than in the nineteenth century. This factor tends to work in favour of promoting savings. But expansion of the system of social security has offset this factor to some extent because the social provision against the contingencies and the exigencies of life weakens the precautionary motive to saving.

The net result of the conflicting tendencies mentioned above seems to be a secular rise in the average propensity to save at full employment. The advanced private enterprise economies are, therefore, faced with an ever more serious problem of how to offset the widening saving leakage. The failure to do that means less than full employment.

4. Factors that Weaken Investment Offsets

A high and rising absolute rate of private net saving at full employment is not, however, by itself a sufficient condition of inadequate demand. There would be no shortage of demand if the investment increased correspondingly to the increase in savings at the full employment level. But in the present day mature private-enterprises economies, there are several factors that tend to weaken the propensity to invest with the result that investment falls short of savings at the full employment level. We briefly discuss below important of such factors.

Large Accumulation of Capital: The mature private-enterprise countries have accumulated huge amounts of capital. The larger the existing volume of capital, the lower would be the prospective rate of return on new investment and hence the weaker the incentives for investment.

Decline in the Rate of Population Growth: In the twentieth century, in most of the mature economies, population growth has considerably slowed down; in some countries the rate of population growth is near zero. In the nineteenth century, population grew at a tremendous rate. Growing population stimulates investment in two ways. Firstly, it require goods and services which give rise to huge amounts of investment. It expands the demand for housing and public utilities like water works, sewerage disposal, gas works, electric works, transportation and communications, etc. Provision of housing and public utilities involves enormous amounts of investment. Secondly, growing population facilitates investment by increasing the supply of labour. In the absence of a growing population, increase in the demand for labour caused by an increase in investment would raise wage rates. Rise in wage rates would lower profits and thereby discourage investment. Even if technical progress throws up new capital-intensive techniques at the required rate, investment may still be retarded by another factor. If capital used per worker *(i.e.,* capital-labour ratio) increases, the ultimate decline in the rate of profit can be prevented only by a rise in the ratio of profits to wages. But a rising profits-wages ratio tends to depress the propensity to consume at full employment.

Development of New Territories: What is true of population growth holds also for the discovery and development of new territories and new resources. Development of new territories requires enormous investment in highways, railroads, means of communication etc. Further a huge amount of investment is required for providing the communities which settle in the new territories with goods, services, housing and public utilities. Expansion of territory furthers the growth of population which in turn stimulates investment. The era of territorial expansion has, now, come to an end. This has resulted into a decline in investment opportunities.

Disappearance of Pre-capitalist Sector: Historically, the adoption of capital-intensive techniques in advanced private-enterprise countries has been associated with capitalist enterprise (one where production is carried on private account with hired as against self-employed workers). In the early stages of capitalist development, the labour supply for the capitalist sector came from the decline of the pre-capitalist sector releasing men, women, and children for employment in the capitalist sector. This facilitated investment in the capitalist sector in the same manner as the increase in the available labour force through natural increase in population. But in advanced countries the scope for such increase in labour supply available to the capitalist sector appears to have more or less exhausted with the virtual disappearance of the pre-capitalist sector.

Relatively Weaker Stimulus of Technological Progress: Technological progress in the form of invention of new products, machines and processes promotes investment by creating new outlets for it. The strength of the stimulus provided by the discovery of new products depends upon the degree of their novelty, the capital intensity of the production process involved, the time dimension (fruition-period) of the investment promoted, and the intrinsic importance of the wants served. Similarly, the investment-generating potential of new machines and processes depends upon their novelty, their capital-intensity, and the intrinsic importance of the wants served. Technological progress provided a powerful stimulus to investment from the second half of the 18th century to about the end of the first quarter of the 20th century. Inventions in the fields of manufacture, transport and mining created products and processes which were very different from the then known products and processes. In the early part of this period, there was the change from handicrafts to 'roundabout' capitalistic methods of production; in the latter part there appeared large, altogether new, electrical, chemical and automotive industries. The novelty of the new products and processes meant that these could not be introduced simply by minor changes in the existing techniques. The new industries, being highly capital-intensive, led to large investments. As a result of the factors mentioned above, the propensity to invest was strong enough relatively to the then rate of saving corresponding to full employment level.

The things, in contrast, are very different today. Some of the important changes bearing on the inducement to investment are briefly stated below:

(i) Highly efficient methods of satisfying man's basic wants—food, clothing, footwear, means of transportation and communication, facilities for recreation or cultural pursuits—have been discovered and adequately employed in advanced countries. The future technological progress, therefore, is likely to relate to intrinsically less important wants or simply to improvements in the existing capitalistic methods of satisfying basic wants. As such, leaving aside the possibilities of 'technological progress' in the field of war, new wants and processes are not likely to stimulate investment as strongly as they did in the nineteenth century.

(ii) While a century back private enterprise economies were by and large competitive, in present days there is growing predominance of imperfectly competitive market structures. The growing monopolization of such economies has had in some ways favourable and in others adverse effects on new investment outlets. The vast resources at the disposal of giant monopolistic and oligopolistic enterprises, for instance, make it possible for them to spend lavishly on research projects which stimulates technological progress and hence new investment. Monopoly profits are an important source of finance for the employment of new techniques of production whereas the competitive enterprises having smaller profits might lack funds for this purpose, particularly where large initial investments

are required and the fruition period is rather long. It is possible that a monopolistic producer may adopt 'risky' innovations of product or technique more readily than a competitive producer. Innovations will presumbly be made by a producer because these are likely to increase profits by increased demand or reduced cost. The larger the profits from a successful innovation and the longer the period for which the producer can enjoy these, the stronger is the incentive to introduce innovations. Under competition, while unsuccessful innovation is as damaging, successful innovation, because of early imitation or entry by others, does not add to profits by as much or for as long as under monopoly which precludes entry and competition.

On the other hand, the growing predominance of monopoly and oligopoly has had adverse effect on investment in several ways. Under such market structures, output is not extended to the level where price equals the marginal cost. Output will thus fall short of what it would be if the monopolised or oligopolised industry were to act like a purely competitive industry. Restriction of output in the monopolised and oligopolised sector decreases the scope for investment in those sectors. It follows that the flow of investment into the monopolised and oligopolised fields stops even when average return on capital is higher than the normal return obtainable in the competitive sectors; to be more concrete, it stops when the marginal return on capital, as distinguished from the average return, falls short of the rate of profit that can be earned in competitive fields. After that the monopolists and oligopolists invest even their own savings in other fields and seek to monopolise and oligopolise them. Thus the tentacles of monopoly and oligopoly spread ever wider, and the restrictive effect on new investment outlets is correspondingly strengthened. Monopolies also delay the introduction of technological innovations because the monopolist while deciding whether or not to adopt them, must take account of the consequential obsolescence of existing capital. Under competitive conditions, the gain from an innovation accrued to the innovator while the loss (as a result of obsolescence of capital) was shared by his competitors. To be more concrete, given the cost-reducing opportunity, the monopolist will make the innovation only when, output being given for future periods, the average total cost of production with the new technique is less than the average variable cost with the existing plant. Under competitive conditions, in contrast, though established sellers will act in the same way, new entrants will tend to introduce new techniques as soon as the average total cost with them is less than the expected market price. Thus under monopolistic and oligopolistic conditions introduction of innovations tends to be delayed. In other words, the technological progress tends to be financed from depreciation accruals instead of from net saving. Taking into account the favourable as well as the unfavourable factors, the conclusion appears to be that the impact of growing predominance of imperfectly competitive market structure would be unfavourable to the inducement to invest.

(iii) In recent periods, the bias of technological innovations appears to be markedly towards capital-saving. The latest development *(e.g.,* air conditioning and television) illustrates the trend towards more complex goods requiring less capital outlay. To cite Samuelson[4]:

> Thus the invention of airliner may make possible the development of Siberia without billions and billions of dollars of investment in public roads and rail-roads...Atomic energy may minimise the need in many parts of the world for costly hydro-electric reclamation projects... Science gives and takes as far as investment is concerned, and Hansen thinks these may continue to be—what he believes to have been true of the 1930's—a preponderance of capital-saving invention.

Since monopolies and oligopolies produce on a relatively large scale, they have a tendency to make greater use of complex, specialised and indivisible equipment to economise capital outlay per unit of capacity or output. Further development of safeguards against breakdowns and excess wear and tear has considerably reduced the replacement demand incident to rapid depreciation. Still further, equipment has often been installed which increased productivity by merely speeding up the operation of the existing equipment. All such capital-saving innovations have inhibited the growth of investment-demand.

(*iv*) Financial prudence is now a commonly accepted tenet of corporate management. In pursuance of this, it is customary for

4. P.A. Samuelson, *Economics,* p. 404.

corporate managements to amortize assets at higher than the actual rate of their depreciation. As such the depreciation provision contains an element of net saving. To the extent net investment is financed from such concealed net saving fewer net investment opportunities remain available to offset the statistically accepted private net saving.

Relatively Weaker Stimulus of Expanding Exports: Expanding exports stimulate investment in the export industries. But the net addition of exports to the aggregate opportunities for domestic investment open to the system depends upon the character of imports obtained in exchange. If the latter consists of commodities which the country must in any case import, (because either it simply cannot produce them or it is not worthwhile for it to produce them because the position of comparative costs is such) expanding exports create new investment opportunities for domestic investment without being offset by the disappearance of potential investment opportunities in other sectors of the economy. For example, during the period from the Indian Mutiny (1857) to the first World War the expansion of British exports of textiles and other manufactured products to India stimulated investment in the export industries concerned, but the expanding imports of foodgrains, raw cotton, raw jute, oil seeds, hides and skins, tea, spices, manganese ore, mica etc. obtained in return from India, did not diminish any investment opportunities in Britain. The stimulating effect of expanding exports on capitalist development is reinforced if the resultant expansion in imports causes a decline of the non-capitalist sectors, so that the capitalist sector is enabled to tap both the labour-power and the demands currently in the non-capitalist sector; it is further reinforced if expanding exports also involve a growing exports surplus. In contrast, if the imports consist of commodities which discourage the growth of industries that could in course of time be expected to become as efficient as the present export industries, the additional investment opportunities provided in the export industries are largely offset by the suppression of potential investment opportunities in other fields. Thus the stimulus to capitalist development from expanding exports is the strongest when they increase at a fast pace and are accompanied by a growing export surplus, and when the resultant expansion of imports not only does not impair potential investment opportunities but also brings about a rapid decline in the pre-capitalist sector. In all these respects, conditions are not so favourable as they were a century ago. Then there was a great scope for the expansion of foreign trade of the few capitalist countries within the pattern-structure most conducive to the development of their respective capitalist sectors, *viz.*, export of manufactured products in exchange for food, raw materials and very simple manufactures. At that time vast territories were available for 'colonization,' which term signifies reduction of a country into a buyer of manufactured goods and a supplier of primary products. Further, there were in these areas till that time large possibilities of the colonial type of development, *i.e.*, development which, being confined to agriculture, mining, transport and communications and public utilities increased their importance as sources of supply of primary products and markets for manufactured products. Exports of capital to these areas for this type of development stimulated the exports of the advanced capitalist countries not only at the time when such exports occurred but also in subsequent years because the increase in exports of primary products from the relatively backward countries increased their capacity to absorb large imports of manufactured products. The stimulus to capitalistic development in advanced countries provided by expanding exports from them is now very much weaker than it was a century back owing to the fact that, relatively to their aggregate output, the scope for expanding exports within the appropriate pattern structure of foreign trade (*i.e.*, exchange of manufactured for primary products) is much smaller because of a number of reasons. In the first place, the relatively backward territories of the world have greatly shrunk in size. Secondly, some development has taken place even in the backward countries. Thirdly, the possibilities of development with the colonial-feudal framework have been largely exhausted; in fact, many of these countries, owing to expanding population and relatively stagnant primary production, have actually become importers of food and agricultural raw materials. Finally, the most important capitalist country of today (*i.e.*, the United States) is a very large producer and also exporter of primary products. Moreover, the stimulus to private investment in the advanced countries has greatly weakened because it is no longer possible for these countries to raise capital exports to backward countries to the level at which they will stimulate a volume of exports from the former sufficient to absorb a significant production of their output.

Lesser Scope for Foreign Investments: Net private saving corresponding to full employment may also be offset by positive net investment abroad. In the pre-World War I period, capital exports provided a significant outlet for net private saving in those private-enterprise countries in which the volume of such saving had begun to press against investment opportunities available at home. From 1874 to 1914, for instance, the foreign long-term investments of the United Kingdom, France and Germany increased from $6,000 million to $33,000 million.[5] But because of the present international political climate and other factors,[6] there is hardly any hope for the revival of capital movements from advanced to the under-developed countries on the required scale.

Decline in population growth, virtual disappearance of territorial expansion, monopolistic competition, capital-saving innovations etc. have considerably decreased investment opportunities and thereby lowered the marginal efficiency of capital. Full employment can be maintained only if the rate of interest declines corresponding to the decline in the marginal efficiency of capital. While the marginal efficiency of capital can fall to zero or go even below that, the rate of interest cannot fall below a minimum level because the demand for liquidity becomes infinitely elastic at very low rates of interest and because of institutional borrowing costs. Thus, in mature economies, there exists a deflationary gap at the full employment level of national income. The result is that national income would fall below the full employment level until the reduced savings are equalised by the investment opportunities forthcoming at this low level of national income. This is the problem of chronic under-employment.

The diagram given below illustrates the secular stagnation thesis. If the full employment is to be maintained, the investment opportunities must be adequate to absorb all the real savings which take place at that level of income—say at OY_0; otherwise there would occur a decline in national income. As the economy becomes more fully developed and investment opportunities decline, the propensity to invest will decline as shown by $C+I'$ curve which gives

5. United Nations, *International Capital Movements during the Inter-War Period*, 1949, pp. 1-2.
6. K.R. Gupta, *Economics of Development* (Delhi, 1967), pp. 215-22.

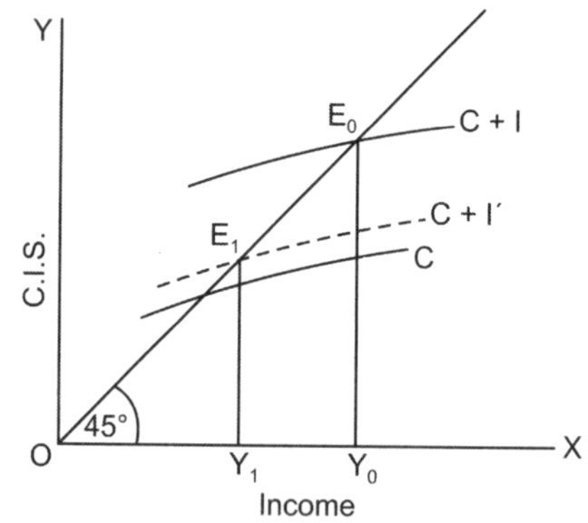

Diagram No. 7.1

us a new level of income at OY_1. Income has declined from OY_0 to OY_1 so that savings would not be larger than those for which the investment opportunities are available. This decline in income from OY_0 to OY_1 causes considerable unemployment and the economy continues in secular under-employment equilibrium for an indefinite period. Thus, we find that in order to maintain full employment, either the investment must be maintained at a level high enough to offset the volume of full-employment savings or savings must decline so as to raise the level of consumption high enough to reduce savings to be offset by investment. Otherwise, the economy will remain in a state of secular underemployment or secular stagnation.

5. An Appraisal

The doctrine of secular stagnation has been sharply criticized by a number of economists. George Terborgh, in a strong counter-attack, labels those who accept the doctrine as 'stagnationists' and 'professional pessimists'. Let us examine the important grounds on which the doctrine of secular stagnation has been criticised.

Some economists have challenged the relation between the rate of population growth and the rate of investment. Purchasing power remaining constant, mere increase in population won't expand market. "An increase in the number of paupers does not broaden the market."[7] Conversely, the decline in the rate of population growth may be accompanied by an increase in the per capita

7. Kalecki, *Theory of Economic Dynamics* (New York, 1954), p. 161.

spending and thus may not lead to a decline in total expenditure. Purchasing power remaining constant, an increase in population may not lead to a considerable increase in effective demand in general. With the same purchasing power, pattern of expenditure, of course, will be different in cases in which population is growing rapidly and in those in which it is growing slowly and the pattern in the former cases will give rise to comparatively more investment.

> Thus a rapidly growing population will demand a much larger per capita volume of new residential building construction than a stationary population. A stationary population with its larger proportion of old people may perhaps demand more personal services; and the composition of consumer demand will have an important influence on the quantity of capital required. The demand for housing calls for large capital outlays, while the demand for personal services can be met without making large investment expenditures. It is therefore not unlikely that shift from a rapidly growing population to a stationary or declining one may so alter the composition of the final flow of consumption goods that the ratio of capital to output as a whole will tend to decline.[8]

Further, population growth may lead to an increase in aggregate income and even to an increase in per capita income if the population is below the optimum level. If population is small in relation to other productive factors, mere increase in population would be accompanied by an increase in income and spending. The tendency for a growing population giving rise to increased expenditure will be stronger where increase in population is accompanied by an increase in income.

The optimist economists believe that there will always be spontaneous changes in the tastes of consumers and in the techniques of production which would create ample investment opportunities for absorbing current savings. Terborgh questions the vital importance of a 'few great innovations' as compared with 'many small ones.'

> There is no real evidence that one 'great new industry' is more dynamic in its impact on capital formation than ten

8. Alvin H. Hansen, "Progress and Declining Population", *The American Economic Review* (March, 1939), p. 7.

> small new industries. The important thing is the total flow of technological development, not its degree of concentration. Given an abundance of rising industries like aviation, mechanical refrigeration, air conditioning, radio, television, rayon, plastics, quick freezing, prefabricated housing, light metals, powered metals, high octave gasoline, gas turbines, jet propulsion, spun glass, cotton pickers, combined harvesters, electronics—to name only a few at random—the total volume of direct and induced investment can be tremendous. There is no evidence of an increasing proportion of capital saving innovations.[9]

No doubt spontaneous changes in the pattern of consumer wants and techniques of production give rise to considerable investment but it is very doubtful if they alone would provide the required investment outlets.

Stagnationists believe that the propensity to consume is more or less stable. This has a considerable element of truth in the short run. But evidence shows that the consumption has a tendency to rise in the-long run. In the long run, country's conception of a minimum, standard of living has a tendency to shift upward. Things which were comforts and luxuries are now considered indispensable necessities. But the secular rise in the consumption function is not likely to be so rapid as to close or considerably reduce the gap between saving and investment at the full employment level.

We have examined above the important arguments of the proponents and opponents of the secular stagnation thesis. As the doctrine refers to a very remote future, it is very difficult to say anything definite about the possibility of the advent of a state of secular stagnation. Further the doctrine refers to a system of free enterprise which does not exist in any part of the world. Now, in almost all countries—whether capitalist or socialist—state plays an important role in economic affairs and tries to maintain full employment by all means at its disposal. Advent of socialist ideology pleading a more equalitarian distribution of wealth will considerably raise the consumption function and thus decrease the volume of savings and consequently the possibility of secular stagnation.

---

9. George Terborgh, *The Bogey of Economic Maturity*, pp. 89-96.

Prof. Martin Bronfenbrenner in a recent article has challenged the very concept of secular stagnation and asserts that it is the danger of secular inflation rather than secular stagnation that threatens the Western capitalist countries in the years to come. He states:[10]

> We look on secular inflation, not as strictly inevitable but as likely to dominate economic life in capitalist countries for the next few years.... The world of secular stagnation is the world of sound finance and of the gold standard. It is not currently in existence. It passed into coma in 1933, when Roosevelt and Hitler came *to* power, and died completely on the several battle fronts of World War II. Its importance today may be largely academic.... The world of secular inflation, however, is the pressure economy of the present, including the political necessity of maintaining high employment at whatever cost.

It is very difficult to say as to whether or not the predictions of secular stagnationists and secular inflationists are true and real. It would take a long time to test these theses against observations. To cite Koivisto, "The future contains too many imponderables. The subject remains a great guessing game...No one can say for sure. This is not a matter of economic analysis, but a prediction of exogenous factors. And the further into the future that we try to predict such matters, the more answers depend on our own particular crystal balls. Such forecasts accordingly must be taken with a large grain of salt, but it is nevertheless interesting to speculate about them."[11] To cite Prof. Samuelson, "Economic analysis must be prepared to understand the policies called for by stagnation; it must be no less prepared to meet the opposite situation of long range inflationary condition."[12]

---

10. M. Bronfenbrenner, "Some Neglected Implications of Secular Inflation" in K.K. Kurihara (ed.) *Post-Keynesian Economics* (London, 1955), pp. 36-37.
11. Koivisto, *Principles and Problems of Modern Economics*, pp. 405-10.
12. P.A. Samuelson, *Economics*, p. 407.

Harrod-Domar Model

8

1. Introductory

Harrod and Domar are mainly concerned with the conditions required for smooth and uninterrupted growth in national income.[1] Both of them developed their models of steady growth independent of each other. Harrod, of course, published his theory earlier than Domar. Though the models of Harrod and Domar differ in details, the basic idea is very similar in the two.

In Harrod-Domar model, capital accumulation plays a crucial role in the process of economic growth. The distinctive feature of this model is that it considers both the sides of the investment process while the earlier writers concentrate only on one side. The classical economists consider only the capacity side of capital accumulation and, believing that supply creates its own demand, do not consider it necessary to pay attention to the demand side. Keynesians, on the other hand, err in the opposite direction. Concerned primarily with the short period, they consider only the adequacy of demand and neglect the problem of increase in capacity through investment in the long run. Harrod-Domar model integrates the classical and Keynesian analysis of economic growth.

The essence of the Harrod-Domar model is, starting from a full employment equilibrium level of income, continuous maintenance of this equilibrium requires that the volume of spending generated by investment must be sufficient to absorb the increased output resulting from investment. Given the marginal propensity to save, the more the capital is accumulated and the larger the initial national income, the larger must be the absolute volume of net investment. Maintenance of full employment, therefore, requires an ever-expanding amount of absolute net investment. This, in turn,

1. R.F. Harrod, *Towards a Dynamic Economics* (London, 1948) and Evsey D. Domar, *Essays in the Theory of Economic Growth* (New York, 1957).

requires a continuous growth in real national income. Capital accumulation and growth of income must go side by side. An increase in capital expands the productive capacity of the economy. If it is not accompanied by an increase in income, any of the following three things may happen: (1) the new capital may remain unutilised; (2) the new capital may replace old capital depriving the latter of its labour and/or markets; (3) the new capital may be substituted for labour (and possibly for other factors). Thus increase in capital unaccompanied by an increase in income would result into an unemployment of capital and/or labour. Harrod and Domar are afraid that excessive accumulation of capital would result into overproduction and consequently into a fall in investment leading to depression.

2. Domar Model

The fundamental question around which Domar builds his model is: Investment leading to an increase in productive capacity and income, what should be the rate of increase in investment which would equalise the increase in income and the increase in productive capacity, so that full employment is maintained?[2] The model is based on the following main assumptions: (1) an initial full employment level of income has already been achieved; (2) absence of government and foreign trade; (3) there are no lags in adjustment; (4) the average and marginal propensities to save are equal; (5) the propensity to save and the capital coefficient (ratio of capital stock to output) are constant. All these assumptions, however, are not necessary. Some of these are made just for simplifying the analysis and can be relaxed in a more complicated analysis. Income, investment and saving are all used in the net sense, *i.e.*, gross minus depreciation. The model is in the form of an equation. Let us set up this equation. Let investment proceed at an annual rate of I and let annual productive capacity per dollar of newly created capital be equal on average to S. In other words, S is the ratio of increase in real income or output to an increase in capital, *i.e.* the reciprocal of acceleration or the marginal capital coefficient. Thus if capital worth 3 dollars is required for producing output worth one dollar, S will be 1/3 or 33.3 per cent per year. The productive capacity resulting from an investment of I dollar will, thus, be IS dollars per year.

---

2. Domar, n. 1, p. 89.

But the operation of new capital may, at least to some extent, be at the cost of previously existing capital. In other words the new capital may replace some of the existing capital by depriving the latter of its market and factors of production (particularly labour). If so happens, the increase in productive capacity resulting from an increase in investment will not be *IS*; it would be a smaller amount say $I\sigma$ dollars per year. Thus *S* stands for the increase in productive capacity per dollar invested in only new plants while σ stands for the increase in productive capacity per dollar invested of the whole economy. Since a part of the increase in capacity in new plants is offset by a decrease in capacity in the existing plants, σ is less than *S*. σ should be distinguished from the traditional concept of the marginal productivity of capital. The concept of the marginal productivity of capital is based on the assumption that the quantity of other factors of production and the state of technique remain unchanged while σ makes no such assumption. Thus σ stands for the productive capacity which *accompanies*, rather than which is caused by, each dollar invested. Further it may be mentioned that σ stands for productive potential of the economy *(i.e.,* capability of the economy to increase output) and not an actual increase in output. Whether or not the productive potential results into an increase in output depends on the behaviour of money income. Domar defines the symbol σ as the potential social average productivity of investment.

The expression $I\sigma$ is the supply side of the system, *i.e.,* the total net increase in output that the economy can produce. The demand side of the economy is the familiar Keynesian multiplier. If investment increases at an absolute annual rate of ΔI and the corresponding absolute annual increase in income is indicated by ΔY,

(1) $\Delta Y = \Delta I \frac{1}{\alpha}$ where α is the propensity to save and, therefore, $\frac{1}{\alpha}$ the multiplier.

If the economy is initially in a state of full employment equilibrium, so that its income equals its productive capacity, the maintenance of the state of full employment requires that the income and the productive capacity should increase at the same rate. $I\sigma$ being the annual increase in potential capacity and $\Delta I\left(\frac{1}{\alpha}\right)$

the annual increase in actual income, the full employment equilibrium will be maintained only if

$$(2)\quad \Delta I \frac{1}{\alpha} = I\sigma$$

Multiplying both sides of the equation by α and dividing by I, we obtain

$$(3)\quad \frac{\Delta I}{I} = \alpha\sigma$$

The left side of the equation (3) is the absolute annual increase (or the absolute rate of growth) in investment —ΔI— divided by the volume of investment itself; or in other words, it is the relative increase in investment, or the annual rate of growth of investment. This shows that the maintenance of full employment requires that the investment should grow at the annual relative rate of $\alpha\sigma$. Let us now turn to the income. Suppose that the marginal and average propensities to save are equal and constant, *i.e.*, income is a constant multiple of investment. Therefore, income must also grow at the same annual relative rate of $\alpha\sigma$. In short, maintenance of a continuous state of full employment requires that investment and income grow at a constant annual relative (or compound interest) rate equal to the product of the propensity to save and the average productivity of investment. Let us illustrate the analysis with the help of a numerical example. Let σ=25 per cent per year, α=12 per cent, and Y=$150 billion per year. The investment required for the maintenance of full employment is $\frac{150 \times 12}{100}$ or $18 billion. This would raise productive capacity by the amount invested σ times: that is, by $\frac{150 \times 12 \times 25}{100 \times 100}$ or $4.5 billion. If unused capacity is to be prevented, national income would have to rise by 4.5 billion. But the relative increase in income would equal the absolute increase divided by the income itself, *i.e.*

$$\frac{150 \times 12 \times 25}{150 \times 100 \times 100} = \frac{12}{100} \times \frac{25}{100} = \alpha\sigma = 3 \text{ per cent.}$$

Thus if full employment is to be maintained and unused capacity avoided, the income must grow at the rate of 3 per cent per annum. The above results are based on the assumption that α, the propensity to save, and σ, the average productivity of investment, remain constant. This assumption, however, is not essential for the analysis and the whole problem can be easily reworked with variable α and σ.

Let us contrast this long-period analysis with the Keynesian short period analysis which neglects growth. In the short-period analysis, to maintain a level of income, investment must offset saving, or the savings of yesterday must be invested today. To maintain full employment over a long period of time, however, offsetting yesterday's savings by today's investment is not sufficient; investment of today must exceed saving of yesterday. Further investment must grow at an increasing absolute rate (or constant compound interest rate).

As is clear from equation 3 the larger is the α, the larger would be the amount of investment required for the maintenance of the income. Similarly, the larger is σ, the greater is the increase in productive capacity resulting from investment and therefore the larger is the rise in income required for avoiding unused capacity. But, since rising income depends on a rising rate of investment, if income is to grow, investment must also grow. The required amount by which the investment must grow is given by the product $\alpha\sigma$.

Thus the economy faces a serious dilemma: if sufficient investment is not forthcoming today, unemployment will occur today; but, if enough is invested today, still more will be needed tomorrow in order to increase demand so that the expanded capacity can be utilised and excessive capital accumulation avoided tomorrow; otherwise, the excessive capital accumulation will cause a fall in investment leading to a depression day after tomorrow. To stay at the same place, therefore, the economy must move faster and faster otherwise it will slip downward.

In contrast to the situation in which a depression occurs, when investment is below the required rate, too rapid a rate of growth strains existing capacity and stimulates investment, which, in turn, accelerates the growth of output and increases the strain on capacity all the more. Elimination of the idle capacity, therefore, requires building of more capital (assuming a given propensity to save or that the propensity to save does not decline sufficiently rapidly).

Avoidance of capital shortage requires a reduction in investment. This conclusion sounds paradoxical. For understanding this paradox, we have to consider the effect that an increase in output or investment has on demand. Too rapid an increase in output or investment will increase the quantity to be sold, but it will also raise the demand even more and, therefore, there would be underproduction and a capital shortage. For eliminating the capital shortage, investment would have to be reduced which would, in turn, reduce demand and the pressure on capacity. Similarly, for eliminating idle capacity, more investment is needed which would, in turn, lead to increase in demand.

After considering the rate of growth of income required for maintaining full employment equilibrium over time, Domar considers the question as to whether or not sufficient investment would be forthcoming for allowing the required increase in income. Unlike the classical analysis leading to the stationary state, or the Marxian analysis leading to the inevitable downfall of capitalism, Domar's model shows that there is no inherent logical impossibility in conceiving a capitalist system enjoying continuous expansion, or in other words, the downfall of capitalism is not inevitable. Nevertheless, it demonstrates that there is no automatic tendency for capitalist system to keep moving 'onward and upward' and that certain special conditions are necessary for continuous expansion.

Domar states that the growth of monopoly leads to increasing unemployment of capital, and by retarding innovation, may also cause unemployment of labour. If this inhibition to new investment resulting from a developing of idle capacity in monopolistic industries is not offset by exogenous forces like territorial, technological and population expansion, there may occur chronic depression and increasing unemployment.

3. Harrod Model

Like Domar, Harrod is concerned primarily with conditions for a steady rate of growth and demonstrates the possible paths along which the economy might grow. He starts his model with the fundamental equation

(*i*) $GC=s$

In this equation G stands for the rate of growth of output, *i.e.*, ratio of increase in output to total output in any unit period or

$\frac{\Delta Y}{Y}$; *C* stands for the increase in capital during the period divided by the increase in output in the period or $\frac{I}{\Delta Y}$; *S* is the average propensity to save or $\frac{S}{Y}$. The equation (1) can be written as $\frac{\Delta Y}{Y} \cdot \frac{I}{\Delta Y} = \frac{S}{Y}$ or $\frac{I}{Y} = \frac{S}{Y}$ or $I = S$. Thus, this equation is a mere truism, that is, *ex post* (or actual or realised) saving equal *ex post* investment.

Harrod then postulates two important behaviour relations, *viz.* (1) savings depend on the level of income and (2) investment depends on the rate of growth of income. Second relation involves the acceleration principle, *i.e.* increase in the rate of output that is taking place induces the increase in the stock of capital that makes it possible. Maintenance of full employment requires that the *ex ante* (or desired or intended or planned) savings out of full employment income must be offset by an equal amount of *ex ante* investment. For inducing the required investment, income must be growing.

Harrod states a second fundamental equation

(*ii*) $GwCr = s$

This equation expresses the equilibrium conditions for a steady growth. *Gw*, the "warranted rate of growth" is defined as the rate of growth $\left(i.e.\ \frac{\Delta Y}{Y}\right)$ which satisfies entrepreneurs and thereby leads to its own perpetuation. *Cr*, the "capital requirement" is defined as the capital coefficient $\left(i.e.\ \frac{I}{\Delta Y}\right)$ required for sustaining the warranted rate of growth. This definition is based on two assumptions, *viz.*, (1) that innovations are neutral and (2) that the rate of interest is constant. Under these assumptions the capital/income ratio will remain constant, *i.e.*, the length of production process will remain unchanged. If capital/income ratio remains constant, existing output can be sustained with the existing capital and the additional output can be required for sustaining only the additional output. Harrod assumes that saving intentions are always realised and, therefore, *ex ante* savings are equal to *ex post* savings, *s*, therefore, is the same in both the equations. Thus in dynamic equilibrium $\left(\text{stable value of } \frac{\Delta Y}{Y}\right)$, $GwCr=GC$; the actual or *ex post* value of $\frac{I}{Y}$ equals the equilibrium value, which is a subjective phenomenon. Further *G* must equal *Gw* and *C* must equal *Cr*.

If *G* (the actual rate of growth) exceeds *Gw* (the warranted rate of growth that would give steady advance), *C* (actual capital accumulation) must be less than *Cr* (required capital accumulation for steady advance). In other words, actual amount of capital goods will be less than the desired amount of capital goods, *i.e.* there would occur a shortage of capital. This situation would lead to a chronic inflationary gap because desired investment would be greater than desired saving, and production would be less than the aggregate demand.

In contrast, if *G* falls short of *Gw*, *C* must be greater than *Cr*. This situation would lead to a chronic deflationary gap, *i.e.* desired saving would be greater than desired investment, and businessmen would not be able to sell all that they have produced.

Deviations of *G* from *Gw* are unstable, *i.e.* once *G* departs from *Gw*, the gap between the two would continue widening cumulatively. "Around the line of advance, which, if adhered to, would alone give satisfaction, centrifugal forces are at work, causing the system to depart farther and farther from the required line of advance."[3] If *G* is greater than *Gw*, desired investment is greater than desired saving, and this, in return, stimulates further growth. In contrast, if *G* is less than *Gw*, desired saving exceeds desired investment, inventories accumulate, entrepreneurs become pessimistic, they keep the rate of increase in output below *Gw*, and this results in a further retardation of growth.

Harrod realises that the equation $GC=s$ may be criticised for laying too much emphasis on the acceleration principle. To avoid this criticism, he suggests that this equation may be rewritten as $GC=s-k$ when *k* is the investment not required by the current

3. Harrod, n. 1, p. 86.

increase in output. k is, in fact, the investment of a long run character and is not justified within a fairly short period. In the long run, k will be zero because in the long run all investment is put to some or the other use and, therefore, is justified.

The third fundamental equation in Harrod's model is

(*iii*) $GrCr = or \neq s$

Gn, the natural rate of growth, is the maximum possible rate of advance determined by the fundamental conditions, *viz.*, growth of population and technological improvements. This is the ceiling above which the rate of advance cannot go "...it excludes the possibility of 'involuntary' unemployment."[4]

Gn may or may not be equal to *Gw*. If *Gn* exceeds *Gw*, there is no reason why G should not exceed *Gw* for most of the time. We saw earlier that when G exceeds *Gw*, there tends to occur a cumulative boom. Therefore, when *Gn* exceeds *Gw*, a boom will tend to develop. In contrast, if *Gw* exceeds *Gn*, G must be below *Gw* for most of the time because the average value of G over a period cannot exceed that of *Gn*. We saw earlier that when G falls short of *Gw*, there tends to occur a cumulative recession. Therefore, when *Gn* falls short of *Gw*, a recession will tend to develop. This sounds a little paradoxical. Apparently, if desired rate of growth exceeds the rate of growth permitted by fundamental conditions, we should expect inflationary pressures. But penetrating analysis demonstrates that, in fact, quite the opposite happens. This paradox is very similar to the contrast between Keynesian economics and classical economics. When *Gw* is below *Gn*, we will have boom conditions and a tendency to approach full employment; but this high employment will be of an inflationary and hence unhealthy character. Under these circumstances, savings are desirable because these enable us to have a high level of employment without inflationary pressures. In contrast, when *Gw* is above *Gn*, savings will have a tendency to accentuate depression.

Harrod uses his analysis to explain trade cycles. While doing so, of course, he fully recognises that no theory of business cycles can be complete without taking into account lags and psychological, monetary and other factors. In the recovery phase, because of the existence of unemployed productive resources, G is above *Gn*.

4. *Ibid.*, p. 87.

When full employment is reached, G becomes equal to Gn. If Gw exceeds Gn at the full employment, slump is inevitable. Since G has to fall below Gw, it will, for the time being, be driven progressively downwards. Further, G itself fluctuates during the course of the business cycle. Savings as a fraction of income, though fairly steady in the long run, fluctuate in the short run. In the short run, savings tend to be residual between the earning and normal consumption. Companies, also, are likely to save a large portion of their short-period increases in net receipts. Thus, even if Gw is normally below Gn, it is likely to rise above Gn in the later stages of advance, and, if it so happens, a vicious-spiral of depression is inevitable when full employment is reached. If Gw does not rise above Gn in the course of advance, there would be continued pressure to advance when full employment is reached; this would lead to inflation and consequently, sooner or later, to a rise of Gw above Gn, resulting, ultimately, into a vicious spiral of depression. Actually, G may be reduced before the full employment is reached, because of immobilities, frictions and bottlenecks and, if it so happens, depression may come before full employment is reached. If Gw is far above Gn, G may never rise far above Gw during the revival and the depression may be precipitated long before full employment is reached.

Actually, business cycles are constrained and are not free to move beyond certain limits. The upper limit is provided by the Gn. In the short run, real income cannot rise beyond the full employment ceiling. The lower limit is set by a 'floor' of autonomous investment, the 'break-even point' of the consumption function, the impossibility of gross investment being negative (disinvestment cannot exceed the rate of depreciation), and eventually replacement investment.

For making allowance for inventions which are neutral, Harrod introduces another symbol in the fundamental equation, d stands for the fraction of income needed for capital involved in lengthening the production process; d will be negative if the inventions are 'capital saving.' To take into consideration such inventions, the equation will have to be rewritten as

$$GwCr=s-d.$$

Capital saving inventions enhance the equilibrium rate of growth (Gw) and thus aggravate any tendency towards chronic unemployment resulting from $Gw>Gn$. Thus, d may be positive because of the nature of inventions or because of falling rate of interest which tends to lengthen the period of production. For preventing depression, we should try to get such a progressive reduction in the rate of interest that

$$GwCr=s-d=GnCn$$

So far we were considering a closed economy. In an open economy, the fundamental equations will have to be rewritten as $GC=s-b$ and $GwCr=s-b$, where b stands for foreign balance. Thus, in a country suffering from a chronic unemployment, $Gw>Gn$, a positive value of 6 (*i.e.*, favourable balance of payments) would, reduce the deflationary gap. In contrast, in a country suffering from an inflationary gap, a positive value of b will accentuate the inflationary gap. Thus a country with $Gw>Gn$ should try to achieve a favourable balance of payments and a country with $Gw<Gn$ should aim at an unfavourable balance.

After explaining business cycles, Harrod discusses policies for filling a chronic deflationary gap. Regarding wage policy, he states that once for all wage reduction is not effective. A year-by-year wage reduction would not affect Gn directly. It would not depress Gw. On the contrary, it would raise Gw by raising the goods value of money and thereby accentuate the tendency towards depression. Harrod considers interest rates to be an effective way of preventing unemployment. But he is doubtful if the system will of its own secure a sufficient fall in the interest rates.

In a later article[5] published in 1960, Harrod stresses the need for elaborating the supply side of his growth equation in order to make it more relevant to the conditions prevailing in underdeveloped countries. He particularly studies the role of the rate of interest in determining the availability of savings and the demand for saving for implementing plans of investment. In his earlier essay C_r indicates the optimum amount of capital required at the warranted growth rate of income. But the amount of savings available and as such the magnitude of investment that is possible are both influenced by the rate of interest. Similarly, the natural rate of growth of income requires a certain volume of savings. Given the other resources in the economy like labour and natural resources, actual rate of growth can reach the level of natural rate only if a

5. R.F. Harrod, "Second Essay in Dynamic Theory," *Economic Journal*, June 1960, pp. 277-93.

corresponding amount of savings is forthcoming. Further, the natural rate of growth itself will not be determinate unless the rate of interest is specified. Harrod, therefore, conceives of natural rate of interest which he defines as the one that conforms to the natural growth of income and is determined by the natural rate of growth of per capita output (P_c) and the elasticity of the schedule of the diminishing utility of income (e). Thus a large value of e means that the utility of income falls rapidly when income grows. Hence the natural rate of interest is

$$r_n = \frac{P_c G_n}{e}$$

With given values of P_e and G_n the natural rate of growth will be low if e is large and *vice versa*. e is supposed to "be generally less than one. The capital intensity of the methods of production employed by the entrepreneurs and as such the amount of capital required will be determined by the rate of interest. Generally C_r or the capital requirements would be a decreasing function of r_n, *i.e.* $C_r = f\ (r_n)$. Corresponding to the natural rate of growth of output there would be the required rate of savings and also the natural rate of interest. It is not necessary that the fraction of income actually saved *(S)* should tend to equality with the social requirement (S_r). S may be greater or small than S_r. In case S exceeds S_r, the warranted rate of growth will be above the natural rate of growth, *i.e.*, the entrepreneurs will like to increase their investment because larger savings are available. There is an important difference in the way the natural rate of growth and the warranted rate of growth are determined. The natural rate of growth is determined by labour and technological resources. Given these resources, the level of natural rate of growth would require a certain rate of savings. The warranted rate of growth is determined by the actual rate of savings (S).

What would happen if S exceeds or falls short of S_r. In case S exceeds S_r, the warranted rate of growth would be higher than the natural rate of growth. As the natural rate is the highest which can be attained in the long run, it is not possible for the excess of warranted rate to continue. The actual rate of growth would hit the full employment ceiling and thereafter it will have to decline below the warranted rate of growth and a depression will ensue. In contrast, if S falls short of S_r, investment will exceed savings and as such there will be a chronic tendency to inflation, which is an important characteristic of developing economies. If the rate of growth is low because of a shortage of savings; there would result underemployment and unemployment. It may, therefore, be expedient to raise S towards the level of S_r by surplus budgeting or compulsory levy. Harrod, however, stresses the need for social and institutional changes to bring about growth in underdeveloped countries. Growth may not be limited by savings. A low rate of growth may be the result not of a shortage of S compared with S_r but of a shortage of technical skill or of institutional and social hindrances. Owing to these reasons, the required rate of savings will be low in underdeveloped countries and the actual level of savings may not fall short of it.

4. Criticism of Harrod-Domar Models

The models assume key parameters, like the propensity to save and the capital-output ratio, to be constant. In reality, these are very likely to change over the long run. Changes in these parameters would change the requirements for steady growth.

Because the variables in the models refer only to aggregates, a model constructed on the basis of such aggregates cannot show the inter-relations between the sectors and as such is not meant for demonstrating the structural changes which constitute a basic aspect of the economic development of underdeveloped countries.[6] Harmonious growth of different sectors of the economy is very important for steady growth. Deviations from steady growth may be caused by a lack of harmony between the growth of different sectors even when aggregative requirements for stability are fulfilled.

The models assume the production function to be fixed and, therefore, there is no scope for substitution between different factors. Actually different factors of production, at least to a limited extent, can be substituted for each other. If labour can be substituted for capital, the requirements for steady growth would not be so rigid. Substitutability between different factors increases the flexibility of the economy and thereby decreases the possibilities of cumulative deviations from the path of steady growth. In fact such substitution is regularly taking place and constitutes an essential feature of economic growth. Technological changes and improvements in the

6. *Economic Bulletin for Asia and Far East* (New York, 1955), pp. 34-40.

methods of organisation bring about a shift in the pattern of production. It is, therefore, not correct to make use of a fixed production function for explaining long-term growth. The capital output ratio and the accelerator are also not constant in the real world. In fact, the contribution of capital to production is not clearly known. Lundberg states that recent statistical studies pertaining to Norway and the United States indicate that contribution of capital accumulation to the growth rate of these economies has been small as compared with the contribution of shifts in the production function, technical research, administration and investment in education.[7] The variables in the models are expressed in real terms which rules out the influence of monetary and price factors on investment, savings and demand. In fact, the accelerator is not a non-monetary element in the business cycle. Businessmen's willingness and ability to invest is influenced by price expectations, interest rates, credit policies and condition of stock market. If these factors influence savings and investment, changes in them may bring about equilibrating adjustments in savings and investment when there is a deviation and check the cumulative working of the forces of deviation. It is held that, in fact, instability is very much exaggerated in the growth models. Small deviations from the equilibrium path need not carry the economy headlong in either direction. Instability, in fact, is caused by the entrepreneurial behaviour and the lag between investment decisions and capital outlay.[8] Yeager criticises the use of the concept of natural growth in Harrod's model.[9] He points out that the upper limit to growth is not rigidly fixed by labour and natural resources. Even if it is assumed that labour and natural resources are fixed, the output that can be obtained from these resources would vary according to the method of utilizing the resources. Improvements in technology and the methods of organisation would increase the productivity of both capital and labour and thus the maximum output possible with a given supply of productive resources can be increased. Yeager also

7. Erik Lundberg, "The Profitability of Investment," *Economic Journal*, December 1959, pp. 653-77.
8. H. Rose, "The Possibility of Warranted Growth," *Economic Journal*, June 1959, pp. 313-32.
9. Leland, B., Yeager, "Some Questions about Growth Economies," *American Economic Review* (March 1944), pp. 53-63.

points out that the cumulative upward and downward movements supposed to describe the real world are only a theoretical derivation from certain basic assumptions and are not supported by empirical evidence. He criticizes models also on the ground that many of the concepts like warranted rate of growth in Harrod are fuzzy and incapable of being assessed objectively.

The concept *Gw* "warranted rate of growth" has an important place in Harrod's model. Harrod, however, has not elaborated the meaning of this concept. He defines Gw "as that over-all rate of advance which, if executed, will leave entrepreneurs in a state of mind in which they are prepared to carry a similar advance."[10] In his earlier article in *Economic Journal*, he defines *Gw* as "that rate of growth which if it occurs, will leave all parties satisfied that they have produced neither more nor less than the right amount." Harrod does not tell as to what are the determinants of *Gw*. It is very important to know as to what determines the *Gw*. C_r depends on *Gw*; in fact, it is defined in terms of *Gw*. The value of *G* and *C* depend on entrepreneurial decisions which in turn depend on *Gw*. *Gw* is, in fact, the core of the model. Though Harrod says nothing regarding the determinants of *Gw*, he, in the course of discussion, gives a number of relationships between *Gw* and other variables. *G* varies (1) inversely with C_r (capital requirements); (2) directly with *s* (the average propensity to save); (3) inversely with the volume of public works; (4) inversely with the volume of investment, that is, independent of the current rate of growth, *k;* (5) directly with the rate of interest *r* (since *k* and G_r, vary inversely with *r,* and *s* probably varies directly with *r).* These relations, however, are not truly causal, with meaning in terms of entrepreneurial behaviour.

5. Applicability of Harrod-Domar Models to Underdeveloped Countries

The growth models as developed in advanced countries are based on three principal concepts, *viz.* (*i*) the saving function, (*ii*) autonomous *vs* induced investment and (*iii*) the productivity of capital. The Harrod-Domar growth models were formulated primarily to illuminate secular stagnation that was threatening the advanced economies in the post-war period. The application of these

10. *Ibid.*, p. 82.

models has now been extended to development problems of underdeveloped economies. To cite Hirschman, "The Domar model, in particular, has proved to be remarkably versatile: it permits us to show not only the rate at which the economy must grow if it is to make full use of the capacity created by new investment but inversely, the required savings and the capital-output ratios if income is to attain a certain target of growth rate. In such exercises the capital-output ratio is usually assumed at some value between 2.5 and 5; sometimes several alternative projections are undertaken; with given growth rates, overall or per capita, and with given population projections in the latter case, total capital requirements for five-or-ten-year plans are then easily derived."[11] Let us show how these models can be used for planning in underdeveloped countries.

Suppose the capital-output ratio is 4:1 and the full capacity growth rate is estimated at 3 per cent per annum for the economy. With the help of either the Harrod or the Domar formula, the planners can find out the saving-income ratio required to sustain the growth rate of 3 per cent per annum. In Harrod's model:

$G_w.C_r = s$ and by applying the assumed rate we get,

$3/100 \times 4/1 = 12/100$ or 12% which is the saving-income ratio. Similarly, in Domar's model:

$$\Delta Y/Y = \alpha\sigma$$
$$= 3/100 \times 4/1$$
$$= 12/100 \text{ or } 12\%$$ (σ being the reciprocal of Harrod's Cr).

Thus, in an economy, if the capital-output ratio is assumed to be 4:1, the community will have to save 12% of its annual income, if its annual growth rate of output is to be 3%. Let us work it out in practice. Given the saving ratio and the capital-output ratio, the Harrod formula for calculating the growth rate is

$$C_w = \frac{s}{C_r},$$ if s is 12% and the value of C_r 4 then,

$$G_w = \frac{12}{4} = 3 \text{ per cent.}$$

11. K. Kurihara, *The Keynesian Theory of Economic Development*, p. 153.

6. Limitations

The models pay attention only to the requirements for steady growth and neglect the rate of growth. The models are more useful for developed countries whose main aim is stability and not the rate of growth. In contrast, underdeveloped countries are interested more in the rate of growth. They would not mind following policies which create fluctuations if these considerably raise the rate of growth.

Preclusion of autonomous investment makes Harrod's concept of 'warranted' rate analytically inadequate for the purpose of underdeveloped economies.[12] Hicks feels that there is too much instability in Harrod's model of an economy advancing at the warranted rate, and, therefore, considers it essential to introduce autonomous investment as a stabilising force.

The 'required' rate of growth of investment in Domar's model fails to solve the problem of structural under-employment. What it meets is the problem of unemployment due to an insufficiency of effective demand. But if population grows faster than accumulation of capital, which is not uncommon in underdeveloped countries, there would arise structural unemployment owing to a shortage of capital equipment.

Domar's attitude towards technology leaves much to be desired. Being primarily concerned with an insufficiency of effective demand, Domar considers technological progress mainly as 'the creator of investment opportunities.' As regards an underdeveloped country, technological progress is desired for its productivity effect, irrespective of whether or not the effective demand is increased thereby.

The models do not describe the development process correctly and, therefore, a point may be reached when they will prove a hindrance rather than a help in the understanding of the reality of underdeveloped countries. The two important variables of the growth equations—marginal propensity to save and the capital output ratio—are more relevant to advanced countries than to underdeveloped countries.

---

12. Kenneth K. Kurihara, *The Keynesian Theory of Economic Development* (London, 1961), pp. 62-73, 153.

In an advanced economy, savings and investment decisions are generally taken by different groups of persons and institutions and therefore are independent of one another. At the same time the level of income is an important factor which determines the supply of savings. Hence, in an advanced economy, the equality of saving and investment is considered to be an equilibrium condition. In contrast, in an underdeveloped economy, saving and investment decisions are generally taken by the same group of persons and, therefore, are largely interdependent. Further, since savings come mostly from the more well-to-do people, additions to savings will depend upon they opening up of investment opportunities and on the removal of various obstacles to investment activity. Thus while savings depend upon the *level of income* in an advanced economy, they depend upon investment opportunities in underdeveloped economies.

The advanced and underdeveloped countries differ in regard to capital-output ratio. In an advanced country, the capital-output ratio may be taken in general as a technological coefficient; at any particular period, entrepreneurs will choose various projects with some kind of balanced distribution of capital coefficients. In an underdeveloped country, it is difficult to apply the concept of capital-output ratio because 'normal productivity' is often held back by shortages and bottlenecks and when the latter are eliminated the productivity of already invested capital increases considerably.

Professor Kurihara is of the view that though "their policy implications are very opposite of what one might expect of an underdeveloped economy," yet "these growth models have this positive lesson for underdeveloped economies, that the State should be allowed to play not only a stabilizing role but also a developmental role, if these economies are to be industrialized more effectively and rapidly than the now industrialized economies did in conditions of *laissez faire*." He further points out that because of the universal character of saving-income ratio and capital-output ratio (or its reciprocal) as measurable strategic variables, the growth mechanism discussed by Harrod and Domar is applicable to all economic systems, although with due modification. That is why, these growth models are applicable to those underdeveloped countries in which the technique of planning with 'balanced growth' is adopted under this technique, saving-income ratio and capital-output ratio remain constant during the plan period.

Joan Robinson's Theory of Capital Accumulation

9

Joan Robinson's model[1] of economic growth is based on two fundamental factors, *viz.*, (*i*) the capital formation depends on the manner of distribution of income and (*ii*) the rate at which labour is utilised depends upon the supply of capital and that of labour. The model is based upon the following assumptions: (*i*) Total income in real terms is distributed between only two classes—the workers and the entrepreneurs. The workers spend their entire income on consumption and save nothing. The entrepreneurs spend their entire income (from profits) on investment or capital formation and consume nothing. If they have no profits, the entrepreneurs cannot accumulate and if they do not accumulate, they have no profits, (*ii*) Capital and labour are the only productive factors. They are combined in fixed proportions and there is no technological change. (*iii*) There is a *laissez faire* closed economy.

In Robinson's Model, net national income is the sum of total wage bill and total profits. Total wage bill is the real wage rate multiplied by the number of labourers. Total profits are the profit rate multiplied by the volume of capital. Algebraically, the net national income may be expressed as

$$Y = wN + pK$$

where Y stands for the net national income, w for the real wage rate, N for the number of workers employed, p for the rate of profit, and K for the amount of capital. The profit rate, which is a strategic factor in the theory of capital accumulation, would, therefore, be

$$p = \frac{Y - wN}{K}$$

Thus profit rate is the ratio of total income minus the total wage bill to the amount of capital utilised. As the profit per labourer employed is the difference between the output per labourer and the

1. Joan Robinson, *The Accumulation of Capital* (London, 1956).

real wage, profit rate would depend on labour productivity, the real wage rate and the quantum of capital per worker or the capital-labour ratio. Hence the profit rate can increase if the income remains constant and the wage rate decreases or if the income increases and the wage rate remains constant. The rate of profit can also rise by a decline in the capital-labour ratio. In. this way the entrepreneurs maximise their profits.

On the expenditure side, net national income (Y) is equal to the sum of consumption expenditure (C) and investment expenditure (I). Algebraically speaking

$$Y = C + I$$

Since Joan Robinson assumes that savings out of wages are zero, savings are done only by the entrepreneurs, and profits are meant only for investment, we have

$$S = I$$

This saving-investment relation may be shown as

$$S = pK$$

and $$I = \Delta K \text{ } (\Delta K \text{ is increase in real capital})$$

$\therefore$ $$pK = \Delta K \text{ } (\because S = I)$$

or $$p = \frac{\Delta K}{K}$$

which is the growth rate of capital or the rate of capital accumulation. The growth of capital ($\Delta K/K$) being equal to p (rate of profit), it depends on the same factors on which depends the latter.

In addition to the rate of growth of capital ($\Delta K/K$), another factor on which depends the rate of growth of the economy is the rate of population growth. An increase in population and in labour force without being accompanied by an increase in capital would lead to a decline in labour productivity, and if the real wages are constant, would lower the margin of profit and thus widen the difference between capital and labour supply. It would also lead to unemployment. Full employment, therefore, is possible only if the growth rate of population is matched by the growth rate of capital. Algebraically speaking, if

$$\frac{\Delta N}{N} = \frac{\Delta K}{K}$$

there would be full employment of both labour and capital. Joan Robinson calls this the 'golden age'. To cite Joan Rabinson:[2]

> When technical progress is neutral and proceeding steadily, without any change in the time pattern of production, the competitive mechanism working freely, population growing (if at all) at a steady rate and accumulation going on fast enough to supply productive capacity for all available labour, the rate of profit tends to be constant and the level of real wages to rise with output per man. There are then no internal contradictions in the system. Provided that political events cause no disturbances, and provided that the entrepreneurs have faith in the future and desire to accumulate at the same proportional rate as they have been doing over the past, there is no impediment to prevent them from continuing to do so. Total annual output and the stock of capital (valued in terms of commodities) then grow together at a constant proportionate rate compounded at the rate of increase of the labour force and the rate of increase of output per man. We may describe these conditions as a *golden age*....

If the economy goes off the path of golden age, there is possibility of its coming back to this path under certain conditions. Thus, if the rate of increase in population exceeds that of capital $\left(i.e., \frac{\Delta N}{N} > \frac{\Delta K}{K}\right)$ a return to the *golden age* equilibrium is possible only if the profit wage relation behaves in an equilibrating manner. Thus excess of labour supply would lower the wage rate and if prices are unchanged, will reduce the real wages, and by increasing the amount of profits may increase the rate of growth of capital so that it would catch up with the increase in population. The equilibrating mechanism, however, will not work if real wages fail to decline either because of rigidity of money wage rates or because price level falls in the same proportion as the money wage rates. Normally, increase in prices assists capital formation so long as there is not a corresponding increase in wages. Increase in unemployment, while prices and wages are rising, is a common phenomenon in underdeveloped countries.

2. *Ibid.*, p. 99.

In contrast, if the capital grows faster than population, it is possible that the equilibrium may be restored through technological improvements and the shifting of the whole production function so that the economy gets itself adjusted to a higher capital-labour ratio. Joan Robinson, however, observes that the "mechanism by which the rate of accumulation is adjusted to the rate of increase in the supply of labour is more reliable when what is required is a reduction in the rate of accumulation than when a rise is required; it is only too easy for a surplus of labour to grow, relatively to the stock of capital, while investment fails to increase and the economy sinks into stagnation; whereas entrepreneurs will not accumulate and maintain redundant capital, so that when the rate of accumulation is too high (relatively to the labour force) one way or another it is certain to be cut down."[3]

Joan Robinson considers an economy in the golden age when the 'potential growth ratio' is being realized. The potential growth ratio is the highest rate of capital accumulation which can be permanently maintained at a constant rate of profit. The conditions of a golden age require the growth ratio to be steady because frequent changes in the growth ratio disturb the tranquility of a golden age. This tanquility, however, may not be possible even when the growth ratio is stable. An increase in the total stock of capital is likely to slacken the urge to accumulate so that a state of stagnation starts and the economy deviates from the path of golden age. The golden age is not an ideal. It only represents a state of equilibrium growth at any conceivable rate so that each rate of growth will have its appropriate golden age.

Though broadly speaking Robinson's Model comes to the same thing as those of Harrod and Domar, there are some important differences between them.[4] Joan Robinson makes capital accumulation depend explicitly on the profit-wage relation and the labour productivity, which brings her theory nearer a real market economy. In contrast, Harrod and Domar make capital accumulation depend on the saving ratio (related to national income and not to profit income alone) and capital productivity (or its reciprocal)

---

3. *Ibid.*, p. 81.
4. Kenneth K. Kurihara, *The Keynesian Theory of Economic Development* (London, 1961), pp. 79-80.

which transcend all economic systems, capitalistic or socialistic. While Joan Robinson approaches the question of capital accumulation from the standpoint mainly of labour, Harrod and Domar approach it from that of capital.

Joan Robinson's principal contribution lies in the fact that she has integrated classical value and distribution theory and modern Keynesian saving-investment theory into one coherent system. This, however, appears to be also the major shortcoming as far as policy application is concerned. Unlike the Harrod-Domar models, the Robinson model is not capable of being modified so as to introduce fiscal-monetary policy parameters—unless labour productivity, the wage rate, the profit rate, and the capital-labour ratio could be considered as objects of practical policy—as they might be so regarded in a completely planned economy.

1. Applicability to Underdeveloped Countries

Joan Robinson, in her theory, studies the problem of population and its effect on the rate of capital accumulation in a developing economy. There is a 'golden age' which any country can achieve through planned economic development.

An underdeveloped economy faces the problem of the rate of population growth being higher than that of capital growth, *i.e.*, $\Delta N/N > \Delta K/K$ as posed by Joan Robinson. It reveals the tendency of progressive underemployment in such economies.

The 'potential growth ratio' is crucial to J. Robinson's theory of economic growth. The golden age depends on the growth ratio. The task of planning becomes easier if the potential growth ratio of an economy is calculated for the planning period on the basis of the growth rate of labour force and of output per head.

In an underdeveloped economy the rate of capital accumulation is always less than its potential growth ratio and as such it is backward and possesses surplus of labour force. The planning authority should, therefore, increase the ratio of capital formation to the level of growth ratio for the economy. An underdeveloped country cannot, however, match the two by following the 'capitalist rules of the game.' On the other hand, it is the responsibility of the planning authority to take the initiative in controlling and regulating not only private investment but also public investment in such economies. Kurihara observes, "Joan Robinson's discussion of capital growth has the subtle effect of discrediting the whole idea of leaving so important a problem as economic growth to the capitalist rules of the game, for her model of *laissez faire* growth demonstrates how precarious and insecure it is to entrust to private profit-makers the paramount task of achieving the stable growth of an economy consistent with the needs of a growing population and the possibility of advancing technology."

Some other shortcomings of Joan Robinson's model are its unrealistic assumptions of a closed economy, no changes in the price level and the absence of institutional factors in the process of economic growth. Underdeveloped countries are not closed but open economies wherein foreign trade plays an important role in accelerating their rate of development. Further, experience shows that development has been accompanied by a rise in the prices. Further, no model can ignore the institutional factors as one of the determinants of economic growth. The development of an economy considerably depends on social, cultural and institutional changes. Thus it is not possible to use the concept of the 'golden age' in solving the problem of development planning because the unchanging continuity required for the golden age is not present in an underdeveloped economy.

Meade's Neo-Classical Theory of Economic Growth

10

Professor Meade's model[1] of economic growth is based on the following assumptions: (1) There is a closed economy without any economic or financial relationships with other economies. (2) There are no state or governmental economic activities involving taxation or state expenditure. (3) There prevails perfect competition (with its corollaries of prices equal to marginal costs and net factor rewards equal to the value of their marginal net products). (4) The production is subject to the law of constant returns. (5) Only two commodities are produced in the economy, *viz.*, consumption goods and production goods. The consumption goods satisfy all final human needs for food, clothing, shelter etc. and capital goods are used to help the further production of consumption goods or capital goods. (6) In addition to machines, there are only two other factors of production, *i.e.*, land and labour. (7) There is a constant money price for consumption goods and full employment of labour and land available at any moment of time is attained by the adjustment of money wage per worker and money rent per acre of land. (8) All machines are alike and the ratio of labour to machinery can be varied with equal ease in the short period as in the long period. (9) There is perfect substitutability in production between capital goods and consumption goods. (10) Each year some percentage of machines wear out which requires replacement.

In an economy of the type envisaged above, the net output produced depends upon four things, *viz.*, (*i*) the amount of the existing stock of machines; (*ii*) the amount of labour available for productive employment; (*iii*) the amount of land or natural resources available for productive use in the economy; and (*iv*) the state of technical knowledge which is assumed to be improving through

1. J.E. Meade, *A Neo-Classical Theory of Economic Growth* (London, 1961).

time. This simple relation may be put in the form of a production function as below:

$$Y = F(K, L, N, t)$$

where Y stands for net output or real national income, K for the existing stock of machines, L for the amount of labour, N for the amount of land and t for time, since the mere passage of time brings technical progress and allows Y to be raised even without any increase in K, L, or N.

With the passage of time, three things can happen to raise Y. In the first place, the stock of machines (K) may increase because the community is saving part of its income and is thereby accumulating real capital. Assume that in a year the stock of machines increases by ΔK. This would lead to an increase in output equal to $V\Delta K$, where V is the marginal net physical product of a machine.

Secondly, the working population (L) may grow. If in any one year the amount of labour productivity employed rises by ΔL, it would lead to an increase in output equal to $W\Delta L$, where W stands for the marginal product of labour.

Thirdly, it is assumed that the amount of land or natural resources available to the community is fixed and, therefore, there is no change in N to affect the level of Y. But with the passage of time (as it grows), Y would rise even if K, L, and N remain unchanged because of technological improvements. The term $\Delta Y'$ may be used to indicate the amount by which net output Y would rise in any one year because of technical progress.

If the changes which occur in any one year are not very great, it can be assumed that total change in net output (ΔY) is equal to the sum of the three influences mentioned above. Algebraically speaking,

$$\Delta Y = V\Delta K + W\Delta L + \Delta Y'$$

The above equation can be written as:

$$\frac{\Delta Y}{Y} = \frac{VK}{Y} \cdot \frac{\Delta K}{K} + \frac{WL}{Y} \cdot \frac{\Delta L}{L} + \frac{\Delta Y'}{Y}$$

where $\frac{\Delta Y}{Y}$ is the annual proportionate rate of growth of the output, $\frac{\Delta K}{K}$ the annual proportionate rate of growth of the stock of machinery, $\frac{\Delta L}{L}$ the annual proportionate rate of growth in the working population, and $\frac{\Delta Y'}{Y}$ the annual proportionate rate of growth of output solely due to technical progress. Let us call these four proportionate rates of growth *y, k, l,* and *r* respectively. The proportion of national income going to each factor in the form of remuneration is the ratio of the marginal product of the factor times the factor to total income. Thus the amount of income paid as profit is *VK/Y*. Let this be called the pioportional marginal product of capital (as distinct from net marginal product) and expressed as *U*. Similarly *Q* represents the proportional marginal product of labour. The basic relationship can, therefore, be written as

$$y = Uk + Ql + r$$

which shows the growth rate of output (*y*) as being the weighted sum of three other growth rates; namely the sum of the growth rate in the stock of machines (*k*) weighted by the proportional marginal product of capital (*U*) plus the growth rate of population (*l*) weighted by the proportional marginal product of labour (*Q*) plus the growth rate of technical progress (r).

The basic relationship $Y = Uk + Ql{+}r$ can be written as:

$$y{-}l = Uk{-}(l{-}Q)I{+}r$$

In the above equation *y–l* is the difference between the growth rate of total output and the growth rate of the working population and, therefore, it approximately measures the growth rate of real income per head. It is the growth rate in this real income per head which is most important. According to our basic relationship, the growth rate in real income per head (*y–l*) is the result of three factors, *viz.* (*i*) it is raised by the growth rate in real capital (*k*) weighted by its proportional marginal product or by proportion of the net national income which would be paid to profits in a competitive equilibrium (*U*); (*ii*) it is depressed by the growth rate in the working population (*l*) weighted by one minus the proportional marginal product of labour (1–*Q*); and (*iii*) it is raised by the technical progress (*v*). The second element — (*l–Q*)*l* which tends to depress the growth rate of real income per head is the familiar tendency for diminishing returns to labour set in as more and more labour is applied to any given amount of land and capital equipment.

In the basic relationship $y{-}l{=}Uk{-}(1{-}\text{Q})\,l + v$ the element *Uk* can be expressed in other forms. *U*, as has been seen, is $\frac{VK}{Y}$· *k*, the growth rate of the stock of machines, equals $\frac{SY}{K}$, where S is the proportion of the net national income which is saved; since SY would equal the amount of net real output which is added to the stock of machines in the course of a year so that $\frac{SY}{K}$ would equal the proportionate increase in the stock of machines over the year. Thus $Uk = US\frac{Y}{K} = SV$, which expresses in three forms the same thing, namely the contribution which capital accumulation is making to the growth rate of final output. The basic relationship can then be expressed between the growth rate of real income per head and its three basic determinants in three different forms:

$$y-l = UK-(1-Q)\,l + v$$

$$y-l = US\frac{Y}{K} - (1-Q)\,l + v$$

$$y-l = SC - (1-Q) + v$$

After discussing the main factors which determine the rate of growth of real income per head, Meade passes on to the conditions which may lead to a rise of economic growth over time. If growth of population and development of technology (*i.e.* l and v) are constant, the change in the growth rate would depend on changes in the values of V, S and Q over time. If population and technology remain unchanged but savings rise, capital per head would increase and the marginal product of capital would decline. This decline in V will, however, be less if it is possible to substitute capital for land and labour. Also if technical progress takes place, the decline in the marginal product of capital will be offset. But the volume of land and labour being fixed in the economy, more capital per head will be used and at the same time technical progress will tend to raise V. Under these conditions, the rate of growth of income per head over time would rise which would in turn tend to raise S. S will tend to rise still further owing to a change in income distribution towards larger profits resulting from the factors mentioned above. In other words, if population above is assumed to be constant, real income per head would depend upon the rate of capital accumulation (VS) and technical progress (r) which can be expressed as:

$$y = VS + r$$

Next, Prof. Meade examines the conditions of a state of steady economic growth, where population is growing at a constant proportionate rate while the rate of technical progress is constant. Obviously the income per head will be constant under these conditions only if the rate of growth of total output is constant. But under what conditions would the growth rate of total output be constant? This question is examined under the following assumptions: (*i*) all elasticities of substitution between the various factors are equal to unity; (*ii*) technical progress is neutral towards all factors; and (*iii*) the proportion of profits saved, of wage saved, and of rents saved are all three constant.

Let the proportion of national income saved out of profits, wages and rents be Sv, Sw and Sg respectively. Then total savings or $S = SvU + SwQ + SgZ$. As l and r are assumed to be constant, the proportional marginal products U and Q will be constant. Since U, Q and Z are constant, and Sv, Sw and Sg are also constant, S as a ratio of Y will be constant.

Now the rate of growth of output is given by our basic relationship

$$y = Uk + Ql + r$$

and y will be constant if and only if k is constant. We have assumed that l and r are constant and also conditions (*i*) and (*ii*) mentioned above mean that the proportional marginal products U and Q will be constant. It is, therefore, only if k is constant, that y will be constant.

But k, the growth rate of the capital stock, equals $\frac{SY}{K}$, since SY represents the amount annually added to the capital stock K through savings. Since conditions (*i*), (*ii*) and (*iii*) above mean that S is constant $\frac{SY}{K}$ or k will be constant, if and only if $\frac{Y}{K}$, the ratio of annual national income to the value of the capital stock, is constant. But $\frac{Y}{K}$ will be constant only if Y and K both grow at the same proportional rate per annum. In other words, $\frac{Y}{K}$ will be constant if

$y = k$. The conclusion, therefore, is that if the growth rate of the capital stock is equal to the growth rate of the national income, the growth rate of income will be constant and hence given a constant proportionate rate of population the per capita growth of income will be constant and steady.

This equilibrium position ultimately depends upon the rate of the capital stock. There is a *critical growth rate* of capital stock which makes the growth rate of income equal to the growth rate of the capital stock. A higher or lower growth rate in the capita stock than this 'critical growth rate' will not bring about the equality of y and k. If the 'critical growth rate' is denoted by a, the basic relationship will be

$$a = Ua + Ql + r$$

or

$$a = \frac{Ql + r}{l - U}$$

If at any time there is any deviation from this level of steady growth, forces will set in to bring the growth rate of the capital stock at the equilibrium level of $\frac{Ql + r}{l - U}$. Suppose k or $\frac{SY}{K} > \frac{Ql + r}{l - U}$. Since $\frac{Ql + r}{l - U}$ is as already seen, the rate of accumulation of capital which causes income (Y) and capital stock (K) to grow at the same proportionate rate, a rate will of accumulation of capital greater than this critical rate will cause the capital stock (K) to grow at a greater proportionate rate than income (Y). So long, therefore, as $\frac{SY}{K} > \frac{Ql + r}{l - U}$, Y will be growing at a lower proportionate rate than K, $\frac{Y}{K}$ will be falling, and with S constant $\frac{SY}{K}$ will be falling. In other words, if k starts above the critical steady growth level of $\frac{Ql + r}{l - U}$, the capital stock will grow more rapidly than income; and since savings grow only in proportion to income, the ratio of savings to the capital stock or the growth rate of capital will be declining towards the critical level $\frac{Ql + r}{l - U}$.

Similarly, if k starts at a figure below the critical steady-growth level of $\frac{Ql+r}{l-U}$, the income would grow more quickly than the capital so that savings would grow more quickly than the capital stock and the rate of growth of the capital stock would in consequence rise towards the critical level $\frac{Ql+r}{l-U}$.

The conclusion, therefore, is that if the growth rate of population is constant, if the three elasticities of substitution between the three factors land, labour and machinery are all unity, if the technical progress is at a constant rate and neutral towards all factors, and if the proportions of profits, of wages, and of rents saved were all three constant, then the growth rates of real income and of the stock of machinery would both tend towards a constant level equal to $\frac{Ql+r}{l-U}$.

The significance of Meade's model lies in showing the influence of population growth, capital accumulation and technical progress on the growth rate of national income and real income per head. The model follows the classical tradition of a closed *laissez faire* economy, there is perfect competition and constant returns to scale. It thus ignores the important role played by social, political and religious institutions and international forces in the process of economic development.

Mahalanobis Model

11

Mahalanobis started with a very simple model, *i.e.,* single sectoral model.[1] In this model, β is the ratio of the increase in net national income per unit of time to the investment associated with this additional income, *i.e.,* inverse of the marginal capital co-efficient; α is the rate of net investment, *i.e.* fraction of net national income used for investment. Thus the rate of the growth of the economy is αβ. If ρ is the rate of increase of population, the rate of increase in income per capita would be αβ—ρ. This model is similar to the growth models of Harrod and Domar. While formulating his model, Mahalanobis, however, was not aware of the existence of the models of Harrod and Domar.

Then he introduced a two sector model. In this model, he divides the total net investment into two components. One part of this investment (say λ_k) is used to increase the production of basic capital or investment goods (which may be called the *K*-sector) and the other part (say λ_c) is used to increase the production of consumption goods (*C*-sector). Because λ_k and λ_c are fractions of the total investment $\lambda_k+\lambda_c = 1$. Appropriate fractions of investment in industries manufacturing intermediate (producer) goods should be allocated to λ_k and λ_c in proportion to the value of such intermediate goods used in the capital goods (*K*-sector) and consumer goods (*C*-sector) industries respectively. The division of investment between the production of consumer goods and capital goods depends upon the choice of the planners. But once the value of the λ_k is decided, the supply of domestic investment goods becomes fixed; the supply of investment goods can be changed only through imports or exports.

Let γ_t=national income, C_t=consumption, and K_t=investment at time *t;* with Y_0, C_0, and K_0 as the corresponding values at the initial

1. P.C. Mahalanobis, "The Statistical Basis of the Plan Frame," *Sankhya* (December 1955).

period. As already mentioned, λ_k and λ_c (with $\lambda_k + \lambda_k = 1$) are fractions of investment allocated to industries producing capital goods (*K*-sector) and consumer goods (*C*-sector) respectively. Let β_k = ratio of increment of income to investment in industries producing investment goods; β_c = ratio of increment of income to investment in industries producing consumer goods; (β=ratio of increment of income generated to total net investment in the economy as a whole.

Thus $\beta = \lambda_k + \beta_k + \lambda_c\beta_c$

We also have $K_{t+1} - K_t = \lambda_k\beta_k K_t$

$$C_{t+1} - C_t = \lambda_c\beta_c K_t$$

We then get $K_t = (1 + \lambda_k + \beta_k)\, K_0$

$$Y_t = Y_0[1 + \alpha_0 \frac{\lambda_k\beta_k + \lambda_c\beta_c}{\lambda_k\beta_k} \{(1 + \lambda_k\beta_k)^t - 1\}]$$

giving national income in terms of the initial income Y_0, the initial rate of investment α_0, and the allocation parameters $\lambda_k + \lambda_c$ (which are not our choice), and the contingent co-efficients β_k and β_c (which are determined by the pattern of investment and conditions of production).

Later on, Mahalanobis introduced a four-sector model. In this model, the allocation to industries producing capital goods (λ_k) is decided with the help of the two-sector model. The industries producing consumer goods and services are divided into three sectors, *viz.* factory production of consumer goods (sector $C._1$); the production of consumer goods (including agricultural products) in small and household industries (sector $C._2$); and services such as health, education, etc. (sector $C._3$).

In this model an additional set of parameters, θ's, the net investment required per engaged person, is introduced. The number of jobs created in any sector, which may be called *n*, is simply $\frac{\lambda}{\theta}$ per unit investment where λ is the fraction of investment allocated to the sector under consideration. Subscript *k* is used for industries, producing investment goods (*k*-sector); subscripts 1, 2, and 3 used for the industries producing consumer goods and services in the three sectors $C._1$, $C._2$, $C._3$ respectively. λ_k, λ_1, λ_2 and λ_3 are fractions of investment allocated to sectors *K*, C_1, C_2 and C_3 respectively; with $\lambda_k + \lambda_1 + \lambda_2 + \lambda_3 = 1$. β_k, β_1, β_2 and β_3 are the ratios of increment of income to investment; and θ_k, θ_1, θ_2 and θ_3 are the net investment required per engaged person respectively in the four sectors. If n_k, n_1, n_2 and n_3 are the number of additional persons engaged respectively in the four sectors over a five-year period and A is the total investment over the same period, then

$$n_k = \lambda_k A/\theta_k,\ n_1 = \lambda_1 A/\theta_1,\ n_2 = \lambda_2 A/\theta_2,\ n_3 = \lambda_3 A/\theta_3$$

If N is the total number of additional persons engaged over the period under consideration, and E is the total increase in income over the whole plan-period, then

$$\begin{aligned} N &= n_k + n_1 + n_2 + n_3 \\ A &= n_k\theta_k + n_1\theta_1 + n_2\theta_2 + n_3\theta_3 \\ &= \lambda_k A + n_1\theta_1 + n_2\theta_2 + n_3\theta_3 \text{ since } n_k\theta_k = \lambda_k A \text{ (as shown earlier)} \\ E &= \beta_k\theta_k n_k + \beta_1\theta_1 n_1 + \beta_2\theta_2 n_2 + \beta_3\theta_3 n_3 \equiv Y_o\,[(1 + n)^5 - 1], \text{ say.} \end{aligned}$$

If we assume a constant annual rate of growth of income of, say η per cent per year, then E can be derived from the initial income per year Y_0 by applying the η ratio to Y_0.

For applying the above model, we will have to substitute statistical estimates for the various algebraic symbols in the equations. The increase in national income E, the investment A, and the employment N, are the variables. The ratio of net income generated to capital investment β_k, β_1, β_2 and β_3 and the net investment required per engaged person θ_k, θ_1, θ_2 and θ_3 respectively, for each of the four sectors behave as parameters, that is, they are given in the sense that their respective values are assumed to remain more or less constant and are not sought to be influenced by planning during the period under consideration. Allocation ratios λ_k, λ_1, λ_2 and λ_3 also are parametric in the sense that they do not change during the period of time under consideration. There is, however, one important distinction. The income-investment ratio β's are determined by the conditions of production (and the pattern of investments within each of the four sectors) and are not directly influenced by planning during the period under consideration. These, of course, are indirectly influenced by planning since the pattern of investment itself is determined by the programme of investments resulting from planning. The allocation ratios λ_s, on the other hand, are at the choice of the planner within certain limits. The proportion of total investment allocated to investment goods industries λ_k must be decided from considerations of long period changes; and the allocation ratios for the other sectors λ_1, λ_2 and λ_3 then be obtained as solutions of the set of simultaneous equations given above. For example, the rate of increase of income or the employment generated may be treated as 'variables' to which desired values may be assigned. The model would then enable us, with the help of numerical estimates of the various parameters, to study how the allocation ratios λ, *s*, that is, the proportions of total investment going into the different sectors should be chosen so that the desired aim can be realized.

1. Assumptions

1. Investment size at the start of the plan is known.

2. Any investment that is made in a project is without any friction. In other words, there is domestic availability of all the required factors, *viz.* advanced technology, designing service, sophisticated capital goods, all raw materials, skilled labour, etc.

3. There is no foreign exchange problem and foreign exchange can be had in as much quantity as it is needed.

4. There is no time lag and various projects and even sectors have different gestation period.

5. Period of rotation of capital is constant.

6. There is a welfare function. But it is not easy to determine various degrees of welfare because it depends upon growth rate and upon the intertemporal distribution and so on. Again the distribution pattern of income affects growth rate differently.

7. All supplies generated by any investment patterns have a ready market. In other words, capital goods to be generated by the basic industries will find a market at the factory gate.

8. A satisfactory supply of wage-goods (consumer goods) has been assumed. Mahalanobis thinks that much investment is not needed on consumer goods industries.

2. Critical Appraisal

It is essentially an operational model. It arrives at an optional solution out of a multiplicity of solutions in relation to a preference or welfare function already prescribed. The numerical solution of the model, however, does not point towards any definite welfare function without which it is not possible to arrive at an optimum allocation of resources.

Mahalanobis assumes the value $\lambda_k = \frac{1}{3}$ but he does not ascribe any cogent reason for this, and simply states that "it would not be possible to go beyond this value under present conditions." The assumption of $\lambda_k = \frac{1}{3}$ is, therefore, somewhat arbitrary and may not help the planners in arriving at correct solutions for the optimum allocation of investments to different sectors of the economy.

The use of λ technique suggests that investment is a single homogeneous fund which is utilised for a single type investment good. Since investment goods are of heterogeneous type, this requires the use of an investment matrix. The λ technique can be applied as long as constant relative prices are assumed. It can not be applied to a model of open economy where the system is not homogeneous.

The Mahalanobis model is based on the supposition that the supply of agricultural produce is infinitely elastic. This is untenable for the supply of agricultural produce has failed to meet the increased demand for food and raw materials since the beginning of the Second Five Year Plan.

It assumes an infinitely elastic supply of labour which does not seem to be correct even though an underdeveloped country like India is faced with a substantial volume of unemployment and underemployment. What is needed for productive structure is not simple labour but skilled and trained labour and managerial personnel.

Mahalanobis, like Harrod, assumes the technique of production to be constant during the Plan period. In fact technological change is bound to occur during the process of development.

The values assigned to the structural parameters (the β's and θ's) are arbitrary. In fact, it is extremely difficult to have a correct estimate of the values of β's and θ's in an underdeveloped country which utterly lacks in adequate and reliable data. Further, the assumption of independence between capital-output ratios and capital-labour ratios is not realistic. These parameters may change in the process of development.

The Mahalanobis model does not provide guidance to planning authorities for deciding the allocation of investment between private and public sectors. It is silent with regard to this important problem of development planning in a democratic country.

It ignores the pattern of factor prices while fixing targets on the basis of his model.

It is confined to closed economy. Mahalanobis assumes that there are no imports or exports of investment goods. Thus he ignores the impact of foreign trade on the variables of the model and deprives it of the element of reality.

It concentrates exclusively on the supply functions and ignores the demand functions altogether. This makes the growth model incomplete.

It assumes away the foreign exchange problem. But this is a serious problem for most of the underdeveloped countries. At every point they have to be cautious about the foreign exchange. This limitation was realised by Raj-Sen who have shown that the real problem is not to show the total use of resources but to show the use of scarce foreign exchange resources. Thus, according to Raj-Sen foreign exchange should be used not only on basic industries (as assumed by Mahalanobis) but on that part of the basic industries which do not produce anything that may be a component for consumer goods industries. In other words, according to Mahalanobis, foreign exchange should be used on basic goods industries but according to Raj-Sea foreign exchange should be used on those industries also which do not directly produce consumer goods. Professor Mahalanobis has very rightly remarked in this connection, "Although in the beginning India will no doubt have to depend on imports of capital goods, the policy would be to make India independent of such imports as far as possible. In the present model, I have, therefore, assumed that there would be no imports and exports of capital goods."

Bhotoj Datt criticises the model on the ground that it does not consider the impact of various distribution patterns on the rates of growth. In does not consider the result of incentives on growth rate which is a very important phenomenon. Not only that growth determines distribution pattern but the latter also determines the former.

Criticising the model Alak Ghosh says, "Actually speaking many important considerations connected with market forces, psychological environment, popular enthusiasm and the emergence of specific pressure points are unavoidably involved in the course of development planning in a backward economy. Mahalanobis model ignores those important problems for the sake of mathematical simplicity."

Domar criticises it by saying, "All basic industries (*K*) will give the same investment ratio or growth rate. It is unscientific to lump together so many sectors and call them '*K*'. *K* is a mixture of greatly varied sectors, the constituents of which give different results."

Lewis' Model of Economic Development with Unlimited Supplies of Labour

12

W. Arthur Lewis' model is based on the fact that in many less developed countries there exist large reservoirs of labour whose marginal productivity is negligible, zero, or even negative. This labour is found in agriculture, petty trades and services, domestic services in the houses of wealthy people who keep retainers because their social position requires so, and in other areas. The labour whose marginal productivity is zero is not available to the industrial employers at a zero wage for the labourers as family members or retainers are provided a subsistence income on peasant farms or by their patrons. But it is available in unlimited quantities at a wage equal to the subsistence level of living plus a margin sufficient to overcome the friction of moving from the "subsistence sector" to the "capitalist sector," which may be called "subsistence-plus" wage. As the supply of labour is unlimited, the new industries can be set-up and the existing ones can be expanded without limit at the ruling wage rate. The capitalistic sector also needs skilled workers. But Lewis maintains that skilled labour is only a temporary bottleneck and can be removed by providing training facilities to unskilled workers.

Since the marginal productivity of labour in the capitalist sector is higher than the ruling wage rate, there results a capitalist surplus. This surplus is used for capital formation which makes possible employment of more people from the subsistence sector. The increase in investment by the capitalists raises the marginal productivity of labour which induces capitalist-employers to increase their labour force till the marginal productivity of labour falls to equality with the ruling wage rate. This process goes on till the capital-labour ratio rises to the point where the supply of labour becomes inelastic.

Technical progress in the capitalist sector may also increase the share of profits in national income so long as there is surplus labour. It is much more likely to do so in a labour-surplus economy than in a full-employment economy because in the former, if the innovation increases the demand for labour, the labour can be obtained without bidding up the wage rates while under many conditions it may lead to a rise in wages in a full-employment economy.

The ratio of profits to national income increases both because the profit ratio within a capitalist sector of a given size may increase through innovation and because the capitalist sector grows. According to Lewis, this is the major way in which the rise in capital formation from "4 or 5 per cent" to "about 12 to 15 per cent" of national income takes place.

Let us illustrate the Lewis model with the help of a diagram. The quantity of labour employed is measured along X-axis and its wages and marginal product are measured along Y-axis. *SS* represents average subsistence earnings and *WW* the capitalist wage. The

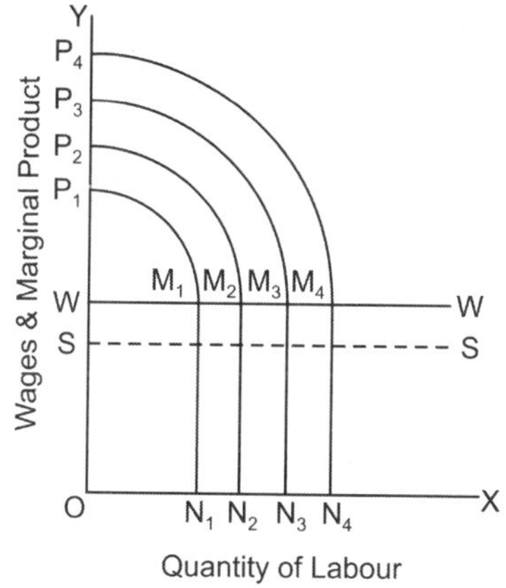

Diagram No. 12.1

marginal productivity of labour in the capitalist sector in the beginning is $P_1 M_1$ for ON_1 labour. $WM_1 Pi$ is the capitalist surplus at this stage. When this surplus is reinvested, the curve of marginal productivity shifts upwards to P_2M_2. The capitalist surplus and employment are now larger than before, being $WM_2 P_2$ and ON_2 respectively. Further reinvestments raise the marginal productivity curve and the level of employment to P_3M_3 and ON_3 and so on, till no surplus labour is left.

Capital is created not only out of profits but also out of bank credit. In an underdeveloped country characterised by abundant unemployed resources and scarcity of capital, the effect of credit creation on capital formation is similar to that of profits. It will expand output and employment. Credit financed capital formation, however, results in a temporary rise in prices. When the surplus labour is employed in the capitalist sector and paid wages out of credit money, prices rise because income increases while output of consumer goods remains unchanged. This is, however, only a temporary phenomenon because prices start declining as soon as the production of consumer goods starts. The inflationary process also comes to an end when voluntary savings rise to the level where they are equal to the inflated level of investment. As the process of capital formation goes on, output and employment expands and so do profits. As larger profits lead to a larger volume of savings, a stage is reached when savings increase to such an extent that new investment can be financed without resort to bank credit.

The process of growth cannot continue indefinitely and must come to an end. According to Lewis, this can happen in the following ways: (*i*) if the continuous process of capital formation leaves no surplus labour; (*ii*) if the expansion in the capitalist sector is so fast that it leads to an absolute decline in population in the subsistence sector which results in an increase in the average productivity of labour in the latter sector and thereby to a rise in the wage rate in the capitalist sector; (*iii*) if the expansion of the capitalist sector relatively to the subsistence sector turns the terms of" trade against the former as a result of the rise in the prices of raw materials and food, the capitalists will have to pay higher wages to the workers; (*iv*) if the subsistence sector adopts improved techniques of production, real wages would rise in the capitalist sector which would lead to a reduction in the capitalist sector; and (v) if the workers in the capitalist sector imitate the capitalist way of living and agitate for higher wages and if they succeed in getting a rise in wages, the capitalist surplus and the rate of capital formation will decline.

When the process of growth is adversely affected by any of the factors mentioned above, the process of capital formation can still be kept going by stimulating immigration or by encouraging export of capital to countries which possess abundant supplies of labour at the subsistence wage rate. Since immigration on a mass scale adversely affects the local labour, it is strongly opposed by the trade unions, and, therefore, is not a very practicable measure. The other best alternative is to export capital over which trade unions have hardly any control.

1. Critical Appraisal

The model assumes existence of surplus labour not in a seasonal sense but over the entire production cycle. But actually surplus labour, by and large, is a seasonal phenomenon; during busy seasons in some countries there is even a shortage of labour in the agricultural sector. Transfer of workers from agricultural sector to the industrial sector may, therefore, be accompanied by a decline in the agricultural production.

Lewis considers shortage of skilled labour only a temporary bottleneck which can be removed by providing training facilities to unskilled labour. Skill formation is not so simple a problem as assumed by Lewis. It poses difficult problems and takes a fairly long time.

Lewis assumes the existence of a capitalist class in the underdeveloped countries. In fact, the underdeveloped countries are characterised by a conspicuous absence of this class.

Lewis does not pay attention to the problem of an adequate volume of aggregate demand. He assumes that the entire production of the capitalist sector is either consumed by itself or exported. In actual practice, the process of growth may come to a halt if there appears a shortage of demand for the products of the capitalist sectors.

Lewis assumes an unlimited supply of labour in underdeveloped countries but this assumption does not hold true in case of many countries of South America and Africa which are sparsely populated.

The model assumes that capital accumulation takes place when the capitalist class continues to invest profits. It, therefore, presupposes operation of the 'investment multiplier' which is not applicable to underdeveloped countries. If profits decline or the prices of wage goods rise the whole process of capital accumulation will halt before all the surplus is absorbed.

Higher capitalist wage may not lead to the movement of surplus labour from the subsistence sector to the capitalist sector. People are so intensely attached to their family and land that they do not like to leave their kith and kin. Further, differences in language and customs, the problems of congestion, housing and high cost of living in the capitalist sector hinder the mobility of labour to this sector. This is a great weakness of the model.

Schultz does not agree that the marginal productivity of labour in overpopulated underdeveloped countries is zero or negligible. If it were so, the subsistence wage would also be zero. The fact is that every worker receives the subsistence wage, may be in kind, if not in cash. It is, therefore, difficult to find out the exact number of surplus labourers who are to move to the capitalist sector.

The Lewis model assumes that when surplus labour is transferred from the subsistence sector to the capitalist sector, the agricultural production remains unaffected in the subsistence sector. But the fact is that withdrawal of workers from the farms will reduce output. Prof. Schultz points out that there is no evidence for any poor country anywhere that would suggest that a transfer of even some fraction, say, 5 per cent of the existing labour force out of agriculture, other things remaining unchanged, could be made without reducing its production.

It is wrong to say that only 10 per cent of the people save. In fact, as Lewis himself admits in the case of Japan, people with low income also save in underdeveloped countries.

Lewis' view that inflation for the purpose of capital formation is self-destructive is difficult to believe in the face of acute shortage of consumer goods. Production of consumer goods does not increase rapidly owing to structural regidities. On the other hand, the marginal propensity to consume of the people is very high so that all increases in income lead to inflationary rise in prices.

Lewis' view that taxation will mop up increasing income cannot be accepted because the tax administration in underdeveloped countries is not so efficient and developed as to collect taxes sufficient enough for capital accumulation.

In spite of the limitations mentioned above, the Lewis model has the outstanding merit of explaining in a clear manner the process of development. The two sector model has great analytical value. It explains how capital formation takes place in underdeveloped countries which have plethora of labour and scarcity of capital. His study of the problems of credit inflation, population growth, technological progress and international trade gives the model a touch of realism.

Leibenstein's "Critical Minimum Effort Thesis"

13

The central idea of the Leibenstein's "Critical Minimum Effort Thesis" is that in order to attain sustained secular growth, it is essential that the initial stimulant (stimulants) to development is (are) of a certain critical minimum size.[1] According to Leibenstein, economic backwardness is characterized by a set of related factors which have a certain degree of stability. The degree of stability is characterised by the fact that some of the crucial variables have equilibrium values that possess at least stability in small though not necessarily perfect stability. The actual values are different from the equilibrium values because the economy is always being subjected to stimulants or shocks. These stimulants have a tendency to raise per capita incomes above the equilibrium level. But in backward economies long-run economic development does not take place because the magnitude of the stimulants is too small. In other words, the efforts to escape from economic backwardness, be they spontaneous or forced, are below the critical minimum needed for sustained growth.

For small values of the stimulant the generated income-depressing factors are, in the long run, more significant than the induced income raising forces but the reverse is the case with high values of the stimulant. This implies the corollary explanation that where economic backwardness persists the stimulants have been small in the past, while in advanced countries there was some point or period during which the magnitude of the stimulant(s) was great.

The income-depressing forces have an upper limit but simultaneously generated income-raising forces have either no upper limit or a higher upper limit. The income-depressing factors

1. Harvey Leibenstein, *Economic Backwardness and Economic Growth* (New York, 1957), pp. 94-110 and 188-93.

may be working autonomously or be generated by the stimulant, and up to some maximum effect they may be more significant than the income-raising factors. But if the income-raising factors are stimulated beyond the maximum of the income-depressing factors, the critical minimum has been reached and economy would be on the road to development. The population growth may be cited as an example of this type of phenomenon. A small increase in capital will stimulate more than equivalent increase in population. Thus, a one per cent increase in capital will generate (through raising incomes and depressing mortality rates) a more than one per cent increase in population and a proportional decline in per capita income. There is, of course, a biologically determined maximum rate of population growth between three and four per cent. As such, a persistent capital accumulation above a certain minimum rate would permit development.

The factors that determine the need for a minimum effort are of four types. Briefly speaking, there is need for a minimum effort so as: (*i*) to overcome internal diseconomies of scale due to indivisibilities in the factors of production, (*ii*) to overcome external diseconomies due to external interdependencies and to attain what is popularly called "balanced growth," (*iii*) to overcome income-depressing obstacles which may be generated by the stimulants to growth, and (*iv*) to generate sufficient momentum in the system so that the factors that stimulate growth continue to play their part.

Certain favourable economic conditions are necessary for the 'growth agents' to expand at a sufficient rate so as to render their contribution more significant than the depressing effects of the retarding factors. By 'growth agents' is meant the quantum of capacities residing in the members of the population to carry out growth-contributing activities. The result of such growth-contributing activities is to increase the quantum of productive capacities of the population, their entrepreneurial capabilities, their skills, their stock of knowledge, etc. A noteworthy point is that while the growth-contributing activities expand the capacities of the labour force, they may, and usually will, in part, expand the magnitude of the growth agents themselves.

Whether or not growth agents expand will depend on the anticipated outcome of such activities, the actual results on the incentives for further expansion or contraction generated by the interaction of the anticipations, the activities, and the results. The motivations and incentives are of two types: (*i*) those that lead to activities which yield increases in national income (positive-sum incentives) and (*ii*) those that do not (zero-sum incentives). In stagnant backward economies the incentives, at the outset, are by and large of the zero-sum type. Also, some of the activities set in motion by positive-sum incentives lead to their degeneration and to the creation of counteracting, zero-sum incentives. But at the same time there will be some members of the economy who will have invested in capital or in the development and expansion of their own economic skill and abilities, whose anticipated gains are fulfilled. Quite naturally it would be expected that activities which result in at least their anticipated gains would give rise to further positive-sum incentives of a similar nature. Also, it seems reasonable to suppose that the greater the actual rate of growth, the greater the extent to which such anticipations are fulfilled. As such, only a fairly rapid rate of growth, as a result of the appropriate stimulants, can lead to an economic environment in which the continually created positive-sum incentives are more important than those that are degenerating as well as more important than the counteracting, zero-sum incentives.

The critical minimum income at which the required rate of growth can be achieved must be sufficiently large to overcome many influences hostile to change as well as those that have the direct effect of decreasing resources per capita. Important of such influences are: (1) the zero-sum entrepreneurial activities directed towards the maintenance of existing economic privileges through the inhibition and curtailment of potentially expanding economic opportunities; (2) the conservative activities of both organised and unorganised labour directed against change, such as feather-bedding, security regulations, and the maintenance of existing techniques; (3) the resistance to new knowledge and ideas and the simultaneous attraction of classical knowledge and old ideas; (4) increase in "essentially non-productive" conspicuous public or private consumption expenditures that use resources which could otherwise be used for capita] accumulation; and (5) population growth and the consequent labour force growth that has the effect, other things being equal, of decreasing the amount of capital available per worker.

The stimulant sufficiently large to raise per capita income above the critical minimum would lead to a rise in the stock of capital as a consequence of the higher per capita income. The initial stimulant and its consequences will simultaneously lead to the following effects: (1) an expansion of the growth agents and as such an expansion in the ability of the economy to take advantage of productive opportunities; (2) a possible increase in the contribution of the growth agents per unit of capital as a result of possible declines in the capital-output ratio; (3) an ultimate decline in the effectiveness of the retarding factors by increasing the rationality of the population, increasing the gains from change, and decreasing the fears from insecurity that may arise because of perspective changes; (4) the creation of social and environmental conditions that can promote physical and economic mobility necessary for development; (5) the expansion of the degree of specialisation and especially the expansion of the secondary and tertiary industries; and lastly (6) the development of an atmosphere that leads to changes in mores conducive to economic and social changes, and especially an environment that leads to ultimate fertility decline and an ultimate decline in the rate of population growth.

1. Population Problem

Professor Leibenstein believes that the underdeveloped countries, whose per capita income is low and rate of population growth is constant owing to high birth and high death rates, are in a Malthusian underemployment equilibrium position based on a subsistence structure.[2] He assumes that the population, is an increasing function of income up to a certain level of income but beyond that it is a decreasing function of income. At very low levels of income, the costs in relation to utility of a large number of children are low. The rate of mortality being high at this stage, a large number of children are to maintain the existing level of population. Also, because children are sent for employment, and as such become gainful, at an early age, the cost of bringing up children is low. In the next stage, when the rate of mortality declines, there is a lag in fertility rate because the social attitudes take time to change. As a larger number of children survive to the

2. Harvey Leibenstein, *A Theory of Economic Demographic Development*; (Princeton, 1954).

productive age, the contribution of children to production as a proportion of the costs of maintaining them will rise. As the income rises further, however, the importance of children as contributors to production declines and at the same time the advantage of having a smaller number of children in rising social and economic status creates a social attitude favourable to a reduction in the size of the family. At this stage per capita income will be high and both birth and death rates will be low and the population growth rate will decline or remain constant.

The underemployment equilibrium which characterizes the overpopulated low income countries relates to the first and second stages mentioned above. Displacement from this equilibrium is possible by obtaining a rise in initial per capita income through the importation of a substantial amount of foreign capital or technological innovations or migration of labour out of the country. This initial rise in income sets in motion two forces, *viz.*, (*i*) an annual rise in aggregate income through an increase in the volume of investment, and (*ii*) an increase in population growth rate. As a consequence of the second force, the per capita income does not increase to the extent that it otherwise would. If the per capita income rises sufficiently high, it would lower the rate of population growth and after a certain stage is reached, further increase in investment and per capita incomes becomes easier. The time that would be taken for reaching this stage depends on (*i*) the magnitude of the initial income gain that displaces the equilibrium; (*ii*) the initial relative magnitudes of capital and labour; and (*iii*) the rate of growth of population. Thus the larger the initial income gain and the slower the rate of population growth, the more quickly would the point be reached after which further growth becomes less and less difficult. In underdeveloped countries confronted with the problem of overpopulation, therefore, economic development is possible only if vigorous attempts, are made in the initial period to start large income generating investment schemes. In this way Leibenstein conceives of a critical minimum in regard to this initial income gain. If the effort falls below this level, economic growth is not only not possible but in fact, becomes more difficult because of increasing population. Given the rate of population growth, the critical minimum effort in the form of investment should therefore be of such an order as to break the population barrier to economic expansion.

2. Diagrammatic Representation

The curve *N* measures the level of per capita income which generates a level of national income growth equal to the growth

Diagram No. 13.1.

rate of population. The curve *P* indicates the rate of population growth at each level of per capita income. Starting from a point which represents the subsistence equilibrium point where there is absence of population and income growth, if the per capita income is raised to Y_b, both the population and income growth rates are 1 per cent. At the Y_e level of per capita income, the rate of population growth is higher than the rate of national income growth, *i.e.*, $Y_e g > Y_e C$, the former is 2 per cent while the latter is 1 per cent. Therefore, the per capita income level should be so raised as to increase the national income by more than the rate of population growth. This is only possible after Y_e level of per capita income whence the rate of population growth starts declining—point *e* the maximum biologically determined growth rate of population 3 per cent assumed by Leibenstein. Y_e is thus the critical minimum per capita income level to generate the process of sustained economic development.

In the case discussed above, the level of per capita income is an income-increasing force while rate of population growth induced by the former acts as a depressing force. For sustained development, it is imperative that the initial investment effort must be above a certain minimum level so as to generate a sufficiently large per capita income level in order to overcome autonomous or induced income-depressing forces. But the critical minimum effort need not be made all at once, according to Leibenstein. It may be more effective if it is broken up into a series of smaller efforts of which the applications to the economy are optimally timed. Diagram 13.2 illustrates Leibenstein's critical minimum effort thesis.

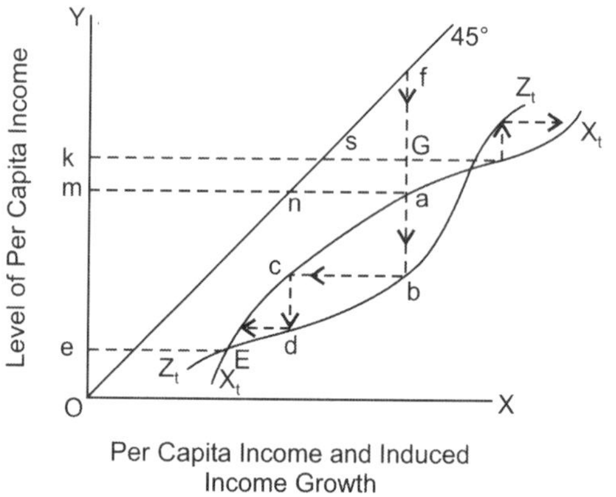

Diagram No. 13.2.

In the above diagram, 45° line measures induced increases and decreases in per capita income. The curve X_tX_t represents all the per capita income-raising forces and the curve Z_tZ_t the per capita income-depressing forces. If the stimulants raise per capita income from the equilibrium level O_e to O_m, the income-raising forces thus generated will raise the per capita income level by *na*. But at this level, the income-depressing forces *bf* are greater than the income-raising forces *af* which will therefore, generate the downward path *abcd*, until it reaches the equilibrium position *E*. It is only when the investment programme raises the per capita income to O_k level that the path of sustained growth starts. Thus if the per capita income level in a period is raised to O_k, the income-raising force generated will raise the income level to *sG* which will in turn generate the path of endless expansion of per capita income as shown by the arrows rising above *G*. Raising the per capita income to O_k level and beyond or point *G* is the critical minimum effort case. It may be pointed out that Leibenstein regards the critical minimum effort as "a *minimum minimorum* of all possible efforts that would lead to sustained real income growth" involving an optimum time pattern of expenditure or effort.

3. Critical Appraisal

In the preface to his book, Leibenstein states that his "aim has been explanation and understanding—not prescription." But his critical minimum effort thesis has caught the imagination 'of economists and planners in underdeveloped countries and is regarded as a prescription to economic backwardness. The Leibenstein thesis is more realistic than Rosenstein-Rodan's 'big push' theory. Giving a big push to the programme of industrialisation all at once is not practicable in underdeveloped countries while the critical minimum effort can be properly timed and broken up into a series of smaller efforts to put the economy on the path of sustained development. This theory is also consistent with the concept of democratic planning to which most of the underdeveloped countries are wedded. The theory, however, is not without its shortcomings.

Suppose a country has succeeded in crossing the population barrier of 3 per cent by increasing the growth rate of income above this. According to Leibenstein when an economy has reached Y_e level of per capita income in diagram 13.1 or *Ok* in diagram 13.2, it enters the path of endless expansion. Myint questions the correctness of this contention. For it is possible to find cases where abortive 'take offs' take place "in which a country may for a time succeed in raising its saving and investment ratio above 10% to 12% and raising the rate of growth in its total income above 3% level, but subsequently relapses into a slower rate of growth and stagnation." The theory does not take into consideration time element which is required for sustained efforts during which fundamental changes in the institutional and productive structure should be taking place for ensuring a successful take-off. To cite Myint, we may therefore question how far this type of analysis, originally designed to illustrate the gear shifts in short-run economic activity of a fully developed engine of growth in the advanced countries, is useful for the study of the problem of the long-term economic development of the underdeveloped countries which are concerned with the construction of the engine of growth itself."

According to Myint the functional relationship between the level of per capita income and the rate of growth in total income is more complex and not so simple as has been shown by Leibenstein. In the first place, the relation of per capita income with the rate of saving and investment depends on the distributional pattern of income and the effectiveness of financial institutions in mobilizing savings. Secondly, the relation between investment and the resultant output is not determined by a constant capital-output ratio as is assumed by Leibenstein, but depends on the extent to which the productive organization of the country can be improved and how far land-saving innovations can be adopted to overcome the tendency to diminishing returns on additional investment even after the growth rate of population has reached the 3% level.

The Leibenstein theory does not explicitly explain the influence of foreign capital and other external forces on the level of income, saving and investment.

Leibenstein's thesis is logically attractive but has only limited practical value. Leibenstein assumes that a small rise in income leads to an increase in the rate of growth of population but a rise in income which is above a certain level has the reverse effect on the rate of population growth. The implication here is that a mere rise in incomes has a direct bearing on population trends. But in reality the population problem in underdeveloped countries is not a simple problem of arithmetic but an intricate social one influenced by customs and traditions and the social attitudes and prejudices of the people. Changes in social attitudes and cultural patterns will, therefore, have a more direct impact on population trends than mere increase in incomes.

Leibenstein does not take into consideration the measures which the state may adopt for attaining a decline in the birth rate. The underdeveloped countries obviously will not wait till a rise in the per capita income above the critical minimum level automatically brings down the birth rate. If the family planning measures adopted in underdeveloped countries result in a decline in the fertility rates before the per capita income rises above the critical minimum level, Leibenstein's thesis may not hold good.

Myrdal on Economic Growth

14

1. International Economic Inequalities

A few countries are highly developed economically and have very high levels of average real income per head. In contrast more than two-thirds of the people in the non-Soviet world live in countries where real income per head is only a small fraction of what it is in highly developed countries and, in fact, in most cases is much smaller than it was in those countries before they started to develop rapidly a century or more ago. Not only that, the disparities between the developed and underdeveloped countries are increasing with the passage of time. It is on the whole the industrialised countries which are industrialising further. They account for a major portion of the non-Soviet world's total savings. Since new inventions constantly raise the demand for capital, almost the entire capital is invested there. In contrast, in underdeveloped countries, where incomes are much lower, capital formation and investment tend to be on a smaller scale, even relatively to their lower incomes. The relatively faster increase in population in these countries worsens the matters still further. The people in underdeveloped countries are becoming increasingly aware of these huge international inequalities and the danger that they will continue to grow. The people in underdeveloped countries have a tendency to blame for their poverty the rest of the world, particularly the better off countries; rather they hold the world economic system responsible for the increasing inequalities between the developed and the underdeveloped countries.

2. Circular and Cumulative Causation

Prof. Myrdal believes that the theoretical approach which we have inherited is inadequate to grip with the problem of inequalities.[1] The theory is based on unrealistic assumptions, an important of

---

1. Gunnar Myrdal, *Economic Theory and Underdeveloped Regions* (Bombay, 1966), pp. 23-34.

which is the assumption of stable equilibrium. The concept of stable equilibrium implies that every disturbance provokes a reaction within the system, directed towards restoring a new state of equilibrium, and the action and reaction will meet in one and the same time-space. An economic system which is not in rest is for this reason always moving towards equilibrium, though not necessarily in the straight way. The concept of stable equilibrium embodies the idea that when a change calls forth other changes as reaction, these secondary changes are counter-directed to the primary change.

In Myrdal's opinion, in contrast, in the normal case there is no such tendency towards automatic self-stabilisation in the social system. The system is by itself not moving towards any sort of balance between forces, but is constantly on the move away from such a situation. In the normal case a change does not call forth countervailing changes but, instead supporting changes, which move the system in the same direction as the first change but much further. As a result of such circular causation a social process tends to become cumulative and often to gather speed at an accelerating rate.

A social process can, of course, be stopped. One possibility is that new exogenous changes may occur which have the direction and strength necessary to bring the system to rest. The position of balancing forces which thus become established is, however, not a natural outcome of the play of the forces within the system. Moreover, the position is unstable. Any new exogenous change will by the reactions in the system again start a cumulative process away from this position in the direction of the new change. Alternatively the position of the rest may have been attained by policy interferences, planned and applied with the intention of stopping the movement. This is, of course, the very opposite of a natural tendency towards equilibrium, endogenous to the system.

Myrdal illustrates the principle of circular and cumulative causation with the help of the Negro problem in the United States. In order to simplify the explanation, he reduces his model to two factors: 'white prejudices' causing discrimination against the Negroes in various respects, and the 'low plane of living' of the Negroes. The two factors are mutually inter-related. The Negroes' low standard of living is kept down by discrimination from the whites while, on the other hand, Negroes' poverty, ignorance, superstition, slum dwellings, health deficiencies, dirty appearance, bad odour, disorderly conduct, unstable family relations and criminality stimulate and feed the antipathy of the whites for Negroes.

White prejudices and low Negro standards thus mutually 'cause' each other. If at a point of time things tend to remain about as they are, this means that the two forces balance each other: white prejudices and the consequent discrimination against the Negroes block their efforts to raise their low plane of living; this, on the other hand, forms part of the causation of the prejudice on the side of the whites which leads them to discriminatory behaviour.

Such a static 'accommodation' is, however, entirely fortuitous and by no means a stable equilibrium position. If either of the two factors should change, this is bound to bring a change in the other factor, too, and start a cumulative process of mutual interaction in which the change in one factor would continuously be supported by the reaction of the other factor and so on in a circular way. The entire system would move in the direction of the primary change, but much further. Even if the original push or pull were to cease after a time, both factors would be permanently changed, or the process of interacting changes would even continue without any neutralisation in sight.

3. Non-economic Factors

Another unrealistic assumption on which the economic theory is based is the notion that there are certain elements of social reality which can be characterised as "the economic factors" and that the theoretical analysis can be rationally restricted to the inter-actions of those factors. This assumption is closely related to the equilibrium assumption. For it is precisely in the field of that large part of social reality, which is left outside the economic analysis by the abstraction from the 'non-economic factors,' that the equilibrium assumption falls to the ground. These non-economic factors cannot be taken for given and static; when they react, they normally do so in a disequilibrating way. The classical economists lumped together the so-called non-economic factors under concepts like the "quality of factors of production" and the "efficiency of production" and normally kept them outside their analysis.

4. Backwash Effects

The free play of market forces normally tends to increase, rather than decrease, the inequalities between regions.[2] If the things were left to market forces unhindered by any policy interferences, industrial production, commerce, banking, insurance, shipping and, in fact, almost all those economic activities which in a developing economy tend to give a bigger than average return—and, in addition, science, art, literature, education and higher culture generally—would cluster in certain localities and regions, leaving the remaining country more or less in a back-water. It is easy to see how expansion in one locality has 'backwash' effects in other localities. To be more concrete the movements of labour, capital, goods and services by themselves do not counteract the natural tendency to regional inequality; they rather accentuate the inequalities.

The regions where economic activity is expanding will attract net immigration from other parts of the country. Since migration is always selective, at least in regard to migrant's age, this movement by itself tends to favour the rapidly growing communities and adversely affects the others.

Capital movements tend to have a similar effect of accentuating inequalities. In regions where expansion takes place, increased demand stimulates investment which in turn increases incomes and demand and causes a second round of investment, and so on. Saving increases as a result of higher incomes but tends to lag behind investment in the sense that the supply of capital steadily meets a brisk demand for it. In the other regions, the lack of new expansionary momentum has the implication that the demand for capital for investment remains relatively weak, even compared to the supply of savings which will be low as incomes are low and tending to fall. Studies in many countries show how the banking system, if not regulated to act differently, tends to become an instrument for siphoning off the savings from the poorer regions to the richer and more progressive ones: where returns on capital are high and secure.

In a similar manner, trade operates with a bias in favour of the richer and progressive regions and against the poor and backward regions. The freeing and widening of the markets often confers such

---

2. *Ibid.*, pp. 38-43.

competitive advantages on the industries in already established centres of expansion, which usually work under conditions of increasing returns, that even the handicrafts and industries existing earlier in the other regions are thwarted. In the latter regions, not only manufacturing industry and other non-agricultural pursuits but agriculture itself shows a much lower level of productivity than in the richer region.

5. Spread Effects

Against the backwash effects there are, however, also certain centrifugal 'spread effects' of expansionary momentum from the centres of economic expansion to other regions.[3] It is natural that the whole region around a nodal centre of expansion should gain from the increasing outlets of agricultural products and be stimulated to technical advance all along the line.

There is also another line of centrifugal spread effects to localities further away, where favourable conditions exist for producing raw materials for the growing industries in the centres. If a sufficient number of workers get employment in these other localities, even the setting up of consumer industries will be stimulated. These, and also all other localities where new starts are being made and happen to succeed, become in their turn, if the expansionary momentum is strong enough to overcome the backwash effects from the older centres, new centres of self-sustained economic expansion.

The spread effects of momentum from a centre of industrial expansion to other localities and regions, operating through increased demands for their products and in many other ways, weave themselves into the cumulating social process by circular causation in the same fashion as the backwash effects in opposition to which they set up countervailing changes. They represent a complication of the main hypothesis that in the normal case the changes in other factors which are called forth as reactions by a change in one factor, always tend to move the system in the same directions as the first change.

Under no circumstances, however, do the spread effects establish the assumptions for an equilibrium analysis. In the marginal case the two kinds of effects will balance each other and a region will be

3. *Ibid.*, pp. 43-45.

stagnating. This balance, however, is not a stable equilibrium because any change in the forces will start a cumulative movement upwards or downwards.

Empirical evidence shows that while regional inequalities have been diminishing in the richer countries of the Western Europe, the opposite has been the tendency in the poorer countries. This phenomenon is explained by and large by the fact that the higher the level of economic development that a country has already reached, the stronger the spread effects will normally be. For a higher average level of development is accompanied by improved transportation and communications, higher levels of education, and a more dynamic communication of ideas and values, all of which tend to strengthen the forces for the centrifugal spread of economic expansion or to remove the obstacles for its operation.

The neutralisation of backwash effects, when a country reaches a high level of development where the spread effects are strong, will itself stimulate economic development and thus become an important factor in the cumulative process. The disappearance of poverty on a large scale is accompanied by a fuller utilisation of the potentialities of the human resources in a country. This is one of the reasons why rapid sustained progress becomes an almost automatic process when once a country has reached a high level of development. On the other hand, an important reason for the low rates of economic development in underdeveloped countries is the weak spread effects.

6. Effects of Trade, Capital Movements and Migration

Trade by itself does not promote equality. On the contrary, it may have strong backwash effects on the underdeveloped countries. A widening of markets often strengthens the rich and progressive countries whose manufacturing industries have the lead and whose competitive position is strengthened by the external economies available to them, while whatever little industry, particularly small-scale industry and handicrafts, exists in underdeveloped countries is constantly threatened of being priced out by cheap imports from the industrial countries if it is not afforded protection. Examples can easily be cited of underdeveloped countries whose entire culture has been impoverished as a result of the establishment of trading contacts with the outside world. The main positive effect of international trade on the underdeveloped countries has in fact been to promote the production of primary products, which has come to form the bulk of their exports. The world demand for these products, however, is inelastic and, therefore, does not grow sufficiently fast.

Nor can the capital movements be relied upon to counteract international inequalities. As already seen, capital will tend to shun underdeveloped countries, particularly because the advanced countries themselves are rapidly developing further and can offer to owners of capital both good profits and security. Labour migration is not an important factor for international economic adjustment as between underdeveloped and developed countries.

At the international level, the backwash effects of trade and capital movements dominate the scene because the countervailing spread effects of expansionary momentum are very much weaker. Differences in legislation, administration and more generally, in language, in basic valuations and beliefs, in levels of living, production capacities and facilities, make national boundaries much more effective barriers to the spread of expansionary momentum than any demarcation lines within one country can be. Under these circumstances market forces will tend cumulatively to accentuate international inequalities.

Rostow's Stages of Economic Growth

15

Most of the rigorous models of growth suffer from the basic defect that they ignore, or do not attach adequate importance, to institutional and social factors, which have a vital bearing on economic development. Prof. W.W. Rostow has made an attempt to incorporate these factors in his theory of growth and to explain economic development in terms of social and institutional set up and the attitudes of the people. Rostow relates social and institutional factors with economic forces of growth through a number of observable propensities of the community, *viz.* (1) propensity to develop fundamental science; (2) propensity to apply science to economic ends; (3) propensity to accept innovations; (4) propensity to seek material advance; (5) propensity to consume; and (6) propensity to have children. These propensities depend on the attitudes, motives and aspirations of the people which in turn depend on the previous political, economic and social factors. The total working force and the magnitude and productivity of the capital available in the economy are the prime movers in the process of economic growth. The size of the working forces and its ability to contribute to output depend on the birth rate and previous and current death rates which determine the rate of growth of population and hence that of working force. It also depends on the role of women and children, that is, whether or not women take jobs in factories and fields and whether children are employed or not. The skill of the working force and the extent of effort made by it depends on its quality and standard of efficiency. The size and productivity of capital is determined by (*i*) the proportion of income saved and invested which in turn depends on the propensity to consume and (*ii*) the technological level reached by the economy. The latter depends upon the volume of resources devoted to the pursuit of fundamental science as well as applied science and also the proportion of the flow and pool of potential innovations accepted for commercial and economic uses. The use of these propensities to explain the quantity and quality of labour and capital available in an economy "involves a frank abandonment of the effort to make economic behaviour solely a function of what are conventionally regarded as economic motives. The propensities exhibit the extent to which the actual economic activities of a society deviate from those which would obtain if 'economic' motives alone were operative."[1]

The actual process of growth is explained in terms of the development of the particular sectors. As the natural resources are relatively fixed, the law of diminishing returns may start operating in some sectors. The prices of products in such sectors would rise relative to those in other sectors. This necessitates the application of science and technology and encourages the search for innovations so as to counteract the tendency to diminishing returns. In the initial stages of economic growth such obstacles arising from natural limitations led to the search for more fertile lands, mines, sheep grazing lands and so on. In more recent times, the application of science and technology towards this end has taken the form of scientific technological research, *e.g.* research in timber substitutes when timber prices rise very high; research in synthetic textiles when the prices of natural textile fibre rise, etc. A noteworthy point is that such possibilities of counteracting the tendency to diminishing returns and increasing output through alternative and more productive ways of using resources arise from the motives and attitudes of the people, particularly their propensity to utilise science and technical knowledge towards this end. If these motives are weak, such innovations will not be possible and the economy would stagnate.

In order to show how growth in some sectors spreads to other sectors and thus to the entire economy, Rostow divides the sectors into three broad classes, *viz.* (*i*) Primary growth sectors, (*ii*) Supplementary growth sectors, and (*iii*) Derived growth sectors. In primary growth sectors, the opportunities for innovations or for the exploitation of newly profitable or unexplored resources lead to a rate of growth which is substantially higher than the average for the economy. The growth of Britain's industrial development in the late eighteenth century and early nineteenth assisted development of

1. W.W. Rostow, *The Process of Economic Growth* (London, 1960), p. 35.

the engineering and chemical industries. In the supplementary growth sectors rapid development takes place in direct response to, or as a requirement of, progress in primary growth sectors. Derived growth sectors are those in which progress takes place in some fairly steady relation to the growth of total real income, population, industrial production, or some other overall modestly increasing parameter. Examples of this category are provided by an increase in food output and provision of housing and other amenities with an increase in population and income.

W.W. Rostow divides the sequence of growth of a society into five stages: (1) the traditional society, (2) the pre-conditions for take-off, (3) the take-off, (4) the drive to maturity, and (5) the age of high mass-consumption.

1. Traditional Society

A traditional society is one in which modern science and technology are either not available or not regularly and systematically applied. It, however, need not be static. Production may increase from an expansion in acreage or from an *ad hoc* application of technical innovations. Composition of production may change. Changes may occur in the volume and composition of domestic and foreign trade. Population may grow or contract. The crucial fact about the traditional society is that there exists a ceiling to the level of attainable per capita output. In such a society, because of limits on productivity, a. very large proportion of productive resources is devoted to agriculture. Such a society exhibits a number of social, political and psychological characteristics, *viz.*, prevalence of joint family system, lack of vertical, mobility, fatalistic attitude, concentration of political power in the hands of land-owning class.

2. Pre-conditions for Take-off

The second stage comprises societies in the process of transition. During this stage the pre-conditions for take-off are developed. A traditional society takes time to reach the stage at which it is in a position to exploit the fruits of modern science, to fend off diminishing, returns, and thus to enjoy the blessing and choices opened up by the march of compound interest. Masses realise that economic progress is possible and desirable. Education spreads. Entrepreneurship develops. Institutions providing banking and credit facilities appear. Investment increases, particularly, in transport, communications and in raw materials required by other nations. Scope for domestic and foreign trade increases. Manufacturing enterprises using modern methods of production appear here and there. Though modern, elements are introduced, the society still remains primarily traditional. In many cases, the traditional society exists side by side with modern activities conducted for limited economic purposes by a colonial or quasi-colonial powers. In addition to changes in the economy and in the balance of social values, decisive changes occur in the political set-up. There emerges a strong centralised national state.[2]

Rostow describes the evolution from traditional society to "take-off" as below:

> We start with a reasonably stable and traditional society containing an economy mainly agricultural, using more or less unchanging production methods, saving and investing productively little more than is required to meet depreciation. Usually from outside the society, but sometimes out of its own dynamics comes the idea that economic progress is possible....More often than not the economic motives for seeking economic progress converge with some non-economic motive, such as the desire for increased social power and prestige, national pride, political ambition and so on. Education, for some at least, broadens and changes to suit the needs of modern economic activity. New enterprising men come forward willing to mobilise savings and take risk in pursuit of profit, notably in commerce. The commercial markets for agricultural products, domestic handicrafts and consumption-goods imports widen. Institutions for mobilising capital appear: or they expand from primitive levels in the scale, surety and time horizon for loans. Basic capital is expanded, notably in transport and communications, often to bring to market raw materials in which other nations have an economic interest.... And, here and there, modern manufacturing enterprise appears, usually in substitution for imports.[3]

---

2. W.W. Rostow, *The Stages of Economic Growth* (Cambridge, 1960).
3. W.W. Rostow, "The Take-Off into Self-Sustained Growth," *Economic Journal* (March, 1956), pp. 29-30.

3. Take-off

This is a crucial stage in the sequence of growth in economy. During this period, hurdles and resistances of steady growth are overcome and the process of growth becomes self-sustained. Industries expand rapidly, yielding profits, a substantial portion of which is reinvested. Expansion of manufacturing industries increases the demand for capital equipment and thus leads to an expansion in capital goods industries. Expansion in capital goods industries stimulates expansion of manufacturing industries through an increase in the incomes of the newly employed people, a part of which is spent on manufactured goods. Expansion of industry increases the demand for minerals and agricultural products. Thus the wave of expansion moves from urban to rural areas. Entrepreneur class expands. New techniques and methods of production spread in industry as well as in agriculture. Agriculture becomes commercialised. In a decade or two, the economic, social and political structure of society changes in a way that makes the process of growth self-sustained.

According to Rostow the 'take off' stage is indicated by: (*i*) a rise in the rate of productive investment from about five per cent or less to over ten per cent of national income or net national product; (*ii*) the development of one or more large manufacturing sectors with a high rate of growth; (*iii*) the existence or quick emergence of a political, social and institutional framework which exploits the impulses to expansion in the modern sector and the potential external economy effects of the 'take off' and give to growth an ongoing character. An allied factor which assists the transformation is an expansion in the supply of loanable funds. This results from shifts in the control over income flows including transfer of capital from landlords and others to the state or to the investing business class through capital markets, redistribution through inflation, increased inflow of foreign capital, large export earnings etc. In addition to transfer of incomes, another factor that helps 'take off' is an adequate supply of entrepreneurship—the rising of social group which is actuated by the profit making and acquisitive motive.

Rostow cites historical examples of the occurrence of 'take off' in several countries. It took place in Great Britain, France, Belgium and the United States during the period covering the last quarter of the eighteenth century and the first half of the nineteenth century. It occurred in Germany, Sweden and Japan in the latter part of the nineteenth century; in Russia and Canada in the twenty to twenty five years preceding the outbreak of the First World War. India and China appear to have entered this stage round the middle of the present century. Different sectors of the economy were responsible for the initial momentum for development in different countries. Cotton textiles played the leading role in Britain. The 'take off' was initiated in the United States, Germany and Russia by the introduction of railroad. The expansion and modernization of the armed forces was an important factor in the 'take off' of Russia, Japan and Germany. The timber industry, shortly followed by the pulp industry, initiated the process of development in Sweden. The domestic manufacture of consumption goods replacing imports accelerated the process of development in Australia and Argentina.

4. Drive to Maturity

The take-off is followed by a long interval of sustained—may be fluctuating—growth. Some 10-20 per cent of the national income is reinvested and the rate of growth of output has a tendency to exceed the rate of growth of population. There is a drive to extend the modern technology to the whole front of economic activity. The composition of production changes continuously. New industries expand and old industries contract. Certain goods previously imported are produced at home. New import requirements develop. New exports emerge to match new imports.

The economy attains maturity in about sixty years after the beginning of take-off or in about forty years after the end of take-off. Comparatively simpler industries and techniques introduced in the take-off period are extended into more refined and complex industries and techniques. The most advanced methods and techniques of production are applied in a substantial part—if not whole—of the economy. The economy acquires technological and entrepreneurial skills which make possible production of, if not everything, anything that it chooses to produce. If it does not produce certain things, it is because of economic choice or political priority and not because of technological or institutional limitations.

5. Age of High Mass-Consumption

In the age of high mass-consumption, leading sectors shift towards durable consumer goods and services. Per capita real income rises to level at which a large number of people can afford consumption transcending beyond basic food, shelter, and clothing. Ratio of urban to total population rises. Development of technology no longer remains the over-riding objective of society. Larger resources are allocated to social welfare and security.

6. Critical Appraisal

Rostow's "The Stages of Economic Growth" is the most widely circulated and highly commented piece of economic literature in recent years. The authenticity of the division of economic history into five "stages of growth" is widely doubted among economists. Are these stages inevitable like birth and death, or do they follow a set 'sequence' like childhood, adolescence, maturity and old age? Can one tell with sufficient precision that one stage is complete and the other has begun? "To maintain that every economy follows the same course of development with a common past and the same future is to over-schematize the complex forces of development and to give the sequence of stages a generality that is unwarranted."[4] Let us briefly comment on these stages.

(*i*) A number of countries like the United States, Canada, New Zealand and Australia were born free of *traditional societies* and they derived the preconditions from Britain, a country already advanced. It is, therefore, not essential for growth that a country must pass through the first stage.

(*ii*) In the case of 'preconditions,' it is not necessary that they must precede the take off. For instance, there is no reason to believe that an agricultural revolution and accumulation of social overhead capital in transport must take place before the take-off. In fact, the experience in many countries tells us that development in agriculture continued even in the take-off" stage. The take-off in the case of New Zealand and Denmark is attributed to agricultural development. Similarly, social overhead capital in transport, particularly in railways, has been one of the leading sectors in take-off as Rostow himself tells, us. This shows that there is considerable overlapping in different stages.

---

4. G.M. Meier, *Leading Issues in Development Economics,* p. II.

(*iii*) The most widely discussed and controversial stage is the takeoff. Professor Cairncross remarks: "The stage that has struck the public mind most forcibly is undoubtedly that of the take-off. Largely, no doubt, because the aeronautical metaphor-prolonged in the phrase 'into self-sustained growth'—suggests at once an effortlessness and finality congenial to modern thought. The reactions of historians and economists have been less favourable. They have grown accustomed to emphasizing the continuity of historical change, to tracing back to a previous age the forces producing a social explosion and to explaining away the apparent leaps in economic development. They are inclined, therefore, to regard Rostow as a latter day Toynbee, stressing a discontinuity that is no more than symptomatic of the underlying forces at work and making the symptoms more decisive than they really were."[5]

Economic historians are critical of the take-off dates suggested by Rostow. The dates also vary from publication to publication. In fact, it will take many years of research to determine the correctness or otherwise of the dates suggested by Rostow. Further, the analysis of the take off ignores the effect of historical heritage, time of entry into the process of modern economic growth, degree of backwardness and other relevant factors on the characteristics of the early phases of modern economic growth in the different underdeveloped countries.

Even the necessary conditions for take-off have limitations.

(*i*) The first condition of a rise in the rate of productive investment to over 10 per cent of national income is arbitrary. To cite Prof. Dasgupta, "What is the sanctity about this particular percentage, except that with 10% annual saving one may expect an economy to acquire higher trend of per capita income unless the capital-output ratio and the rate of population growth are abnormally high. A demarcation along this line is surely arbitrary."[6] Further, there is no historical data to justify a sharp increase in the saving-income ratio at the beginning of industrialization. On the contrary, this ratio has been increasing gradually as growth proceeded.

---

5. A.K. Cairncross, "Essays in Bibliography and Criticism, XLV: The Stages of Economic Growth," The *Economic History Review* (April, 1961), p. 464.
6. A.K. Dasgupta, *Planning and Economic Growth*, p. 58.

(*ii*) The second condition relates to rapid development of leading sectors. Rostow has laid stress on a limited number of leading sectors like textiles, railroad etc. But economic growth has not always been governed by the development of a few leading sectors. Cairncross questions the utility of this idea in helping us to understand the take-off. There appears to be no basis on which to recognise a leading sector *ex ante.* Cairncross asks, "What connection is there between the conception and later stages? Why must the leading sector be in manufacturing? If railway building can qualify, why not retail distribution or agriculture?"[7]

(*iii*) The last condition for take-off is the existence or emergence of a cultural framework which gives to growth an outgoing character. According to Rostow the necessary condition for this is the 'capacity to mobilize capital from domestic sources,' and this is in fact nothing else but the first condition of take-off restated. Further, as Cairncross remarks, "A definition in these terms tells us nothing about the factors at work since we can only deduce their existence from the fact of take-off, never the likelihood of take-off from the ascertained fact of their existence."[8]

The *stage of 'self-sustained' growth* is a little puzzling and misleading. It contains all the features of the take-off—rate of net investment over 10 per cent of national income, development of new production techniques, leading sectors and institutions. Naturally a question arises where lies the need for a separate stage where growth process is sustaining. It can be self-sustained even in the take-off stage. In fact, as observed by Kuznets, no growth is purely self-sustaining or self-limiting. The characterization of one stage of growth as self-sustained and of others, by implication, as lacking that property, requires substantive evidence and analysis not provided by Rostow.

The age of *high mass-consumption* is so defined that certain countries like Australia and Canada have entered this stage before even reaching maturity. According to one critic, "the period of mass consumption is nothing else but communism *minus* its ideological overtone."

---

7. *Op. cit.,* p. 142.
8. *Ibid.,* p. 143.

According to Prof. Higgins, "All this is very general and far indeed from a tight and systematic theory of economic development. No doubt, historians will raise once again their objections to 'stage theories' and insist that the documentary evidence does not permit any precise division of economic history into any such neatly defined periods. Rostow would no doubt agree, but we can also agree with him that his conception of the three stages of growth does correspond roughly to the data and general information about economic development of various countries, however difficult the dating of these stages may be. We can also agree that the lessons of history are more easily assessed if we do make such a distinction among the three stages; for we will not then make the mistake of looking for historical evidence of the causes of take-off during a period when all we can hope to find is evidence on causes of establishing *preconditions,* a mistake to which economic historians have been addicted; nor will we make the mistake committed by so many economists of looking for historical evidence on the take-off in statistics covering only the period when the process of *self-sustained* growth has already set in."

To cite Professor A.K. Cairncross, "The stage that has struck the public mind most forcibly is undoubtedly that of the takeoff: largely, no doubt, because of the aeronautical metaphor—prolonged in the phrase "into self-sustained growth" suggests at once an effortlessness and a finality congenial to modern thought. They have grown accustomed to emphasizing the continuity of historical change, to tracing back to a previous age the forces producing a social explosion, and to explaining away the apparent leaps in economic development. They are inclined therefore to regard Rostow as , stressing a discontinuity that is no more than symptomatic of the underlying forces at work...."[9] Ian Drummond writes, "Many scholars have found the stages—especially the take-off—inherently plausible. It is easy to believe in an industrial revolution especially if one's historical knowledge is scanty and out of date. But historians are almost certain to reject the take-off's implication of sudden change....Years of research and controversy will be required to determine whether the idea of take-off is

9. A.K. Cairncross, "Essays in Bibliography and Criticism, XLV: The Stages of Economic Growth," *The Economic History Review* (April, 1961), p. 454.

empirically sound, and whether Rostow's own take-off dates are correct. Rostow himself has marshalled some evidence—plausible, but insufficient to prove his case. Unfortunately, he has defined his criteria so vaguely that they will stretch to cover any likely instance. And he seems willing to admit "exceptions" when take-off occurs at a time different from the time his tests would suggest. The stages of growth are not defined with sufficient precision."[10]

Professor Simon Kuznets, in a paper entitled "Notes on the Take-off" presented at the International Economics Association in 1960, at Lake Constance, concluded: "Unless I have completely misunderstood Professor Rostow's definition of take-off and its statistical characteristics, I can only conclude that the available evidence lends no support to Professor Rostow's suggestions."

7. Importance of Take-Off for Underdeveloped Countries

The concept is very useful for the industrialization of underdeveloped countries. To cite Prof. Dasgupta, "The term lacks precision and yet it is suggestive and can be given interpretation which is useful for an understanding of the process of economic development of an underdeveloped country. It is indeed the vagueness of the term that gives it strength for one can put an interpretation upon it to suit the conditions of the economy in which one is interested." Prof. Higgins writes, "It is with both the problems and the cyclical movements of national income in such growing economies in the fourth stage that the bulk of modern theoretical economics is concerned. The students of the contemporary underdeveloped countries are more likely to be concerned with the economics of the first three stages. If we are to have a useful and adequate theory of economic growth, it must obviously be comprehensive enough to embrace these three stages as well, especially the economics of take-off. Thus the concept of take-off is more suitable for the industrialisation of poor countries."[11]

Of the three necessary conditions for take-off, the first two, namely, capital formation over 10 per cent of national income and the development of one or more leading sectors, are helpful in the

10. Ian Drummond in his review of *The Stages of Economic Growth: A Non-Communist Manifesto in Canadian Journal of Economics and Political Science* (February, 1961), pp. 112-13.

11. *Op. cit.*, p. 156.

process of industrialization of underdeveloped countries. So far as the first condition is concerned, there can be little doubt about attaining that percentage. But the second condition can be moulded to suit a country's environments. For instance, the leading sectors can be in agriculture or in the production of primary products for exports. The last condition is more important in the context of underdeveloped countries where monetary and political institutions, and skills and technology are at a low level whereby they restrict the growth of the modern sector.

In estimating the total capital requirements for poor countries, Prof. Rostow takes a constant capital-output ratio. This means constant returns to scale. This assumption is valid in case of advanced countries. But underdeveloped countries are characterized by the predominance of agriculture and primary production. Given unchanged techniques and growing population, their natural resources result in diminishing returns to scale for the growth of the economy as a whole.

Prof. Dasgupta considers the 'elimination of an accumulated backlog of unemployment' as 'the minimum that the take-off must accomplish' in an underdeveloped economy. According to him, 'once full employment is secured the economy is raised to a level where growth is self-sustained and spontaneous.' Regarding India, he says, "Judged by the employment criterion, despite all the investment that has taken place over the period, our economy seems to be receding." Hence, it is imperative for an over-populated country to have the elimination of unemployment as one of the conditions for take-off.

There is an element of ambiguity in the concept of 'take-off' when it is applied to an underdeveloped country. During the take-off investment increases with a rise in the national income without reducing the average propensity to consume. Technically speaking, there is an excess of the marginal rate of saving over the average rate of saving so that the average rate keeps on rising and the final level is characterized by a constant, though high, average rate of savings. Prof. Dasgupta says, "This does not seem to be a sensible interpretation. For even in a highly developed economy the average rate of saving may not remain constant."

The concept of take-off suggests an element of spontaneity which is of little significance in the context of an underdeveloped economy. But "a take-off is not an instantaneous process. It is an exercise that requires time and from which, after a certain speed has been attained and a portion of the runway used up, there is no turning back or even safe throttling down."[12]

Professor Bicanic does not agree with the symbolical presentation of the take-off because it appears to him like a light flying animal just got cut off from the earth and floating in the air. It is like creeping over a very difficult threshold of economic development. One has to creep over it, one cannot fly over it. It is not a take-off but a very painful process which every underdeveloped country has to go through.[13]

8. Rostow and Marx

Describing his system as "A Non-Communist Manifesto" Rostow presents his analysis as an alternative to Marx's theory of modern history. He poses his five stages of growth against Marx's stages of feudalism, bourgeois capitalism, socialism and communism.

Some broad similarities can be recognised between the analysis of Rostow and Marx. Both are bold attempts to interpret the evolution of whole societies, primarily from an economic perspective. Both recognise that economic change has social, political, and cultural repercussions.

In other respects, however, their analyses differ, diametrically. The basic Marxian problems of class conflict, exploitation, and inherent stresses within the capitalist process do not find a place in Rostow's analysis. Rostow, unlike Marx, does not reduce the complexities of man to a single economic dimension. He recognises that, in terms of human motivation, many of the most profound economic changes must be viewed as the consequence of non-economic human motives and aspirations. Instead of limiting human behaviour to simply an act on maximisation, he interprets net human behaviour "as an act of balancing alternative and often conflicting human objectives in the face of the range of choices men perceive to be open to them." He avoids the Marxian assertion that

12. John P. Lewis, *Quiet Crises in India.*

13. R. Bicanic, in A. Datta (ed.), *Paths to Economic Growth.*

the behaviour of societies is uniquely determined by economic considerations. He rejects Marx's assumption that a society's decisions are merely a function of who owns property and maintains that "one must look directly at the full mechanism of choice among alternative policies; including the political process—and, indeed, the social and religious processes—as independent arenas for making decisions and choices."[14]

14. *Ibid.*, p. 150.

Production Function Approach to Growth

16

An important way of measuring growth is by making use of the production function. This method is helpful in understanding the sources of growth and in quantifying the contribution of these sources to any measured growth rate. This approach has been employed widely and usefully in advanced countries. Now underdeveloped countries have also started using it, though some would say not very fruitfully because the major sources of growth in these countries are institutional and non-measurable. In spite of the fact that institutional change plays an important role in growth, production function approach is still useful to know the rough contribution that growth of, say, capital and labour has made to measured growth in the past, if only to put the growth debate in perspective. No doubt, there are problems of calculations and estimation, but they are not insuperable. In addition to the difficulties of specifying the sources of growth precisely, and measuring accurately both the dependent and independent variables, the major problem is a methodological one of fitting the appropriate production function to the data; that is, the function relating output to inputs.

1. The Production Function

An important and highly desirable property of production function approach to growth is that it is consistent with, and derivable from, microeconomic analysis. It borrows the concept of the production function from the theory of the firm. Just as we can say for a firm that output is a function of the factors of production—land, labour, capital and the level of technology (or factor efficiency) so we can express aggregate output as a function of factor inputs and the prevailing technology, *i.e.*,

$$O = f(R, K, L, T)$$

where R stands for land, K for capital, L for labour and T for technology.

The problem is how to separate empirically the contribution to growth of the growth of factor inputs from other factors which can lead to higher output, included in *T*, such as economies of scale (resulting from both technical change and increase in factor supplies), improvements in the quality of factor inputs, advance in knowledge, improved organisation of factors, and so on. The task is to fit a suitable, correctly specified, production function which, if possible, will not only separate the contribution of factor inputs to growth from the contribution of increases in output per unit of inputs (increases in 'total' factor productivity) but will also distinguish between some of the factors that may contribute to increases in the productivity of factors such as education, improvements in the quality of capital and economies of scale.

2. The Cobb-Douglas Production Function

There are three broad sources of growth which can be distinguished by using the production function framework, *viz.* (*i*) increase in factor supplies, (*ii*) increasing returns, and (*iii*) technical progress interpreted in the wide sense of anything that increases the productivity. The production function most commonly fitted to aggregate data to distinguish empirically between these three broad sources of growth has been the unconstrained form of the Cobb-Douglas production function. This function may be expressed as

$$O_t = T_t K_t^{\alpha} L_t^{\beta} \qquad \text{... } (i)$$

where O_t stand for real output at time *t*, T_t for an index of technology, or 'total' productivity, K_t for an index of the capital services, at constant prices, L_t for an index of labour input (preferably man-hours), α for the partial elasticity (responsiveness) of output with respect to capital (holding labour constant), and β for the partial elasticity of output with respect to labour (holding capital constant). It is assumed that changes in technology are exogenous and independent of changes in factors inputs, and the effect of technical progress is neutral on the factor intensity of production. T_t, α and β are constants to be estimated empirically if the function is unconstrained. If α and β are assigned values prior to the use of the function for estimating purposes, the function is said to be constrained. Generally, α and β are less than unity on the assumption of diminishing marginal productivity of factors. The sum of partial elasticities of output with respect to the factors of production gives the scale of returns, or the degree of homogeneity, of the function. $\alpha+\beta=1$ represents constant returns, $\alpha+\beta>1$ represents increasing returns and $\alpha+\beta<1$ represent decreasing returns, and the function is said to be homogeneous of degree one, greater than one and less than one, respectively.

If α and β are not estimated empirically and their sum is assumed to be equal to unity, in which case the function would be constrained, then increasing or decreasing returns will be reflected in the value of T_t which is the index of total factor productivity. Obviously the existence of increasing returns would bias the value of T_t upwards, and decreasing returns would bias the value of T_t downwards. This has been pointed out because in practice the Cobb-Douglas function is often employed in this constrained form with the sum of α and β put equal to unity. Then values are assigned to α and β according to the share of capital and labour in the national income. The underlying assumption is the perfectly competitive one that if production is subject to constant returns and factors are paid the value of their marginal products, then factor shares will reflect the value of a factor's marginal product. In spite of the fact that the conditions in developed and underdeveloped countries alike are far removed from perfect competition, it is interesting to note that empirical estimates of α and β frequently do not vary much from the estimates of factor shares of the national product. This has been used as a justification for assigning values to α and β on the basis of factor shares to avoid the problem of making empirical estimates.

In order to use equation (*i*) for separating out the influence of the three broad sources of growth mentioned earlier, we have to take first logarithms of the variables and then differentiate with respect to time.

This gives $$\frac{d\log O_t}{dt} = \frac{d\log T_t}{dt} + d\frac{d\log K_t}{dt} + B\frac{d\log L_t}{dt} \qquad \ldots (ii)$$

For simplicity, equation (*ii*) may be expressed as

$$rO = rT + \alpha rK + \beta rL \qquad \ldots (iii)$$

where rO stands for the rate of growth of output per time period, rT for the rate of growth of total productivity or technical progress, rK for the rate of growth of capital, rL for the rate of growth of labour and α and β are the partial elasticities of output with respect to capital and labour, respectively, as before. To express this equation in words, the rate of growth of output is equal to the rate of growth of 'total' productivity plus the rate of growth of capital weighted by the partial elasticity of output with respect to capital plus the rate of growth of labour weighted by the partial elasticity of output with respect to labour. With knowledge of rO, rK, rL, α and β, it becomes possible as a first step to separate out the contribution of factor inputs to growth from increases in output per unit of inputs represented by rT.

3. Criticism

The use of Cobb-Douglas function has been criticised on four main counts. In the first place, it is held that since only one combination of factor inputs can be observed at any one time, it is not possible to distinguish shifts in the function (technical progress) from movements along the function (changes in factor intensity) unless the assumption of neutral technical progress is made. But technical progress may not be neutral and therefore the effects of technical progress and changing factor intensity become confused, biasing the results of the contribution of factor inputs and technical progress to growth. Secondly, the assumption that technical progress is independent of increases in factor inputs has been questioned. This, however, is not a specification error of the function itself and the Cobb-Douglas function can be used making technical progress a function of the rate of growth of inputs—so-called endogenous models of technical progress. Thirdly, the Cobb-Douglas function cannot represent a change in the case of substitution between capital and labour because it contains the restrictive property of constant unitary elasticity of substitution between factors whatever the factor intensity. This may be serious if the elasticity of substitution of factors differs significantly from unity and there are wide discrepancies in the growth rate of factors. For instance, if the elasticity of substitution between capital and labour is significantly less than unity and the growth of capital is faster than that of labour, this would lead to an overestimate of the contribution of capital to growth and an underestimate of the contribution of other factors. The reason for this bias is that the smaller the elasticity of substitution the more difficult it is in practice to obtain increased output just by increasing one factor because diminishing returns set in strongly. Fourthly, some point out that what meaning can be attached to a function which aggregates so many heterogeneous items; particularly, what is the meaning of an aggregation of capital goods built at different times, at different costs and with varying productivities? How are such capital goods to be equated in an aggregate measure of capital?

All the criticisms mentioned above are mainly of theoretical importance and do not have much practical significance. None of these is so damaging as to suggest the abandonment of the function. Studies of the nature of technical progress, at least in advanced countries, show that the assumption of neutrality is a fair working hypothesis. The fact that technical progress may be dependent on factor accumulation is easily accommodated within the Cobb-Douglas framework. The elasticity of substitution would matter much only if the capital and labour grow at very different rates but case studies show that it is close to unity. Finally, although the aggregation of heterogeneous outputs and inputs, particularly the aggregation of capital, is a matter of concern, none the less capital and labour aggregates appear to do well in production function studies as measured by the correct picture they convey of relative factor shares.

Applicability of Economic Theory to Underdeveloped Countries

17

1. Different Environments

It is often held that most of the existing economic theory has been developed in the advanced countries and, therefore, is not applicable to the underdeveloped countries. The formulators of the existing theory had in view the environments and problems of the advanced countries which are very different from those of the underdeveloped countries.

> ...all over economic speculation, including the theory of international trade, was originally framed in the setting of interests and ideals of the then most prosperous country, Great Britain, and there even consciously conceived of as a theory for the welfare of the British nation. Thereafter and until very recently, it was almost exclusively developed further by theorists who were the nationals of those few countries which were rapidly progressing, economically under conditions of expanding mutual trade and large movements of capital and labour....
>
> ....It is common place in the sociology of knowledge that social and economic theories rarely escape from becoming to some extent a rationalization of the interests and the aspirations of the milieu where they grow; if not so much by commission, the more by omission.[1]

The applicability of the existing economic theory to underdeveloped countries is challenged primarily on two grounds. Firstly, there is a marked difference between the economic data available in the developed and underdeveloped countries. Because of the insufficiency and imprecise nature of the economic data available in underdeveloped countries, the techniques of economic

1. Gunnar Myrdal, *Development and Underdevelopment* (Cairo, 1956), pp. 79-80.

analysis existing in developed countries cannot be applied to underdeveloped countries. In the absence of sufficient and reliable data, the underdeveloped countries have to depend on certain crude techniques of analysis. In making policy recommendations, economists have to depend more upon intuition and common sense than upon fine tools of economic analysis developed in advanced countries. Secondly, the general environments of underdeveloped countries remarkably differ from those of developed countries. The term 'general environments' refers to such elements as banking and credit system, transportation and communication system, land-holding and property system, structure of markets, for commodities and for factors of production, legal system, political set-up, social institutions, education system, and culture, human attitudes etc. Further, the existing system of economics is based on some assumptions. The assumptions which hold in developed countries may not be realistic in underdeveloped countries.

2. Theory Widely Applicable

In contrast, there are economists like Bauer who hold that the existing economic theory is widely applicable to all countries, developed or underdeveloped.

> I am now convinced of the wide applicability to underdeveloped countries of the basic methods of approach of economics and of the more elementary conclusions stemming from these. I am thinking especially of the elements of supply and demand analysis and its simpler conclusions, the tendency of people to seek activities and occupations which yield the highest net advantage within the opportunities open to them, the implications of the concept of complementary and competitive relationships between productive resources and many others. Some of these propositions are direct corollaries of the limitation of resources, so that their wide applicability to underdeveloped countries is not in question.
>
> Those who dispute the relevance of the propositions of economics to underdeveloped countries usually base their arguments on the differences in attitudes and institutions between the underdeveloped world and the Western

countries. Usually, however, these views reflect incomplete observation or imperfect understanding of economics.[2]

In examining the applicability of economic theory to underdeveloped countries, distinction should be made between the tools of economic analysis and the conclusions drawn by the application of these tools. Some economists doubt the applicability to underdeveloped countries of even the tools developed in advanced countries. "The tools and techniques of economics of developed countries, when applied to an analysis of the problems of these (underdeveloped) countries, would lead to a number of conclusions which are bound to be unrealistic."[3] This, however, is going too far. In fact, the tools of economic analysis are widely applicable to all countries, developed or underdeveloped. Of course, some tools may be more suitable to one set of countries than to the other set of countries. The difference is only of degree and not of kind. Suitability of the same tools differs even within different advanced countries. Some tools may be more suitable to one advanced country than to another advanced country. Similarly, the same tools do not suit equally well to all underdeveloped countries.

The general applicability of the conclusions drawn with the help of tools is less than that of the tools themselves. The basic economic data in advanced and underdeveloped countries differs remarkably. The conclusions drawn from one set of data may not hold in case of another set of data. The difference is, again, of degree and not of kind. The conclusions drawn from the data of one advanced country may not hold true in case of another advanced country. Similarly, the conclusions drawn from the data of one underdeveloped country may not hold true in case of all other underdeveloped countries. The basic economic data differs from country to country and, therefore, the conclusions drawn from one country may not be completely applicable to another country. The basic economic data differs not only in different countries but also in different regions of a country. This is particularly so in the case of large-sized countries like India. But the similarity between the data of two advanced or

2. P.T. Bauer, *Economic Analysis and Policy in Underdeveloped Countries* (London, 1557), p. 15.

3. C.N. Vakil and P.R. Brahmanand, *Planning for An Expanding Economy* (Bombay, 1956), p. 197. Words within parenthesis added.

between that of two underdeveloped countries is likely to be more than that between the data of an advanced and an underdeveloped country. Therefore the conclusions drawn from one advanced country would be more applicable to other advanced countries than to underdeveloped countries.

Differences in the economic data of different countries do not prevent the formulation of certain generalisations widely applicable to all countries. "The discernment of uniformities underlying diversity of circumstances is the primary task of scientific enquiry and indeed, of all systematic enquiry into phenomena."[4] Once it is accepted that a different theory is required for underdeveloped countries because their economic data differs from that of developed countries, it cannot be denied that there is no theory applicable to all underdeveloped countries because the economic data widely differs in different countries; and to stretch it further, there is no theory applicable even to a single country because economic data widely differs in different regions of the same country. Further, a different theory will be required for the country from one phase of development to another.

While claiming a substantial degree of generality of economic theory to all countries, developed and underdeveloped, it cannot be denied that the developments in economic theory during the fifty years before the Second World War are much more useful to advanced than to underdeveloped countries. During this half century, developments in economic theory were largely in the field of equilibrium analysis and subjects related to it.[5] Economists were primarily concerned with theory of value, the theory of firm and the theory of income distribution which were explored by the method of equilibrium analysis. Main concern was with formal conditions of equilibrium situations which were defined as situations that continue unchanged unless disturbed by external factors. Trade cycle theory and theory of employment were also concerned with movements away from and towards equilibrium. The emphasis was on short period oscillations in economic activity around an assumed trend. Problems of economic development received very little

4. Bauer and Yamey, *The Economics of Underdeveloped Countries* (London, 1957), p. 8.
5. *Ibid.*, pp. 9-10.

attention. Factors affecting the level, efficiency and growth of resources did not receive much attention.

> The discussion was generally at a high level of abstraction, so much, indeed, that the principal long-term determinants of income and wealth, such as the factors underlying the growth of capital, the size of population, the attitudes towards work, saving and risk-bearing, the quality of entrepreneurship and the extent of markets were considered as institutional forces or facts given, as data, to the economist. In his technical or professional capacity he was not directly concerned with the data as such, or with the causes or course of changes in the data. Such studies of these forces and facts as were made by some economists were largely outside the main stream of the subject.[6]

In recent years, the problem of economic development of underdeveloped countries has received considerable attention in underdeveloped as well as in advanced countries. Attention has been paid not only to the allocation of resources but also the growth of resources. It has been realised that the theory developed before the Second World War did not take into consideration some very important factors which substantially influence economic phenomenon. An attempt is being made to incorporate into economic theory factors and influences which were relegated to institutional literature or to other disciplines.

3. Conclusion

Economic theory as it exists may not be completely applicable to underdeveloped countries. This, of course, does not mean that it is useless and should be discarded. It would be suicidal on the part of underdeveloped countries to throw away the rich knowledge existing in developed countries. They should take full advantage of it. What is required, in fact, is the adaptation and modification of the existing theory to make it more suitable to the conditions prevailing in underdeveloped countries and the development of additional principles catering to the specific problems of underdeveloped countries in which the formulators of the existing theory were not interested.

---

6. *Ibid.*, p. 10.

What is an Underdeveloped Economy?

18

1. Introductory

In the existing literature on economic development, the term 'underdeveloped' has been used in a vague, loose and indefinite manner. In fact, it is almost impossible to precisely define an underdeveloped economy. W.W. Singer thinks that any attempt at defining an underdeveloped country is waste of time and effort. "An underdeveloped country is like a giraffe—difficult to describe but you know one when you see one."[1] A number of criteria of underdevelopment have appeared in the current literature. Let us briefly examine the important ones.

2. Poor Countries

In popular discussions, all poor countries are designated underdeveloped. The level of development of a country is measured by its per capita income.

> We use the term 'underdeveloped countries' to mean countries in which per capita real income is low when compared with the per capita real incomes of the United States, Canada, Australia and Western Europe. In this sense, an adequate synonym would be 'poor countries.'[2]

Meier and Baldwin also write, "Because of the ambiguities involved in using the term 'underdeveloped,' and because we wish to focus on low per capita real income, we may better adopt the less confusing term 'poor country'."[3]

---

1. H.W. Singer, 'Reply' to A.N. McLeod's 'Comment' on Singer's paper "The Distribution of Gains Between Investing and Borrowing Countries," *American Economic Review* (June 1951), p. 419.
2. United Nations, *Measures for the Economic Development of Underdeveloped Countries* (New York, 1961), p. 3.
3. Gerald M. Meier and Robert E. Baldwin, *Economic Development* (Bombay, 1964), p. 9.

This definition of an underdeveloped economy, however, is not appropriate. The term 'underdeveloped' involves the implication that the concerned country has certain known potentialities for development which have not been utilised so far. A poor country may or may not have potentialities for development. A poor country with little potentialities for development cannot be called underdeveloped. A desert country having no minerals and no scope for irrigation, for instance, cannot be called underdeveloped even if its per capita income is extremely low.

3. Backward Countries

The term 'underdeveloped' must also be distinguished from the term 'backward.' Till the Second World War, the term 'underdeveloped' was not very common, and all such regions were designated as backward. But recently the term 'backward' has given place to the term 'underdeveloped.' The term 'backward' appears negative and static in nature. It merely indicates absence of progress and does not signify the existence of development potential. In addition, it has some indirect reference to the cultural aspect of life in these regions. It lacks dynamism because it does not bring into focus the desirability of exploiting the potential of the 'backward' regions for raising their standard of living. Gunnar Myrdal writes:

> It is interesting that we have now all come to refer to this majority of very poor countries as 'the underdeveloped countries.' The dynamic term, which has gained its present prevalence only after the Second World War, itself indicates the great change in the world political situation.... The use of the concept...implies the value judgment that it is an accepted goal of public policy that the countries so designed should experience economic development.[4]

4. Age of a Country

The 'age' of a country is an equally unsatisfactory criterion of underdevelopment. "We avoid calling a country poor merely because it is a young country."[5] Some of the oldest countries like India and China are underdeveloped while some of the youngest countries like

4. Gunnar Myrdal, *Economic Theory and Underdeveloped Regions* (Indian Edition, 1958), pp. 19-20.
5. Gerald M. Meier and Robert E. Baldwin, *Economic Development: Theory, History, and Policy* (New York, 1957), p. 9.

the United States and Canada are highly developed. "The familiar fact is that today's underdeveloped countries, with a few exceptions, are all areas of ancient civilisation."[6] No doubt, time factor is important in the process of economic development, but it does not bring in development of its own.

5. Low Ratio of Population to Area

Sometimes, a country is labelled as underdeveloped merely or mainly because it has a low ratio of population to area. Because the term 'underdeveloped' implies that development is possible, to the extent there exist empty or thinly populated areas lacking potentialities for development, the criterion is not very appropriate. This criterion overemphasises the importance of mere space. History shows that it is only fertile soils and good climate which have attracted settlers. Density of population is very low in the tropical jungles, the Arctic, the Antarctic and the Sahara Desert because, in the present state of technology, it is not possible to raise much production in these areas.

6. Scarcity of Capital

Scarcity of capital exhibited in the form of high interest rates is another criterion used to identify underdevelopment.[7] Interest rates, however, are not a satisfactory index of the level of development. Before the breakdown of the international capital market in thirties, borrowers of equal creditworthiness could borrow at almost the same rates irrespective of their location and the level of development of their country. Before 1914, India, Canada, the United States, Argentina, and Austria raised long-term loans in the London money market at almost the same rates of interest. High interest rates may be artificially manipulated by monetary and/or fiscal measures. Interest rates may be high because of high marginal productivity of capital. But the available evidence shows that the marginal productivity of capital is higher in developed than in underdeveloped countries. This is mainly because the producers in developed countries have access to certain production facilities (*viz.*, efficient means of transportation and communications, skilled labour, banking and credit facilities, etc.) which are not available to producers in

6. Jacob Viner, *International Trade and Economic Development* (Oxford, 1953), pp. 94-95.
7. *Ibid.*, pp. 95-96.

underdeveloped countries. Sometimes even known unexploited potentialities are larger in advanced than in underdeveloped countries.

Another form of the criterion of scarcity of capital is the ratio of the capital supply to the supply of other factors of production.[8] A.N. McLeod defines an underdeveloped country as "...a country or region with a relatively low ratio of capital and entrepreneur-ship to other factors of production but with reasonably good prospects that additional capital could be profitably invested."[9] This criterion has considerable practical validity but, theoretically, low ratio of capital to other productive resources may not always be accompanied by the high marginal productivity of capital. Because of certain reasons (*e.g.* bad government) marginal productivity functions of all the factors may be low. Because of this and certain other reasons, economies can be conceived, at least theoretically, where marginal productivity of capital is low beyond a fairly early stage of investment even though natural resources are abundant and good in quality.

7. Ratio of Industrial Output to Total Output

Ratio of industrial output to total output or of industrial population to total population is a widely used criterion of economic development.[10] The terms 'developed' and 'industrialised' are, often, used interchangeably.

> The most striking feature which we observe when comparing a census of rich with a census of poor countries, whether they be different countries at the same date or the same country at different dates, is the sharp fall in the proportions recorded in agriculture as we pass from poverty to riches. The poorest countries show seventy per cent or more engaged in agriculture, whereas the richest can feed themselves twice as well with only twelve to fifteen per cent in agriculture.[11]

But history also tells us that "The degree of industrialisation may be and often is a consequence rather than a cause of the level of

8. *Ibid.*, pp. 96-97.
9. A.N. McLeod, "Trade and Investment in Underdeveloped Areas: A Comment," *American Economic Review* (June 1951), p. 411.
10. Viner, n. 7, p. 97.
11. W. Arthur Lewis, *Theory of Economic Growth* (London, 1954), p. 333.

prosperity." Prosperous agriculture creates conditions for the growth of tertiary and service industries. Higher productivity in agriculture creates disposable surplus which can be used for industrial development. High per capita productivity in agriculture decreases the need to import foodstuffs and agricultural raw materials and increases the capacity to export these commodities and thereby enlarges the foreign exchange resources which are very essential for importing capital equipment, technical know-how and essential raw materials required for any programme of industrialisation. Japan's success in raising agricultural production and utilising the surplus for building industry provides a good example of agricultural prosperity preceding or to some extent running parallel to the programme of industrialisation.

A high proportion of agricultural population to total population will act as a dead weight to development, however, if it is not accompanied by raising production trends in agriculture.

8. Backward Technologies

Sometimes an underdeveloped country is defined as one applying backward technologies. "Regions, the productivity of which increases or could increase by the simple implantation of already known techniques, would be considered to be at different levels of underdevelopment."[12] This definition overemphasizes the role of technology in economic development and neglects all other factors.

9. Stagnant Economies

Often the term 'underdeveloped' has been taken to mean a stagnant economy.

> ...the most significant difference between an underdeveloped and a developed economy is that a normally functioning underdeveloped economy does not grow, whereas a normally functioning developed economy grows.[13]
>
> In an underdeveloped economy whenever an increase in real gross national product occurs, either it is not sustained

12. Celso Furtado, "Formacao de Capital Desenvolvimento Economico," *Pevista Brasileira de Economia* (September, 1952) 15 Cf. G.F. Loeb, *Industrialisation and Balanced Growth* (Netherlands, 1957), p. 9.
13. Hyman P. Minsky, "Implications of the Development Status of An Economy," *Economic Development and Cultural Change* (January, 1959), p. 152.

> or it is quite rapidly offset by a rise in population. A limiting form of underdevelopment is found in the stagnant economies in which net savings, net investment, and the net change in population are all zero.[14]

This is not correct. In fact an underdeveloped economy may "be in a stagnant or in a developing state. All underdeveloped countries can be classified into two categories, *viz.*, (1) developing countries and (2) stagnant countries. A developing country is that which is exploiting its development potentialities while a stagnant underdeveloped country is one which has not started exploiting its development potentialities.

10. Unutilised Development Potentialities

The term underdeveloped is a relative term. In its absolute sense, all countries are underdeveloped because every country possesses some unutilised potentialities for development. No country is fully developed in this sense. But with the known natural resources and technology, different countries offer varying degrees of scope for development. In developed countries the known resources and technology are being exploited more fully than in underdeveloped countries. In developed countries the scope for further development depends mostly on the discovery of new technologies and natural resources. In underdeveloped countries, on the other hand, income can be considerably raised by applying the modern methods of production to the known natural resources. As no country is fully developed or fully underdeveloped, it will be more appropriate to use the term 'comparatively more developed' or 'comparatively less developed' or 'comparatively more underdeveloped.' All countries can be arranged in an ascending order according to the amount of known unutilised development potentialities existing in these. For terminological convenience, however, we may draw some arbitrary line in the array and designate all countries above the line as developed and all countries below the line as underdeveloped. The position of different countries regarding their comparative state of economic development may change with the change in the technology or with the discovery of new natural resources. Our earlier mentioned fully developed desert country, for instance, may become underdeveloped if vast mineral

14. *Ibid.*, p. 152.

resources are discovered below the desert. Similarly, with development in technology, uses may be found for certain known resources which were previously considered almost useless. If a country possesses vast amount of such resources, its potentialities for development will considerably increase, *i.e.*, it will become comparatively underdeveloped.

According to our above mentioned definition, a country can be in a developing state without any rise in per capita income. Let us take a hypothetical example to illustrate such a situation. Suppose the increase in total income from the exploitation of development potentialities is followed by a proportionate increase in population and consequently the per capita income remains constant. A part of the potentialities for development has been utilised (*i.e.*, the degree of underdevelopment has decreased) without any increase in per capita income. If this process continues, a country may exhaust all its known development potentialities and thus become fully developed without any increase in the per capita income. Similarly, a country can be in a developing state even with falling per capita income if the rate of increase in population is faster than the rate of increase in income from the utilisation of development potentialities. But the fundamental objective of development is an increase in the welfare of the people. This objective can be achieved not by merely raising total income but by raising the per capita income. Care should, therefore, be taken that the increase in total income resulting from the development of the country is not counterbalanced by an increase in population. Jacob Viner defines an underdeveloped country as:

> A country which has good potential prospects for using more capital or more labour or more available natural resources, or all of these, to support its present population of a higher level of living, or, if its per capita income level is already fairly high to support a larger population on a not lower level of living.[15]

11. Development and Growth Distinguished

There is a tendency to use the terms economic development, economic growth, economic progress, and secular change interchangeably. Though these terms refer to more or less the same

15. Viner, n. 6, p. 93.

phenomenon, it is possible to make some fine distinctions among them. Some economists have made a distinction between economic development and economic growth. According to them, economic development refers to the problems of backward nations while economic growth refers to those of the advanced countries. According to Schumpeter, development is a discontinuous and spontaneous change in the stationary state which for ever alters and displaces the equilibrium state previously existing while growth is gradual and steady change in the long run which comes about by a general increase in the rate of savings and population.[16] Mrs. Hicks points out that the problems of underdeveloped countries are concerned with the development of unused resources, even though their uses are well known, while those of advanced countries are related to growth, most of their resources being already known and developed to a considerable extent.[17] According to Professor Bonne, "Development requires and involves some sort of direction, regulation, and guidance to generate the forces of expansion and maintain them. This is true of most of the underdeveloped countries while the spontaneous nature of growth characterises advanced free trade enterprise economies."[18] Everyman's Dictionary of Economics makes the distinction as follows. "Generally economic development means simply economic growth. More specifically, it is used to describe not quantitative measures of a growing economy (such as the rate of increase in real income per head) but the economic, social or other changes that lead to growth. Growth is then measurable and objective: it describes expansion in the labour force, in capital, in the volume of trade and consumption. And economic development can be used to describe the underlying determinants of economic growth, such as changes in techniques of production, social attitudes and institutions. Such changes may produce economic growth."

12. Growth and Progress

H. Mynit makes a distinction between natural resources and human resources. He uses the term underdeveloped for natural

---

16. J.A. Schumpeter, *The Theory of Economic Development* (Cambridge, Mass, 1934), pp. 63-66.
17. U. Hicks, "Learning about Economic Development", *Oxford Economic Papers* (February, 1957), p. 1.
18. A. Bonne, *Studies in Economic Development* (London, 1957), p. 7.

resources and backward for people.[19] Barrere makes a distinction between growth and progress.[20] Progress refers to an increase in per capita product while growth refers to an increase in both population and total real income. Progress can occur without growth, *e.g.* total income remaining the same, there occurs a decrease in population, or decrease in total income is smaller than the decrease in population. Such progress occurred in France during the first half of the century. This kind of progress, however, is of little interest to the underdeveloped countries. Growth can also occur without progress, *e.g.* the rate of increase in population is higher than the rate of increase in total income. Barrere distinguishes between (a) progressive growth, *i.e.* the increase in total income is larger than the increase in population; (*b*) regressive growth, *i.e.* the increase in population is larger than the increase in total income; (*c*) stationary growth, *i.e.* population and total income increase at the same rate. Dr. Loeb defines development in the sense of Barrere's progressive growth, *i.e.* increase both in total income and per capita income.[21] Sometimes the term 'growth' is used for an increase in total and per capita income of the advanced countries and the term 'development' for an increase in total and per capita income of the underdeveloped countries. Schumpeter defines economic development as "only such changes in economic life as are not forced upon it from without but arise by its own initiative, from within."[22]

13. Definition of Economic Development

There are three important definitions of economic development. According to Meier and Baldwin, "economic development is a process whereby an economy's real national income increases over a

---

19. H. Mynit, "An Interpretation of Economic Backwardness," A.N. Agarwala and S.P. Singh (ed.), *The Economics of Underdevelopment* (Oxford, 1958), p. 93.
20. Alain Barrere, "A Teoria do Crescimento e do Desenvolvimento Economico", *Revista Brasileira de Economica* (June 1953), pp. 17-18. G.E. Loeb, *Industrialisation and Balanced Growth* (Netherlands, 1957), p. 10.
21. G.E. Loeb, *Industrialisation and Balanced Growth* (Netherlands, 1957), p. 10.
22. Joseph A. Schumpeter, *The Theory of Economic Development* (Cambridge, 1951), p. 63.

long period of time".[23] In this definition we should underline for special attention the words 'process', 'real national income' and 'long period'. Process implies the operation of certain forces; these forces operate over the long period and embody changes in certain variables. The most important of these are changes in fundamental factor supplies and changes in the structure of demand for products. Particular changes in factor supplies include (1) discovery of additional resources, (2) capital accumulation, (3) population growth, (4) introduction of new and better techniques of production, (5) improvement in skills and (6) other institutional and organizational modifications. Particular changes in the structure of demand for products are associated with developments in (1) size and age composition of population, (2) level and distribution of income, (3) tastes, and (4) other institutional and organizational arrangements. Real national income refers to the country's total net output of final goods and services, expressed not in money terms but in real terms: the money expression of national income must be corrected by an appropriate price index of both consumer and capital goods. The increase in an economy's net national product must be a sustained increase over a long period of time in the midst of cyclical fluctuations and not a short-period expansion as occurs within a business cycle.

Criticism: This definition ignores the point that economic development generally refers to an improvement in the standard of living of the people. Per capita income, therefore, is a good measure of economic development. It cannot be said that development has taken place if the growth of population exceeds the growth of output or net real national income so that each person is worse off than before, or if the two growth rates are equal so that the increase in net real national income is spread over the increased population, keeping the average standards unchanged. Thus if the economic development is to have some significance, that the rate of increase in real national income must be higher than the rate of growth of population so that per capita income also increases.

23. Gerald M. Meier and Robert E. Baldwin, *Economic Development* (Bombay, 1964), p. 2.

We should be careful in identifying an expansion in total output with enrichment because the composition of the total output is also important. Whether a large total output contributes to economic welfare depends as much on what is produced and its quality as it does on the quantity produced. Further, an expansion of total output could be accompanied by a depletion of natural resources.

In this indication of economic development, allowance has to be made for changes in the real national income owing to cyclical swings and for changes in the value of money. Further, there are certain conceptual difficulties relating to the measurement of national income, particularly in underdeveloped countries.

The second definition refers to an increase in the per capita real income of the economy over the long period. Professor Meier defines economic development "as the *process* whereby the real *per capita income* of a country increases over a *long period* of time." Prof. Bran says, "Let economic growth (or development) be defined as an increase over time in per capita output of material goods.[24] To cite Buchanan and Ellis, "Development means developing the real income potentialities of the underdeveloped areas by using investment to effect those changes and to augment those productive resources which promise to raise real income per person."[25]

Criticism: This definition is not free from objections. If an increase in per capita income was taken as the measure of development, we would be in awkward position of having to say that a country had not developed if its real income had risen but population had also risen at the same rate. For instance, if over a given period, country A's national income quadrupled, and country Y's national income only doubled, but growth of population prevented per capita income from rising in either country, then according to per capita income criterion we would have to say that neither country had developed. But it does some violence to our ordinary notions of development to deny that country A developed more than country B.

If per capita income is the measurement, the population problem may be concealed since population has already been divided out. To

24. P.A. Baran, *The Political Economy of Growth* (New York, 1957), p. 20.
25. N.S. Buchanan and H.S. Ellis, *Approaches to Economic Development* (New York, 1955), pp. 21-22.

cite Kuznets, "the choice of per capita, per unit, or any similar single measure to gauge the rate of economic growth...carries with it the danger of neglecting the denominator of the ratio. In a sense such neglect is an inevitable consequence of the operation: we divide national product by total population largely to eliminate changes in the former 'produced' by mere changes in the latter.... To put it bluntly, in insisting on gauging economic growth by such per-unit measures, economists are treating the population factor either as an extremely simple variable that can be handled by mere division...or, what is worse, as an exogenous factor, beyond the ken of the economist as a student of economic growth...In arguing for the total volume of national product rather than the per capita, I am suggesting a change that should symbolize and give effect to the real widening of the field of required attention."[26]

An increase in per capita income may not raise the real standard of living of the masses. While the per capita income is increasing, it is quite possible that the per capita consumption might be falling. People might be increasing the rate of saving or the government might itself be using up the increased income for military or other purposes.

An increase in per capita income may be accompanied by any type of distribution of income. Along with the increase in per capita income, the rich might be getting richer and the poor getting poorer. Economic welfare cannot be said to have increased even if real per capita income has risen, unless the resultant distribution of income is also considered good. Further, from a welfare point of view, consideration should be paid not only to what is produced but also to how it is produced. Along with the increase in real national output, the real costs—the pain and sacrifice and the social costs involved in producing this larger output might also have risen. In such cases, increase in national output is not an unmixed blessing.

The third definition refers to an increase in economic welfare. Economic development is viewed as a process whereby the real per capita income increases accompanied by reduction in inequalities of income and satisfaction of the preferences of the masses as a whole.

26. S. Kuznets, "Problems in Comparison of Economic Trends," in S. Kuznets, W.E. Moore, J. J. Spengler (eds.), *Economic Growth: Brazil, India, Japan* (Durham, 1955).

To cite Okun and Richardson, economic development is "a sustained, secular improvement in material well being, which we may consider to be reflected in an increasing flow of goods and services."[27] In the words of Colin Clark, "Economic progress can be defined simply as an improvement in economic welfare. Economic welfare, following Pigou, can be defined in the first instance as an abundance of all those goods and services which are customarily exchanged for money. Leisure is an element in economic welfare and more precisely we can define economic progress as the attaining of an increasing output of those goods and services for a minimum expenditure of effort, and of other scarce resources, both natural and artificial."[28]

Criticism: The identification of economic growth with increase in economic welfare leaves out of account a considerable portion of total output which bears no relation to welfare, *e.g.* currently produced investment goods, armaments, net exports etc. Equation of economic welfare with an increase in the output of goods and services customarily exchanged for money is untenable. Economic welfare may be greatly improved by an increase in the supply of goods and services which are customarily not exchanged for money, *e.g.* services rendered by educational institutions, hospitals, roads etc. On the other hand, many goods and services which are customarily exchanged for money may not contribute to human welfare, *e.g.* beauty parlours, narcotics, items of conspicuous display etc. Economic welfare can be increased without an increase in the output of goods and services through changes in its structure and distribution. To cite Meier and Baldwin, "Although an increase in output per head is in itself a significant achievement, nevertheless we cannot equate this with an increase in economic welfare, let alone social welfare, without additional considerations. To specify an optimum rate of development we must make value judgements regarding income distribution, composition of output, tastes, real costs and other particular changes that are associated with the overall increase in real income."[29] Therefore, in order to avoid

27. B. Okun and R.W. Richardson, *Studies in Economic Development*, p. 230.
28. Colin Clark, *The Conditions of Economic Progress*, p. 1.
29. Gerald M. Meier and Robert E. Baldwin, *Economic Development* (Bombay, 1964), p. 8.

value judgements and for the sake of simplicity, most of the modern economists use the real net national income as a measure of economic development making due allowance for the increase in population.

14. Characteristics of Underdeveloped Countries

The above discussion leads to the conclusion that it is not possible to precisely define an underdeveloped country. It is difficult even to draw a picture which reflects every underdeveloped economy. Still more difficult is to locate a typical country on the world map, possessing the representative characteristics of underdevelopment.

There is a marked difference in the rate of growth of the various underdeveloped countries. The rate of growth is higher in some countries than in others. India, for instance, has progressed faster than Pakistan but slower than Burma and Thailand.

The underdeveloped countries remarkably differ in respect of the technological levels reached by them. The systems of land tenure differ from communal tenure to individual tenure. There is a wide difference regarding demographic patterns. There is a significant difference in the rate of growth of population between India and China. Some countries are overpopulated while others are underpopulated. India and China are examples of the first type and Sudan and Morocco of the second type. The demographic differences have considerably influenced total real income, per capita income, population policies, rate of development, etc. Consequently "there is much variation in their ripeness or suitability for economic development or promise of profitable returns to capital investment in the near future...it is wrong to infer that all or even most of the countries in question are particularly suitable for early development on economic terms or at an otherwise reasonable cost."[30] Some countries have more efficient government and law and order than others.

Though it is not possible to draw a common picture of underdeveloped countries or to locate a representative underdeveloped country, it is certainly possible to describe some

30. P.T. Bauer and B.S. Yamey, *The Economics of Underdeveloped Countries* (Chicago, 1957), p. 6.

fundamental characteristics which are common to many underdeveloped countries. The extent of these features, of course, may not be uniform in these countries; nor are these the only features of an underdeveloped country. But, broadly speaking, they do describe a typical underdeveloped country. This is what is briefly attempted below.

15. Underdeveloped Natural Resources

The existence of underdeveloped natural resources is one of the most conspicuous characteristics of an underdeveloped country. The underdeveloped countries are not so because of poor endowment of natural resources.

> The Creator has not divided the world into two sectors—developed and underdeveloped—the former being more richly blessed with natural resources than the latter. All developed countries began by being underdeveloped by modern standards, which are the operative ones, indeed they remained in this state until quite recently.[31]

W.S. Woytinsky and E.S. Woytinsky remark: "Core of the problem of the carrying capacity of the earth is not the scarcity of fertile land in comparison with the number of mouths that must be fed but the insufficient ability of men to make full use of their available resources."[32]

A question may be raised as to why these countries have remained underdeveloped if they have got plenty of unutilised natural resources. The answer is that the natural resources themselves cannot lead to economic development. For that matter, no single resource (or factor of production) can produce anything or assume economic value. Two basic conditions must be met before the natural resources can assume economic value. Firstly, complementary factors of production must be available in adequate quantity and at an economic price. Secondly, there should be sufficient demand for the resultant product.

The natural resources may remain unutilised because of a number of reasons. These may be economically inaccessible. The

---

31. *Ibid.*, p. 46.
32. W.S. Woytinsky and E.S. Woytinsky, *World Population and Production* (New York, 1953), pp. 533-34.

cost of the required complementary factors may be prohibitive. The resources may remain unutilised because of monopolistic restriction of production. Sometimes institutional factors may stand in the way of efficient utilisation of natural rescources. The caste system, for instance, inhibits occupational mobility of labour and thereby creates artificial shortages and surpluses of manpower in certain occupations. Ill planned or wrongly enforced official measures (*e.g.*, moratorium orders, market regulations) may also obstruct a fuller utilisation of productive resources.

16. Deficiency of Capital

Since, as seen above, the underdeveloped countries have not been able to fully utilise their natural resources, it has not been possible for them to create enough means of production. Their stock of capital, therefore, is very inadequate to meet their development requirements. It is insufficient in relation to their resource potential at the prevailing standards of technology. The inadequacy is felt more acutely if the growth of population is taken into consideration. The growth of population without a corresponding rise in the rate of capital formation further lowers the standard of living.

Not only the existing stock of capital is small but the current rate of capital accumulation is also very low. The average rate of capital formation does not exceed 5 per cent. In contrast it is 15 to 18 per cent in the United States, Canada and Western Europe.

Because of a shortage of capital, there is a tendency to invest the available capital in staple farming and light labour-intensive; consumer goods industries rather than in the heavier capital intensive capital goods industries.

The unskilled labour being cheaper than the capital, the producers have a tendency to substitute the former for the latter. Consequently, the techniques of cultivation, manufacture, marketing and domestic work are in a primitive state as compared with those of rich countries. The peasant cultivators are unable to use power-propelled machines. The implements used in ploughing, levelling, water-lifting, crop-cutting, winnowing, etc. have remained primitive. The poor farmers rarely use chemical fertilisers, superior varieties of seeds, crop protectives and cattle of good breed.

Manufacturing industries are also labour-intensive. Handicrafts and small scale industries using more labour and less capital account for the production of a considerable portion of the consumers goods. Even in the large scale sector, the capital-intensity is low as compared to that in the advanced countries. Often the plant and machinery employed is obsolete. There is a tendency to prolong the life of capital equipment beyond justification. The export of second-hand machinery from advanced to underdeveloped countries substantiates this fact.

The same phenomenon prevails in trade and marketing. The trade suffers from shortage of storage facilities and working capital. Inadequate transport and storage facilities and insufficient working capital often results into regional and seasonal shortages and surpluses and consequent variations in prices.

The deficiency of capital in underdeveloped countries is more serious if the term capital is interpreted broadly. According to broader interpretation, capital formation means investment of current income that augments future output. The stock of capital includes, in addition to physical equipment, the body of knowledge and the capacity of the people to utilise it. The outlays on education and training, research, public health and social services, the aim of which is to raise people's future productive capacity, are treated as capital expenditure. Since the expenditure on these heads in underdeveloped countries is much smaller than that in the developed countries, the difference in the proportion of capital formation to national income would be much larger in the two sets of countries. Kuznets suggests that instead of a difference in net capital formation proportions between 10 per cent in rich and, say, 3 per cent in poor countries, the true difference is more likely to be between 30 per cent or over and 3 per cent.[33]

There are two basic reasons for the capital deficiency, *i.e.*, (1) shortage of savings and (2) the tendency of the meagre savings to go into prodigal consumption or short term speculative investment rather than productive investments. The extreme inequalities in the distribution of wealth existing in these countries aggravate this

33. S. Kuznets, "Towards a Theory of Economic Growth" in R. Leckachman (ed.) *National Policy for Economic Welfare at Home and Abroad* (New York, 1955), pp. 39-40.

difficulty. The inequalities in the distribution of income are greater in underdeveloped countries than in developed countries. The percentage of total income received by the poorest 60 per cent of the people is 28 per cent in India, 30 per cent in Ceylon and 24 per cent in Puerto Rico—compared with 34 per cent in the United States and 36 per cent in the United Kingdom. The percentage of total income received by the richest 20 per cent is 55 per cent in India, 50 per cent in Ceylon, and 56 per cent in Puerto Rico—compared with 44 per cent in the United States and 45 per cent in the United Kingdom.[34]

Normally it is believed that the larger inequalities in the distribution of income would lead to a higher rate of capital accumulation. But this does not hold true in the case of underdeveloped countries because the top income class in these countries consists of landowners and traders who have a tendency to invest more in land, real estate, speculation, capital flights, or inventories rather than in industries or public utilities. A number of factors are responsible for this type of tendency, *viz.*, the greater desire for quick gains than for long-term gains, the higher rate of return which the moneylender or landlord, can obtain by short-term lending to small cultivators, the difficulties in obtaining trained labour and machinery and other factory equipment, the investor's desire to have liquid assets as a hedge against currency devaluation and price inflation, the general uncertainty regarding government's economic policies which may suddenly increase costs or reduce the domestic market or invite foreign competition, the fact that in underdeveloped countries ownership of land is a means of social and political power, and all the social, legal, and political institutions which restrict initiative and enterprise, inhibit the mobilisation of savings, and prevent an effective channeling of those savings into more productive outlets.

17. Underutilisation of Capital

Whatever capital exists is not fully utilised. Under-utilisation of capital is particularly marked in agriculture. A large number of holdings are too small to fully utilise even a single unit of agricultural equipment, *viz.*, one plough and a pair of bullocks. A

34. S. Kuznets, "Economic Growth and Income Inequality," *American Economic Review* (March, 1955), pp. 20-21.

large part of the agricultural area is single-cropped and consequently the idle period in agriculture is very long.

18. Subsistence Farming and Plantation Economy

Primary production for local consumption is the predominant feature of a rural economy. Though there exists some industry, it consist mostly of the processing of agricultural products, the production of agricultural implements, the simple manufacture of textiles, and light industries of minor importance. Traditional handicraft industries account for most of the manufacturing employment. Key industries like iron, steel, coal, chemicals etc. which promote and feed manufacturing and subsidiary industries are more or less non-existent. An overwhelming majority of the population is engaged in producing foodgrains for the growing population. The fast growing population requires more food which means greater pressure on land. The increasing pressure on land leads to decline in production and consequently to increasing poverty. The conditions are no better in the tropical regions, where the plantation economy predominates, because the profits are drained out of the national economy by the foreign investors and the native population does not benefit significantly.

Foodstuffs and raw materials occupy a place of pride in the economy. Agricultural and other primary industries like plantations and mining account for a major portion of the total national income. Roughly speaking, from two-thirds to more than four-fifths of the population of the underdeveloped countries earns their livelihood from agriculture and allied occupations.

An important point related to primary production is the low agricultural productivity in the underdeveloped countries. The level of output per acre is much lower than that in advanced countries. The level of output per worker is still lower because of a very high density of farm population per acre. A number of factors are responsible for low agricultural productivity in the underdeveloped countries, *viz.*, low ratio of land to worker, inferior soils, inefficient land-use patterns, low efficiency of the worker, low ratio of capital to land and labour, inefficient techniques of production, inadequate .knowledge of better methods of production, poor organization of agricultural production, etc.

In the tropical parts of Asia, plantation agriculture exists side by side with subsistence cultivation. It plays a predominant role in

Indonesia and Malaya; to a less extent it prevails in parts of India, Siam, Burma, Ceylon, Indo-China and the Philippines. The plantation economy differs from ordinary agriculture in regard to size of holdings, type of crops, capital investment, management, relation with industry, marketing products, nature and time of returns and the status of labour employed. The former requires high standards of cultivation, large capital investment, superior management and extensive distributing and servicing organisations. Most of the plantation products are exported to world markets. While the subsistence farming is owned and operated by the local population, the plantations are mostly owned and run by foreigners and have been developed by foreign capital.

Minerals are another primary product of some poor countries. Modern mining industry requires for its efficient operation and development large amounts of capital, and enterprise of unusual financial risk-bearing capacity, industrial research, organisational ability and technical skill. The underdeveloped countries being short of these factors, the mines are owned mostly by the foreign interests. Further, since industry has not made much progress in the underdeveloped countries, only a small portion of the mineral output can be used locally and the major portion is exported to the industrially advanced countries. The result is a heavy drain of nation's profits abroad leaving underdeveloped economies still poorer. "From standpoint of country's development the direct physical effect of the mineral industry is, therefore, less significant than the benefits derived from its role as an earner of foreign exchange."[35]

19. Dependence on Exports

The underdeveloped countries heavily depend on exports. In all underdeveloped countries taken together, the ratio of exports to the national income appears to be not less than 20 per cent.[36] Excessive dependence on exports may not in itself be serious but it becomes so when exports consist primarily of raw materials. The situation becomes still more serious when considered in the light of the fact that most of the underdeveloped countries heavily depend on the export of one or a few staple commodities.

35. Meier and Baldwin, n. 3, p. 276.
36. United Nations, n. 2, p. 71.

> ...rice has recently accounted for about 80 per cent of the value of exports from Burma. Ninety per cent exports from Pakistan have consisted of jute, cotton, tea, wool, hides and skins. Exports from the Federation of Malaya consisted almost exclusively of rubber and tin. Seventy-six per cent of Indonesia's exports have been petroleum, rubber and tin. Over 80 per cent of Philippine exports are covered by sugar, copra and oil form about 90 per cent of the entire exports of Ceylon, while Thailand's rice, rubber and tin exports account for 80 per cent of total exports.[37]

> ...in Venezuela, exports of petroleum account for 97 per cent of the credit side of the balance of payments, and for almost 60 per cent of the revenue of the fiscal budget. If to this part of the revenue is added the 18 per cent of the revenue received from customs duties paid on merchandise imported with foreign exchange produced by petroleum, the contribution of petroleum to the budget amounts to about three-quarters of the total. In Chile, to cite another case, copper produces almost 50 per cent of the credit side of the balance of payments, and directly and indirectly, a sum approximating 33 per cent of the budget revenue; for each American cent by which the price of a pound of this metal varies, the Chilean Treasury receives or loses the approximate amount of $4 million in tax revenues. In Egypt, cotton in either fiber or seed form contributes 88 per cent of the credit side of the balance of payment; in Turkey, tobacco and fruit 53 per cent.[38]

The heavy reliance on exports exposes the underdeveloped economies to the business cycles originating in advanced countries.

The underdeveloped countries also heavily depend on imports which consist primarily of manufactured products, textiles, light consumer goods, foodstuffs, capital equipment and essential raw materials. Not only the marginal propensity to import is high but also the average propensity to import tends to rise over the long period as a result of the operation of the demonstration effect.

---

37. United Nations, *A Study of Trade Between Asia and Europe* (Geneva, 1953), p. 10.
38. United Nations, n. 2, p. 71.

20. Factor Disequilibrium

Under conditions of perfect factor mobility, factors of production move from one industry to another until their marginal productivities become almost equal in all industries. This leads to an optimum allocation of productive resources and maximum productive efficiency in the national economy.

The underdeveloped countries are characterised by a high degree of factor immobility. Labour, for instance, utterly lacks mobility in the underdeveloped countries. Often, the workers cluster around a few occupations even when they are capable of earning higher wages in other professions. The occupational pattern of a village in India is determined mainly by the caste system and very few can cross the frontier. Differences in customs, habits, attitudes, language etc. inhibit the desire for mobility. The poverty of the workers is another factor inhibiting mobility.

In addition to factor immobility monopolistic practices, ignorance of existing domestic and international market possibilities, lack of specialisation, rigidity of price and production structure and unprogressive social set-up create various imperfections resulting in sub-marginal allocation of resources.

21. Dualistic Development

In its earlier phase, the Industrial Revolution influenced the growth of Western economies. But in its later phase, its impulses penetrated into the underdeveloped world with varying effects. The penetration took three forms. First form is the emigration and permanent settlement of European labour and capital in temperate lands. The sparse population in these areas offered good scope for permanent settlement. The primitive order in these areas was either destroyed or isolated to die its natural death. The result was a cohesion in the economic and social institutions of the country. Canada, U.S.A., Australia and New Zealand are typical examples of such areas.

The second form was the opening up of old tropical countries by the industrial powers for securing a cheap and regular supply of valuable articles like textiles, spices, bullion, products of fine arts. Until the middle of the nineteenth century, the economies of the tropical countries were not much affected. Simply the process of export of valuables from the Oriental countries was accelerated.

But, thereafter, the policy of converting them into bases of supplies of raw materials and grounds for dumping manufactured goods through political domination brought about a drastic change in the colonial economies. Gradually the economies were divided into two sectors—the subsistence economy sector and the market economy sector. Since most of these countries were already having large populations and their tropical climate was not very suitable to the Europeans, the number of Europeans migrating to these countries was very small. This type of countries are represented by India, China, Indo-China, Malaya, Siam, Indonesia, some areas of South Africa and the Pacific Islands.

The third form of penetration is represented by certain regions of Africa, West Asia, Central America and Oceania (excluding Australia and New Zealand). These areas had potentials of plantation and minerals and sufficient supply of unskilled labour. But they were short of capital and managerial and technical skill. They were also unable to buy the European manufactured goods because they had nothing to offer in exchange. In such a situation, European capital and management moved in these regions to exploit their potential and to develop exports of plantations and minerals. A typical example of this trend is the movement during the inter-war period of foreign capital and enterprise into the Middle East countries to exploit their oil resources. These enterprises employed indigenous labour and foreign capital and technical know-how. They appeared like oases in vast stretches of underdevelopment. Their income was mostly drained out of the country in the form of profits and wages of the foreign technical personnel. They, therefore, failed to make any significant contribution towards the development of the country.

In the case of the first type of penetration, the emigrant labour, capital, enterprise and socio-economic institutions became an integral part of the new countries and led to their development in an integrated manner. The other two types of penetration led to division of the economy into two broad parts, *viz.*, (1) the modern part and the primitive part. The modern part contains primarily the large scale industry, mines and plantations and is confined to urban centres. It is highly monetised. It is well organised. It. uses modern techniques and processes of production. It is highly capital intensive. It has up-to-date facilities in respect of public utility services and external economies. It has up-to-date banking, and credit facilities. The markets for commodities as well as for factors of production are well organised. Workers and employers are well organised. Labour and capital are highly mobile. Monetary and fiscal measures of regulation are considerably effective. This part exhibits more or less the features of an advanced country. It, however, forms only a small part of the whole economy.

The primitive part consisting primarily of agriculture and confined to rural areas is very backward. Money does not play an important role in this sector and most of the transactions are of a barter nature. There prevails a high degree of self-sufficiency and the people do very little buying and selling. There are no organised markets for commodities and for factors of production. Banking and credit facilities are scanty. A large part of the credit is supplied by the time-honoured moneylender who, besides charging a very exorbitant rate of interest, indulges into a number of malpractices. Techniques and processes of production are highly primitive and consequently the productivity is very low. Monetary and fiscal measures of regulation are not very effective. There is a marked degree of disguised and seasonal unemployment. Methods of production are highly labour-intensive. Incomes being very low, the rate of saving and investment is extremely low, almost zero.

The mobility between the two parts is very low. Price mechanism is not very powerful in bringing about a shift in the allocation of resources and, therefore, the rates of return considerably vary in the two parts. There is a considerable divergence in the rates of wages between the two parts of the economy. There is no tendency towards an equilibrium between the two parts even in the long run.

Disparity in the development of different sectors of the economy obstructs the smooth growth of the underdeveloped countries. The less developed sector acts as a break on the growth of the developed sector. The less developed sector being a subsistence economy sector employs primitive techniques of production, obstructs factor mobility and the people employed in this sector have comparatively lower incomes. The demand of this sector, therefore, is smaller in quantity and poor in variety. It, therefore, fails to create sufficient demand for the manufacturing industries. The emphasis in their production shifts from the socially necessary commodities to luxury goods demanded by the people with higher incomes.

22. Population

The discovery of modern drugs and the introduction of modern methods of public sanitation and health have led to a significant decline in the death rate in the underdeveloped countries. Without a corresponding decline in the birth rate, the population has a tendency to expand at a very fast rate.

Another striking feature of the demographic pattern in underdeveloped countries is that a much larger proportion of the total population is in the younger age group. In Asia, Africa and Latin America, population below 25 years of age accounts for 40 per cent of total population while it ranges between 23-25 per cent in the United States and the United Kingdom.

The average expectation of life is very low in poor countries. While it is 55 years in the United States and Canada, 69 years in Norway and 67 in England, it ranges between 32-40 years in Asia, Latin America and the Middle East. It has two consequences. Firstly, the number of persons dying at a younger age is larger in the underdeveloped countries than the developed countries. Secondly, the span of productive years for survivors is shorter in underdeveloped countries than in developed countries. The result is a larger population of non-producers to producers and the consequent heavy burden on national economy for their birth, upbringing, education etc. Alfred Bonne states:

> Economically speaking, the underdeveloped countries suffer a considerable loss of investment—material and immaterial—in upbringing and educational efforts in respect of a substantial number of young people who never reach the prime of life. Even if the amount invested per capita is below the equivalent of the cost of education, clothing and food customary in Western countries, the outlay lost in the aggregate is staggering.... An earner in Western countries is easily able to repay to society the cost of his upbringing, training, etc., since he has a fair chance of reaching the end of his productive years and, therefore, of contributing his share for a period of about 40 active years or more.[39]

It may, however, be mentioned that all underdeveloped countries do not suffer from overpopulation. Some underdeveloped countries

39. Alfred Bonne, *Studies in Economic Development* (London, 1957), p. 24.

are underpopulated and the problem there is of increasing the hands to make possible a better exploitation of the natural resources, *e.g.*, Latin American countries, Australia, Africa excluding certain areas like Eastern Nigeria, Union of South Africa and some parts of Kenya, Middle East excluding river zones.

23. Unemployment

There exists large unemployment, underemployment and seasonal unemployment, particularly in agriculture. The agricultural farms have working force larger than that required by their size, crop pattern and the amount of capital equipment. Often four persons are seen working on a farm where three can do the job well.

> An ideal, or optimum, distribution of workers does not exist so long as some workers would be more productive in employments other than those in which they are present; in more technical terms, so long as the marginal product of labour is higher in some occupations and industries than in others, net national product may be increased by the transfer of labour from less productive to more productive situations. As long as such transfers remain possible, 'hidden', or 'disguised' unemployment may be said to exist.[40]

A certain quantity of manpower can be withdrawn from agriculture without effecting the production at all. An increasing number of members of a farmer's family work on the same piece of land adding virtually nothing to farm output. In such a situation, it is difficult to identify any particular person as under-employed or unemployed in the family.

> In an over-populated peasant economy, we cannot point to any person and say he is unemployed in disguise. The people may all be occupied, and no one may consider himself idle. Yet the fact remains that a certain number of the labour force on the land could be dispensed with, without making any difference to the volume of output.[41]

---

40. J.J. Spengler, "Demographic Pattern" in H.F. Williamson and J.A. Buttrick, *Economic Development* (Englewood Cliffs, 1954), p. 68.
41. Ragnar Nurkse, *Problems of Capital Formation in Underdeveloped Countries* (Oxford, 1957), p. 33.

It may, however, be mentioned that all underdeveloped countries do not suffer from unemployment or underemployment.

> Disguised unemployment or underemployment is not the common characteristic of all the underdeveloped countries. There are sparsely populated countries and regions in Latin America and Africa which are underpopulated but do not have to face the problems of over-population or unemployment. The presence or absence of such unemployment cannot provide a criterion of underdevelopment.[42]

Large-scale underemployment is a characteristic mainly of densely populated countries in the area ranging from South-Eastern Europe to South-Eastern Asia. Quantitative measurement of underemployment is difficult and observers differ in their estimates of its extent. A United Nations Report states:

> In a study made by the Royal Institute of International Affairs... the lowest estimate of surplus population, based on pre-war data, was placed between 20 and 25 per cent for the Eastern European region. Recent estimates on a similar basis made for Southern Italy also yield high figures of a surplus population. An estimate based on the actual labour requirements of cultivation in Egypt placed the surplus in that country in 1937 at about one-half of the farm population. Similar estimates have not been made for Asiatic countries; it seems, however, safe to assume that for many regions of India and Pakistan, and for parts of the Philippines and Indonesia, the surplus cannot be less than the pre-war average for East European region.[43]

While analysing the problems of capital formation in relation to population growth, Nurkse also accepts this approximation.[44] Describing Indian conditions, Lewis has concluded that at least a quarter of the agricultural population is surplus to requirements.[45]

---

42. P.T. Bauer and B.S. Yamey, *The Economics of Underdeveloped Countries* (Chicago, 1957), p. 75.
43. United Nations, *Measures for the Economic Development of Underdeveloped Countries* (New York, 1951), pp. 8-9.
44. Nurkse, n. 41, p. 35.
45. Lewis, n. 11, p. 327.

24. Occupational Structure

The occupational structure in the underdeveloped countries is rigid and stagnant. The lack of mobility of factors of production hinders specialisation and industrialisation which are very important for economic growth.

> The occupational structure is thus a datum of primary importance in the analysis of the economic conditions of backward areas, and a point of departure in every practical scheme for the promotion of economic progress in such areas.[46]

25. Backward Human Resources

The underdeveloped countries have economically backward population in the sense the quality of the people as productive agents is low. Important manifestation of this are low labour efficiency, factor immobility, limited specialisation in occupations and trade, lack of entrepreneurship, economic ignorance, and a value structure and social structure that minimise the incentives for economic change.

The low efficiency of labour is mainly explained by malnutrition, low standards of health, illiteracy, lack of training, obstacles to occupational mobility, and the low value placed on work as against leisure. The efficiency of labour is also impaired by endemic disease and inadequate medical and hospital care.

Labour is immobile among different occupations. Caste system obstructs occupational mobility and makes vertical mobility difficult. Labour mobility is also low because of low response among workers to income incentives. An increase in the relative wages of some occupations may not cause workers to move to higher wage occupations.

It is maintained that a small rise in wage rates may actually induce a worker to work less and enjoy more leisure.

> Many workers (do) not want to work for wages regularly five or six days a week all the year round.... They prefer to have a lower standard of living and more leisure; they are not educated to appreciate a higher standard of living, and

46. Bonne, n. 18, p. 27.

> would rather take life more easily than add to their material comforts.[47]

The people lack knowledge. They are ignorant about the available natural resources, alternative production possibilities, the required skills and the market conditions. They lack not only technical knowledge but also knowledge of social relations. Social knowledge is no less important than the technical knowledge, because development depends as much upon learning how to administer large-scale organisations, or how to create institutions that favour economising effort and economic rationality, as it does upon the knowledge of how to breed new seeds or learning how to build bigger dams.[48]

Another element of backwardness manifests in the form of social structure and value of an underdeveloped country. Often, the structure of social relations is hierachical and the social cleavages are pronounced. Importance is attached not to the individual but to the family or class as the special unit.

> An individual's status is ascribed in terms of who he is or who his antecedents were, rather than being achieved by his own efforts. An ascribed status, in contrast with an achieved status, means that people are evaluated not according to what they can do but according to their position in a system of social classification—by age, sex, kin, clan, caste, etc.[49]

The value system minimises the importance of economic incentives, material rewards, independence and rational calculation. Such a value system hampers the development and acceptance of new ideas. It fails to evaluate the costs and benefits of alternative methods of achieving certain objectives.

Material welfare is subordinated to other worldly ends. Some religions consider austerity and resignation as ideals and desire an evil. There is a widespread belief that a man's fortune is decided by God and not by his own efforts. There is an attitude of resignation

---

47. T.S. Simek, *Welfare and Planning in the West Indies* (Oxford, 1946) pp. 33-34.
48. Lewis, n. 11, p. 164.
49. Meier and Baldwin, n. 3, p. 302.

rather than of innovation. People have a tendency to accept what happens rather than attempting to change it.

Even if a country has good natural resources, adequate supply of labour, technical know-how and capital, its potential productivity will not materialise unless there are entrepreneurs who are economically motivated and who have the ability to organise other factors of production for the creation of economic goods. The term "economically motivated" means guided by the objective to maximise gains, with money as a measure of the degree of successful achievements. But the culture of the underdeveloped countries hampers entrepreneurship. In these countries, the motive to produce wealth is not so strong because the social prestige that people desire can be acquired in non-economic ways. The production of wealth is actually looked down upon, by many people. Entrepreneurship is inhibited where society is stratified by caste, colour, or creed and where custom or Jaw restricts the activities of the large sections of the population and makes the introduction of change difficult. Absence of good law and order is not conducive to entrepreneurship. The underdeveloped countries do not have a large class of people interested in long-term productive achievements. They have instead a small class of businessmen engaged primarily in distribution activities, real estate, speculation and money-lending.

If an adequate number of entrepreneurs was not coming forward from among the private individuals, the question may be asked as to "why the government did not fill up the gap by assuming the functions of an entrepreneur. The reply lies in the fact that governments themselves have been backward and weak in the underdeveloped countries. "After all, the government is composed of individuals, and there is no obvious reason why these individuals should necessarily be more entrepreneurial in spirit than private individuals."[50]

There is a lack of really competent and well trained civil servants. The salaries offered by the government are not very attractive. The civil service system is inadequate for selecting and training personnel and corruption is rampant.

50. Meier and Baldwin, n. 3, p. 305.

26. Fiscal and Monetary Organisation

A common characteristic of the fiscal system of the underdeveloped countries is the high ratio of revenue derived from indirect taxes and customs duties which are regressive in incidence. Taxes on land or the income from it are low and account for only a small proportion of the government's total revenue. Progressive income taxes are either non-existent or low in yields. The collection of taxes is inefficient and costly and there is considerable tax evasion.

The money markets are underdeveloped. Monetary policy is not an effective instrument of regulating the economy. Most of the underdeveloped countries lack an organised, highly liquid call loans market and few of them possess a commercial bill market of any significance. Different parts of the money market are loosely connected and there is hardly any integration in the structure of money rates.

Because of the underdeveloped money markets, the functions of the central bank are severely limited. The central bank does not have an effective control over the activities of the commercial banks. Because of the absence of a bill market and call-loans market, open market operations are not possible. Since the banks do not generally maintain fixed ratios between their cash reserves and deposits and often allow considerable fluctuations in their cash ratios, the banks are not likely to react to the small changes in their cash balances which are brought about by whatever open market operations are possible in these narrow security markets.[51]

27. Development in Pioneer and Presently Developing Countries

The presently developing countries have to traverse the path in years which was traversed by the present developed countries in generations. In advanced countries, the development process was spread over several generations. Underdeveloped countries cannot afford to wait for such a long period. It is maintained that the presently developing countries are in a privileged position as compared with the countries which developed in the past. Pioneer countries had to start from a clean slate. Presently developing countries have at their disposal a vast store of experience and

---

51. S.N. Sen, *Central Banking in Underdeveloped Money Markets* (Calcutta, 1952), p. 28.

knowledge existing in advanced countries. They can use it without any substantial cost. Developed countries took centuries to evolve the modern techniques of production. Presently developing countries are receiving vast amounts of technical and financial aid from the advanced countries which was not available to countries pioneer in the field of economic development.

Along with the facilities mentioned above, presently developing countries have to face certain difficulties which were not faced by the pioneer countries. Pioneer countries developed under conditions of expanding world markets, absence of strong competition, availability of imported cheap food and raw materials. These easy conditions no longer prevail. Underdeveloped countries have to face strong competition from developed countries in procuring raw materials as well as in selling final products.

The entrepreneurs in pioneer countries had vast investible funds obtained from land rent, domestic and foreign, commerce, foreign investments, etc. Wages were low, working hours long, welfare expenses almost nil and profits extremely high. The tradition of frugal living, thrift and hard work facilitated a high rate of investment. Such favourable conditions do not exist in the presently developing countries. With the emergence of the ideology of socialism and welfare state and the awakening created in labour, it is not possible to completely ignore the demands of labour regarding higher wages, better working conditions and health and social security measures. The present underdeveloped countries have no foreign incomes. A major portion of world commerce is in the hands of nationals of the advanced countries and therefore profits go to the nationals of these countries. Often, even highly lucrative industries like mining and plantations are in the hands of foreigners and consequently the profits are transferred abroad. Demonstration effect of the high standard of living in advanced countries adversely affects the rate of voluntary savings. Wealthy classes are not much interested in productive investments. Investment in gold, jewellery, real estate and speculation is very popular.

In advanced countries, the development took place primarily through a continuous and self-propelling process of capital formation under conditions of free economy. The presently developing countries, however, cannot depend on this type of automatic process of capital formation. Their fast growing population eats away whatever little capital they can accumulate out of their limited national income. A policy of *laissez faire* in these countries would mean keeping them where they are. The government, therefore, has to play a more positive role in these countries in respect of initiative, pioneering, capital formation, supply of entrepreneurial factor, direction and quantum of investment, foreign trade policy, choice of technique and above all, objectives of development.

The private entrepreneur cannot be expected to lift the economy out of a state of stagnation. His strength can hardly match the dimensions of the task.

Pre-requisites for Economic Development

19

1. Introduction

An underdeveloped country aspiring to make its way up the economic ladder should necessarily possess some pre-requisites for economic development. But in order to attain economic development it is not enough to remove the obstacles to development. According to Prof. W.A. Lewis, the proximate causes of economic growth are: the effort to economise, the increase of knowledge and its application in production, and increasing the amount of capital or other resources per head. These three causes, though clearly distinguishable conceptually, are normally found together. Naturally, according to Lewis, an underdeveloped country should do something to acquire these three pre-requisites for economic development. But since economic growth is closely tied with human endowments, political conditions and social attitudes and historical accidents, only economic pre-requisites for growth are not enough. Social, political, cultural and psychological requirements are as important as economic requirements. As Professor Cairncross rightly remarks, "Development is not just a matter of having plenty of money nor is it purely an economic phenomenon. It embraces all aspects of social behaviour, the establishment of law and order, scrupulousness in business dealings, including dealings with the revenue authorities, relationships between the family, literacy, familiarity with mechanical gadgets and so on."

2. Availability of Abundant and Rich Natural Resources

The availability of abundant and rich natural resources required for production is a great advantage. A country which possesses such resources will have better scope for development than country which lacks them. But this does not mean that a country with poor endowment of natural resources cannot attain a high level of development. Japan and Switzerland provide examples of countries which have attained a high level of development inspite of their poor natural resources. We simply want to point out the decisive advantage which a country enjoys if it possesses good and abundant natural resources. The domestic availability of natural resources reduces its dependence on other countries and this imparts certainty to schemes of economic development.

3. Removal of Market Imperfections

Market imperfections restrict transfer of factors from less productive to more productive forms of employment, handicap the expansion and development of markets and restrict the impact of expansion in one sector on another sector. They must, therefore, be removed. Alternative forms of social and economic organisations are needed to remove the market imperfections. The opportunities for greater productivity within the existing state of knowledge and with the existing resources should be more widely exploited. The knowledge of market opportunities and new techniques of production should also be increased. Monopolistic practices through the domestic production and marketing sectors should be curbed. The capital market should be widened; better credit facilities should be made available to peasants, small traders and small businessmen. The entrepreneurial horizons of the small traders and manufacturers should be widened by spreading new knowledge, workers should be made aware of better employment opportunities elsewhere and producers should be made aware of existing domestic and international market opportunities. The removal of market imperfections is particularly necessary if development in one sector is to spill over to other sectors. If rigidities and inflexibilities are reduced foreign trade would have much greater impact throughout the economy.

4. An Indigenous Base

The process of growth should have an indigenous base within the underdeveloped economy. If the forces of growth are implanted from outside, the stimulating effect will not be lasting. "The implanted forces can, at the most, ginger up the growth process for a short time but they can hardly initiate the process of feed-back within the economy."[1] Meier and Baldwin also observe, "If the

1. D.S. Nag, *Problems of Underdeveloped Economy* (Agra, 1962), p. 111.

process is to become cumulative and long-lasting, the development forces must be fundamentally based within the developing country."[2] All parts of the economy should grow in proportion to their importance in the functioning of the economy. An excessive growth of any part would ultimately inhibit the smooth growth of economy.

5. Structural Changes

The process of growth has not only to make a fuller use of existing resources but also to expand resources. The problem has to be attacked at two fronts. In the first place, the productive opportunities within the existing resources and know-how have to be exploited to the maximum possible extent through our optimum allocation of resources. Secondly, the 'production frontier' has to be widened through sizable structural changes.

The amount of development that can be achieved by a mere better allocation of the existing resources, however, is very much limited. Schultz has aptly remarked, "in most poor countries there is not much economic growth to be had by merely taking up whatever slack may exist in the way of the available resources being utilised."[3] In fact, the supply of the productive factors has to be expanded to give an outward push to the production frontier. For this a number of structural changes have to be brought about.

The structural change in the underdeveloped agricultural countries may begin with a reduction in the proportion of population engaged in agriculture and an increase in that employed in non-agricultural activities. "The speed or rate of economic development may then be described by the rate at which the 70:30 ratio in economic structure is approximated to the 20:80 ratio which represents ultimate equilibrium at a high level of development."[1] The transfer of agricultural population to the non-agricultural sector has to be accompanied by an increase in agricultural production to provide food and raw materials for the latter sector and for the mutual increase of population in both the sectors. This requires sizable changes in the agricultural set-up, *viz.*, land reforms,

---

2. Gerald M. Meier and Robert E. Baldwin, *Economic Development, Theory, History and Policy* (New York, 1957), p. 112.
3. T.W. Schultz, *The State of the Social Sciences* (1956), p. 372.
4. H.W. Singer, "The Mechanics of Economic Development," *Indian Economic Review* (August, 1952).

new credit institutions, increase in the supply of productive factors in agriculture, dynamic market mechanism, new incentives, changed socio-economic relationship, etc.

Economic phenomena are interwoven in the social system. This is particularly true of underdeveloped countries where productive activities and expenditure patterns are substantially influenced by social institutions, habits and attitudes. The pattern of savings and investment, for instance, is considerably shaped by cultural and social considerations. Any structural change in the economy of the country will, therefore, necessarily require a change in the social structure of the society. A dynamic economy and a static social set-up cannot pull together. Meier and Baldwin aptly remark, "New wants, new motivations, new ways of production, new institutions need be created if national income is to rise more rapidly. Where there are religious obstacles to modern economic progress, the religion may have to be taken less seriously or its character altered."[5] Professor Gadgil also states:

> All attitudes, habits of mind, patterns of behaviour, etc. are-born out of chiefly historical institutional modes of living. These modes of living in most underdeveloped countries have had in the past little direct connection with economic development. If now rapid economic development is to become the main objective of these societies, their attitudes and habits of mind must change correspondingly.[6]

6. Favourable Environments

Economic development cannot be achieved unless the prevailing atmosphere is conducive to it. There must exist among the people a desire for economic progress and the political, legal and religious institutions should be conducive to it. Development is not a function simply of capital and technology. If the atmosphere in a country is not very conducive to development, mere investment cannot lead to economic development. Investment in such an economy can at the best give it a kick and it will return to its original position after some time. Investment can lead to self-sustained development only if the general atmosphere is favourable

5. Meier and Baldwin, n. 2, p. 112.
6. D.R. Gadgil, "Pre-Conditions of Economic Development," *Indian Economic Review* (February, 1952), p. 19.

to development. When atmosphere is favourable, initial investment leads to automatic cumulative growth.

7. Belief in Possibility of Development

People must be convinced that development is possible. Development will not be desired in a country where people are doubtful about the feasibility of achieving it. Belief in the possibility of development leads to a scientific and experimental outlook. Human beings experiment with different techniques of production, different techniques of organisation, different social institutions and so on. Experimental attitude is very essential for economic development. Modern methods of production, methods of organisation and social institutions existing in advanced countries are the result of experiments carried over centuries.

8. Desire for Development

Even when it is widely believed that development is possible, it won't be realised if there does not exist a strong desire among the people for material advancement. The religious philosophy in several backward countries teaches people to be less materialistic and to care more for the other world than for the world in which they are living. Meditation and worship of God is considered to be a more fruitful use of life than the production of goods and services. People are taught to strictly limit their wants and to lead a simple life. Such philosophy is not very conducive to economic development and its eradication is very essential for rapid economic development.

After elementary needs have been met, the marginal leisure-preference becomes very high. This kind of attitude is not very favourable to economic development. Such behaviour prevails, primarily, because of lack of education, social mores and prejudices. It is rigid but not unalterable.

9. Absence of Taboos and Prohibitions

Economic development may be inhibited by a series of taboos and prohibitions. Use of certain products and the adoption of certain processes may be made difficult by these. Progress in certain occupations, very essential for economic development, may be inhibited because these are ranked low. Even where there exist no social or religious prohibitions, economic development may be inhibited by traditions and habits built through practices continuing since generations. Self-employed workers on farms and in cottage industries, for instance, are not accustomed to punctuality in hours of work and regular attendance which are very essential for factory life. Unless these traditions, attitudes and habits are shed off, people won't be very responsive to economic development.

10. Favourable Social Values

Urge to work for producing wealth will be lacking if the social prestige which people desire can be acquired more easily in other ways. In a feudal or aristocratic society where inherited wealth is far more important than the earned wealth, the urge to produce wealth will be lacking. People born outside feudal and aristocratic families cannot acquire their status and prestige however hard they may work for producing wealth. On the contrary, work for producing wealth is often considered to be contemptuous and below the prestige of well-bred people. In such societies, people ambitious of social prestige, therefore, turn to professions other than producing wealth, which command high social esteem and give them power, *viz.*, military, law, literature, theology, journalism, music, etc. For economic development, it is essential that those people should be held in the highest esteem who are actively engaged in the production of wealth. Social status of a person should depend upon the wealth produced by him and not upon that inherited by him.

11. Law and Order

Strict maintenance of law and order is very essential for economic development. Incentive to produce wealth will be lacking if the people are not sure to enjoy the fruit of their labour. In several underdeveloped countries governments are weak and internal disorders frequent.

12. Economic, Social and Legal Institutions

Prevalence of joint family system acts as a disincentive to enterprise. A person won't have the incentive to work hard if he knows that he has to share the fruit of his hard labour with a number of other persons. Individualistic system of society is more conducive to economic development. The institution of veil deprives the economy of a considerable portion of the working population.

Incentive for enterprise will be lacking if the legal system of the country is defective and fails to secure a person the fruit of his efforts. A tenant, for instance, will have no incentive to make investment in land if the law does not provide for compensation for the unexhausted investments at the time he vacates the land.

Under private enterprise system, communal ownership of property is not very conducive to enterprise. An enterprising cultivator, for instance, cannot effect improvements on land if it is held jointly by the whole community. Institution of the individual ownership of property is very essential for economic development.

Innovation should not be hindered by law or by custom. In certain societies, techniques and rituals in agriculture are prescribed by priests and any person introducing innovations is considered to be committing sacrilege. Even in advanced countries, there exists considerable opposition to the introduction of improved technology.

Every person in society should be provided full scope for economic advancement so that talent potentialities do not go unutilised in persons who are denied opportunity to show their worth. In many backward countries, persons born in poor families do not get an opportunity to demonstrate their abilities. If provided with an adequate opportunity, some of them may contribute to the national product far more than that contributed by most of those who get opportunity simply because they are born in rich families. Opportunity for economic advancement is denied to a large section of society not only by inequalities in the distribution of wealth but also by caste, colour and creed bars. Rapid economic development is not possible if vertical mobility is hindered either by law or by custom.

Potential enterprisers should not be denied opportunity to organise new units of production. Opportunity to potential enterprisers may be denied in a number of ways. Enterprisers coming from certain classes may not be permitted to buy land. Banking concerns may discriminate against certain classes of enterprisers. Horizontal mobility of resources is no less important than the vertical social mobility. In certain industries, entry of new enterprisers may be excluded by the existing monopolistic organisations.

Above all, leaders of the country at all levels—politicians, teachers, engineers, doctors, business leaders, trade unionists, priests, journalists—should desire advancement of the country and work for it honestly and sincerely. No progress can occur if the leaders who are to guide and inspire the masses are corrupt and selfish.

The economic, social, political and institutional obstacles to rapid economic development mentioned above should not discourage us in launching a development programme in underdeveloped countries. In their earlier stages of development, Western countries were not free from such obstacles. Experience shows that once the development process starts, these obstacles start disappearing gradually. Calculation replaces traditions and deep-rooted habits. The force of social and religious prohibitions weakens. People develop a strong desire for material advancement. New techniques and products become more acceptable. Economic and materialistic values get higher place in life. Vertical mobility increases. Nuclear families replace joint families. Rural workers get accustomed to factory discipline. Appropriately designed education and publicity can considerably help in rapidly removing social and institutional obstacles.

Factors Inhibiting Growth

20

1. Introductory

The underdeveloped countries do not present a uniform pattern of underdevelopment nor do they pose problems of the same nature. It is, therefore, not possible to locate a set of common factors which inhibit development in these countries.

Broadly speaking, the reasons for the underdevelopment of the underdeveloped countries are implicit in the characteristics of these countries described in chapter 17. Keeping aside the abnormality caused either by local conditions or historical forces, it is certainly possible to lay hand on sufficient common forces which have inhibited the growth of these economies. There may be differences in the intensity of various inhibitory factors but all the same they have hindered development in most of the underdeveloped countries. An analysis of such common factors is attempted below.

The historical forces and inhibitory factors have worked for such a long time in underdeveloped countries that it has become difficult to distinguish between cause and consequence of underdevelopment. Further, the process of circular causation has been going on in poor countries for such a long period and has affected their economies so deeply that many obstacles to development are both a cause and consequence of poverty. There appears to be a lot of justification in Nurkse's remark "a country is poor because it is poor."[1] Thus poverty, the main characteristic of underdevelopment, is both a cause and consequence of underdevelopment in poor countries.

2. Vicious Circle of Poverty

Market imperfections, underdeveloped resources, illiteracy, low technological levels and capital deficiency operating in a combined

1. R. Nurkse, *Problems of Capital Formation in Underdeveloped Countries* (Oxford, 1957), p. 4.

manner result in low productivity in the underdeveloped countries. Lower productivity means low real incomes which in turn means small savings and investment or deficiency of capital leading to low productivity. "Thus, deficiency of real resources and low productivity constitute the basis for the saying 'a country is poor because it is poor'."[2] Ragnar Nurske explained this phenomenon as below:

> It implies a circular constellation of forces tending to act and react upon one another in such a way as to keep a poor country in a state of poverty. A situation of this sort, relating to a country as a whole, can be summed up in the trite proposition: 'a country is poor because it is poor.'[3]

The things are made worse by the cumulative nature of the phenomenon.

> The poignancy of the situation becomes more clear when it is discovered that causative circular reactions of these negative factors are of a cumulative nature. A push downward releases forces which depress the country to a still lower level. The tragic process of levels sliding downwards goes on operating continuously resulting in further depression of a poor economy. The common saying 'nothing succeeds like success' (emanating from the concept of an upward spiral) has its opposite counterpart, too, 'nothing fails like failure.'[4]

3. Inhibited Capital Growth

Underdevelopment is more or less synonymous with deficiency of capital which gives rise to adverse effects in the entire national economy. It is very important to analyse as to how the accumulation of capital has been inhibited in the underdeveloped countries. Investible funds come from three classes of society: the poor people, middle class and the rich.

The poor class has hardly any surplus to invest. It consists mostly of cultivators depending on subsistence farming for their livelihood. They are mostly uneducated and ruled by habits and

2. Gerald M. Meier and Robert E. Baldwin, *Economic Development, Theory, History, and Policy* (New York, 1957), p. 319.
3. Nurkse, n. 1, p. 4.
4. D.S. Nag, *Problems of Underdeveloped Economy* (Agra, 1962), p. 94.

customs of the old order. They do not have much desire for economic development. A paper prepared by the Secretariat of the Food and Agriculture Organisation of the United Nations sums up the position as below:

> A major limitation on the amount of internal investment in underdeveloped countries is their very low production and incomes per capita and their low rate of saving out of that income. Almost all that they produce is actually needed, either directly or through interchange in international trade, to maintain or increase an exceedingly low standard of living. It is difficult to restrict consumption further to increase capital. That is why even very inexpensive equipment, such as a scythe or wheel hoe, or a simple draught animal is beyond the means of millions of small farmers. The available data suggest that net voluntary savings in most underdeveloped countries are usually very low.[5]

The middle class is a second source of investible funds. The numerical strength of this class is very small in industrially backward countries. A large middle class is the result of industrialisation and consequent urbanisation. The entrepreneurial element in this group has a tendency to follow the policy of minimum risk. They engage themselves mostly in occupations of a stable and secure nature like marketing and other services. Their individual savings are not adequate for the sizeable capital requirements of modern large scale industrial establishment. As the corporate and institutional finance is not adequately developed, they are handicapped in mobilising capital from the money market. They find it difficult to compete with foreign manufactured goods on the basis of their small factories built mostly with their personal savings. They are also handicapped in securing technical personnel of the right type. They, therefore, have a tendency to invest, whatever they can save, in traditional activities, hoarding in the form of bullion and ornaments, building house property, etc.

Most of the savings in the underdeveloped countries come from high-income group people. The high-income people belong mostly to the landed class which lacks entrepreneurial spirit. The

5. United Nations, *Methods of Financing Economic Development in Underdeveloped Countries* (New York, 1949), p. 72.

environments in which they have been living and their traditional attitudes are not very congenial to the entrepreneurial ventures in the field of industry and manufacture. The savings of this class tend "to be put into real estate, gold, jewellery, commodity hoards and hoards of foreign and domestic currency."[6] The hoarding tendency appears to be strongest in South and South-East Asia and in the Middle East. It has been estimated that in some countries in this area, private gold hoards are as large as 10 per cent of the national income.[7]

Another class of items on which the rich people have a tendency to spend their savings are residential dwellings and buildings, land, purchase, church buildings, temples, tombs and monuments. The landed class does not have much interest in using savings for productive investment.

Export trade is another field in which the rich people invest their savings because they believe that it involves less risk than investment in industries catering to potential domestic demand. The foreign rulers also developed the colonial countries into foreign trade-oriented economies. Local capital was given several facilities and protection if invested in promoting the export of raw materials and the import of finished goods.

So far we were discussing the process of capital formation in the private sector. The question arises that if the private sector has failed, why has the Government not come forward to accelerate the rate of capital formation. For answering this question, the underdeveloped countries have to be divided into two categories, one having national governments and the other ruled by foreign governments. In the latter type of countries, the primary interest of the foreign governments was to develop these countries as sources of raw materials required, and the markets for manufactured goods produced, by the industries of the ruling countries. They, therefore, made investments to facilitate the export of raw materials rather than to develop the country in an integrated manner. The development of railways, ports, canals and commercial crops in India was guided by the self-interest of the imperial governments.

---

6. Nurkse, n. 1, p. 26.
7. United Nations, *Measures for the Economic Development of Underdeveloped Countries* (New York, 1951), p. 35.

The same was true of investments in the plantations in Ceylon, rubber plantations in Malaya, sugar plantations in Indonesia and the tin mines of South-East Asia and the teak and oil industry of Burma.

A different set of factors was responsible for lack of capital accumulation on the part of politically independent countries. The political instability consumed a substantial part of government's resources and energies. These countries were mainly engaged in defending their territories either against foreign attack or against internal disorder. The rulers had a tendency to indulge in conspicuous consumption. Pomp and show at the court rather than the economic welfare of the masses determined their pattern of expenditure. A major portion of the expenditure, therefore, was of an unproductive nature and failed to develop the economies.

4. Backwash Effects of Internal Forces

During the period of last hundred and fifty years, the operation of economic and non-economic forces, through trade and capital movements, has produced 'backwash effects' on underdeveloped economies. The cumulative process has led to positive gains for advanced countries and those for the underdeveloped countries.

The opening of trade brought a substantial expansion in the export of raw materials from the underdeveloped countries. This promoted production of primary products employing mostly unskilled labour and exposed underdeveloped countries to the business fluctuations originating in advanced countries.

Though, during boom periods, the prices of raw materials rise more than those of manufactures, the underdeveloped countries are not able to take benefit of these. Because of market imperfections, structural maladjustments and lack of overhead capital, the plentiful foreign exchange earnings are dissipated. Often the foreign exchange is spent on the import of consumption goods rather than on that of capital goods and technical know-how.

Depression brings misery to the underdeveloped countries because the prices of raw materials decline more rapidly than those of manufactures. Foreign exchange earnings decline steeply. The inflow of foreign capital also declines under such conditions. The balance of payments becomes unfavourable.

Myrdal rightly maintains that expansion of the exports of primary products tends to have 'backwash' effects and to strengthen the forces maintaining 'stagnation or regression.'[8] The economic history of every country bears testimony to the fact that expansion of exports of primary products drains out national resources if the foreign exchange earned therefrom is not invested productively.

The same is true of foreign investments. These were made mostly in the production of primary goods meant for export. A substantial amount of foreign capital was invested in railways and other public utilities made secure through the guarantee system followed by colonial governments. As the enterprises in which foreign capital was invested were owned and controlled by foreigners, there was a heavy outflow from the national income in the form of interest charges, profits and salaries of foreign personnel.

5. Impact of Imperialism

To take an objective view of the effects of colonial policies, it may be mentioned that the foreign governments did build up profits, roads, railways, irrigation projects etc. Though the primary objective of these activities was to expand the colonial type of trade and to help in the maintenance of law and order, these did create a frame, which could be used for economic development. The machinery for law and order created by them is a prerequisite for economic development. They also paid attention, though on a limited scale, to public health and sanitation and primary higher education.

The adverse effects of the colonial policies, however, far outweighed the beneficial effects. The ruling countries developed the colonies as a perennial source of raw materials and a market for the manufactured goods of the mother country. The cheap local labour and natural resources were ruthlessly exploited to serve the interests of the imperial economies. Several measures were taken to ensure these markets to the manufacturing industries of the 'mother country.' Protective duties discriminating in favour of imports from the 'mother country' were levied. Measures were taken to obstruct the growth of local industries. The ruling power more or less monopolised the colonial country's trade. This limited the scope of

8. Gunnar Myrdal, *Economic Theory and Underdeveloped Regions* (Indian Edition, 1958), p. 64.

markets in which the colonial country could buy and sell which resulted into a deterioration in its terms of trade.

Fortunately, the colonial system is, now, under liquidation. Many colonies have obtained independence and are in a position to launch development programmes on progressive lines.

6. Market Imperfections

The market imperfections like factor immobility, price rigidity, ignorance of market conditions, rigid social stucture, and lack of specialisation have created frictions and inhibited the achievement of an optimum allocation of resources. The productive resources have remained unemployed and employment has been misdirected leading to a lower efficiency of production.

In a world of perfect factor mobility, the factors of production have a tendency to move from one industry to another till their marginal productivities are equalised in all industries. In the under-developed countries, however, there are a number of workers whose marginal productivity is almost zero and yet they do not move to industries where their productivity would be higher. Similarly, capital is also not efficiently allocated. Customs, habits, and attitudes towards alternative employment are powerful obstacles to the easy movement of capital and labour. Poverty is another factor which inhibits mobility of labour. Many workers are too poor to bear the costs of movement and re-employment.

Another imperfection is the lack of knowledge of market opportunities. Workers are unaware of better employment opportunities elsewhere and producers are unaware of existing domestic and international market possibilities. Monopolistic practices create still another set of imperfections which cause malallocation.

In such a situation, it is possible for an underdeveloped country to increase its national income through a more efficient allocation of resources without any change in its capital stock, natural resources, and population.

Factors in Economic Development

21

1. Economic Factors

The important economic factors which affect economic development are:

(1) Land.

(2) Labour.

(3) Capital.

(4) Entrepreneurship.

(5) Technology.

(6) Mechanisms and other circumstances which determine the allocation of factors of production and of finished goods and services, *viz.*, price system, extent of market, division of labour, inter-sector balance and aggregate demand, etc.

(7) Major economic decision makers and the environments in which economic decisions are made.

Factors other than the first, fourth and seventh have been discussed in detail in later chapters. Let us briefly discuss these three factors one by one.

2. Land

The term 'land' is used here in a wider sense including not only soil but everything bestowed by nature. The quantity and quality of the available natural resources is an important factor determining the rate of economic development. Natural resources include character of the soil, the forest resources, topography as favouring or hindering cheap transportation, mineral resources, the availability of water-power, and rainfall and temperature. The geographical situation of the country considerably influences the opportunities for profitable trade. Countries situated near foreign markets and sources of supply have greater opportunities for foreign trade.

The recent emergence of trade restrictions has increased the importance of natural resources still further. In the golden days of free trade, a country could achieve a high per capita income even without possessing rich natural resources. It could import raw materials and export them in processed form at highly profitable prices. Herein lies the secret of the prosperity of the United Kingdom and some other European countries. With the emergence of trade controls, the opportunities for this kind of trade have considerably decreased.

The importance of land has a tendency to decrease with the advancement of an economy. As the economy advances, capital accumulates and technology improves. Improvements in technology reduce the input of land per unit of output. These make possible substitution of other factors of production, particularly capital, for land. With the advancement of an economy, services requiring little land from a larger and larger portion of the total product. But land is fixed in quantity while the supply of other factors of production can be increased. Consequently, other things remaining the same, growth of an economy will have a tendency to increase the relative scarcity of land. If the rate of discovery of unknown land and/or the rate of improvement in technology economising lands and substituting other factors of production for land is greater than that of the growth of other factors of production, the relative scarcity of land may not increase. "... despite the increasing importance of 'services' in the total product of economically advanced countries, a fairly large amount of 'goods' appears to be a necessary prior condition."[1]

3. Entrepreneurship

Schumpeter in his theory of economic development assigns a central role to the entrepreneur. Entrepreneur is the main driving force in economic development. Describing the functions of an entrepreneur, Schumpeter writes:

> ... the function of entrepreneurs is to reform or revolutionize the pattern of production by exploiting an untried technological possibility for producing a new commodity or producing an old one in a new way, by opening up a new

---

1. Joseph L. Fisher, "The Role of Natural Resources" in H.F.Williamson and J.L. Buttrick (ed.), *Economic Development* (New York, 1954), p. 22.

> source of supply, of materials or a new outlet for products, by reorganising an industry and so on.... This kind of activity is primarily responsible for recurrent 'propensities' that revolutionize the economic organism and the recurrent 'recessions' that are due to the disequilibrating impact of the new products or methods. To undertake such new things is difficult and constitutes distinct economic function, first, because they lie outside of the routine tasks which everybody understands and, secondly, because environment resists in many ways that vary, according to social conditions, from simple refusal either to finance or to buy a new thing, to physical attack on the man who tries to produce it. To act with confidence beyond the range of familiar beacons and to overcome that resistance requires aptitudes that are present in only a small fraction of the population and that define the entrepreneurial type as well as the entrepreneurial function. This function does not essentially consist in either investing anything or otherwise creating the conditions which the enterprise exploits. It consists in getting this done.[2]

In underdeveloped countries, the central role is played not by the entrepreneur but by the government acting in social and national interests. Welfare of the masses rather than the maximisation of profits of the entrepreneur is the main guiding force. In underdeveloped countries, the divergence between social and private returns is so wide that the entrepreneur interested only in maximising his private profits cannot be assigned a central role. Initiation of the development process requires considerable investment in social and economic overheads, the return from which is mostly indirect and not taken into account by the entrepreneur. In underdeveloped countries, the innovating class of entrepreneurs is not very important because innovations do not play an important role and the process of development primarily involves the application of known technology existing in advanced countries. The emergence of planning has thrown the entrepreneur in the background.

> No longer is he the hero of the piece, admired by economists, and, more important, by his compatriots. The law does not

2. Joseph A. Schumpeter, *Capitalism, Socialism and Democracy* (London, 1944), p. 132.

> aid and abet him and his property interests on all sides, as it did during the hey-day of capitalism. He seems to be regarded as a byproduct of economic development, to be tolerated because of his usefulness but to be watched and curbed because of his selfish propensities. If in most of the less developed countries his wealth escapes heavy taxation, it is mainly due to administrative inadequacies.[3]

Loss of faith in *laissez faire* policy and the emergence of socialistic ideology has considerably decreased the importance of entrepreneur even in developed countries. Schumpeter himself predicted the ultimate fall of the entrepreneur.

> A more or less stationary state would ensue.... There would be nothing left for entrepreneurs to do. They would find themselves in much the same situation as generals would in a society perfectly sure of permanent peace.[4]

> The social function (of an entrepreneur)[5] is already losing importance and is bound to lose it at an accelerating rate in the future even if the economic process itself of which the entrepreneur was the prime mover went on unabated. For, on the one hand, it is much easier now than it has been in the past to do things that lie outside familiar routine—innovation itself is being reduced to routine. Technological progress is increasingly becoming the business of teams of trained specialists who turn out what is required and make it work in predictable ways. The romance of earlier commercial adventure is rapidly wearing away because so many more things can be strictly calculated that had of old to be visualized in a flash of genius.... Thus, economic progress tends to become depersonalized and automatized. Bureau and committee work tends to replace individual action.[6]

---

3. Henry C. Wallich, "Some Notes Towards a Theory of Derived Development" A.N. Agarwala and S.P. Singh (eds.), *The Economics of Underdevelopment* (Bombay, 1958), p. 191.
4. Schumpeter, n. 2, p. 131.
5. Words within parentheses added.
6. Schumpeter, n. 2, pp. 132-33.

4. Decision-makers

In a private enterprise economy, most of the important decisions are made by the private entrepreneurs. In a planned economy, state is the primary decision-making authority. Decisions have to be made regarding the allocation of resources between various sectors, selection of techniques, the ratios in which the different factors are to be combined, division of the product into saving and investment etc. The decision maker is expected to accomplish what the impersonal price mechanism cannot. Decision-makers play the central role in economic development. If the decision makers are not efficient and competent, considerable productive resources may be wasted. Productive resources may remain unemployed or employed in less productive fields and consequently the rate of development slowed. On the other hand, even if productive resources are limited, competent decision-makers can raise the rate of development by making the best utilisation of the available limited resources and also, in the long run, by raising the supply of resources themselves.

The decision-makers, however, may not be able to give the best to society if in exercising their skill and ability, they are hindered by the prevailing environments. The environments refer to elements like the state of arts; law and order: monetary and fiscal systems; the talent recruitment system and the reward system; the land-holding and the property system; price, income and market structures etc. The state can play an important role in improving the environments in which the decision-makers have to function.

5. Non-economic Factors

In addition to economic factors, non-economic factors play an important role in economic development. Economic and non-economic factors act and react on each other. Economic changes have far-reaching political and social consequences. Similarly, political and social changes have important economic consequences. Ignoring or assuming away non-economic factors leaves the economic theory extremely sterile. The motivation for economic development is provided as much by non-economic forces as by economic forces. The non-economic factors are crucial to the theoretical explanation of differences in growth rates in the advanced and poor countries. The distinction between economic and non-economic factors has aroused sharp criticism from several economists. Jacob Viner remarks:

> It is incumbent on the economist...to recognise and proclaim that economic improvement is not merely a matter of more capital, or more coal in the ground, but also of a growth of effectiveness of management and of manual effort through better education, better health, better motivation, and better political and social organisation. If he fails to do so, he is liable to himself throwing the blame for national poverty wholly on physical circumstances beyond human remedy, or on factors external to that economy, to the neglect of internal human, social, political and moral factors which may carry a large part of the true responsibility.[7]

Gunnar Myrdal states:

> In reality there is no distinction between facts corresponding to our traditional scholastic division of social science into separate divisions. A realistic analysis of problems can never stop at such lines of division. The distinction between factors that are 'economic' and those that are 'non-economic,' is, indeed, a useless and non-sensical device from the point of view of logic.... It will have to be discarded as illogical and, consequently, misleading. Economic analysis will have to deal with all the relevant factors if it wants to be realistic; general economic theory will have to become social theory...concrete problems are never simply economical, sociological, psychological and political. A theory of underdevelopment and development which works only with 'economic variables' is for logical reasons doomed to be unrealistic and thus irrelevant.[8]

There is, however, the problem that if all factors—economic, political, social, cultural, religious and psychological—are considered together, the phenomenon becomes so complex as to make any generalisations almost impossible. Because social, political, cultural,

---

7. Jacob Viner cited in J.W. Williams, *Economic Stability in a Changing World,* p. 16.
8. Gunnar Myrdal, *Economic Theory and Underdeveloped Regions,* pp. 22, 112, 175.

psychological and several economic elements are not amenable to rigorous treatment, there is a tendency on the part of the economists to concentrate only on a few variables, assuming away all other variables. Recently, it has become a fashion to build elegant models taking into consideration only a few variables and assuming away all realities. If the assumptions behind these models are not fully kept in view, use of these may lead to wholly unrealistic and grossly mistaken conclusions and policy recommendations. As the economy advances, however, the influence of non-economic factors diminishes.

> In backward countries, exogenous or non-economic factors exercise relatively most influence; the autonomy of an economic system as such increases as the society including it progresses, and therewith the applicability of economic theory.[9]

9. Joseph J. Spengler, "Economic Factors in Economic Development," *American Economic Review, Papers and Proceedings*, 47 (May, 1957), p. 42.

Population and Economic Development

22

1. Introductory

The economic well-being of a country depends more than anything else on the quality of its inhabitants. Adam Smith wrote, in the opening words of *The Wealth of Nations,* "The annual labour of every nation is the fund which originally supplies it with all the necessaries and conveniences of life...." The past and present human effort and ability are the ultimate source of all economic goods and services.

As recently as ten or fifteen years ago, it was a matter of lively discussion and controversy as to whether or not the underdeveloped countries of South Asia were overpopulated and in what sense. But, now, it is generally accepted that these countries have entered a critical phase of sharply accelerated population growth, and that the prospects for successful economic development are crucially related to population trends.

The rapidly rising population is a phenomenon common to all underdeveloped countries. But as regards the anticipated increase in the size of the labour force in relation to natural resources, particularly, land resources, the emerging population crises are more specifically an Asian phenomenon so far as poor countries are concerned.[1] Outside of South Asia, only China, North Africa (including Egypt), and the Caribbean part of Latin America are confronted with a similar situation. Most parts of the continental Latin America are sparsely populated and possess substantial untapped natural resources which can be exploited at manageable costs by modern technology. In West Asia, the same is the case with Turkey, Syria, Iraq and probably, Iran. In most parts of Africa, a large labour force would not only be compatible with economic development but may be a pre-condition for it.

1. Gunnar Myrdal, *Asian Drama*, Vol. II (New York, 1958), pp. 1392-93.

2. Dimension of Population

Population has a number of dimensions influencing economic development of which the following important may be mentioned:

(*i*) Quality of population referring to factors like level of education, quality of health etc.

(*ii*) Size of population, *i.e.,* the number of persons occupying the country or any other specified territory.

(*iii*) Rate of growth of population, *i.e.,* the percentage by which the population is increasing or decreasing each year.

(*iv*) Composition of population, *i.e.,* the proportion of population which is male or female, the proportion of population falling into different age groups etc.

(*v*) Distribution of population, *i.e.,* the proportion of working force attached to different occupations of the economy, the proportion of population living in different regions—say rural and urban etc.

(*vi*) Growth differentials, *i.e.,* differences in the rate of growth of different elements of population. We shall briefly discuss below the first four dimensions which are more important.

3. Quality of Population

Quality of population refers not only to racial or biological differences, which scientists have shown to be of minor importance, but also much more important differences arising from historical and cultural factors, from environments, quality of health, nutrition, and education, and from the quality of leadership provided by government and social elite. Quality of working population, including the rank-and-file of industrial and agricultural labour, the skilled engineers and technicians and the managerial and entrepreneurial elite, is an important factor determining the rate of development. For raising productivity of labour, it is very essential that masses are literate, healthy, and well fed, well clothed and well sheltered to be strong and energetic. In case labour force is inefficient, it will not be possible to take full advantage of rich natural resources, huge amounts of capital and superior technology.

4. Size of Population

Given the total product, the larger the size of the population, the lower will be the per capita income. Thus given the total product, the smaller the size of the population, the better it is. Large population, however, helps production in a number of ways. It provides a large market and thereby offers incentive for investment. Large population and large market provide greater scope for the division of labour which brings in a number of economies. Large population makes possible the exploitation of indivisible resources which cannot be exploited by a small population.

Size of Working Force: 'Working force' refers to that part of the population which is available for employment for productive purposes. The higher the proportion which the working population forms of the total population, the larger the possibilities for development. Size of the working population depends upon a number of factors, *viz.*, sex composition of the population, number of married women, distribution of population between different age groups, wants and tastes, degree of industrialisation or urbanisation, productivity, etc.

5. Change in Age Structure

The high fertility rates experienced in the South Asian countries have caused the age distribution of population to be skewed in the direction of high dependency burden. The populations of these countries contain a large number of children. A reduction in fertility rates would have the direct effect of decreasing the dependency burden. There would be fewer children to support.

A lower dependency burden would raise the per capita income. A rise in per capita income would mean a better standard of diet, clothing, housing, education and medical facilities which would be more pronounced in the poorest countries where particularly low levels of nutrition, health, and education depress the duration and efficiency of work. Further, at higher levels of per capita income, more can be saved and devoted to direct investment and the government can also squeeze out more in "forced savings" through taxation and other means. Both forms of saving would, after some time, tend-to increase per capita income still further, with cumulative effects similar to those of the initial rise in per capita income owing to a decline in the fertility rates. The decline in fertility rates would lower the costs and interruptions of work incidental to births. Lower fertility rates would also cause a decline in the mortality rate owing to a number of reasons, *viz.*, smaller number of maternal and infant deaths, better standards of living, and with progressively rising incomes, a broadened financial base for public health work. A fall in mortality rates, in turn, will raise incomes on account of the decline in illness associated therewith. There would also be a decrease in economic inconveniences and costs associated with every death, which are quite high in underdeveloped countries.

6. Rate of Growth of Population

Rate of population growth is an important factor determining the rate of economic development. History shows that growth in income has been followed by an increase in the rate of population growth. It is feared that, unless a comprehensive policy of population-control is vigorously followed, every increase in income may be dissipated by an increase in population. Effective control of population is considered to be an important pre-requisite for economic development.

All advanced countries have passed through three phases of population growth. In the first phase, both birth and death rates are high. During the second phase, birth rate continues high but death rate declines because of health services, more nutritious food, sanitary living etc., made possible by an increase in incomes; this results into a rapid increase in population. In the third phase, both birth and death rates become stable at a low level. Birth rate declines in the third phase because of a number of reasons. Urban industrial life removes ignorance and creates an awakening among the masses. Calculation takes the place of tradition. People start calculating the comparative pleasure from an additional child and from a rise in the standard of living. Availability of a large range of goods and means of recreation decreases the importance of sexual pleasure in life. Economic development increases social mobility. A person with a smaller family stands a better chance of not only raising himself but improving the status of his children. With economic advancement, children become less of an asset and more of an expense. The opportunities for child labour decrease and the cost of bringing up children increases because of the availability of greater opportunities for education and training. Advancement in civilisation brought about by economic development and urbanisation tends to replace joint family system by nuclear families consisting of wife and husband and their children. In a joint family, the responsibility for supporting children of a couple is widely diffused; this encourages early marriage and a large number of children. In a nuclear family, the obligations for supporting children are exclusively of the parents. People, therefore, tend to marry only when they can support a family; this tendency raises the normal age of marriage. Rise in the marriage age considerably lowers birth rate because the fertility is far higher in the earlier than in the latter period. Further, when parents alone are responsible for supporting their children, they tend to have a smaller number of children. When the death rate is high, people tend to have larger families to cover the risk of death of some children at one or the other stage. In trying to cover the risk of death they, often, overcompensate themselves. Decline in death rate brings a decline in birth rate by decreasing the need for having children to cover the risk of death.

Most of the advanced countries have passed through the first two phases of population growth and are living in the third phase of low birth and low death rates. Countries in the early stage of development are, generally, in the second phase of population-growth. In the early stages of development, birth rate continues high but death rate declines. Sometimes, birth rate may even rise because with the increase in income, people can afford larger families. Forces which reduce the birth rate have to overcome strong social resistances while the forces reducing death rate do not meet any such resistances. At this stage of development, if the rate of increase in income is not faster than the rate of population-growth there is the risk that the process of development may be frustrated. Rapid increase in population decreases the capacity to save. In some countries, savings are not sufficient to maintain even the per capita income with the population growing at current rates; per capita income in such countries is maintained with the funds borrowed abroad.

It is held by some that no development is possible till population growth has been controlled. Does it mean that we should wait for the development programme till the population growth is effectively controlled? Certainly not. Some population growth will occur even if the state does not follow a deliberate development policy. Growth in population through a decline in death rate cannot be checked by refraining from economic development. With the spread of medical knowledge, decline in birth rate is inevitable. No doubt, medical services will be availed of more fully at higher incomes, these won't remain unavailed at unchanged incomes. Medical services are a bare necessity and it is very probable that a part of the expenditure will be diverted to these from other less important items. Even in underdeveloped countries, some classes are well off and will make full use of the medical service with the spread of medical knowledge. Provision of medical services is considered to be one of the important functions of a government and every popular government will make best efforts to provide these even at unchanged incomes by diverting a part of its expenditure from less essential heads. Medical services are also provided by charitable organisations. Thus to a certain extent, spread of medical services is independent of the rate of growth in income; consequently, population will grow through a decline in death rate whether or not economic development takes place. If the efforts are not made to develop these countries, the growth of population will be checked by the Malthusian misery. Malthusian misery and catastrophes do not check the population-growth permanently. Population cut by the misery, epidemics, starvation, etc. retains its potentiality for growth. This may lead to repeated cycles of growth and decline in population.

If the growth of population is met by the same or by a quicker rate of economic development, the growth of population will be permanently checked after some time through the operation of forces which bring a decline in birth rate. If the rate at which income rises is more rapid than the rate of population-growth, standard of living will rise. Rise in the standard of living combined with new ways of life associated with economic development causes a decline in the birth rate. Ultimately, both birth and death rates become stable at a low level and development takes place at an accelerated rate. The second phase is likely to be shorter in presently developing countries than it was in the case of countries which were pioneers in the field of economic development. Evolution of ideas in the pioneering countries was a very slow process and took a long time. Once the ideas are evolved, these spread quickly. Mere spread of education will lower the birth rate irrespective of whether or not economic development is taking place. It is, of course, true that economic development will expedite the decline in birth rate. In spite of the comparatively advantageous position of the presently developing countries, stabilisation of birth and death rates at a low level through natural forces will take a long time. Meanwhile there may occur a large increase in population. Measures to control population, therefore, are very essential if the development is to be achieved at a fairly rapid rate.

Use of contraceptives is an important method of controlling the birth rate. In a primarily rural country, it, however, involves a number of difficulties. Most of the women are uneducated and, therefore, it is difficult for them to learn and practise contraception. People are too poor to afford the high cost of contraceptives. Training of women in the use of contraceptives requires a large number of lady doctors which are not available in most of the underdeveloped countries. Use of contraceptives is, often, bitterly opposed on moral and religious grounds.

There are certain underdeveloped countries which suffer not from overpopulation but from underpopulation. The problem of both underpopulated and overpopulated countries can be simultaneously solved by encouraging migration. International migration was an important factor in the development of newly settled regions. In present days, however, because of certain political and economic factors, it is doubtful, if international migration can be achieved on a sufficiently large scale. Movement and resettlement of labour requires considerable expenditure in the emigrant as well as in the immigrant countries. Any migration on a fairly large scale requires considerable expansion of transportation. Most of the demand in advanced countries is for skilled labour of which there is shortage within the underdeveloped countries themselves. Immigration is not welcome in advanced countries even when faced with a fear of stagnation. Stimulation of consumption, increase in public expenditure and foreign investments are preferred to immigration for dispelling stagnation. The prejudice against the immigration of non-white people is particularly marked. Partly it is because of the fear that low standard of living of the non-white people will lower the wage rates and thereby the standard of living of the local labour. Racial complexes is another factor obstructing labour movements.

Further, if migration is permitted, it is mostly the young, enterprising and adventurous people who will migrate abroad.

Local development of the country will suffer if the efficient labour migrates abroad and only the aged, incapable and incompetent labour is left behind.

Sometimes it has been suggested that population-growth be controlled through fiscal devices. It is, however, difficult to devise a system which discourages larger families and is also equitable.

Development will be followed by an increase in the rate of growth of population only if the consumption is permitted to rise alongwith the increase in incomes. Increase in the rate of growth of population can be checked by diverting the increased incomes towards investment rather than towards consumption. This method of controlling population-growth will have the additional advantage of accelerating the pace of development. Once the development has reached the stage at which the factors which restrict population growth—urbanisation, education, break-up of the joint family system, etc.—have become operative, increase in consumption can be permitted without any risk of explosive growth of population.

Population-growth, however, is not an unmixed evil. In certain respects it helps the development process. Economies with growing population can adjust to changed conditions more easily than the economies with stationary populations; newcomers can adapt to changed conditions more easily than the old ones. High rate of population growth expands markets and thereby offers incentive for investment. Increase in population lowers wage rates and thus raises the share of profits in total output which stimulates investment. Profits constituted an important source of investment during the development phase of the present developed countries. At the same time, we should not neglect the possibility of lower wages encouraging substitution of capital and thus slowing the rates of capital formation.

Most of the advantages of growing population, however, relate to latter stages of growth when the supply of savings tends to exceed investment opportunities. At this stage, the growing population maintains the growth process by expanding markets. Expanding markets are essential for maintaining the marginal efficiency of capital. In the absence of expanding markets, the economy will move towards a state of secular stagnation. Growing population, however, is not the only way of expanding markets. In the absence of a growing population, markets can be expanded through fiscal and monetary measures which stimulate consumption and investment. Gap between savings and investments opportunites can be filled up by government expenditure.

7. Population Policy

In framing a policy for fighting the problem of overpopulation, the South Asian countries are bound by one rigid value premise which has important practical consequences, that is, the efforts to check the rapid rate of growth of population have to be concentrated only on the fertility factor. Complacency about or even tolerance of a high rate of mortality because it keeps down the rate of growth of population is simply not permissible. All that is reasonably possible must be done to check diseases and premature deaths irrespective of its effect on the rate of growth of population. This value premise is accepted throughout the civilised world.

Measures to lower the birth rate have to be based on the principle of voluntary parenthood, which is, in fact, the basis of population policies in almost all countries. People have to be induced through various ways to have a smaller number of children. Knowledge about birth control must be spread widely and the most effective means to carry it out made available to the masses.

For creating a motivation for birth control, some people have suggested economic penalization of the families with a larger number of children or rewarding those having a smaller number of children. But no country has done this in actual practice. The maximum that has been done is to deprive larger families of certain benefits available from the government, *e.g.*, denial of maternity leave after a certain number of births, limiting health facilities to a certain maximum number of children etc. The reason is obvious. Since having a larger number of children is the major cause of poverty, such measures would penalise the relatively poor and subsidize the relatively well off. Such a result would not only be contrary to principle of equity but would also be detrimental to the health of the poor families and thus to that of the growing generation.[2]

On the other hand, the South Asian countries should avoid, as far as possible, redistributional reforms in favour of families with a large number of children, who will tend to be poorest and most in need of aid, lest they thereby encourage childbearing. The two

---

2. Gunnar Myrdal, *Asian Drama*, Vol. II. (New York, 1968), pp. 1502-04.

objectives of checking fertility and improving the living conditions of children therefore appear to conflict with each other. But the conflict arises mostly when redistributional reforms are carried out by means of cash payments to parents. No doubt, there is an element of redistribution in everything that is done for children, from expanding health, educational, and training facilities to providing school meals, the risk of stimulating childbearing is minimized if the benefits are provided to children in kind and not to parents in cash.

Once the fertility rates are brought down, the population policy should be directed towards an improvement in the quality of population and the welfare of families. The policy of bringing down the birth rate would in itself improve the quality of population and the welfare of children. The children will share the increase in per capita income resulting from a decline in the fertility rate. Further, it is natural that the birth control efforts would be concentrated more on parents who are poor and already have a large number of children. If these efforts are successful, living conditions for the children already born will be improved.

In recent years, many South Asian countries have been groping towards a public policy of bringing down fertility through birth control. India and Pakistan have already started a birth control programme with great vigour. Ceylon and Thailand have permitted or sponsored studies and pilot projects, and Ceylon and Malaya have given government support to private organisations for 'family planning.' Some other countries have also shown interest in formulating a policy of population control. But no country in South Asia has yet succeeded in bringing down the fertility rates to any significant extent. Fertility rates have not declined even in India, which has pursued the policy of birth control most vigorously. The meagre gains from birth control policy have been offset by a decline in mortality rates and a relaxation of fertility-depressing customs.

Occupation Structure and Economic Development

23

1. Classification of Production

For analytical purposes, production is, generally, divided into the following three main classes: (1) primary production including agricultural and pastoral production, mining, fishing, forestry and hunting; (2) secondary production including manufacturing, building construction and public works, and gas and electricity supply and (3) tertiary production covering the rest of the activities, the principal of which are distribution, transport, public administration, domestic services and all other activities producing non-material goods.

2. General Principles

An analysis of the statistics of occupation structure of various countries leads to the following general principles[1]: (1) Per capita, real income is low in which the percentage of total population employed in primary production is high. (2) Barring a few exceptional cases (*e.g.*, New Zealand, Australia, etc.), per capita value productivity is higher in secondary and tertiary occupations than in primary occupations. (3) Agricultural productivity itself (both per acre and per capita) is higher in countries in which the percentage of total population employed in agriculture is lower than in those in which percentage of agricultural population is higher. (4) In industrial countries, secondary employment tends to fall and tertiary employment tends to rise.

3. Optimum Occupation Pattern

An occupation pattern will be non-optimum if the national output can be increased by transferring workers from certain occupations to others. There are certain occupations, however, which may be less productive but are still very essential for the

1. Bhabatosh Datta, *The Economics of Industrialisation* (Calcutta, 1957) p. 68.

country. Take the case of defence services. If the workers employed in defence services are transferred to agriculture or industry, total national output will be increased. Transfer of workers from defence to other occupations, however, may not be very desirable for political reasons. To take another case, it is considered desirable for a country that it should, as far as possible, be self-sufficient in food and essential raw materials. Free trade and multilateral balancing permanently assured, no country need produce its own food and agricultural raw materials if the workers can be employed more productively in other occupations. In the actual world, a country may find it difficult to obtain the required quantity of food, and raw materials because of a number of reasons, *viz.*, export restrictions, payment difficulties, strained political relations with food-producing countries, overall shortage of food, war, transportation difficulties etc. Thus while considering changes in occupation-structure, care should be taken that production of essential goods and services is not decreased.

A more appropriate and more realistic criterion for judging the desirability of a change in occupation-structure, therefore, is that total net output can be increased without any decrease in the output of goods and services considered essential for the country. According to this criterion, occupation structure in most of the underdeveloped countries is non-optimum. Marginal productivity of labour in agriculture is almost zero (sometimes even negative). If a portion of workers is transferred from agriculture to other occupations, production in agriculture, even with unchanged techniques, capital and skills, will remain unaffected. This was well demonstrated during the war when the transfer of a portion of workers from agriculture to war occupations left the agricultural output almost unaffected. In cases in which the marginal productivity of labour is negative in agriculture, transfer of workers from agriculture to other occupations will increase production not only in other occupations but also in agriculture itself. Experience in advanced countries shows that a decline in agricultural population has, generally, been associated with an increase in total net output, increase in agricultural output per worker, and increase in total agricultural output.

A change in occupation structure cannot be considered in isolation. It has to be considered along with the change in the stock of capital, technology and other resources. In most of the underdeveloped countries, there is little possibility of changing the occupation-structure without a vast amount of expenditure on the formation of capital and skills. The increase in output from a change in occupation-structure may be partly or wholly because of a change in the stock of capital and technology that is associated with the change in occupation-structure. Larger output per worker in secondary and tertiary occupations may simply be owing to a larger amount of capital associated with workers in these occupations. Desirability of a change in occupation-structure will be established only if it can be demonstrated that more output can be obtained by using a particular amount of productive resources combined with a particular number of workers from certain occupations than from others. Mere existence of surplus workers in agriculture is no proof of a non-optimum occupation structure. This demonstrates simply the existence of unemployment and tells nothing about the appropriateness of the occupation-structure. In underdeveloped countries, because of the existence of vast unemployment and underemployment, the marginal social cost of labour is almost zero. So long as marginal social cost of labour remains zero; optimum occupation-structure will be determined solely in reference to the marginal productivity of productive resources other than labour in different occupations. Case for a change in the occupation-structure will be established if it can be shown that the marginal productivity of productive resources other than labour is high in secondary and tertiary occupations than in primary occupations.

4. Productivity in Tertiary Occupations

It is widely believed that income per capita is the highest in the tertiary occupations and a transfer of workers from primary and secondary occupations to tertiary occupations constitutes economic progress.

> ... in every progressive economy there has been a steady shift of employment and investment from the essential 'primary' activities, without whose products life in even its most primitive forms would be impossible, to secondary activities of all kinds, and to a still greater extent into tertiary production.... The shifts of employment towards

> secondary and tertiary production revealed by the census are the inescapable reflection of economic progress.[2]
>
> Studying economic progress in relation to the economic structure of different countries, we find a very firmly established generalisation that a high average level of real income per head as always associated with a high proportion of the working population engaged in tertiary industries.... Low real income per head is always associated with a low proportion of the working population engaged in tertiary production and a high percentage in primary production, culminating in China, where 75-80 per cent of the population are primary producers. High average real income per head compels a large proportion of producers to engage in tertiary production.[3]

The proposition that per capita income is lowest in primary production, higher in secondary production and the highest in tertiary production does not hold good in all countries. In Australia and New Zealand, for instance, the *per captia* income is higher in primary occupations than in secondary and tertiary occupations. In several underdeveloped countries, the percentage of workers employed in tertiary occupations is fairly high. But this does not mean much. There is a marked difference between the tertiary occupations in developed and those in underdeveloped countries. In developed countries, tertiary occupations emerge out of a high level of incomes in other sectors. In underdeveloped countries, employment in tertiary occupations emerges out of a number of factors without the existence of high incomes in other occupations. Personal services form an important part of tertiary employment in underdeveloped countries. This is the result of gross inequalities in the distribution of wealth and income. Labour being very cheap, rich people have a tendency to keep a whole army of servants, often, just for prestige purpose. This kind of employment is not possible in developed countries because of very high wage rates. Distributive services form another important part of tertiary employment. Increase in primary and secondary production increases the demand

---

2. A.G.B. Fisher, *Economic, Progress and Social Security* (London, 1964), pp. 6-7.
3. Colin Clark, *The Conditions of Economic Progress* (London, 1940).

for distributive services but the mere existence of a large number of persons in distributive services does not mean prosperity.

> Petty retail trading is...enormously expanded in overpopulated economies; each trader makes only a few sales; markets are crowded with stalls, and if the number of stalls were greatly reduced the consumers would be no whit worse off....[4]

In developed countries, tertiary employment is mostly in occupations like commerce, transport, banking, entertainment and recreation, etc. which exist along with prosperity of the whole economy.

> We should thus distinguish between the 'low-income' type of tertiary employment and the high-income types, between service occupations, that are poverty induced and those that are prosperity induced. An overpopulated agricultural country requires not only a shift in its occupation structure from primary employment to secondary and tertiary, but also from low-income varieties of secondary and tertiary employment to high-income types.[5]

Tertiary occupations in advanced countries are highly capital-intensive, *e.g.*, transportation, banking, commerce, etc. Tertiary occupations in underdeveloped countries, on the other hand, require very small amount of capital, *e.g.*, personal services, retail trading, etc. Because of the requirement of lesser capital, it is easier for people to enter such occupations. Employment in such occupations, in fact, is a serious problem and there is need for shifting workers from such low-productivity occupations to high-productivity occupations.

---

4. W. Arthur Lewis, "Economic Development with Unlimited Supplies of Labour" A.N. Agarwala and S.P. Singh (eds.) *The Economics of Underdevlopment* (Bombay, 1958), p. 402.
5. Bhabatosh Datta, *The Economics of Industrialisation* (Calcutta, 1960) p. 129.

Capital Formation: Domestic Sources

24

1. Definition of Capital Formation

For a proper understanding of the problems of capital formation, it is very essential to be clear about the term capital formation. Capital is that part of the current produce which is used for further production instead of being immediately consumed. Capital formation means that a part of the current produce, instead of being used for immediate consumption, is directed to the making of goods which facilitate production, *viz.*, tools and instruments, machines, means of transportation and communications, canals, etc. Capital formation, thus, involves a sacrifice of immediate consumption for obtaining a larger flow of consumable goods in the future.

Capital formation may take the form of material goods or that of non-material goods, like health, knowledge, skill, etc. embodied in human beings. In what follows, we shall be concerned only with material goods. This, of course, should not be taken to mean that capital formation in the form of non-material goods is less important. We are here limiting ourselves to material goods because capital formation in the form of non-material goods is dealt with in a later chapter.

2. Importance of Capital

Emphasizing the importance of capital formation in economic development, Professor Lewis remarks:

> The central problem in the theory of economic development is to understand the process by which a community which was previously saving and investing 4 or 5 per cent of its national income or less, converts itself into an economy where voluntary saving is running at about 12 to 15 per cent of national income or more. This is the central problem because the central fact of economic development

> is rapid capital accumulation (including knowledge and skills with capital).[1]

It is a matter of common knowledge that, generally, per capita income is higher in countries employing a larger amount of capital per worker. Countries in which rapid progress is occurring have a considerably high rate of capital formation. Often, an important reason for the underdevelopment of the underdeveloped areas is the lack of capital to exploit the natural resources.

As our main interest lies in an increase in per capita income and not in total income alone, the factor which brings about the increase in production is very important. If the increase in total production is brought about by an increase in population, the per capita income may not rise or may even fall if the production is subject to the law of diminishing returns. On the other hand, if the increase in production is brought by an increase in the amount of capital or by an improvement in technology or by an expansion of entrepreneurship, total increase in production will be accompanied by an increase in per capita income. Thus the increase in total production brought about by an increase in the capital will add to economic welfare more than that brought about by an increase in the number of workers.

The role of capital formation, however, has often been overemphasized. Rate of economic development depends in addition to the rate of capital formation, on a number of other factors, *viz.*, economic and social institutions, natural resources, behaviour of the people, size and composition of the population, knowledge, historical accidents, political conditions etc. Provisions of capital alone may fail to develop a country if there does not exist suitable framework for its fruitful utilisation.

3. Forces Governing Accumulation of Capital

Formation of capital is determined by the demand for and supply of capital. The demand for capital depends upon the incentives to invest. The supply of capital depends upon the ability and the willingness to save. In underdeveloped countries, there

1. W. Arthur Lewis, "Economic Development with Unlimited Supplies of Labour," *The Manchester School* (May, 1954) reprinted in A.N. Agarwala and S.P. Singh (eds.) *The Economics of Underdevelopment* (Bombay, 1958), p. 416.

exists a vicious circle on both the demand and supply side of the capital formation. On the supply side, the capacity to save is low because of low incomes. Lack of savings leads to lack of capital in production. Lack of capital leads to low productivity and hence low incomes in turn mean low capacity to save. Thus the lack of capital moves in a vicious circle. On the demand side, there is a lack of incentives for investment because of low purchasing power of people. Lack of incentives for investment lead to lack of capital in production. Lack of capital leads to low productivity and hence low incomes. Low incomes in turn mean small purchasing power. It may be noted that low productivity and consequent low income is a factor common to both circles.

Demand Side: Apparently, it may seem ridiculous to talk of lack of demand for capital in underdeveloped countries, whichare marked by an acute shortage of capital. Lack of demand for capital does not refer to the need for capital from the point of view of the economy as a whole. Lack of demand for capital exists from the point of view of private investors. There is a lack of incentives for private investors. Lack of incentives for private investment arise primarily from the small size of the domestic market. It will not be profitable to instal modern capital equipment for the production of a commodity for which the demand is too small to keep the equipment, working for a fairly long period in the year.

The nature of the shortage of demand in undeveloped countries is widely different from that in developed countries. In developed countries the shortage of demand arises from oversaving. Such a shortage of demand can be easily remedied by monetary expansion. Shortage of demand in underdeveloped countries arises not from oversaving but from low incomes and consequent small purchasing power of the people. In other words, shortage of demand arises from shortage of supply to offer in exchange in the market. Mere monetary expansion cannot remedy such a shortage of demand. It will lead simply to inflation.

Size of market can be enlarged through a number of ways, *viz.*, monetary expansion, public expenditure, high-powered methods of salesmanship and advertising, increase in population, enlarging the country's territory, formation of customs unions or free trade areas between the adjacent countries, increase in productivity, etc. Raising productivity is the best and the most effective method of enlarging the size of the market. High-powered salesmanship and advertising cannot increase market if the people have no purchasing power to purchase additional goods. Increase in population will increase demand only for bare necessities for which there already exists sufficient market. Other things remaining unchanged, increase in population will lower the per capita income and further decrease the demand for goods other than bare necessities leading to a decrease in incentives for investment. Enlarging the territory won't increase demand for a commodity if the people inhabiting the old as well as the new territory are too poor to buy this commodity. The same holds true in case of the formation of customs unions and free trade areas. Further, the increase in demand brought about through an extension of the territory, or through the formation of customs unions and free trade areas, does not provide a coherent market. If the demand is thinly scattered over a wide area, considerable costs, of transportation will be involved. Transportation facilities are not sufficiently developed in most of the underdeveloped countries. Because of the lack of transportation facilities, it might not be possible to exploit the market which is scattered over a very wide area. Development of the transportation system in itself will increase the size of the market. Measures other than raising productivity can do very little towards enlarging the market for most of the commodities. Any considerable increase in the size of the market can be achieved only through raising productivity.

Ragnar Nurkse proposes simultaneous investment in a number of industries as method of enlarging the size of the market.

> A wave of capital investment in a number of different industries can economically succeed while any substantial application of capital by an individual entrepreneur in any particular industry may be blocked or discouraged by the limitations of pre-existing market.[2]

Say's law of demand applies more to underdeveloped than to developed countries. In underdeveloped countries, because of the very low standard of living, marginal propensity to consume is almost unity. When an overwhelming majority of people are living just on subsistence level, any increase in incomes will be utilised for

2. Ragnar Nurkse, *Problems of Capital Formation in Underdeveloped Countries* (Oxford, 1955), p. 9.

immediate consumption. Production thus creates its own demand and the size of market depends upon the volume of production. Say's law will hold only if the increase in production is spread over a number of industries so that the people employed in these industries provide demands for each other's products. "Every increase of production, distributed without miscalculation among all kinds of produce in the proportion which private interest would dictate creates, or rather constitutes, its own demand."[3] Say's law won't hold true in case the whole increase in production is concentrated in a single industry. Let us illustrate this point by taking Nurkse's example of a shoe industry. Suppose a shoe industry is set up in an underdeveloped country. People employed in this industry won't spend whole of their income on shoes. They require a number of other things, too. If the incomes of the people other than those employed in the newly set up shoe industry remain unchanged, the demand for shoes will be very small. Only a small part of their unchanged incomes will be diverted from other products to shoes. Shortage of demand for shoes may lead to a failure of the shoe industry. On the other hand, if a simultaneous investment is made in a number of industries producing mass consumption goods, people employed in these industries will provide demand for each other's products. Thus, production will create its own demand if it is spread over a number of industries proportioned in a manner which corresponds with the pattern of consumers' preferences.

In addition to the small size of the market, there are a number of other factors which limit the demand for capital. Some such important factors are mentioned below:

Lack of entrepreneurship: There is an acute shortage of Entrepreneurship in underdeveloped countries. Even if there exist highly profitable opportunities for investment, there may be no demand for capital because of dearth of entrepreneurs, who are to exploit these investment opportunities.

3. J.S. Mill, *Essays on Some Unsettled Questions of Political Economy* (London School of Economics Reprint, 1948), p. 73. *Cf.* Nurkse, n. 2, p. 9.

Lack of skilled labour: Underdeveloped countries suffer from a dearth of skilled labour. Investment might be inhibited by a shortage of skilled labour.

Lack of basic facilities: Investment is inhibited by a lack of basic facilities, *viz.*, transportation and communications, ancillary and auxiliary industries, electricity, etc.

Legal framework: Incentives for investment will be lacking if the legal framework does not ensure that investors will obtain the full fruit of their investments. Defective system of land-tenure in underdeveloped countries, for instance, discourages investment in agriculture. A tenant who is always insecure of his holding cannot risk capital in it. Further a part of the fruits of investment is taken by the landlord while cost of investment is borne by the tenant alone.

Size of holding in agriculture: Small size of holdings in agriculture limits the scope for investment. It is not profitable to use up-to-date machinery if the size of the farm is small.

Political conditions: Underdeveloped countries, often, lack a stable government. Unstable political conditions discourage investment.

Taxation policy: Several underdeveloped countries have recently considerably raised taxes on incomes and profits to obtain additional funds for the government treasury and to decrease inequalities in the distribution of income. Extremely high taxes on incomes and profits discourage investment.

High interest rates: Interest rates are comparatively higher in underdeveloped countries. Other things being the same, high interest rates discourage investment.

Availability of cheap labour: Availability of labour at extremely cheap rates tends to encourage substitution of labour for capital and thus decreases the demand for capital.

Supply Side: Supply of capital comes out of two sources, *viz.* domestic savings and net capital imports. In this chapter, we shall limit ourselves to domestic savings only because foreign capital has been discussed separately in the next chapter. Foreign capital may be helpful in initiating and accelerating the process of economic development, but sustained growth cannot be achieved without increasing domestic savings.

> Unless the habits of consumption, and saving, the institutions and legal framework for accumulation, lending and investing can be adapted to the building and maintenance of capital, foreign aid can bring only transitory benefits. A permanent basis for higher living standards must be created *within*[4] the society; indeed, this is the very meaning of economic development. Unless the chief nature of growth is indigenous, the society is constantly exposed to retrogression.[5]

The most important reason for the dearth of savings in underdeveloped countries is the low level of per capita income. An overwhelming majority of population lives just on the subsistence level. People having somewhat higher incomes lack saving habits. They lavishly spend on ceremonial consumption, *i.e.,* ostentatious weddings, funerals and religious celebrations. People having still higher incomes try to emulate western ways of life.

4. Hoarded Savings

In underdeveloped countries, the rate of investment is low not because there is no surplus but because both individuals and governments have a tendency to invest their savings in unproductive channels like real estate, gold, silver, jewellery, foreign exchange balances etc. Lewis aptly observes:

> No nation is so poor that it could not save 12 per cent of its national income if it wanted to; poverty has not prevented nations from launching upon wars, or from waste. Least of all can those nations plead poverty as an excuse for not saving, in which 40 per cent or so of the national income is squandered by the top 10 per cent of income-receivers, living luxuriously on rents.[6]

This tendency is generated and nourished by certain socio-economic factors prevailing in the underdeveloped countries. When the general environment is not favourable to productive investment, savings tend to flow into ornaments, precious metals and stones, domestic and foreign currency because they can be easily concealed

---

4. Emphasis added by the author.
5. Norman S. Buchanan and Howard S. Ellis, *Approach to Economic Development* (New York, 1955), p. 301.
6. W.A. Lewis, *The Theory of Economic Growth* (London, 1954), p. 236.

and moved in times of trouble. In addition, they can be easily converted into purchasing power and used in times of crisis. They also provide insurance against currency inflation. Inadequate financial organisation and lack of education contribute to this tendency. Further, a set of complicated social factors has encouraged the holding of savings in the form of hoarded wealth. Hoarding gold is an ancient habit in the orient because gold is considered to be the best form of wealth. Many Syrians, for instance, prefer to have recourse to bank overdrafts for which they pay heavy rates of interest rather than invest capital, that lies idle with them in the form of gold.[7] Palaces and temples in Asian countries possess large hoards of precious stones and metals.[8]

Not to talk of individuals, even governments in some underdeveloped countries were hoarding on a large scale by backing their domestic currency with foreign exchange. Backing domestic currency with sterling was very common in the British colonies. Luckily, most of the erstwhile British colonies have now more or less exhausted their sterling balances and have, therefore, discontinued or substantially diminished the use of sterling as backing to domestic currency.

It is difficult to assess the size of these hoards because they are scattered over vast regions and among all sections of the people. They cannot easily be requisitioned because information about their whereabouts is scanty. A notable point about the hoards is that they can be used only once and are not perennial source. According to a U.N. estimate, if used over a period of five years, they would contribute 2 per cent of the national income to capital formation during: five years.

There is no simple way of mobilising these hoards. Compulsion will not be of much help. This is particularly so in a democratic country. The governments have to court hoards for development investment. Through vigorous publicity, people should be made development-and-investment minded. They should be explained the significance of development schemes for their economic well-being. Since hoarding of gold is encouraged by inflation, the monetary

7. United Nations, *Final Report of the U.N. Economic Survey Mission for the Middle East,* Part I (New York, 1949), p. 41.

8. Alfred Bonne, *Studies in Economic Development* (Bonne, 1957), p. 198.

policy of government should create confidence in people's mind about the stability of the domestic currency. Adequate financial institutions, suited to requirements of the different sections of society should be provided. An attractive rate of interest may be offered on gold bonds purchased with dishoarded gold.

5. Saving Potential of Different Social Classes

We briefly study below the saving potential of different social classes. This type of study is very helpful in devising effective measures for the mobilisation of savings.

Land Owners: The landowning class or rent earners have a tendency to direct their income into unproductive expenditure or conspicuous consumption. They spend their income mostly on estate, land purchase, construction of monuments and religious buildings, lavishness and charity. Their place in the traditional economic order prevents them from developing an outlook for productive investment. They have got power to save but lack will to save. To channel rent income into productive investments, very high taxes should be imposed on rent incomes and wasteful and conspicuous consumption.

Peasants: Though peasants have a tendency to be thrifty, their thriftness is not out of their desire for productive investment but to provide for hard days. Agriculture being a gamble in rains and other natural phenomenon, they have to be ready for a crisis any time. Whatever meagre savings they have are invested in bullion and ornaments or in lending to other peasants which does not result in capital formation.

Though peasants lack the power to save large amounts, they are certainly capable of saving small amounts. It is very desirable that savings of the peasants are mobilised and used for improvements on agricultural lands. Lewis emphasizes that "the more farmers can finance themselves the better. This gives special point to savings campaigns and savings institutions in rural areas."[9]

Middle Classes: In underdeveloped countries, the middle class wage earners and salaried persons constitute only a small proportion of total population. Though their incomes are higher than those of peasants, they are more spending-minded than saving-minded. In

9. Lewis, n. 6, p. 226.

colonial countries, or countries in which foreign rule existed till recently, the middle classes have a tendency to imitate foreign tastes with a view to attain higher status in society. Further, lack of suitable opportunities for investment leaves little incentive for the middle class to save. Modern industrial establishments require sizable capital outlays, technological and managerial skills of a high degree, and well organised marketing institutions and services which are obviously beyond the means of the middle class. The small establishments find it difficult to survive against the competition of imported products turned out by giant concerns in advanced countries. The desire to imitate the consumption standards of the high-income groups gets the first priority in the budgets of the middle-class people. Next come building of residential houses, education of children, provision for old age and sickness, etc. If the income is a little higher and the entrepreneurial spirit awakened to some extent, investment is made into marketing and other service industries of a routine nature.

Measures should be taken to mobilise the saving of the middle class. Saving habit in this class should be encouraged through education and publicity. The principle of insurance appeals easily. People should be encouraged to save for sickness, old age, house purchase, marriage or funeral, etc. Attractive rate of interest should be offered on saving accounts.

Historical evidence shows that the rate of saving is highly sensitive to inflation. A United Nations Study states that:

> ...in a number of countries (of Asia and Far East)[10] some net disinvestment has been noted in postal savings, while in none of the countries is the rate of increase in such savings very considerable. Moreover, the volume of Saving Certificates sold and the net annual increases are quite small. This may be partly due to inflationary pressures, which directly affect the group using these facilities.[11]

Inflationary tendencies considerably influence the forms which the savings take. When prices are rising, investment in holding stocks of goods, gold, foreign currency, real estate promises large speculative

10. Words within parentheses added.
11. United Nations, *Mobilisation of Domestic Capital in Certain Countries in Asia and Far East* (New York, 1951), p. 54.

gains which cannot be obtained from productive investments for domestic development.

Steps should be taken to control inflationary pressure as soon as these reach a level which discourages savings. In case, the use of inflation for fast development becomes unavoidable, the real value of savings should be ensured through increased interest rates or other direct methods. Lewis states:

> ....If the community is also using inflation for the purpose of capital formation, with the result that the value of money is falling, there is something to be said for guaranteeing the real value of small savings; otherwise, small savers are discriminated against (since the value of other assets rises as prices rise), and small savings are discouraged.[12]

Profit Earners: The history of the advanced countries shows that profits, distributed and undistributed, have been the major source of financing economic development. Regarding the meaning of profits in this context, Lewis states:

> We do not refer only to private capitalists, but use the term also to refer to State capitalism, or to any other form of economic organisation where capital is used to employ people, and where, after payment of wages and salaries, a substantial surplus remains of which a large part is reinvested productively. In practice, judging by the U.S.S.R., the State capitalist can accumulate capital even faster than the private capitalist, since he can use for the purpose not only the profits of the capitalist sector (described as taxation) but also what he can force or tax out of the peasants, or squeeze out of the economy, as a whole by inflation.[13]

Thus 'profits' do not refer to a choice of any particular type of economic system. They simply imply a process of obtaining a surplus in production which can be used for capital formation. The process involves two things. In the first place, the rising productivity should be prevented from flowing to classes who have a tendency to increase their consumption rather than savings, *viz.*, peasants, wage earners, salaried classes, aristocracy. Secondly, conditions should be

12. Lewis, n. 6, p. 229.
13. *Ibid.*, p. 236.

created, through taxation, or regulation of private enterprise, or both, under which profits are used for further capital formation.

The profit making class is the major source of saving in any economy due to its place in the social hierarchy, its high income level, and its special type of ambitions. They are able to acquire social prestige as employers and owners of wealth without indulging in wasteful consumption. Their incomes considerably exceed their accepted standards of consumption, and, therefore, they are in a position to keep a high rate of saving. Being aware that money is the key to power, they do not compete with the aristocracy in conspicuous consumption. Their ambition is to earn more and more money through profitable investments. They exploit new techniques, extend the scale of production, explore new markets and do so many other things to raise the momentum of profit yielding productive investments. Lewis states:

> The capitalist is therefore the only person whose ambition drives in the direction of using his income to create an empire of bricks and steel; all other classes fulfil their ambitions in other ways—the salaried middle classes by conspicuous consumption, and the agricultural classes by buying land or by holding office. In the later stages of capitalism these distinctions are blurred: ...thrift and productive investment spread to all classes of the community, but in origin productive investment is essentially the mark of the capitalist class.[14]

To earn profit and plough it back into the business is almost an article of faith with the entrepreneur. In fact, he inhales the virtue of saving and investment from the very atmosphere in which he lives. Some pre-requisites will have to be fulfilled for the smooth and fast expansion of the capitalistic sector. The social framework should favour increase in the share of profits in the national income. The capital investments should be politically secure and should not be subject to sudden and arbitrary levies.

Special tax concessions and other facilities may be offered for encouraging the reinvestment of profits. Reinvestment of profits, however, may not result into an optimum allocation of resources. Firms possessing profits will have a tendency to invest these in their

---

14. *Ibid.*, p. 232.

own lines of production of which they possess a knowledge and other lines of production which are more important from the point of the national economy may not obtain sufficient funds. A part of the distributed profits would be saved automatically. Tax concessions for encouraging reinvestment of profits deprive the government of revenue. Loss from a diminution of public revenue will have to be weighed against the benefit from additional savings. Encouraging reinvestment of profits will be more useful in case of foreign companies which would otherwise transfer their profits abroad.

Government: In underdeveloped countries, the government has to play an important role in mobilising resources for long-term agricultural and non-agricultural development, for social overhead capital, for pioneering and resource surveys, for social services and in many cases for supplying the entrepreneurial factor. Because of the large demand from current expenditure, particularly on defence and the maintenance of internal law and order, the contribution of government to capital formation has been limited in most of the underdeveloped countries. Expenditure on defence accounts for 30 to 50 per cent of the total expenditure of most of the countries in South-East Asia. In underdeveloped countries the share of the government in total national income is as small as 5 per cent while in advanced countries the same ranges between 20 to 40 per cent. The recent trends show that, in the development-dominated twentieth century, the government may exceed all other sources of saving, even in countries wedded to free economy. It is high time that governments of the underdeveloped countries realise the significance of this trend and increasingly participate in capital formation with added zeal.

6. "Demonstration Effect" and Propensity to Save

A person's savings are influenced not only by his absolute income but also by his relative income. An absolute increase in a person's income may not necessarily lead to an increase in his savings if his relative position recedes in the nation's income scale because of the rise in the average national income per head. This phenomenon is explained by the human psychology underlying consumer behaviour. With the rise in average per capita income, consumption standards rise in the higher income groups. The people in the lower group (whose real incomes are also rising) "come into contact with superior goods or superior patterns of consumption, with new articles or new ways of meeting old wants, they are apt to feel after a while a certain restlessness or dissatisfaction. Their knowledge is extended, their imagination stimulated, new desires are aroused, the propensity to consume is shifted upwards."[15]

Inequality in the distribution of income is, however, an important obstacle to the operation of 'demonstration effect' in the underdeveloped countries. An overwhelming majority of the people is too poor to afford even bare necessaries of life. The demonstration effect operates particularly in the middle income groups. It is very essential to control its operation. Otherwise it may make deep inroads into the saving habits of the people. Institutional factors, ideas and practices like a sense of responsibility towards members of family, charity for institutions of social importance, saving for the old age and for the education of the children, contributions to village funds, *swadeshi* spirit, etc. should be invigorated to strengthen frugal living and the saving habit among the people. Luckily, India has a long tradition of these virtues. An important safeguard against the "demonstration effect" would be to protect such social institutions against the western way of living; and to reconstruct them to fit into the development setting.

7. Financial Institutions

An appropriate financial organisation is very essential for promoting savings. A study of the role of financial institutions concludes:

> However poor an economy may be there will be a need for institutions which allow such savings as are currently forthcoming to be invested conveniently and safely, and which ensure that they are channelled into the most useful purposes. The poorer a country is, in fact, the greater is the need for agencies to collect and invest the savings of the broad mass of persons and institutions within its borders. Such agencies will not only permit small amounts of savings to be handled and invested conveniently but will

---

15. Nurkse, n. 2, p. 57.

> allow the owners of savings to retain liquidity individually but finance long-term investment conveniently.[16]

The saving institutions affect the rate of saving through their numerical spread-over, sections of the population approached, accessibility, popularity, nature and extent of facilities offered and the rate of interest paid. In underdeveloped countries, the number of saving institutions is very small and their working is not satisfactory. We briefly discuss below the various financial institutions and the measures required to make them more effective and useful in mobilising savings.

8. Commercial Banks

The commercial banks form the most organised sector of the financial organisation. But most of them are not much interested in attracting local deposits, in developing the local capital market, or in financing internal trade. By and large, their offices are concentrated in large towns. They attract deposits primarily from urban people and do not play any significant part in mobilising saving of the rural population.

Provision of adequate banking facilities is very essential for mobilising savings. Banking system should be extended by establishing branches of government banks, using local authorities as agencies of government banks, extending banking facilities through such decentralized government agencies as post offices, guaranteeing to hold government accounts in new branches of banks or new unit banks, providing premises for strong rooms, allowing initial expenses of opening new banks as a charge against profits before assessing taxation, providing training to bank officers etc. The government should take measures to improve the effective provision of banking facilities by formulating and enforcing appropriate banking legislation, to control the establishment of banks, or supervise their operations and to facilitate the spread of banking system to cover a wider population, particularly in remote rural areas. Such measures may include liberalisation of bank laws by eliminating or reducing initial minimum capital requirements but at the same time maintaining supervision over banks to their solvency, avoidance of special taxes on bank deposits and cheques,

16. Edward Nevin, *Capital Funds in Underdeveloped Countries* (London, 1961), p. 75.

popularisation of cheques by the use of cheques by government departments in paying salaries and in settling other expenditures and by accepting cheques by the government in payment of taxes and other dues. Travelling banks may be used to cover remote and sparsely populated areas.

Safety of deposits is very essential for building confidence of the people in the banking system. In the initial stages of the growth of banking, any happening undermining the confidence of the people will give a setback to the development of banking. Government as well as private depositories of savings should be very careful in their investment policies. They should not embark upon risky and less liquid investments without taking measures to safeguard the interests of the depositors. Such measures may include deposit insurances, liquidity and rediscounting facilities, and provision of guaranteed government or other public securities. Investment policies of the depositories should be properly supervised and regulated by the central bank.

Provision of banking facilities alone is not enough. Ignorant and illiterate masses are not habituated to saving. Mass education and publicity should be used to spread the habit of saving and of depositing savings. Prevalence of usury is great hinderance to the development of institutionalised banking. For attracting deposits banks cannot afford to pay so high rates of interest as the moneylenders can. To safeguard banks from unfair competition, appropriate legislation should be formulated and enforced for the suppression of usury.

9. Stock Exchanges

At a certain stage of development of a country, stock exchanges play an important role in promoting savings and channelling these into productive enterprises. Most of the underdeveloped countries lack stock exchanges. To a large extent, lack of stock exchanges exists because the conditions are not yet ripe for the functioning of stock exchanges. This is mainly because of dearth of savings, preference for investment in real estate and gold, unfamiliarity with corporate securities, lack of confidence of public in corporate securities, close holding of stock by wealthy families to avoid sharing profits with others, taxation and other impediments to corporate form of organisation, unwillingness of banks to give loans on the collateral of securities, and preference of corporations to obtain finance from the money market rather than issuing stocks.

It is sometimes held that premature establishment of stock exchanges may do more harm than good by encouraging unhealthy speculation instead of promoting productive enterprises. Stock exchanges in presently advanced countries came into existence only at a certain stage and played an important role in furthering economic development. Before the establishment of stock exchanges, company reform and improvement of company accounts is essential to enable the prospective investors to have a fairly good idea of the state of the company and to prevent undersirable speculation. If the volume of transactions is not sufficiently large, it becomes easy for the speculators to manipulate the market to the detriment of the interests of the innocent investors.

Contrary to the above view, it is held by some that stock exchanges have an important role to play in the development of a country and these should be established as soon as there are securities to be marketed.

Speculation is not peculiar to any stage of development. Steps should, of course, be taken to improve the functioning of the stock exchanges and to check the malpractices. Agencies may be set up to supervise the form of securities issued, their proper issuance and the whole system of security sales and purchases. Supervision and the control of security markets, however, should not be carried to the extent that it impedes the normal growth.

10. Co-operative Institutions

It is generally accepted in the underdeveloped countries that the co-operative institutions are the best media of mobilising and channelling savings. But the co-operative movement has not made much progress. In most countries, it has reached only a small portion of the population. It has failed to mobilise savings or to meet credit requirements of a large portion of population. A number of factors are responsible for the extremely slow growth of the co-operative movement, *e.g.*, people's indifference, past record of the movement, shortage of trained staff, organisational defects, dominance by the government etc. The co-operative societies have failed to mobilise the savings of their members. Their paid up capital, surplus and deposits are generally a small part of their total working capital which consists largely of borrowings from the central financing agencies.

A number of measures have to be taken to put the co-operative movement on a smooth path of growth. Institutions should be set up for the training of co-operative officials so as to make them capable of shouldering greater responsibilities as whole-time paid workers. The provincial or federal banks, in co-operation with the Central Bank, should provide financial and administrative guidance to the primary societies and should also effectively supervise their working. The functions of primary societies should be broadened so as to make them a live organism reaching the very door of the agriculturist. A vigorous drive should be launched for education and publicity in co-operation right to the village level.

11. Saving Banks

Postal saving facilities encourage thrift among the middle and low income groups and supply funds for the Central Governments. The facilities are generally limited to deposit and to purchase of government saving certificates. Several types of restrictions are placed even on these facilities, *e.g.*, ceiling on total amount of deposits, restrictions on frequency of withdrawals, only a single type of deposits etc.

Postal facilities should be used more effectively for mobilising rural savings. The number of postal offices should be substantially expanded. The rate of interest offered on deposits should be increased wherever it is inadequate. The services offered to the depositors should be improved. A wide-spread and effective educational campaign should be launched for savings and bond investments.

Mobilisation of rural savings deserves special attention because of two reasons. In the first place, in most of the underdeveloped countries, at least in the initial stages, the development projects will have to be rural-oriented. As a result, the major benefit will accrue to rural sections of society. It is quite reasonable that those who receive benefit should contribute to the finances of the development. Secondly, mobilisation of rural savings will make the rural population development minded. The objectives can be achieved by linking zonal savings schemes with local development projects. The people would judge the significance of their small savings by the benefit which accrues to them from the sacrifice which they have undergone. The direct relation between savings and investments, instead of the circuitous relation via the capital market, encourages savings for local projects. The All India National Congress Small Savings Committee aptly observed, "Local funds invested in remote places via the market mechanism will fail to arouse local interest, for the majority of the people is illiterate and is afraid of losing hard-earned money through hazardous investments in distant places."[17]

Savings drive should be particularly intensified in those rural areas where intensive development schemes are being carried out, *e.g.*, areas recently 'opened up' by means of transport and communications, areas recently brought under irrigation, localities created on newly reclaimed lands, belts of cash or commercial crops, dairy areas, areas near the long-term multipurpose projects, etc.

Simultaneously with the reinforcing of measures to encourage savings, measures should be taken to weaken the force which dampen the enthusiasm to save. Conspicuous expenditure of the richer classes, for instance, discourages the poor classes to save. The poor classes can accept self-denial only when the well-to-do class sets an example of sacrifice. Often, the government also indulges into wasteful and conspicuous expenditure. The richer classes and the government departments should make it a policy to avoid wasteful and conspicuous expenditure. Indian traditions of simple living and self-sacrifice should be revived among the rich people and the government officials. Institutional factors like mutual aid saving prompted by the family responsibility, and the community feeling can certainly prove helpful in mobilising savings for development.

12. Insurance Companies

Life insurance is an important instrument of mobilising the savings of the people. It develops a recurrent saving habit and provides fund for long-term investment. It creates a strong urge in the policy-holder not to allow the policy to lapse and to compulsorily save for the payment of the premium. In most of the underdeveloped countries, life insurance has not been used effectively for mobilising savings. It is limited to urban areas and to a small number of persons. A number of factors are responsible for the slow growth of

17. All India Congress Committee, *Report of the Congress Small Savings Committee* (New Delhi, 1956), p. 35.

life insurance, *viz.*, lack of general education, traditional prejudice against life insurance, past record of insurance companies, poor legal protection to investors, the urban character of insurance business etc. With a view to inspire people's confidence in life insurance, the Government of India has nationalised life insurance in the country. Policies in regard to investment of insurance funds and maintenance of reserves have been reshaped to protect investors' interest and to suit the requirements of development. Life insurance should, however, be extended to rural areas and to those sections of urban population which yet remain uncovered. Possibilities of selling insurance policies through post offices and co-operative societies should be investigated. Additional incentive should be provided to the policy holders. A vigorous publicity campaign should be launched to educate people about the benefits of life policies.

In some underdeveloped countries, a major portion of the life insurance business is in the hands of the foreign insurance companies. National ownership of the insurance business not only inspires more confidence among the people but also makes funds available for national business. Steps should, therefore, be taken to gradually transfer the insurance business from foreigners to the nationals. In the meantime, legislation may be enacted requiring foreign insurance companies to keep and invest in the country a prescribed percentage of their legal reserves for policies written in the country. Other factors undermining people's confidence in insurance include control of insurance companies by speculative financiers, interlocking of interests between insurance and banking companies, high expense ratios and hazardous investment of insurance funds. Legislative measures should be taken to curb such practices.

13. Profit-making Public Enterprises

In some countries, profits made in government or government-sponsored enterprises have been used for financing economic development. It is desirable that the highly profitable fields are reserved for government and the profits from these fields are used for the country instead of enriching a few people. Public enterprises bring the government closer to economic realities and thus enable it to control the process of development, to formulate development programmes and to improve economic policies. Public enterprises would serve as a yardstick to measure the efficiency, tax-paying capacity and product prices of private enterprises. There is, of course, the problem that if the government invests its limited funds in profit-making enterprises, it may fall short of funds for investment in development activities. It should, therefore, enter only those fields which do not require much capital. In fields requiring larger capital, it should permit private enterprises and share their fabulous profits through taxation, licence fees, etc.

14. Compulsory Saving

In spite of very low incomes, masses in underdeveloped countries incur a lot of wasteful expenditure. Considerable amounts are spent, for instance, on social and religious ceremonies. If such wasteful expenditure is restricted considerable amounts of funds can be made available for development purposes.

Wealthy people in underdeveloped countries spend considerable amounts on luxury articles. Taxes, howsoever high these may be, are not effective in discouraging such consumption because additional taxes are paid not by cutting consumption but by decreasing savings. Such wasteful consumption can be discouraged only by direct measures. Direct measures for checking inessential consumption include selective import control, rationing, licensing, allocation priorities for labour and materials and direct conduct of production by state in socialist economies.

Enforcement of compulsory saving, of course, is not so easy in democratic countries as in dictatorial countries.

15. Capital Formation Through Unemployed Manpower

The underdeveloped countries are characterised by a marked degree of unemployment and underemployment of manpower, particularly in rural areas. The unemployed persons, however, are not being starved. They are being fed by the productive members of family. This is made possible by the joint family system prevalent in the underdeveloped countries. In fact, it is not possible to separate the productive and unproductive manpower. The common phenomenon is that of the attachment of a large number of persons than that required for doing the job because of lack of alternative employment for the surplus persons. A considerable number of persons, for instance, can be removed from land without adversely affecting the production. The number of shops or hawkers is far larger than that necessary for efficiently serving a locality. To the extent the unproductive persons are being fed by the produce of the productive workers, there exists saving potential which can be used for capital formation. All reproducible capital is ultimately the product of labour. Availability of abundant labour, therefore, offers the means of creating capital. The surplus manpower can be made to work on capital projects like irrigation, drainage, land reclamation, roads, houses, factories, training schemes etc. Utilisation of surplus labour for capital formation creates additional employment in two ways. Firstly, workers are employed for building capital goods. Secondly, availability of additional capital goods makes possible the employment of additional labour. Prof. K.N. Raj distinguishes between these two kinds of employment and gives them separate labels. He calls first kind of employment as the "revolving employment" and second as the "sedimented employment."[18]

Mobilisation of surplus manpower for capital formation raises a number of problems. Firstly, there is the problem of materials and equipment with which the labourers are to work. This is not a very difficult problem. In underdeveloped countries, there exists enough scope for productive work which can be done with indigenous tools and equipment. China provides a glaring example of how manpower can be used to do the work of machinery. Roads, drainage, canals, houses and factories can be constructed and land reclaimed with indigenous tools and materials and without the use of modern complicated machinery. If even indigenous tools are not available, the surplus manpower can in the beginning be set to the making of tools.. In actual practice, in underdeveloped countries, the available equipment is not fully utilised. Often farms are small and scattered. Considerable amount of equipment can be relieved if the farms are consolidated and enlarged in size. Further most of the farm equipment remains unutilised during the slack season in agriculture.

In many underdeveloped countries, machinery is being used to do a number of jobs which can be done by the manpower. Most of the consumer goods presently being produced with modern machinery can be produced in cottage industries with indigenous equipment. If manpower is substituted for machinery wherever possible, a considerable amount of capital can be released for equipping the

18. K.N. Raj, *Employment Aspects of Planning in Underdeveloped Economies* (Cairo,1957), p. 19.

additional labourers with indigenous tools. This, however, is not possible in a private enterprise economy. Private entrepreneurs are guided by the private money costs and not by social costs. Their objective is to minimise the money costs which requires substitution of machinery for manpower. Substitution of manpower for machinery is possible only in a socialist economy which is guided by social costs, and not by money costs. In a private enterprise economy, labour will be employed only up to the point where its marginal productivity is equal to the ruling wage rate. It will be unprofitable to employ labour beyond this point. In contrast, in a socialist economy labour will be employed only up to the point where its marginal productivity is equal to the disutility involved in it which may be far below the ruling wage rate. Socialist economies, thus, can employ more manpower than the private enterprise economies. Herein lies the secret of full employment in socialist economies. In spite of a very large population, China, unlike India and other private enterprise underdeveloped economies, does not suffer from the problem of surplus manpower. Utilization of surplus manpower for capital formation, thus, requires a fundamental change in the organisation of society.

Secondly, the surplus labour must be of a type which can be used for the construction of capital goods. Most of the surplus labour available in undeveloped countries is of an unskilled type. This, however, is not a very important hinderance in the mobilisation of surplus labour. Many jobs require unskilled labour. Skilled workers like supervisors, machines, engineers, designers etc. will be required only in a small number. Even if this small number of skilled persons is not available, we can start the process from training labour instead of starting it from building capital equipment.

Thirdly, mobilisation of surplus labour will require considerable changes in the distribution of land holdings. At present, several families possess land-holdings of a size which is not sufficient to provide full time employment to these families. Before surplus labour can be mobilised, all such holdings must be grouped into standard holdings, *i.e.*, holdings of a size which is sufficient to provide full time employment to an average sized family. After allocating these standard holdings to certain families, the remaining families can be mobilised for working on investment projects. A better way of freeing the surplus labour would be to replace individual farming by co-operative farming.

The fourth, and the most important, problem relates to the transfer of surplus manpower to the capital projects and to supply it with food and other consumables which they were consuming in their previous position. As it is assumed that the production does not, decrease with removal of the surplus manpower, this does not require any cut in the consumption of the population remaining behind. This only requires that the population remaining behind should not be permitted to increase its consumption and the consumables which were being consumed by the surplus labourers should be mobilised for feeding them when employed for work on capital projects.

The problem of mobilising the surplus consumables does not arise if the surplus labour is utilised for constructing projects confined to a household, *viz.,* digging a well, raising a fence, building a cattle shed, etc. In a household, consumption of different members does not depend, to any significant extent, on their contribution to the family product. Idle members are supported by the productive members and they will continue being fed as usual while working on investment projects. In underdeveloped countries, there exists considerable scope for increase in production through such investment.

The problem of mobilisation of consumable surplus is not very difficult in case of projects confined to a limited locality. Idle members in different households can be utilised for constructing village tanks, irrigation drains, paths and roads, school buildings etc. The surplus manpower employed on the local projects will continue to be fed as usual by the productive members of their respective households. A proper balance between the contributions of labour by different households and expected benefit to these from the completion of the projects is very essential for the continued success of the scheme. The possible extent of the divergence between the contributions from and benefits to different households depends upon the strength of the ties and bindings between different households in a locality. If the main benefit from the projects accrues to households different from those which are in a position to contribute labour, the system cannot go very far without involving the problem of payment, for the contribution of labour. In such cases if the households likely to benefit are not in a position to make immediate payment to the labour employed on the projects, a system of deferred payments may be introduced. When the projects are complete, the income of the beneficient households will increase and they would be in a position to' make payment out of their increased income to the labour which worked on the projects in the past. Recruitment of labour on deferred payment for local projects is not likely to be very difficult. It would be in the interest of the unemployed labourers to accept work on deferred payment rather than remaining idle. India has launched a scheme of 'community projects' for utilising the idle manpower for productive purposes on projects confined to particular localities. A similar attempt has been made in China under the leadership of party cadres. Utilisation of surplus labour for investment on projects confined to the households, and to a limited extent to the localities, can considerably contribute, particularly in the agricultural sector, to the national product, but the amount of surplus labour that can be utilised for such projects is strictly limited. Utilisation of surplus manpower on a large scale, particularly for industrialisation, is not possible without transferring workers from their homes to other places.

The transfer of surplus labour to projects away from their homes raises two important problems, *viz.*, (1) payment to labour working on investment projects and (2) mobilisation of consumables. Regarding the first problem, when the labourers are working on projects at distant places which do not directly benefit them or their families, they will have to be paid wages for the work. Thus the transfer of surplus workers to projects at distant places raises all the complications involved in an exchange economy. The problem of wage payment can, of course, be solved by the earlier mentioned system of deferred payments. The most important problem relates to the mobilisation of consumable surplus.

> Thus to assume (as Professor Nurkse does) that the saving necessitated by the additional consumption of the newly employed will, or can be done by household which previously sheltered the surplus labour is to leave out of account almost all the essential features of the problems.[19]

19. *Ibid.*, p. 23.

Because of the very low standard of living and consequently extremely high marginal propensity to consume, people are not likely to voluntarily save the whole surplus. In a primarily agricultural economy with individual farming, taxation is not very effective. Further the level of taxation required to completely mop up the surplus will be so high as to considerably adversely affect production. Any decease in production will lead to a breakdown of the whole system designed to utilise the surplus manpower for capital formation. In Russia, the consumable surplus has been mobilised through compulsory measures. The system of collective farming and state operation and/or control of industry has facilitated the working of such measures. These have checked the adverse effect of such measures on production. An extremely high level of taxation, for instance, does not adversely affect production because the amount of work to be done by any individual is determined not by the individual himself but by the collective body or the trade union which receives directives from the state. Some element of compulsion is very essential for mobilising the consumable surplus. Each family may be required to surrender that amount of consumables against deferred payment which was being consumed by the members who left home for working on projects at distant places. The labourers working on these projects will be given these consumables against the payment to be deducted from the wages due to them.

In an economy in which a small minority is rolling in wealth, it will be a gross injustice to ask the majority, which is living just at the subsistence level, to work and to surrender consumables against deferred payments. In fact the burden of development should fall more on the well-to-do classes which have incomes far higher than those required for the subsistence level. The poor classes cannot agree to make sacrifices for the development of the country when a small minority is enjoying all sorts of comforts and luxuries simply because it was fortunate enough to be born in rich families. For enlisting the co-operation of the poor classes it is very essential that the wasteful consumption of the richer classes is restricted and a part of their income utilised for feeding the people who work on new projects. Mobilisation of rental surplus in China made possible investment on a considerably large scale. In case it is not possible to mop up hundred per cent surplus, or a little increment in the consumption of newly employed workers is required to induce them to leave their homes to work on capital projects, or workers require more consumption because now they are putting in a larger amount of work, there would appear a shortage of consumables which may result in a breakdown of the whole process of mobilising surplus manpower for development. In this connection Nurkse's observation is very pertinent.

> It seems to be a question of all or nothing. Either the whole of the food surplus that becomes available on the land through the withdrawal of the surplus labourers is mopped up to feed them in their new occupations or nothing can be done at all.[20]

Because of lack of excess capacity and other bottlenecks, it is not possible to immediately increase the supply of consumables. For the success of the scheme it is absolutely necessary either to mobilise hundred per cent surplus and to prevent a rise in consumption or to arrange additional consumables from abroad. Foreign assistance, if available, can be of great help in easing the process of mobilising the surplus manpower for capital formation.

Finally, it may not be possible to make payment to the labourers working on the new projects at the ruling wage rates because it is not justified by the productivity of labour on these projects. Under such circumstances, an element of compulsion may be necessary to make the labourers work at wage rates which are lower than the ruling wage rates. Nurkse is convinced that:

> Whatever the machinery employed may be, some form of collective saving enforced by the state may prove to be indispensable for the mobilisation of the saving potential implicit in disguised unemployment.[21]

To avoid discrimination against the labourers working on the new projects, the wage structure as a whole may be readjusted. Affecting of such measures, however, requires fundamental changes in the organisation of society.

To conclude, the capital formation in underdeveloped countries is being hindered not by a shortage of funds but by a defective organisation of society. If society is properly organised, the capital formation can be financed from within the system itself.

---

20. Nurkse, n. 2, p. 40.
21. *Ibid.*, p. 43.

Capital Formation: Foreign Sources

25

1. Role of Foreign Capital

Foreign capital has played an important role in the development of most of the countries of the world.

> Nearly every developed state has had the assistance of foreign finance to supplement its own meagre savings during the early stages of its development. England borrowed from Holland in the seventeenth and eighteenth centuries, and in turn came to lend to almost every other country in the world in the nineteenth and twentieth centuries. The United States of America, now the richest country in the world, borrowed heavily in the nineteenth century, and is in turn called upon to become the major lender of the twentieth.[1]

So far, there have been two striking cases in which the countries, have developed without any significant foreign capital, *viz.*, Japan and Russia. Though Japan imported foreign capital, the amount was not very large. Japan could do without considerable amounts of foreign capital because of certain favourable factors which do not exist in most of the present underdeveloped countries. Firstly, Japan had a large export surplus with the continental countries mainly because of their huge demand for Japanese silk; this enabled her to import capital goods and technical know-how required for the development programmes. Secondly, most of Japan's industry was on a small, scale requiring less capital and more labour which was available in plenty at extraordinarily cheap rates. Thirdly, the rate of domestic savings was very high because of the absence of conspicuous consumption among the wealthier classes owing to the prevalence of different social values. Regarding

---

1. W. Arthur Lewis, *The Theory of Economic Growth* (London, 1966), p. 224.

the technology and know-how which generally accompany foreign investments, Japan hired foreign technicians and sent her own people abroad for training. So far as Russia's case is concerned, she inherited an industrial base built during the period 1881-1913 with the import of foreign capital particularly from France. In addition, the rate of forced domestic saving was extraordinarily high which cannot be achieved in a democratic society.

There exist vast disparities between the standard of living of the advanced and the underdeveloped countries. This is a great threat to world peace. The rapid development of underdeveloped countries is very essential for the maintenance of permanent world peace. It is not, however, possible for these countries to develop rapidly with domestic resources alone. The rate of saving is very low in these countries. An overwhelming majority of the people is living on the subsistence level. Any significant increase in the rate of domestic saving is not possible without lowering the standard of living below the subsistence level. Foreign capital, therefore, is indispensable if these countries are to develop at a fairly rapid rate.

Even if the domestic savings are enough to achieve a satisfactory rate of development, the foreign capital might be needed to avoid deficits in the balance of payments. Rapid development, generally, has a tendency to cause a deficit in the balance of payments. Besides the indirect effects, rapid development affects the balance of payments adversely, mainly speaking, in two direct ways. Firstly, import of huge quantities of capital goods, technical know-how and essential raw materials is required to carry on the development programmes. Secondly, many goods which were previously available for export may now be consumed by the newly created domestic industries. In addition to the above mentioned direct effects, rapid development affects the balance of payments adversely, mainly in two indirect ways, *viz.*, through income-effect and price-effect.

The underdeveloped countries suffer not only from a shortage of capital but also from a lack of technology, managerial ability, skill etc. Foreign capital in equity form brings with it these complementary factors which are very essential for the development of the underdeveloped countries. Foreign investments create opportunities for technical training for the local people. These create an industrial atmosphere which induces indigenous capital and enterprise.

Prospecting and promotion of new industries involves a good deal of risk. Pioneering companies might suffer huge losses if the projects are unsuccessful. Foreign capital performs the important function of starting new lines of business and bears huge losses inherent in new ventures. If the new ventures are successful, the indigenous capital may also participate and reap benefits without suffering the initial losses.

2. A Limitation of Foreign Capital

Foreign capital cannot accelerate the rate of development of a country which lacks the capacity to absorb it. The lack of capacity to absorb foreign capital might arise from a number of factors. It might be because of a lack of well thought out and planned projects. It might arise out of a shortage of competent administrative, managerial and technical personnel required to utilise the foreign capital. It might not be easy to train the domestic labour for industry or it might not be easily amenable to factory discipline. Economic, political and social institutions might resist the new methods of production. The absence of economic and social overheads (*viz.* transportation and communications, electricity and other pubic utilities) is another important factor which limits profitable investment in manufacturing and, heavy industries.

3. Disadvantages of Foreign Capital

It is feared that the foreign investors might interfere in the political affairs of the country. If foreign capital exists in substantial amounts, it can exert considerable influence on the politics of the country. The foreign investors might give financial assistance to the political parties supporting their vested interests. These fears have increased with the division of the world into two blocs, each anxious to attract as many countries as possible into its own orbit. The governments of the capital exporting countries might internationally direct and help the investors in their hectic activities through well-trained diplomatic and consular services. The fears of some people go to the extent that flag follows the foreign capital. These people support their fears with historical examples which are available in plenty. These fears are particularly marked in countries which have recently won their freedom after a good deal of struggle. These fears, however, have little basis in the present day world. Most of the capital-importing countries are strong enough to resist any such interference. The existence of the United Nations is another safeguard against any such happening.

If foreign capital dominates the basic industries, the whole economy will be made dependent on foreign investors. Natives will depend for their livelihood on foreigners. Business cycles originating in the capital-exporting countries will be transmitted to the capital-recipient countries.

Foreign investments will decrease the scope for potential domestic investors by utilising the available most profitable opportunities for investment in the country concerned. Somewhat late utilisation of investment opportunities by domestic capital might be in the long-run interest of the country than the immediate utilisation of these by the foreign capital.

Given unrestricted freedom, the foreign investors might oust the domestic investors who are comparatively less efficient. The superior efficiency of the foreign investors is primarily not because of their inherent qualities but because of historical reasons. In course of time and provided with equivalent facilities, efficiency of the domestic investors might rise to the level of that of the foreign investors.

In the past, foreign capitalists indulged in discrimination against the local personnel and in favour of the nationals of their own country. The local personnel were kept out of high administrative and technical positions. The industrial techniques and processes were kept absolutely secret from natives.

It has been alleged that in the past foreign capital exploited the countries in which it was invested. Most of the gain was reaped by the foreign investing countries. An overwhelming part of the foreign capital was invested in extractive industries producing raw materials for manufacturing industries working in the mother country of the foreign investors. The exploitation of exhaustible mineral resources decreased the potentialities of development of the capital-importing countries. The foreign capital failed to develop the recipient countries in a balanced and integrated manner.

> Thus the economy of the underdeveloped countries often presents the spectacle of a dualistic economic structure: a high productivity sector producing for export co-existing

> with a low productivity sector producing for the domestic market.[2]
>
> ...could it not be that in many cases the productive facilities for export from under-developed countries, which were so largely a result of foreign investment, never became a part of the internal economic structure of those underdeveloped countries themselves, except in the purely geographical and physical sense? Economically speaking they were really an outpost of the economies of the more developed investing countries. The main secondary multiplier effects, which the text book tells us to expect from investment, took place not where the investment was made physically or geographically located but (to the extent that the results of these investments returned directly home) they took place where the investment came from.[3]

The progressive part of the economy offering a greater scope for technical progress and the economies of large scale production is in the hands of the foreign investors whereas the natives are engaged in the production of food and raw materials.

Foreign capital did not go in manufacturing for the local market in spite of several advantages in it. Manufacturing industries require initial investment of an amount far smaller than that required by the extractive industries. Manufacturing industry can be initially started on a small scale and then gradually expanded through the reinvestment of profits. Manufacturing industry is not required to invest in building roads, railways, pipelines etc., to handle its products as is the case with the extractive industries. Risks are also greater in extractive industries because huge amounts have to be spent in surveying and locating minerals. Sometimes, the investment might go waste if no deposits are found or if found, exploitation is not profitable due to certain reasons. According to Prof. Nurkse, the factors inhibiting foreign investments in manufacturing industries were the shortage of local market for manufactured goods and the

2. H.W. Singer, "The Distribution of Gains Between Investing And Borrowing Countries," *American Economic Review, Papers and Proceedings* (May, 1960), p. 474.
3. *Ibid.*, p. 475.

expanding markets for primary products in advanced countries rather than any conspiracy on the part of foreign investors.

> The general reluctance of private business capital to go to work for the domestic markets in the less developed countries, in contrast with its eagerness in the past to work there for export to the industrial creditor states, does not reflect any sinister conspiracy or deliberate policy, still less any concerted attempt of the rich countries to exploit the poor.... The explanation lies, on the one hand, in the poverty of the local consumers in the underdeveloped countries, and on the other, in the large and, in the nineteenth century, vigorously expanding markets for primary products in the world's industrial centres.[4]

To strengthen his argument, he points out that the foreign investments in more advanced countries like Canada and Western Europe went into industries manufacturing for the local market because of the availability of local market for manufactures.[5] Without belittling the importance of the inducement effect of the size of the market, it might be mentioned that the non-availability of local market for manufactures alone cannot explain fully the pattern of past foreign investments. In every underdeveloped country, there was enough local market for some manufactures like cloth, shoes, etc., which are consumed by the masses, yet the foreign capital did not develop these industries. With the spread of railways in India there was a great scope for a locomotive industry; no foreign investor, however, developed this industry. In addition to certain genuine reasons, discussed below, for this lopsided pattern of foreign investments, the part played by the deliberate policies of the foreign investing countries to exploit the capital receiving countries, particularly those of the colonial type, cannot be denied.

A second reason offered for the concentration of foreign investments in extractive industries is that investment in these industries does not give rise to the problem of foreign exchange for the repatriation of profits and amortization funds because the minerals are generally meant for export and thus directly earn foreign exchange. It might be contended that the investment in

---

4. Ragnar Nurkse, *Problems of Capital Formation in Underdeveloped Countries* (Oxford, 1956), p. 25.

5. *Ibid.*, p. 28.

industries manufacturing for domestic market will not give rise to the foreign exchange problem because local manufacturing decreases the need for imports and thereby the foreign exchange expenditure. This, of course, is not true to the extent local manufacturing requires imported raw materials or utilises domestic raw materials which were being exported previously. The foreign exchange problem, however, has often been overemphasized. Foreign investments in underdeveloped countries were made mostly in export industries even in earlier times when the foreign exchange difficulties were unknown in these countries.

> But the tendency of direct business investment to go into export industries in these countries has been equally marked in earlier periods. It can, I believe, be observed in the case of British investment in the nineteenth century. It was an outstanding feature of American capital exports in the 1920's at a time when exchange control was non-existent and no one paid much attention to the risk of transfer troubles on private foreign investments.[6]

Further, in times of foreign exchange difficulties, the transfer risks are the same for all foreign investments, whether working for export or for the domestic market. Foreign exchange difficulties, generally, lead to the institution of foreign exchange control. Exporters are not permitted to utilise their foreign exchange earnings in their own way. These have got to be deposited with the exchange control authority in exchange for the domestic currency. All foreign investors have got an equal approach to the exchange control authority for foreign exchange for the repatriation of profits and amortization funds.

Thirdly, foreign investments have a tendency to go mainly in extractive industries producing for export because of lack of internal means of transportation and the existence of a well developed, transportation system between the main commercial centres and ports. The foreign rulers in underdeveloped countries paid more attention to the development of the transportation system between the ports and the main commercial centres than to the internal transportation system. In India, for instance, during the

6. *Ibid.*, p. 83.

British rule, the railway rates between the main commercial centres and ports were lower than those within the country.

Fourthly, the profit rates in extractive industries are generally much higher than those in manufacturing industries. Even when, transportation and other basic facilities are not available, the investors in extractive industries can afford to invest money in providing these facilities for themselves. In contrast, profits in manufacturing industries are not so large as to justify investment in these basic facilities. The cost of adequate basic facilities needed for manufacturing industries producing for local market will be much more than that for extractive industries producing for export. For export, for instance, transportation is required only between the production centres and the port whereas manufactures for local market require an extensive network of transportation within the whole country. No single manufacturing industry can afford to build this network of transportation for itself. The size of investments in extractive industries is much larger than that in manufacturing and, therefore, the extractive industries can afford the overcosts of providing basic facilities more easily.

Fifthly, the foreign investments are concentrated in extractive industries because many foreign investments were made by the manufacturing concerns in advanced countries for supplying raw materials to their manufacturing plants working in mother country.

There is, often, a tendency to overemphasize the harmful effects and to underestimate or neglect altogether the beneficial effects of the foreign investments in extractive industries.

> The extent to which a foreign business enterprise helps to promote a country's development does not depend in any simple fashion, if at all, on whether it works for export or for domestic consumption. Much depends on how far it increases the demand for labour and other local resources, on how much of its profits it reinvests in the country, and on a variety of other factors.[7]

Foreign investments even in extractive industries benefit the capital-recipient country to the extent these employ local labour and other resources. In addition, these create external economies in the form of trained labour, means of transportation and communications, etc.

---

7. *Ibid.*, p. 86.

which can be availed of by the domestic industries. The amount of such benefits to the capital-recipient country, however, differs for different types of extractive industries. The benefits from petroleum industry, for instance, are far less than those from iron or coal industry. First, in petroleum industry, the ratio of capital to labour is very high. Secondly, a considerable amount of capital is invested in laying down pipelines to pump oil from the production to the consumption centres which are of no use to the community at large. In contrast, roads and railways built to carry coal and iron from the production to the consumption centres are useful to the community at large, too. Investment in export industries in the initial stages of development is necessary to some extent to step up exports for earning sufficient foreign exchange for the import of equipment and technical know-how required to execute the development programmes.

Moreover, the past unhappy experience should not deter us from availing of the foreign capital. All these unhappy things happened in a period of *laissez faire* and foreign rule. If the national governments invite foreign capital in a planned and regulated manner, it is not difficult to avoid these unhappy experiences. Care should, however, be taken that these rules and regulations are not such as inhibit the inflow of foreign capital.

4. Joint Participation

One way suggested to avoid the unhappy consequences of foreign capital is the joint participation of domestic capital with foreign capital. Many advantages are claimed for this for the foreign investors as well as the country in which the investments are made. Native investors have better knowledge about the local conditions. They know the cheapest sources of labour. They know better the techniques of advertising the products which will be most successful in the local market. Participation of the national capital will improve the attitude of the natives towards the foreign capital. It will also diminish the fears of discrimination against foreign investors. On the other hand, this will ensure the capital recipient country that the foreign capital does not indulge in anti-national activities. Local investors collaborating with foreign investors will have the opportunity to learn their superior techniques and methods of business.

Joint participation, however, has its own limitations. If a sufficient amount of native capital is not available or the native investors do not agree on a sufficiently large scale to collaborate with foreign capital, narrow limit will be set to the import of foreign capital. Secondly, if the share of the native capital is small, its voice might be ignored. Thirdly, foreign investors might not agree to the participation of native capital. They might be afraid of the possibility of emergence of differences at any time with the native participants in the policy of the enterprise regarding prices, profit margins, reinvestment of earnings, recruitment of personnel etc. which is very harmful for the efficient working of the enterprise. This difficulty is greater in the case of subsidiaries whose policy is decided by the head office; these can accept the participation of national investors only as sleeping partners. Foreign investors may also refuse national participation because of their unwillingness to disclose their business secrets to others who might set up their independent business afterwards.

Foreign capital is of three types, *viz.*, (*i*) private, (*ii*) intergovernmental, and (*iii*) institutional. Let us discuss these types in detail.

PRIVATE FOREIGN CAPITAL

1. Scope

Since the depression of the thirties, the flow of private foreign investment has considerably dwindled. Private foreign investments have not been able to recover from the death blow given by the great depression in spite of the best efforts of the borrowing and lending countries and of the international financial institutions. The expectation of a large scale movement of foreign capital from advanced to the backward countries in the post-war period to avoid the occurrence of secular stagnation in advanced countries has been falsified by the facts. War adversely affected the countries which were the traditional investor of foreign capital. These deliberately restricted the outflow of capital in order to conserve it for domestic reconstruction and to rectify deficits in their balance of payments. Political insecurity has increased in the international field as well as within the underdeveloped countries. Nationalisation of foreign investments without adequate compensation in home countries has increased the risks of investment in foreign countries. The independence of colonies is another factor responsible for the decline in private foreign investments. Colonies attracted large amounts of capital from the metropolitan countries. The private investors were secure against the risks of expropriation, nationalization, discrimination etc. because of their own government ruling the country. Since the Second World War, most of the foreign capital has been invested either on government-to-government basis or by international institutions. Whatever private foreign investments have been made have been restricted mainly to a few areas and to extractive industries producing for export; a good number of private investments have gone into the production of petroleum. A large proportion of the private foreign investments which have occurred in recent years has gone mainly to countries already developed to some extent rather than to those which are very backward and need it badly. Most of the new private foreign investment has been out of the income earned by the parent concern in the capital-exporting country or by its subsidiaries in foreign countries.

2. Role of Private Foreign Capital

Many capital-exporting countries, particularly the United States and international financing organisations attach great importance to private lending. Economic policy statements of United States have stated and restated their faith in the private enterprises. One of the reasons for the great importance attached to private investment is their belief that private enterprise is essential for the maintenance of a democratic system of society. The qualitative aspect of the private foreign capital is more important than the quantitative aspect.

> Discussions on the role of private investment frequently emphasize the quantitative contribution in terms of the magnitude of capital flow, rather than the qualitative advantages to the less developed countries. The private investor from an industrially advanced country not only brings with him capital, technology, and managerial experience, but he introduces new business concepts which help to revolutionize the thinking and practice of the area. The introduction of modern marketing methods, of a policy of low margin and high volume, and of various measures for increased productivity, have repercussions which extend far beyond the business operations of the

> foreign investors. Economic growth is in part a sociological phenomenon which can be transported and encouraged to spread throughout the economically backward areas by socially responsible foreign investors.[8]

Private investment being guided mainly by the profit motive is likely to be more productive than the intergovernmental and institutional loans.

3. Disadvantages of Private Foreign Capital

By its very nature, it is not possible to plan the volume, timing and the regional and functional distribution of private foreign capital. With the end of the *laissez faire*, the emergence of planning and the extension of the public sector, the role that private foreign investment can play in the development of the underdeveloped countries has become considerably less important. The fundamental motive of the private capital is the maximisation of profits and not the development of the country. Investment will be made in industries promising the highest rate of return whether or not these are essential for the development of the country.

4. Factors Impeding Private Foreign Investment

Lack of Basic Facilities: Many backward countries lack in basic facilities, *viz.*, roads, railways, ports, electricity, etc. Each foreign investor willing to invest in a particular enterprise cannot be expected to invest huge amounts in providing these basic facilities for himself. Construction of the basic facilities is not attractive to foreign capital because of the requirements of huge initial investment and low yield. In addition, the investment in these is comparatively more immobile and starts yielding after a long period. The benefit from these facilities being mostly indirect Government is the best agency to provide these.

Regulations Providing Compulsory Local Participation: In some countries there exist restrictions on the hiring of foreign technical, administrative and other personnel, and the employment of local personnel in a certain ratio is compulsory. This discourages foreign investment if the employment of local personnel is not economical. This is particularly so in the initial stages when the

---

8. Raymond F. Mikesell, *Promoting United States Private Investment Abroad* (Washington, 1957), pp. 8-9.

trained local labour is not available. Investment in educating and training the domestic labour does not pay particularly when the labour receiving training at the cost of the enterprise cannot be bound to it for a sufficiently long period. Some countries require that the natives should hold the majority stock in the enterprise to keep its control in their hands. This seems to be an unjust demand. Foreign investors bringing technical knowledge, patents, copyrights etc. cannot agree to a minority share in the enterprise. In addition, if efficient local managerial personnel is inadequate, majority local participation might lead to inefficiency and losses not only for the local but for foreign investors, too.

Absence of General Convertibility: In the past, convertibility of the main currencies was an important factor facilitating the movement of capital. The disappearance of the general convertibility after the depression and more so after the Second World War has proved to be a great hindrance to the movement of capital. To illustrate the hindrance to the movement of capital caused by the disappearance of the convertibility, suppose that country A has surplus savings and wants to invest these in some foreign country and country B requires foreign capital. In the absence of general convertibility, country A can invest in country B only if it can supply the equipment and services required by country B and further if A requires certain goods and services from B by exporting which the capital and return thereon can be transferred back to country A. If there exists general convertibility, country B can borrow from country A and import equipment and services with the borrowed funds from any country. Similarly, it can repay the loan and the interest thereon by exporting its goods and services to any third country which requires these.

Nationalisation: Recently nationalisation of domestic and foreign enterprises has occurred on a large scale in many countries. Not only there has occurred an expansion of the public sector but the private sector has also seen an increased government intervention in the name of planning. This wave of nationalisation and Government intervention is a great deterrent to foreign capital.

International Political Tension: There exists great political tension on the world horizon. Any minor conflict might lead to a third war. This is a great deterrent to foreign investments.

Law and Order: Maintenance of strict law and order is a very important pre-requisite for attracting foreign capital. In many backward countries the absence of law of a standard equivalent to that of the law existing in the advanced and the so-called civilized nations is a great hindrance to the inflow of foreign capital. In addition, the execution of whatever law exists is not very efficient. In some countries the governments themselves are not very stable. Foreign investors will not agree to invest if their personnel and property are not very secure even if there exist highly profitable opportunities for investment. Fabulous profits are of no use if these cannot be taken back home safely. This is one of the explanations for the more private capital going to the comparatively advanced countries with a better standard of law and order and to colonies where the law and order is maintained by the ruling country according to its own standards.

Ignorance about Investment Opportunities: Very often the foreign investors do not know about the profitable opportunities for investment existing in backward countries. Risks of foreign investments have often been exaggerated in advanced countries. On entering the field, many investors discovered that the real risks were not so large as imagined in foreign countries. Generally, the foreign investors acquire knowledge about opportunities for investment through trade in commodities. This, however, is a very slow process. The countries needing foreign capital should make publicity about the opportunities for investment existing in their countries.

Defaults of Payments: The credit of certain countries has been impaired by their repeated failure to honour their debts. In some cases the default was because of reasons beyond the control of the borrowing countries. The great depression of the thirties brought many such defaults. In other cases the defaults have been intentional by the Goverment capturing power by a revolution. The governments established after the revolution in Russia, China and Mexico repudiated almost all their debts to foreign countries.

Low Yield: Contrary to the general expectation of a higher average rate of return in underdeveloped countries because of large unexploited potentialities, the actual average rate of return is lower than that in many developed countries. The comparative rate of return is higher in underdeveloped countries only in a few selected industries. There are several reasons for the average rate of return being lower in underdeveloped countries. Firstly, there is lack of basic facilities, *viz.*, means of transportation and communications, electricity, skilled labour etc. A considerable amount of money might have to be spent in training the local labour. Secondly, the foreign investors have to pay higher salaries and provide other facilities to the staff they need from their own country. Thirdly, the lack of ancilliary and auxiliary activities raises the cost of production. Fourthly, the size of the available market is generally smaller in underdeveloped countries which raises the cost of production.

Labour Legislation: Recently some countries have passed labour legislation conferring extensive favours on the national labour in industries owned and operated mainly by foreign investors.

Economic Instability: Many underdeveloped countries have recently seen frequent changes in taxation, labour laws, exchange rates, import and export policy etc; this increases the risks for the foreign investors. Depreciation of capital importing country's currency, for instance, decreases the value of the repatriated profits and amortization funds in terms of the national currency of the foreign investors. Economic instability, no doubt, is unavoidable to some extent in the developing economies passing through a transitional period, yet attempts should be made to achieve and maintain stability as far as possible without hindering the development process.

Difficulties in Recruiting Personnel: The foreign investors find it difficult to recruit the required personnel in their national country which is willing to work in foreign backward countries. To some extent it is because of a lack of adequate housing, recreational and shopping facilities, sanitary conditions, etc., in most of the backward countries. Lack of adequate education facilities for the children of the foreign employees is another difficulty in their way of accepting a job in backward countries.

Attitude of the Natives towards Foreign Capital: In several underdeveloped countries there exists a hostile attitude towards the foreign investors which has grown out of the memories of the past exploitation by them. Howsoever profitable and secure the investment may be, the foreign investors will not invest if the attitude of the people of the country is not welcome and sympathetic towards them. If they fear a boycott by consumers and strikes by labourers, they will not be willing to invest in spite of the best assurances by the government. Creation of a favourable public opinion towards foreign capital is, therefore, very essential for attracting it.

Restrictions on the Import of Goods and Services: Foreign investment, often, requires goods and services from foreign countries. Restricions on these are a great hindrance in the way of foreign investors. There is, also, the fear that import of materials required for manufacturing might be restricted in future in case the foreign exchange position of the country deteriorates.

Non-availability of Competent Labour at Reasonable Rates: Availability of local labour, having the aptitude and ability to learn factory techniques and skills, at reasonable rates is very essential for attracting foreign investments. Many underdeveloped countries, however, lack in this respect.

Lack of Banking and Credit Facilities: Lack of local well developed banking and credit facilities is a great hindrance to foreign investments.

Inconvertibility of the Domestic Currency: The fear of inconvertibility of the domestic currency for the repatriation of profits and amortization funds is a great deterrent to foreign investments. It might be contended that the lack of convertibility has increased foreign investments because the inability to repatriate profits and amortization funds, compelled the foreign investors to reinvest their earnings in the capital recipient country. The deterrent effect of inconvertibility on the inflow of foreign capital, however, has far outweighed the additional investments brought about through the reinvestment of earnings because of the lack of convertibility facilities. Foreign investors in some countries have to bear the additional burden of paying taxes in their home country on their assets and income earned in foreign countries because their governments give no relief or give inadequate relief to those who cannot repatriate their assets and earnings to their mother country because of the lack of convertibility facilities. In order to diminish the fear of inconvertibility, every effort should be made to maintain a strong balance of payments position. In addition to the adoption of a sound economic policy; a screening system might be instituted for the import of foreign capital to avoid the repayment problem. Foreign investments might be permitted only in those fields which add to the foreign exchange earnings or decrease foreign exchange expenditure of the country.

Expansion of Public Sector: Recently, with the advent of planning, public sector has considerably expanded in several underdeveloped countries; this has decreased the scope for foreign private investments.

Restrictions on Foreign Investment in Capital Exporting Countries: Some countries impose restrictions on the export of capital with a view to conserve the savings for domestic development. Some other countries impose restrictions on the export of particular kinds of funds for the security of the investing enterprises.

Requirement for the Reinvestment of Profits: In some countries there exist limitations on the remittance of profits and the investors are required to reinvest a part of their profits.

Unequal Treatment before the Law with Respect to Property Holding: Many underdeveloped countries prohibit the ownership of land by the foreign private investors. This hinders the investments for which ownership of land is very essential.

Multiple Exchange Rates: Some underdeveloped countries use multiple exchange rates to mop up the fabulous profits of the foreign investors. Burden of taxation can be shifted on the foreign investors more easily through the use of multiple exchange rates than the manipulation of tax system.

Taxation: The deterrent effect of taxes has often been overemphasized. Recent investigations show that the taxes are not a very important hindrance to foreign investments.

> We found no evidence to suggest that United States taxes had been an impediment that had prevented particular investments in foreign countries. More important we found no instance where executives believed that total exemption of foreign income from United States taxes would have tipped the balance and changed a decision that had been made against a particular investment. There was no indication that the greater return that lower taxes on foreign income would allow counterbalance the influence of certain factors limiting investment. Where a company was reluctant to invest in a particular country because of the exchange situation, or the opinion of management about the climate in the particular country, the higher

> return on the investment from lower taxes would not be sufficient to overcome this reluctance.[9]

The clamour of private investors for tax concessions is more out of their desire for higher profits and less because taxation is a genuine hindrance to private foreign investments.

Taxes might be a barrier to foreign investment either because their absolute level is very high or because these discriminate against the foreign investors. Regarding the first type of barrier, the problem is to lower taxes not only against foreign investors but against the domestic investors, too. Special concessions to foreign investors alone might be argued on the ground of additional expenditures and risks involved in investing in foreign countries. It is doubtful, however, if the national sentiments in underdeveloped countries will allow the governments to offer special tax concessions exclusively to foreign investors. In addition, it is contended that there is no justification for it because the special expenditures and risks involved in foreign investments are counterbalanced, or even more than that, by the superior techniques and business methods of the foreign investors which are not available to the domestic investors. The cost of lowering the general level of taxation might outweigh the benefit from increased investments if suitable alternative sources of revenue are not available. Another method of decreasing the deterrent effect of the taxation is to modify the tax-structure in such a way as decreases the deterrent effect without involving any loss of revenue. The stimulant effect of this method depends upon the scope for substituting taxes with a smaller deterrent effect and the same yield.

Regarding the second type of barrier, *i.e.,* discriminatory taxation, the observation of the Fiscal Division of Department of Economic Affairs of the United Nations is worth noting:

> Discriminatory taxes do not loom very large as effective barriers. What differences there are in the tax treatment of residents and non-residents (or nationals and aliens) are mostly due to inherent differences in their position. Two of the most frequent measures of this kind are the imposition of a higher flat income tax rate on non-residents than the

9. E.T. Barlow and Ira T. Wender, *Foreign Investment and Taxation* (Englewood Cliffs, 1952), p. 215.

> lowest rate imposed on residents, and the exclusion of the former from the benefits of family allowances and other deductions which are granted to the latter. The reason for such apparent discrimination is two-fold: the inability of tax administration to check on the family status of a non-resident taxpayer or on his total income for the purpose of calculating the proper allowances or the correct progressive tax rate; and the greater facilities for tax evasion open to such taxpayers who are beyond the reach of national tax authorities.[10]

Sometimes the discrimination might arise out of the efforts of the capital-importing countries to channelise foreign investments in particular sectors of the economy in conformity with the general plan of development of the country. International multiple taxation is another important factor which gives rise to discriminatory taxation against the foreign investors. Multiple taxation arises when more than one state claim jurisdiction over the same taxable items. We shall discuss this problem later in a separate section.

Once the case for tax concessions to foreign capital is admitted, there arise a number of questions. Firstly, should the tax concessions be given to new investments or to the old, too? On equity grounds, it is unjust and unreasonable to give tax concessions only to new investments. Discrimination against old investment might arouse fears of discrimination in future against new investments to attract still more investment. In addition, it is very difficult to distinguish between the new and old investments. An enterprise might sell its property and repurchase it to transform the old investment into a new one. If these things are to be avoided, the tax concessions will have to be given to the new as well as the old invesments. On the other hand, if the concessions are given to the new as well as the old investments, the cost of concessions might far outweigh the benefit from the additional flow of capital brought about by these concessions; this will particularly be the case when there exists a large volume of old foreign investment. Barlow and Wender conclude that as most of the additional investments are out of reinvestment of earnings, the greatest stimulus to foreign investment

10. United Nations, *Effects of Taxation on Foreign Trade and Investment* (New York, 1953), p. 15.

with least cost to treasury can be provided by giving concession only to the reinvestment of earnings.[11]

Secondly, in what ratio should the loss from tax concessions be shared between the capital-importing and the capital-exporting countries. Most of the benefit from capital movements is likely to accrue to the capital-importing countries. On this ground it might be contended that the major loss from tax concession should be borne by the capital-importing countries. It is, however, difficult for the underdeveloped countries to give considerable tax concessions because of their meagre budgetary resources in relation to the expenditure they are required to incur for the rapid development of their economies. The loss from tax concession, therefore, will have to be born mainly by the advanced countries which can afford to forego a part of their revenue with less difficulties and smaller injury to the welfare of their people. This contention is strengthened by the acceptance of advanced countries of their obligation to help the underdeveloped countries in their programme of development by all possible means. It is of great satisfaction for the underdeveloped countries to note that in recent discussions on the subject, the representatives of the advanced capital-exporting countries were among the foremost to propose that the concessions should come mainly from the capital-exporting countries.[12]

Thirdly, should the tax incentives be general or selective ? Tax incentives to be more effective and less costly should be selective. General tax incentives are more costly and less effective. "Such incentives are the more valuable to the taxpayer, the greater his income, *i.e.*, the less by definition he is in need of them. The marginal investors, however, and the one who operates at a loss during his first years of operation, will garner little or no benefits from the incentives which presumably were designed especially to attract him.[13] Tax incentives should be given only to those investors who are highly responsive to such incentives. The foreign investors who come to capture certain markets or to exploit certain natural resources required for their plants working in the advanced country need not be given any tax concessions. Similarly, incentives need not be given for investments in industries which are highly lucrative and

11. Barlow and Wender, n. 9.
12. United Nations, n. 10, p. 5.
13. *Ibid.*, p. 20.

can attract foreign capital without tax concessions. Tax concessions should be limited only to those industries which are essential for the development of the country and cannot attract sufficient foreign capital without such inducements. Tax concessions might be given for foreign investments in particular regions of the country which fail to attract domestic investors. Investors introducing new industries essential for the development of the country might be given tax concessions for a specified initial period in which the profits are likely to be small.

Another useful method of providing tax concessions is to negotiate special agreements with individual investors. This has been the most important method in the past. This method has the advantage that the concessions can be negotiated for each project according to its expected contribution toward the development of the economy. This, however,, has the disadvantage that the powerful foreign enterprises might succeed in exacting unreasonable concessions out of the dire necessity for foreign capital in most of the underdeveloped countries.

5. International Multiple Taxation

International multiple taxation arises when two or more governments simultaneously claim the jurisdiction over the tax base. The jurisdiction for income tax, for instance, may be claimed by the investor's national country, by the country of his residence, or by the country in which the enterprise is located. Multiple taxation will be a great deterrent to foreign investment if the cumulative taxes levied by different governments render the enterprise unprofitable. The distribution of tax revenue and the jurisdiction over the tax is a highly controversial problem.

Methods of Relief from International Multiple Taxation: Relief from international multiple taxation can be provided either through unilateral action or through international agreements between the countries concerned. The former has the advantage that relief can be provided without the concurrence of the other governments. Many capital-exporting advanced countries have provided tax relief to encourage the outflow of capital towards the underdeveloped countries with a view to help them in their programme of development. The scope for unconditional unilateral action, however, is limited by the self-interest of each state. Unilateral relief, therefore, has generally been provided on the condition of reciprocal treatment by the beneficiary countries. Another defect of the unilateral relief is that it cannot be provided by the borrowing country if the lending country requires its investors to pay taxes at the higher rates whether these are of the national country or that of the borrowing country; under this-system, the tax concessions given by the borrowing country go to the treasury of the lending country and not to the private foreign investors. Execution of multilateral agreements, however, is very difficult because of the diversity of the existing tax systems and because of the varying interests of different countries in the stimulation of capital movements. Most of the relief provided so far has been through bilateral agreements. Unilateral relief provided on the condition of reciprocal treatment by the beneficiary country is also a sort of bilateral agreement. Conclusion of bilateral agreements is less complex and easier than that, of multilateral agreements.

6. Guarantees

Risks of inconvertibility and expropriation are a great hindrance to the inflow of foreign capital into the underdeveloped countries. One method of insuring against these risks is the provision of guarantee against inconvertibility and expropriation either by the capital-importing or by the capital exporting, or jointly by both the countries.

Guarantee against Inconvertibility: Provision of a guarantee[14] against inconvertibility raises a number of questions. Firstly, should the guarantee be provided by the capital-importing, or by the capital-exporting, or jointly by both the countries? The ability of the capital-importing country to honour the guarantee and the extent of the inducement which this undertaking provides for the prospective investors depends upon the anticipated position of the balance of payments of the importing country. The balance of payments position of the underdeveloped countries being what it is the guarantee given by the capital-importing countries is not likely to inspire much confidence. Guarantee by the capital-exporting country, on the other hand, might weaken the incentive in the

14. Guarantee may be given for the repatriation of the whole of the compensation in case of nationalisation by the government.

borrowing country to create favourable conditions for attracting foreign capital. In addition, the capital-exporting countries can agree to provide guarantee only if these get a guarantee from the borrowing countries to the effect that the foreign capital will receive fair treatment in all respects and that they will take all measures needed to honour the guarantee given by the capital-exporting countries on their behalf.

Secondly, should the guarantee cover only the new foreign investments or the old, too, which came before the announcement of the guarantee provisions? On equity grounds, it is unjust and unreasonable to give guarantee only to the new capital. Discrimination against old capital might arouse fears of discrimination against the new investors after some time when they become old with a view to attract still more capital. In addition, it might lead to a conversion of old capital into new capital through the sale and repurchase deeds. On the other hand, coverage of old capital, too, might considerably increase the obligations of the guarantor if there already exists a large volume of foreign-capital in the country. Foreign investors having a large amount of blocked funds might avail of the opportunity and rush for foreign exchange which might endanger the stability of the currency.

Thirdly, should the guarantee against inconvertibility be given for funds arising only out of a previous investment of capital in investors' own country or for those arising from all sources? If the guarantee is provided for funds arising from all sources, the opportunity might be exploited by persons other than the investors, too, whereas the purpose of the guarantee is to provide convertibility for investors only. The guarantee, therefore, should be limited to the import of capital in investor's currency and the reinvestment of profits made in the borrowing country. The foreign investments, generally, require some foreign personnel. The foreign investors might agree to invest on the condition that the employment of some foreign personnel in the enterprise is permitted. In such cases, the guarantee will have to cover the saving of the foreign personnel, too.

Fourthly, should the guarantee be given for the convertibility of profits and gradual amortization of capital or for the withdrawal of investments, too? Should the foreign investors be allowed to sell their investments and repatriate the capital at any time they like?

Any such guarantee might lead to a wholesale repatriation of foreign capital at the slightest panic and endanger stability of economy. The mere expectation of a crisis or of a variation in the exchange rate might become a reality because of a rush for foreign exchange for the repatriation of capital. The guarantee, therefore, should be given only for the convertibility of profits and the gradual amortization of capital. This, also, should be subject to the provision that foreign exchange will be provided only after the demand for it for the importation of necessary commodities (*e.g.* food, medicines etc.) has been met. The definition of the necessary imports, however, is a controversial issue. Certain imports might be considered necessaries by the borrowing countries while the same might not be recognised to be so by the lending countries. In addition the determination of profits and amortization funds depends to a large extent on the owners of the enterprise. The value of profits and amortization funds can be considerably magnified by the manipulation of accounts by the foreign investors.

The fifth question relates to the rate of exchange at which the convertibility of the funds is to be guaranteed. A lowering of the rate of the exchange will decrease the value of the funds to be repatriated in terms of the national currency of the foreign investors. The foreign investors will prefer the guarantee at the stable rate of exchange. Guarantee, at the stable rate of exchange will increase the burden of the guarantee in case the currency has to be devalued for certain reasons.

Finally, it is very difficult to precisely define the term convertibility.

> ...in the convertibility type of guarantee the restrictions on convertibility may not present themselves in such clear cut form as an outright blockage of all dollar remittances. Partial blockage of remittances by imposition of unfavourable or even confiscatory exchange rates are more likely to be encountered than complete prohibition of profit repatriation. Also, it is difficult to define with precision the point at which imposition of a multiple exchange system constitutes the 'inconvertibility' against which the guarantee is intended to insure.[15]

15. Staff papers presented to the Commission on Foreign Economic Policy 1954 (Washington, 1954), p. 129.

Guarantee against Expropriation: It is very difficult to precisely define the term expropriation.

> ...there is no unambiguous definition of the term 'expropriation.' Would, for instance, an excess profit tax be regarded as expropriation? Would the regulation by a government agency of utility rates or railway freight charges be regarded as such? Would an injunction on monopolistic practices be regarded as undue or expropriatory interference? In the case of nationalisation, one scheme of compensation may be considered expropriatory, while another scheme may be considered quite fair. In fact, we could continue to name debatable cases like these indefinitely. The concept of expropriation reflects an agglomeration of terms such as 'legitimate profits,' 'fair return,' 'just compensation,' etc., which do not possess any generally accepted meaning, and which may mean different things at different times or under changed circumstances even to the same persons.[16]

A difference of opinion as to the interpretation of the term 'expropriation' is very likely to arise between the lending and the borrowing countries as the desirable degree of state intervention in economic affairs differs between the two. The development of underdeveloped countries requires a degree of state intervention larger than that existing in many developed countries.

Guarantees might cover not only the risk of expropriation and inconvertibility but certain other risks too, *viz.,* risk of war, damage to property of the foreign investors from insurrection and internal revolution, etc. The need for guarantee against these risks arises from the increased international tension and from the instability of governments and absence of strict law and order in many backward countries. Regarding the coverage of investments, guarantees might "be provided not only for equity investments but also for investment in securities issued by foreign governments." Guarantees, however, should not cover the genuine commercial risks involved in any business enterprise.

The guarantee by the governments of the capital-exporting countries might arouse protests from the public of these countries.

16. Yan-Liwu, "Government Guarantee and Private Foreign Investment," *American Economic Review* (March, 1950), p. 67.

The public might contend that investment being a private business, the governments should not use public funds for meeting obligations arising out of the provision of guarantees; if the guarantee is to be provided, it should better be provided by some private institution working on commercial principles, *i.e.*, it should charge a reasonable premium for the service. The governments of the capital-exporting countries, however, are justified in providing guarantees to the extent these encourage private foreign investments and lessen the need for direct governmental assistance. The guarantee by the governments of the capital-exporting countries might be misused by those countries for attaining certain economic and political objectives by favouring certain types of investments and certain investors and discriminating against other types of investments and other investors. Provision of guarantee by the government will also give it some right of control over the enterprise and an access to its books. This might not be liked by the foreign investors. Guarantees by the governments of the capital-exporting countries, on the other hand, have the advantage that these are likely to diminish the chances of international defaults by the capital-importing countries because of the fear of the use of sanctions by the guaranteeing government. In case the guarantees are provided by some private institution the interests of the government are affected indirectly and, therefore, the chances of the use of sanctions against the defaulting government are smaller.

If the guarantee is to be provided on the charge of a premium, there arises the question as to what should be the level of this charge. If the charge is very low, it might not be sufficient to meet all the losses and the tax-payers might have to bear a part of the burden. On the other hand, if the charge is high enough to build up a fund capable of meeting all the prospective losses, it might discourage foreign investments by decreasing their profitability. Further, should the premia for guarantees vary from industry to industry and from country to country according to the degree of risk involved? The answer will be in the affirmative if the principle of equity is to be applied. Different rates for different industries might, however, arouse criticism of favouring certain industries against others. Similarly, different rates for different countries might lead to an embitterment of international relations. Differential rates system, of course, has the advantage that guarantees can be used to channel the private investments in those sectors which are likely to add maximum to the productive capacity of the capital-exporing country.

7. Code of International Investment

The best way to encourage the movement of capital is the formulation of a code of 'fair practices' for international investments and the establishment of the machinery for the settlement of disputes in the light of the provision of this code. There exists, however, a vast divergence between the views of the capital-importing and capital-exporting countries as to the contents of such a code. According to the capital-exporting countries, the purpose of the code should be to ensure complete convertibility, non-discriminatory treatment, and security against nationalisation and expropriation of foreign investments. On the other hand, according to the capital-importing countries the main purpose of the code should be to ensure against exploitation and interference in domestic matters and to impose obligations on foreign investors to work for the smooth and balanced growth of their economies. If such a code is to be framed and adopted, each party will have to forego some of its demands and give concessions to the other party. The contents of the code must be acceptable to all the main capital-importing and capital-exporting countries. The code should cover the equity as well as the portfolio investments. The code might be prepared, more or less, on the following principles:[17]

(*a*) Foreigners should enjoy the same inviolability of their persons as nationals, along with same non-political rights.

(*b*) Non-discrimination must be applied in good faith; there should be no apparently general laws that apply in fact only to foreigners.

(*c*) Foreigners must have the same right and capacity as nationals to enter into contract on their behalf or for the account of another, to repurchase, lease, inherit, hold, use, transfer and convey personal and real property (provided this does not threaten national security) and to appear as plaintiff before the domestic courts.

17. (a) to (i) have been cited from Cleona Lewis, *The United States and the Foreign Investment Problems* (Washington, 1948), pp. 257-58.

(*d*) Restrictions on foreigners for reasons of national security must not become disguised protection to private domestic interests. Government should permit leases and concessions, management contracts, and other special arrangements.

(*e*) The burden of taxation be equitably apportioned. Discriminatory, extra-territorial, and double taxation of foreigner should be avoided.

(*f*) Non-discriminatory practice should apply to the treatment of labour by domestic and foreign concerns and in general to the employment of foreigners and nationals; *i.e.*, to the employment of foreign and local labour, technicians and executives.

(*g*) The status of foreign firms should be similar to that granted to domestic firms:

(1) the accounts of a foreign branch showing transactions with the rest of the enterprise should be kept in the same form as that adopted for transactions with separate firms;

(2) resident manager should be given sufficient discretion to conduct business;

(3) the legal status of the subsidiary corporation as a separate entity from its foreign parent should be fully recognised in all business, judicial and tax matters, subject to legal remedy incase of illegitimate transactions.

(*h*) Special law regarding the proportion of nationals in any business association, the proportion of capital to be subscribed by nationals, the minimum number of seats on boards of directors to be held by nationals, are other instances of discrimination, and should be removed.

(*i*) Where policies of nationalization are adopted by a capital-importing country the properties of foreign investors should not be nationalized without due process of law and they should be guaranteed a fair compensation for their nationalized properties. This compensation should be paid in cash and be freely transferable within a reasonable time.

(*j*) Foreign investors should not interfere in the domestic affairs of the country in which they are making investment.

(*k*) In the recruitment of the personnel in all capacities, they should not discriminate against the nationals of the country. Recruitment should be on purely commercial considerations, nationals of the investing and the capital-recipient countries having equal chances of employment.

(*l*) Foreign investors should abide by all the domestic laws of the country.

(*m*) They should not discourage domestic investors by unfair competition.

(*n*) In case of severe foreign exchange difficulties, the loan contracts should be modified and the borrowing countries be enabled to repay the loan and the interest thereupon in suitable installments keeping in view their foreign exchange position. In case of repeated foreign exchange difficulties owing to factors beyond the control of the borrowing country, the debts might even be scaled down by the proposed international tribunal to be set up.

In addition to the above principles, a moral (not legal) obligation should be imposed on the foreign investors to help the capital-recipient country in its programme of development by all means as far as possible. They should train the nationals in all capacities, encourage joint participation of domestic capital and disclose their secrets to the domestic entrepreneurs as far as possible. They should also try that their investments develop the country in a balanced and not lopsided manner. The capital exporting countries should encourage the import of goods and services from the capital-importing countries to facilitate the repatriation of profits, amortization funds, etc.

8. Machinery for the Settlement of Disputes

The settlement of all disputes arising between the investing and the capital-recipient countries by arbitration should be made obligatory on all countries accepting the code. A tribunal should be set up to arbitrate between the disputant parties. This is in the interest of both the parties. At present the investor has to seek justice through local laws. He cannot invoke the interference of his government till all the local remedies have been exhausted. Under the proposed system, he can expect a better standard of justice from the tribunal proposed to be set up. The judges of the tribunal will also be of a higher status than those of the local courts. On the other hand, the borrowing countries will be ensured against the use of force by the powerful investing country in case of a dispute.

There arises the question as to how should the international tribunal be constituted. International Court of Justice cannot serve the purpose because, by its very statute, it is restricted to act only in case of disputes arising between states. The parties to the code should set up a separate independent tribunal based more or less on the principles of International Court of Justice.

9. Screening of Foreign Investments

It will be harmful for the capital-recipient countries to permit foreign investments in each and every field. A proper machinery should be set up for screening the foreign investments. Foreign investments, generally, should not be permitted in the following fields:

(*a*) Those reserved for the government.

(*b*) Where it is competitive with the local industry whose production is adequate to completely meet the local demand.

(c) Luxury industries.

(*d*) Industries exploring exhaustible minerals for export which will be needed for country's development in the future.

(*e*) Which are likely to be undertaken by the domestic capital in the near future.

Foreign investments might be encouraged in the following fields:

(*a*) Industries considered to be vital for the country's economic development.

(*b*) Which fail to attract adequate domestic capital.

(*c*) Which strengthen the balance of payments position by earning foreign exchange directly or indirectly.

(*d*) Which employ and train maximum national personnel.

(*e*) Those bringing advanced technology.

(*f*) Which can be integrated with the domestic economy and will not remain the floating parts of the foreign economies.

INTER-GOVERNMENTAL LENDING

1. Role of Inter-governmental Lending

Governmental lending is the most important of all the sources of foreign capital, today. One reason for the increase in governmental lending since the Second World War is the increased state participation in economic development in most of the underdeveloped countries. Public utilities and basic industries which require vast investments are under public control and management in almost all the countries. Governments in many underdeveloped countries have embarked on several light manufacturing industries and even on trading.

> ...even in the golden age of private international investment a large proportion took this form. Loans to governmental authorities (Central, State and Municipal) accounted for over half of French and German investments outstanding in 1914. In the case of Britain, 30 per cent of the total outstanding at that time consisted of government bonds.[18]

Without undermining the importance of private investment, it may be emphasized that governmental lending is very essential for building social and economic overheads, *viz.,* transportation and communications, power, land improvement, schools and public works of all kinds. These require long term loans at cheap rates of interest which can be provided only by the governments. Investment in these is very essential also for attracting private foreign investments.

> It was not until the 1920's that Japan began to receive any considerable direct investments from abroad, while government borrowing from abroad virtually ceased. The sequence is interesting. First in the country's development came government investments financed in part by foreign loans, much later, in the 1920's, came direct foreign investments. By that time the market had grown, the public overhead facilities were established, and so the inducement for private entrepreneurial investments had become substantial.

18. Nurkse, n. 4, p. 89.

The same sequence can be observed in certain other countries that have attained a substantial degree of development.[19]

2. Disadvantages of Inter-Governmental Lending

A large proportion of the governmental loans are distributed among different countries not on the basis of their need but on political considerations. A large proportion of the loans given by the government of Russia goes to the communist countries. Similarly, the major proportion of the loans provided by the U.S. Government goes to countries outside the Russian bloc.

This source of capital is not very reliable for the borrowing countries. Any change in their economic or political policy not liked by the lending country might lead to a stoppage of the flow of the foreign capital.

3. Inter-Governmental Lending—A Supplement or a Substitute for Private Investments

Governmental lending can be a supplement as well as a substitute for private foreign investments. Loans to private foreign investors will be a great stimulus to private foreign investments. Some private investors might find profitable opportunities for investment in foreign countries but might not possess sufficient capital to exploit these. Even if they possess enough capital, they might not be willing to risk a large part of their capital and prefer their government sharing a part of the risk by advancing loans. Participation by the government will also provide a better security to the foreign private investors against the arbitrary treatment of the governments of the capital-recipient countries. Sometimes government initiative might be followed by huge private investment which would have not been made otherwise.

Governmental loans will be a substitute for private foreign investment. If they are made for projects which would have been undertaken by the private investors. It is frequently maintained by the government of the United States that its loans do not decrease the scope for private investors because they are made only for those projects for which private investments are not forthcoming. Governmental loans, however, can be substituted indirectly for

19. *Ibid.*, pp. 90-91.

private foreign investments. Borrowing governments, for instance, might utilise their own funds for projects which the private foreign capital is ready to finance and get governmental loans for projects which cannot be financed by private foreign investors. The contention of the U.S. Government will be valid only if the borrowing government does not invest in any enterprise for which private foreign investors are ready to provide finance. Expectation of governmental loans might encourage the underdeveloped countries to bring more and more enterprises under public sector and thus lessen the scope for private foreign investments. Governmental lending might remove the incentive, to some extent, for improving the climate to attract private foreign capital. The increased taxation by the lending government to collect funds for giving loans to the underdeveloped countries will decrease the inevitable funds with the private investors.

INSTITUTIONAL LENDING

1. Benefits

The best method of channelling funds from advanced to the underdeveloped countries is the establishment of international lending institutions. The international lending institutions will distribute the available funds on the basis of the need and the scope for fruitful utilisation of the funds and not on political considerations. The loans from international institutions are free from political strings. Self-respect of the borrowing countries is maintained when the loans come from organisations of which they themselves are members. When many countries are looking for funds from the same institution, they will act as a check on each other's extravagant claims. The chances of the violation of the contracts are less with international organisations than with the individual governments because a country violating a contract with an international institution incurs the displeasure of all the countries member of the institution and not of a single country. International institutions can draw on a greater variety of experience and technical personnel than can any individual country.

PORTFOLIO VS. EQUITY INVESTMENT

1. Definition

Portfolio investment means loans at a fixed rate of interest usually without any share in the ownership, control and management of the enterprise to which the loans have been made. In case of equity investments, the investors participate in the ownership, management and control of the business and are responsible for the losses and profits. This distinction, of course, is not very hard and fast. The World Bank, for instance, interferes in the control and management of the enterprise for which it has given loans to ensure that the loans are utilised economically and only for the purpose for which they have been sanctioned. It often provides technical know-how which is one of the characteristics of equity investment. Similarly, some equity investors, particularly those having small shares, may not participate actively in the control and management of the enterprise in which they have invested funds. Several countries allow foreign capital subject to the condition that the majority shares in the enterprise are held by the local investors. This weakens the voice of the management of the enterprise.

2. Advantages of Equity Investment (Disadvantages of Portfolio Investment)

The private foreign investors prefer equity to portfolio investment "because they can control the policy and management of the enterprise in which they have invested their capital.

Equity investments bring with them experience, technology, patents, copyrights etc., the importance of which cannot be overemphasized for the development of the underdeveloped countries. Sometimes the foreign loans have been utilised inappropriately or have remained even unutilised because of the non-availability of managerial ability and technology in backward countries.

Capital markets in certain countries might not have developed to the extent of dealing with the floatation of foreign issues but certain enterprises in these countries might be ready and competent to invest in some industries in foreign countries. Such investments can be made only if these take the form of equity investment. The absence of these might lead to a monopoly of foreign investments by a few countries possessing well developed capital markets, the consequences of which might not be very pleasant for the capital recipient countries.

Equity investments generally lead to the reinvestment of earnings from the initial investments and thus increase the stock of foreign investment. In addition, if required, the foreign enterprises can raise the additional funds in their capital markets more easily than the local enterprises.

Equity investment is more permanent than the portfolio investment. Portfolio investment has got to be repaid after a fixed period of time whereas the equity investment may go on for ever.

In case of equity investment, risks are shouldered by the foreign investors. The risk of a loss is particularly important in the initial stages of an industry. Once the success of the industry has been demonstrated at the risk of the foreign capital the domestic capital may enter the industry.

The rate of return on equity investments generally rises in booms and falls in depressions. The fixed liability of the portfolio investment, in contrast, might create difficulties for the borrowing underdeveloped countries in a depression when their foreign earnings from the export of primary products decline considerably.

Substantial contractual obligations fixed in terms of foreign currency might rule out devaluation of the domestic currency when it would have been desirable otherwise.

3. Advantages of Portfolio Investment (Disadvantages of Equity Investment)

In the past, the average rate of return on equity investments has been much higher than that on portfolio investments. Thus the portfolio investment is cheaper than the equity investment for the borrowing countries.

Portfolio capital can be used according to the wishes of the borrowing countries. Recently, most of the underdeveloped countries have embarked on planning. Portfolio investment can be fitted into the national plans. It is difficult to channel the equity investment according to the national plans of development of the borrowing countries. Equity investment will go into those fields which offer the highest rate of return whether or not those are provided in the national plans.

The time of repayment of capital and interest thereupon of the portfolio investment is known before hand and the borrowing government can make arrangements for these payments. The time of repatriation of equity investment and profits thereupon, in contrast, is unknown and uncertain. There might arise huge demands for foreign exchange for the repatriation of capital and profits thereupon in times of scarcity of foreign exchange and no demand might be made when the balance of payments position is very easy and foreign exchange available in plenty.

In case of portfolio investment, the management and control of the concern in which the foreign capital has been invested remains in the hands of nationals and, therefore, there is no fear of foreign interference in the internal affairs of the borrowing country. In the past, several borrowing countries had the unpleasant experience of foreign investors interfering in the political affairs of the country. One of the reasons for the delay in India's freedom was the opposition of the vested interests created by foreign investments to any movement for freedom.

The increase in the public sector in most of the underdeveloped countries has limited to some extent the scope for the equity investments.

Investors of equity capital with their superior technology and business methods might oust the domestic enterprises and establish a monopoly over a major part of the borrowing country. Such possibilities do not arise in case of portfolio investment.

4. Decline of Private Portfolio Investment

Most of the portfolio loans made recently have come either from international financing institutions or from the governments of the advanced countries. Private portfolio investments have declined considerably. In the past, floating loans in the international capital markets, by issuing bonds was an important method of borrowing from foreign countries. Floating loans by this method is not possible, now, in spite of substanial differences in the return on the domestic and foreign bonds. Following are among the main factors responsible for the drying up of this source of foreign capital:

(*a*) Repeated defaults by the borrowing governments.

(*b*) Frequent deficits in the balance of payments of the underdeveloped countries and the consequent devaluation of their currencies. Devaluation of the currency of the borrowing country decreases the value of the bonds in terms of the currency of the lending country.

(*c*) Lack of convertibility.

(*d*) Independence of colonies. The bonds issued by the colonies, were bought mainly by the persons and institutions of the metropolitan country because of their great familiarity with the borrowing country and the security provided by their own government ruling the borrowing country.

(*e*) Restrictions on some types of institutions in some countries on investing in foreign bonds.

(*f*) Inflationary trends in almost all the countries. Rise in the prices of commodities decreases the real value of bonds. This has discouraged investment in domestic as well as in foreign bonds.

(*g*) Decrease in the importance of individual savers. Individual savers were important investors in bonds. Decrease in individual saving is mainly because of increased taxation and the replacement of individual savings by corporate savings. Corporations reinvest the earnings instead of distributing these in the form of profits.

(*h*) Countries traditionally experienced in investing in foreign bonds are suffering from shortage of capital and deficits in their balance of payments. Investors in the United States, the country having the maximum saving, are not experienced in this business.

(*i*) Increase in international political tension.

REPAYMENT PROBLEM

1. Process of Repayment

The repayments arise out of interest, profits, amortization funds, repatriation of certain investments and the furlough salaries and old age pensions of the foreign employees accompanying foreign capital.

The difficulties involved in the repayment have often been overemphasized. Foreign investments raise the income of the borrowing countries. History tells that the rise in the national income of a country increases its foreign trade and thereby the foreign exchange transactions. With the increase in the foreign exchange transactions, the relative burden of the repayment of capital and the interest thereupon falls.

Foreign investments in export and import-substitute industries increase the capacity to export and hence the foreign exchange earnings and decrease the need for imports and hence the foreign exchange expenditure. Foreign investments in other industries may also increase indirectly the capacity to export and hence the foreign exchange earnings. Investment in transportation, for instance, increases the capacity to export the commodities which could not be exported previously owing to a shortage of transport facilities. Shortage of wagons and shipping facilities is an important factor hindering the export of several commodities in India.

One way of easing the repayment problem is to encourage foreign investors to settle permanently by adopting the citizenship of the country in which they make investments and to reinvest their profits instead of taking these back to their mother country. Permanent settlement of the investors is one of the reasons why the repayment problem did not arise in the case of countries of recent settlement, *viz.*, U.S.A., Canada, Australia, Argentina, etc. In these countries, a large part of the inflow of capital was accompanied by the emigration of investors who settled there permanently. Adoption of the citizenship of the country in which investments are made also decreases the fears of discrimination. Those who have huge investments in their mother country, too, however, cannot be induced to accept the citizenship of the foreign country where they are investing a part of their capital. In addition, patriotic feelings might prevent investors from changing their nationality.

Capital-Output Ratio

26

1. Definition

The concept of capital-output ratio has been employed in the well-known models of Harrod, Hicks, Domar and others. It is very essential to distinguish between the average and the marginal capital-output ratio. The average ratio is the value of the total stock of capital divided by total annual income. The marginal or incremental ratio for the whole economy is the value of the addition to capital (net investment) divided by the addition to income (net national income). The marginal ratio need not be equal to the average ratio. Even if any change in the average ratio is slow, the marginal ratio can vary much more.

The concept is, often, used to determine the current rate of national income growth. Current rate of national income growth can be obtained by multiplying the current investment rate by the reciprocal of the marginal capital-output ratio. To express it algebraically let Y be the net national income, ΔY the absolute increase in the national income, I the investment, $\frac{I}{Y}$ the investment rate and $\frac{I}{\Delta Y}$ the marginal capital-output ratio. The rate of net national income is $\frac{I}{Y} \cdot \frac{\Delta Y}{I} = \frac{\Delta Y}{Y}$. To take a numerical example, if the rate of net investment is 12 per cent and the marginal capital-output ratio 4, the rate of national income growth will be 12/4=3 per cent.

2. Gross and Net Capital-Output Ratio

The usefulness of the concept of capital-output ratio as a tool of economic analysis is very much limited because of its dependence on the behaviour of a number of other variables. The rate of growth of national income depends, in addition to rate of investment, upon a number of other factors. Capital is normally used in combination with other agents of production. An important factor determining the capital-output ratio is the amount of other agents combined with a certain amount of capital. The same rate of investment will lead to different rates of growth of national income according to the different amounts of other factors combined with a certain amount of capital. Capital-output ratio may be changed by changes in the nature of availability of 'free factors,' *viz.*, rainfall, climate etc., which play an important role in the production process. A favourable change in natural factors will lower the capital-output ratio and an unfavourable one will raise it. Capital-output ratio may be changed by changes in the extent of the utilisation of installed capacity. To separate out the effect of changes in capital on the changes in the rate of growth of income, we may use the concept of net capital-output ratio which means capital-output ratio on the assumption that all factors other than capital remain constant. Because normally changes in capital are associated with a change in other agents of production, to be nearer to reality, we may use the concept of adjusted capital-output ratio which means capital-output ratio when a change in capital is combined with a specified change in other factors of production. In what follows, we won't use the modified concept mentioned above and use the concept of gross capital-output ratio, *i.e.*, ratio between the change in the rate of investment and the rate of growth of income irrespective of changes in other variables.

3. Capital-Output Ratio in Economic Planning

The concept of capital-output ratio has been widely used in discussions on planning for economic development. Professor Harrod gives a formula explaining the forces which determine the rate of growth of an economy. The formula is expressed in the form of the equation $g=s/c$ where g is the rate of growth of national income, c the inverse of capital-output ratio (*i.e.*, output-capital ratio) and s the ratio of savings to total income. A similar formula was introduced by Professor Domar: $d=s\delta$ where d is the rate of development, s the proportion of savings and δ the average productivity of capital. According to the above equations the rate of growth of income depends upon two factors: (1) ratio of savings to income and (2) the capital-output ratio. Given different values of s and c, different rates of growth of income can be obtained. For obtaining the maximum rate of growth, what a country has to do is to manipulate the economic forces in such a manner that the value of *s* is raised to the highest possible level and that of *c* lowered to the lowest possible level.

Capital-output ratio is not an infallible measure of capital productivity. It may not always be in the interest of a country to make investment in fields in which capital-output ratio is the lowest one. Capital-output ratio may be very high in the case of public utilities like roads, railways, irrigation, electricity, yet the importance of these cannot be overemphasized for accelerating economic development. The concept of capital-output ratio does not take into acccount the indirect contribution of capital to output. Public utilities facilitate production and thus contribute to production mostly indirectly. The concept of capital-output ratio does not take into account the contribution to production of an equipment over its whole period of life. In the long run, durable machinery which gives service for a long period may turn out to be more productive and cheaper than the non-durable one which is cheaper but gives service only for a short period.

Capital-output ratios calculated from past data can be used for forward planning only if they remain constant over a long period. They, however, remain changing along with changes in other variables, *viz.*, level of utilisation of capacity, interest rates, prices of factors of production, technological developments, type of economic organisation etc. They differ not only in a country over time but also from country to country. The usefulness of the concept of capital-output ratio as a tool of economic planning, therefore, is very much limited.

4. Relation between Capital-Output Ratio and Economic Development

What is the relation between the capital-output ratio and the economic development? Does capital-output ratio increase, decrease or remain constant with the increase in per capita income? Very little statistical information is available on the subject. Analytically speaking, some factors suggest that capital-output ratio is likely to decline with economic development while other factors suggest quite the reverse. On the whole, the former kind of factors seem to be more forceful than those of the latter kind and, therefore, there is the likelihood that the capital-output ratio will decline with economic development. Let us consider the important arguments on both sides. First we start with the considerations which suggest a rise in the capital-output ratio.

Economic development generally leads to an increase in the demand for labour and thereby to a rise in wage rates. Productivity of labour rises with economic development. This supports the demand of labour for an increase in wages. Rise in wage rates encourages substitution of capital for labour. Substitution of capital for labour will raise capital-output ratio. Wage rates may not rise if the increase in incomes is followed by a considerable increase in the rate of growth of population which generally happens in the initial stages of economic development. Ultimately, however, economic development is followed by a decrease in the rate of growth of population and, therefore, wage rates are likely to rise.

Economic development consists of a utilisation of known potentialities. Gradual utilisation of exhaustible and non-replaceable natural resources raises their price. Capital-output ratio will rise to the extent such resources enter into the production of capital goods. The argument is based on the assumption that known natural resources are fixed in volume or that the rate of utilisation of resources is higher than that of the discovery of new resources. The natural resources of underdeveloped countries, however, have not been properly surveyed and investigated. If sufficient outlay is made in discovering new natural resources, the rate of the discovery of natural resources may be higher than the rate of utilisation of these. In case it is so, economic development will be associated with a fall an the price of natural resources. In fact, it is very difficult to say anything definite about the rate of discovery of new natural resources.

Because of the existence of abundant unexploited opportunities in the field of technology capital will be highly productive in the early stages of economic development. Modern techniques developed in advanced countries cannot be used in underdeveloped countries because of lack of capital. If capital is available, production can be spectacularly increased by the introduction of modern techniques. Once the latest known techniques have been used, additional capital will not lead to so rapid advances in production.

Let us now examine the arguments which suggest that the economic development is likely to lead to decline in the capital-output ratio.

Colin Clark held that the capital-output ratio should decline because economic development consists in a shift of production from primary to tertiary industries which use comparatively lesser capital.[1] But economic development also consists in a shift of production from primary to secondary industry which are comparatively more capital intensive. This kind of shift will tend to raise capital-output ratio.

A rise in incomes increases efficiency of labour in a number of ways. It enables labour to acquire more knowledge and skills, to consume better food, to avail of greater medical facilities, to live in better housing, all of which add to efficiency. Expenditure on the improvement of human beings is generally classified as consumption and not as investment. Availability of larger capital increases the scope for division of labour which increases its productivity. Increase in the productivity of labour decreases the capital-output ratio.

An increase in production, generally, leads to a number of internal and external economies of production which tend to lower capital-output radio.

Generally, the more durable the capital, the higher will be the capital-output ratio. In the initial stages of development, a large part of the capital is invested in the construction of economic and social overheads which are more durable than the industrial machinery which accounts for considerable expenditure in the latter stages.

As development proceeds, the demand for fixed factors increases. An increase in the demand for fixed factors leads to rise in their rent. Rent component in the total cost (and total volume of output), therefore, will be smaller in the early stages of development than in the later stages.

In the initial stages of development, countries are more efficient in the production of consumption goods than in that of capital goods; this raises the cost of capital in relation to income.

In the early stages of economic development, the countries do not know the proper use of capital and this leads to a considerable

1. Colin Clark, *Conditions of Economic Progress* (London, 1951), pp. 500-04.

wastage of it. Workers are not properly trained and they handle the equipment less carefully. Depreciation rates are very high because the roads, buildings and machines are not properly maintained. Capital is not properly allocated between different sectors and between different industries in each sector. This is partly because of lack of knowledge about the profitability of different investment opportunities. Capital tends to stick to beaten tracks even if there exist more profitable opportunities in other lines.

5. Standardisation and Capital-Output Ratio

Standardisation of products and processes is an important method of economising capital, and thus of lowering the capital-output ratio. This is particularly so in the manufacture of industrial intermediates, spare-parts, necessaries, and certain common tools, equipment and machinery used in industries. A fuller use can be made of fixed capital in many interlinking units by standardising their output.

Unemployment in an Underdeveloped Economy

27

1. Introductory

Unemployment is a great economic waste. More serious are its moral consequences. The feeling of not being wanted by society demoralises a person. Unemployment breeds hatred, despair, fear and corruption. Full utilisation of the available manpower is very essential on economic and social grounds.

2. Concept of Full Employment

What does the term full employment mean? The concept of full employment is a very ambiguous one. Different authors attach a different meaning to the concept. Literally speaking, full employment would prevail when every able bodied adult worked the number of hours considered normal for a fully employed person at the current return to labour. It is not, however, possible to attain this level of employment ir private enterprise economies. In such economies quite a few have enough unearned incomes to be in a position to afford a life of well-paid idleness. Pigou, therefore, defined full employment as one when "everybody who at the ruling rate of wages wishes to be employed is in fact employed." But even Pigouian full employment appears to be unattainable because, at any given time, there is bound to be some seasonal and frictional unemployment. There will be a certain amount of irreducible unemployment as workers shift from one job to another and as plants are shut down for model changes, repairs and cleaning. The amount of unemployment necessary to reflect these adjustments within the economy may perhaps be set at one figure under certain circumstances and another level in a different environment. Any attempt to give specific meaning to the concept of full employment must necessarily be an arbitrary one. For the sake of illustration, we may assume that an economy operating within a range of 3-5 per cent of its resources unemployed is operating within the full employment range. They would mean that with 96-97 per cent of its resources at work, an economy might be regarded as being at practical full employment. Whatever the exact figure may be, any economy which consistently moves at levels above this full employment range would bring upon itself the accompaniments of a condition of overfull employment, including rising price levels. The report of the delegation on economic depressions of the League of Nations suggested the concept that "in so far as possible, no man or woman able and willing to work should be unable to obtain employment for periods of time longer than is needed to transfer from one occupation to another or, when necessary, to acquire a new skill."[1] Keynes defined full employment as the absence of involuntary unemployment. He defines involuntary unemployment as a state in which "in the event of a small rise in price of wage goods relatively to the money-wage, both the aggregate supply of labour willing to work for the current money-wage and the aggregate demand for it at that wage would be greater than the existing volume of employment.[2] Thus full employment is reached when the real wage is equal to the marginal disutility of employment. No worker would offer himself for employment at a lower real wage. If a person does not work at this wage, it is evident that he is not interested in employment and therefore is voluntarily unemployed. Keynes considers both "frictional" and "voluntary" unemployment as consistent with his definition of full employment.[3] In fact, frictional unemployment, being involuntary (and not voluntary), cannot be consistent with full employment in Keynes' sense, i.e., absence of involuntary unemployment. An alternative definition of full employment given by Keynes is "a situation in which aggregate employment is inelastic in response to an increase in the effective demand for its output."[4] The policy proposed by Keynes for achieving full employment is that of increasing effective demand to the appropriate level.

1. League of Nations, *Economic Stability in the Post-War World* (Geneva, 1945), p. 21.
2. J.M. Keynes, *The General Theory of Employment, Interest and Money* (London, 1957), p. 15.
3. *Ibid.*, pp. 15-16.
4. *Ibid.*, 26.

Beveridge's definition of full employment is broader than that of Keynes. According to him, full employment "means having always more vacant jobs than unemployed men.... It means that the jobs are at fair wages, of such a kind, and so located that the unemployed men can reasonably be expected to take them."[5] The policy proposed by Beveridge for achieving full employment consists not only of maintaining total outlay at an adequate level but also includes measures for securing controlled location of industry and organisational mobility of labour.[6] Measures for securing controlled location of industry and organisational mobility of labour considerably decrease frictional unemployment. Frictional unemployment, therefore, is less consistent with the full employment concept of Beveridge than with that of Keynes. Mrs. Robinson goes still further and refuses to consider frictional unemployment as being consistent with full employment.

> It is commonly said that there is 'full' employment when the only unemployment which consists can be described as frictional. But it is impossible... to give precision to the concept of specifically 'frictional' unemployment, because it is impossible to make a hard-and-fast distinction between unemployment which is due to frictions and unemployment which is due to deficiency of effective demand.
>
> ... It seems preferable to say that full employment, in a precise sense, can never be attained so long as frictions exist, rather than to use 'full employment' in an imprecise sense in which it can be said to be attainable such unemployment as remains being vaguely attributed to frictions.[7]

Lerner's definition of full employment is similar to that of Keynes. "Full employment is, therefore, that level of employment at which any further increase in spending would result in an inflationary spiral of wages and prices."[8] He considers full employment to be consistent with frictional unemployment.

---

5. William H. Beveridge, *Full Employment in a Free Society* (London, 1945), p. 18.
6. *Ibid.*, p. 125.
7. Joan Robinson, *Essays in the Theory of Employment* (Oxford, 1953) pp. 41-42.
8. A.P. Lerner, *Economics of Employment* (New York), p. 24.

> The unemployment which results from a general insufficiency of jobs may be called 'deflationary unemployment' and the unemployment due to workers having the wrong skills or being located in the wrong places to get jobs is called 'frictional unemployment.' The frictional unemployment is the unemployment which exists when there is full employment.[9]

He maintains that the measures intended to reduce frictional unemployment do not contribute to full employment; these only raise the full employment level.

> All such improvements in the functioning of the economy in particular situations are ways not of moving towards full employment, but of raising the full employment level itself.... It permits a greater level of employment to be attained before inflationary point is reached. The full employment level comes to mean a greater level of actual employment. There is less residual frictional unemployment.[10]

The concepts of full employment mentioned above are not very relevant in the context of an underdeveloped economy. In an underdeveloped economy, a labourer employed in the physical sense may be unemployed in the economic sense, *i.e.,* his marginal productivity may be zero. This type of unemployment, often referred to as disguised unemployment, is particularly marked in the agricultural sector. The removal of a part of labour from the agricultural sector won't affect total production. Such unemployment cannot exist in a capitalistic economy because a capitalist won't employ an additional labourer if his productivity is zero or even positive but less than the prevailing wage rate. The problem in underdeveloped countries is not so much of increasing the quantity of employment as that of improving its quality (or productivity). In an underdeveloped economy, absence of lack of effective demand and frictions cannot mean a state of full employment in the economic sense. Disguised unemployment is perfectly consistent with the concept of full employment of both Keynes and Beveridge. But this constitutes the main problem of unemployment in an

9. *Ibid.*, p. 18.
10. *Ibid.*, p. 25.

underdeveloped economy. Full employment in the Keynesian sense—increase in effective demand leading to inflation—is reached at a very early stage because of lack of complementary factors. The main problem is not of reaching the full employment level but of raising the full employment level by increasing the amount of complementary resources. The emphasis in underdeveloped countries, thus, shifts from increasing effective demand to increasing complementary resources.

3. Overfull Employment

Full employment is reached at different times in different parts of the economy. During the early approaches to general full employment, only a few parts of the economy reach that level, with demand for their products in excess of their capacity. Firms in such industries find customers bidding for their products which are in short supply and as a result prices start rising. In a situation of rising prices the management attempts to expand output by paying for overtime work; this increases the cost of production; the result is that the prices are pushed up by costs and pulled up by demand. Profits may rise for a while but excessive profits will lead to demands for higher wages. Thus, within this industry, the cost-price spiral starts gathering momentum.

The wage patterns established in the full-employment industry and the prices charged for its products affect other industries also. A cumulative disequilibrium spreads to more and more parts of the economy. Some firms may attempt to tackle their problems by undertaking the construction of new facilities. But this simply leads to diversion of resources into the construction industries from other parts of the economy; and these, in turn, find themselves in a situation of full employment. Ultimately, most of the economy enters the full-employment situation and at this stage various rigidities become apparent.

When the full-employment level is reached, all factors of production become short in supply. Faced with backing orders, the business firms will be reluctant to remove units of equipment for normal overhauling and maintenance, and tend to use such equipment on a round-the-clock basis. Overworking of equipment will lead to break-downs in the production line which would tend to raise production cost and lower the general plant efficiency. Retired workers will be added to the labour force. There will follow a general decline in efficiency and a rise in cost structure.

Because of the excessive purchasing power which, by definition, is present in the economy at such times, consumers will not mind paying higher prices for goods in short supply. Being aware of this, the producers have a tendency not to resist the labour's demand for higher wages. They would prefer to grant an increase in wages rather than running the risk of a suspension of production. Promotion standards may be relaxed, piece-rate standards may be downgraded and other supervisory standards may be relaxed. Such measures would tend to raise costs and prices.

Over-full employment raises cost of production in other ways also. As materials become short in supply, the resulting scramble for goods leads to a great deal of crosshauling and of searching in distant supply markets, so that even when there is no increase in the price of materials, their cost to producers rises because of the increased costs of transportation involved in bringing them into the factory from distant sources. In view of the conditions, there is a tendency at all levels—producers, distributors, retailers, and even consumers, to build larger inventories of scarce goods. In this way the pressure builds most heavily upon those sectors of the economy where those pressures are already great.

Ultimately, all these problems have a tendency to result in a disparity between the supply of money and that of goods. This imbalance leads to a rise in prices and profits which in turn push and pull wages and other costs to higher levels. There develops a general sellers' market not only for goods and services but also for factors of production. Such a situation leads to a wage-price spiral which results in a cumulative inflation. This is the danger inherent in any attempt to stabilise at too high a level of employment.

4. Nature of the Unemployment

The nature of the unemployment problem in an underdeveloped country is widely different from that in a developed economy. In developed countries, unemployment is caused mostly by business cycles. Cyclical unemployment is not very important in an under-developed country. Recession affects mostly the money incomes and not the real output and incomes. Further the hardships caused by a decline in money incomes in underdeveloped countries are not very important because of an overwhelming degree of self-sufficiency. Producers retain most of their production for their own consumption and sell very little in the market. Similarly, they buy very little from the market. The most important factor responsible for the comparative stability of real income during the business cycle is the predominance of agriculture in these economies. Production in agriculture is comparatively stable not only in underdeveloped but also in developed countries. A major part of the total costs in agriculture consists of fixed costs and variable costs are small. Variable costs being small, prices during the recession, generally, do not fall below the marginal cost and consequently the restriction of production is unprofitable. Because of the competitive nature of agriculture, it is not possible to raise prices by restricting production. Further, in agriculture, the timelag between inputs and outputs is very long and, consequently, the limits within which production can profitably be restricted in the short period are comparatively narrower. On the contrary, there is some evidence to show that the supply curve in agriculture is backward sloping, *i.e.*, supply increases during the recession and falls during the boom. In developed countries, the number of wage earners is very high. Further wages are very inflexible because of contracts, social connections, legislation, trade union pressure etc. Business fluctuations, therefore, manifest themselves, mainly in variations in employment and not in incomes. The incomes of those who are lucky enough to retain their employment remain almost unchanged. In underdeveloped countries, on the other hand, a predominant part of the population is self-employed. Business fluctuations in such economies, therefore, manifest themselves primarily in changes in money incomes and not in employment. Most of those who are employed on wages in factories, plantations and mines continue their contacts back in their villages and during a recession can go back to their homes and share agricultural employment along with their other family members. Cyclical unemployment, thus, is not very important in underdeveloped economies. Unemployment in underdeveloped countries is primarily of a secular nature and arises from inappropriate factor endowments, *i.e.*, excessive manpower in relation to capital and land. Inappropriate factor endowments won't be a cause of unemployment if different factors of production were technically substitutable for each other. In actual practice, however, the possibilities for the substitution of different factors of production are considerably limited. Lack of flexibility in the co-efficients of production combined with abundance of labour relatively to other factors makes unemployment inevitable. The distinction between the nature of unemployment in advanced and underdeveloped countries has been well brought out by Majumdar:

> In contrast to the situation in advanced industrial countries visualised by Keynes, the problem in an underdeveloped country is one of underemployment; rather than of unemployment; it is primarily agricultural rather than industrial; the phenomenon is chronic rather than cyclical; and moreover the incidence of unemployment spreads widely over the bulk of the population instead of being concentrated among a relatively limited number of workers.[11]

Unemployment in underdeveloped countries can be classified into four major categories, *viz.,* (1) cyclical unemployment, (2) disguised unemployment, (3) seasonal unemployment, and (4) technological unemployment.

5. Disguised Unemployment

Disguised unemployment exists primarily in two forms *viz.* (1) employment of people in less productive works than they are capable of or, in other words, an underutilisation of skills possessed by people; (2) employment of people in a number larger than that required for doing the job. Mrs. Robinson uses the term 'disguised unemployment' to describe a situation in which the wage-workers take to less productive jobs because they lose their regular jobs owing to cyclical ebb in economic activity. The nature of the disguised unemployment, however, is very different in underdeveloped countries. Firstly, it is chronic and not cyclical. Secondly, it relates more to self-employed workers than to wage-earners. Thirdly, it is caused by a shortage of complementary resources and not by a deficiency of effective demand. The experts of the report on 'Measures for the Economic Development of Underdeveloped Countries' prefer to use the term under employment to the term 'disguised unemployment.'

11. N.A. Majumdar, "Some Aspects of Unemployment," *Indian Economic Journal* (July, 1957), p. 3.

> The use of the word 'unemployment' in this connection is, therefore, somewhat misleading, since it is more often confined to wage labourers whose status is recorded in unemployment statistics. We prefer to use, hereafter, the less precise but more familiar term 'under-employment.'[12]

Loss from disguised unemployment in developed countries arises primarily from an underutilisation of existing skills and de-skilling of labour during the period of unemployment. This kind of loss is not very important in underdeveloped countries. The main problem in these countries is not of preventing a waste and underutilisation of existing skills but of positive utilisation of underemployed manpower for the creation of skills and the formation of capital.

The fundamental reason for disguised unemployment in underdeveloped countries is that the capital and skill resources of these countries have not developed along with the growth of population. Population is increasing at a tremendous rate. Employment opportunities outside agriculture increase very slowly. The result is a growth in the number of people employed in agriculture. The additional labour force in agriculture adds little to the total output. Techniques, amount of capital and other complementary factors and the organisation remaining unchanged, a part of the working force can be removed without being followed by a decrease in total output. With minor changes in the organisation, techniques and the amount of capital, it is possible to remove a considerable portion of the working force without affecting production. Establishment of optimum sized holdings, for instance, will render surplus a considerable portion of the agricultural working force. The surplus manpower in agriculture is a great hindrance in increasing productivity in agriculture. A part of the output which is consumed by the surplus mouths can be used for investment in agriculture for raising its productivity. Increase in number in agriculture increases the subdivision and fragmentation of land-holdings which is an important cause of low productivity in agriculture in underdeveloped countries. Mechanisation is not possible because it will render a large number of workers unemployed.

12. United Nations, *Measures for the Economic Development of Underdeveloped Countries* (New York, 1951), p. 7.

In underdeveloped countries, production is carried on, mainly, in family units. Almost all members of the family are associated in different capacities with the production processes Consumption of different members of the family has very little relation to their contribution to the family product. If the productive unit is not sufficiently large to provide employment to all members of the family and cannot be expanded because of lack of land or capital, some members of the family may remain underemployed. These underemployed members continue being fed out of the family product without their underemployment being manifested to an outsider. Often, the underemployed workers themselves may not be conscious of their underemployment. Thus the underemployment remains concealed or disguised, leaving its impact on the incomes. As the workers are not completely unemployed, they cannot be available for alternative employment at other places.

Disguised unemployment exists in underdeveloped countries not only in agriculture but also in other vocations, *e.g.* retail trading, personal services etc. In each locality, there is a large number of petty traders, each making a few sales. The number of shops in a locality can be reduced without causing any inconvenience to the buyers. The buyers may even gain if the retail margins are reduced with the increase in the amount of business conducted by each shop. Overcrowding of porters at railway stations, at bus stands, in markets and other places is a very common phenomenon. The same is true in case of several other casual jobs. Rich people keep an army of domestic servants just for prestige purposes. Reduction in the number of such workers won't affect national product.

Disguised unemployment though primarily existing among the self-employed workers is not absent in case of hired workers. Of course, it looks a little strange that an employer should employ labourers whose contribution to production is less than the wage paid to them.

> Social prestige requires people to have servants, and the grand seigneur may have to keep a whole army of retainers who are really little more than a burden upon his purse. This is found not only in domestic services but in every sector of employment. Most businesses in underdeveloped countries employ a large number of 'messengers' whose

> contribution is almost negligible; you see them sitting outside office doors, or hanging around in the courtyard. And even in the severest slump the agricultural or commercial employer is expected to keep his labour force somehow or other—it would be immoral to turn them out, for how would they eat, in countries where the only form of employment assistance is the charity of relations.[13]

Solution: Wherever there exists scope, more land should be brought under cultivation for affording employment to the additional workers. The solution of the disguised unemployment in underdeveloped countries lies in rapid economic development which creates employment opportunities outside agriculture and thus makes possible a diversion of surplus labour from agriculture to other sectors. "The only remedy for this form of disguised unemployment is economic development, which constitutes the major economic problem of the world."[14]

6. Seasonal Unemployment

Seasonal unemployment arises either from seasonal variations in demand or from those in production conditions. It is the later factor which causes the most serious problem. Seasonal unemployment is far more marked in agriculture than in any other sector of the economy. This is, to some extent, inevitable so long as the agricultural operations continue to depend on climatic conditions. The amount of work during sowing, transplanting and harvesting seasons is far larger than in other seasons. During busy seasons, the workers have much more than the normally required work; there, often, occurs even a scarcity of labour in some regions. But, owing to a number of reasons, the volume of seasonal unemployment is far larger in underdeveloped countries than in the developed ones. In underdeveloped countries, the agricultural operations are highly labour-intensive. The difference in the demand for labour between the busy and the slack seasons, therefore, is very large. In developed countries, on the other hand, the mechanisation of agriculture has

---

13. W. Arthur Lewis, "Economic Development with Unlimited Supplies of Labour," A.N. Agarwala and S.P. Singh (eds.), *The Economics of Underdevelopment* (Bombay, 1958), p. 40.
14. United Nations, *National and International Measures for Full Employment* (New York, 1949), p. 12.

considerably decreased the gap in the demand for labour between the busy and the slack seasons. In underdeveloped countries, the large demand for labour during the busy seasons gathers a large volume of labour around agricultural occupations. Because of a number of reasons, the labour force gathered during the busy seasons gets permanently attached to these occupations. In underdeveloped countries occupation-structure is comparatively rigid. Because of certain economic and social factors, mobility of labour between different occupations is extremely low. There exists a bias for agricultural occupations. After elementary needs have been met, the marginal leisure preference of the agricultural labour becomes very high. In advanced countries the difference in demand for labour during different seasons has been considerably reduced through intensive cultivation, double cropping, mixed farming and dovetailing of agriculture with other subsidiary occupations. Because of comparatively higher incomes, seasonally unemployed labour in developed countries can better afford leisure as a consumer good.

Seasonal unemployment exists, also, in the industrial sector. Employment in rice mills lasts for only a few weeks. Work in sugar mills lasts for four to six months. More important is the seasonal unemployment in cottage industries which either depend on seasonal supplies of perishable raw materials or cater to seasonal demand. Seasonal unemployment in industry, however, is not so important in underdeveloped countries because the total number of workers employed in industry is not large.

Seasonal unemployment results in an underutilisation not only of manpower but also of the available capital equipment. Underutilisation of the available capital presents a serious problem for an underdeveloped country marked by an extreme shortage of capital. The indigenous capital equipment used in underdeveloped countries is not very durable and, therefore, the rate of depreciation merely because of the passage of time is very high. Capital in the form of cattle not only depreciates with the passage of time but also requires a considerable amount of positive expenditure for maintaining it. Cattle have got to be fed and looked after even during the slack season.

Seasonal unemployment is another form of the underemployment in underdeveloped countries. While disguised unemployment is primarily confined to self-employed workers, seasonal unemployment concerns both the self-employed and the hired workers. Disguised unemployment is concealed whereas the seasonal unemployment is visible.

Remedies for Seasonal Unemployment: The best remedy for seasonal unemployment lies in making the agriculture full-time job. Measures should be taken to extend the period of employment in agriculture itself. Lengthening of employment period, however, should not be for its own sake but for increasing production. Lengthening of employment period for its own sake will deprive the people of leisure (which is an important consumer good) without providing them any compensation in the form of additional goods. The employment period in agriculture can be fruitfully extended through intensive cultivation, double cropping, mixed farming, dry farming etc. This, of course, requires large investments for providing the cultivators with several facilities, *viz.,* irrigation, fertilisers, modern equipment, technical know-how, etc.

A second remedy lies in reducing the demand for labour in busy seasons by mechanising the agriculture. This remedy will be useful only if employment opportunities can be created outside agriculture for absorbing the labour rendered surplus by the mechanisation of agriculture. Creation of employment opportunities outside agriculture requires stupendous amounts of investment which can be made only over a very long period of time.

Thirdly, to the extent the busy seasons occur at different times in different regions, the volume of seasonal unemployment can be decreased by facilitating inter-regional mobility of labour. If, however, labour is to work at different places during different seasons, it will give rise to several social and economic problems. There will be the problem of providing the labour with housing at different places. Food arrangements will have to be made for the migratory labour. If the labourers take their families with them from place to place, labour movements will involve considerable costs. If they do not keep their families with them, the family life will be disturbed.

Fourthly, the seasonal unemployment in agriculture should be dovetailed with the seasonal employment in the industrial sector. Seasonal unemployment in cane-growing, for instance, can be dovetailed with work in sugar factories. Sugar factories, however, can employ only a small portion of the cane-growing labour. A far larger amount of labour can be employed if the cultivators themselves produce sugar in small home units. Seasonal unemployment in tea-growing has been successfully dovetailed into tea-manufacturing. This has been possible because tea-growing and tea-manufacturing is done not only by the same firms but also by the same work-units. Seasonal unemployment in cotton-growing can be eliminated by combining cotton-growing with spinning and weaving. Cottage-industries, particularly those using primarily agricultural raw-materials, have, often, been suggested as the best measure for providing employment to the seasonally unemployed labour in agriculture.

Encouragement of cottage industries, however, raises a number of difficult problems, *viz.*, provision of finance, raw materials and technical know-how, protection from competition from the mill sector, marketing products etc. It will result into an underutilisation of capital resources. Capital equipment of cottage industries will remain idle during the agricultural season and agricultural equipment will remain idle when the equipment of cottage industries is being used. A country highly deficient in capital cannot afford such a waste of its capital resources. A stupendous amount of investment will be required for providing the agriculturists even with the simplest form of equipment for cottage industries. An equivalent amount of investment in mill sector may contribute much more to the national income. The ultimate interest lies not in mere full employment of labour but in the total production that can be had with the available productive resources. The efficiency of persons who work as cultivators during certain seasons and as artisans in other seasons is likely to be lower than that of the full-time cultivators and full-time artisans. Agriculture-cum-handicraft system will forego the benefits which arise from specialisation. For a fuller utilisation of limited capital resources and for reaping the benefits of specialisation, it is better to have full time cultivators and full time artisans. Extending employment period in agriculture, on the other hand, has the advantage that it not only avoids duplication of equipment but also uses the existing agricultural equipment more fully. In case cottage industries are to be developed for affording employment to the seasonally unemployed labour it will be better to develop such cottage industries as can be run either with the existing agricultural equipment (*e.g.*, dairy farming) or as require mostly manpower and little capital equipment (*e.g.*, basket making, soap making).

Fifthly, as far as possible, the government should concentrate its public works during the agricultural slack season.

Sixthly, seasonal unemployment in cottage industries producing non-perishable goods can be remedied to some extent if certain arrangements are made for the provision of finance to the artisans. If finance is available for purchasing raw materials, the artisans can produce during the slack season for building stocks.

7. Technological Unemployment

Technological unemployment arises from developments in technology. Other things remaining the same, the unemployment caused by changes in technology will be permanent if the new technology requires a smaller number of workers. Unemployment will be transitional if the new technology requires the same number of workers; in this case the problem will be only that of adapting to the new techniques. The workers experienced in old techniques may have to remain unemployed or seek employment in unskilled jobs till they learn the new techniques. Technological unemployment will be considerable if the changes in technology are very rapid and the difference between the old and the new technology is considerably large.

Normally, the technological unemployment is not a serious problem in developed countries because the change in technology in these countries is very slow and regular; the workers can adapt to the new techniques without much difficulty and distress. In underdeveloped countries, in contrast, the primitive technology has got to be replaced by an altogether new technology, existing in advanced countries. The difference between the old and new technology is so large that the knowledge of the old technology becomes almost useless. Further the new technology requires a number of workers far smaller than that required by the old technology. For these reasons, unless new employment opportunities are created for absorbing the unemployed workers, the technological unemployment is likely to be a serious problem in underdeveloped countries. Artisans employed in handicrafts in underdeveloped countries are the worst victims of technological unemployment caused by the introduction of the modern mill sector. Handicrafts unable to face competition from domestic and foreign modern mills are decaying fast. Technological unemployment may be caused not only by changes in the techniques of production but also by those in the techniques of organisation. In underdeveloped countries, the organisation of production is very defective. In some industries, it is possible to obtain the same output with the same amount of equipment, the same technique of production and a smaller amount of labour if the production is organised and managed more efficiently. Application of modern methods of management and organization will render a considerable amount of labour unemployed. The amount of technological unemployment depends upon the rate at which the underdeveloped country concerned wants to modernise its method of production.

Changes in technology not only cause unemployment among workers but also render old capital equipment useless. Mechanisation of agriculture, for instance, renders useless the indigenous equipment and cattle.

Advances in technology increase the productivity of labour, capital and land. Increases in productivity increase the investible resources. Increase in investment increases the volume of employment. Thus advances in technology which initially cause unemployment would ultimately increase the volume and productivity of employment. This conclusion, of course, is based on the assumption that the increased productivity is utilised, if not fully, at least partially, for investment. If whole of the increased productivity is used for raising the consumption standards, the ultimate increase in the volume of employment through increased investment may fail to materialise. Advances in technology may also fail to increase the volume of employment if the increased productivity is utilised for increasing leisure instead of increasing total production. Somewhat different situation will arise if the leisure is involuntary in the form of forced unemployment. In underdeveloped countries, the possibilities of involuntary leisure through forced unemployment are much larger than those of voluntary leisure. In case the leisure is involuntary, the profits of the entrepreneurs are likely to rise because the same amount of output will be produced with a smaller amount of labour. Profits may rise further if the wages are flexible and with the decrease in demand for labour, wage rates are lowered. Changes in the distribution of income in favour of profits and against wages, howsoever justifiable on economic grounds, cannot be approved on political and social grounds.

Remedies for Technological Unemployment: The best remedy for technological unemployment lies in the creation of new employment opportunities through the rapid development of the country. "Rapid economic development is paradoxically the greatest cause of and the greatest cure for technological unemployment."[15]

Secondly, underdeveloped countries should be a little cautious in employing the techniques which have been developed in advanced countries keeping in view, primarily, their own needs. The need in advanced countries is to economise labour and to find out outlets for savings. The techniques which require more capital and less labour, therefore, best suit such countries. The needs of underdeveloped countries are quite the reverse. These countries possess vast amounts of unemployed and underemployed labour and are very short of capital. The techniques best suited to these countries, therefore, are those which employ more labour and less capital. But the problem is from where to obtain such techniques. Development of new techniques is a very long-term process. The modern techniques in advanced countries have been developed over centuries. Development of new techniques suited to the needs of underdeveloped countries requires huge investments and talents of a very high calibre. It is doubtful if the underdeveloped countries can afford to spend so much on research for developing new techniques. Still more difficult is the problem of finding talented persons for carrying on such research programmes.

8. Conclusion

The only satisfactory solution of unemployment in underdeveloped countries lies in creating additional employment opportunities through rapid overall economic development. "It will be seen that we are led by the analysis both of technological unemployment and of underemployment to the same point, namely, that new employment must be created rapidly. This is the task of economic development."[16]

---

15. United Nations, *Measures for the Economic Development of Underdeveloped Countries* (New York, 1951), p. 27.

16. *Ibid.*, p. 9.

Balanced and Unbalanced Growth

28

1. Introduction

The problem of transforming an underdeveloped economy into a self-generating economy calls forth the adoption of a suitable strategy of economic development. The economists have put forward two different strategies of economic development. Economists like Nurkse and Rosenstein Rodan are of the opinion that pattern of investment should be so designed as to ensure a balanced development of the various sectors of economy. In contrast, economists like Singer and Hirschman, are of the view that rapid economic development follows concentration of investment in certain strategic industries rather than an even distribution of investment among the various industries. The two strategies which the two schools have put forward are known as 'Balanced Growth' and 'Unbalanced Growth'.

2. Meaning of Balanced Growth

Balanced growth does not mean equal percentage growth in output or equal increase in resources allocated or simply that different fields grow at what is considered a 'natural rate'. The most generally accepted definition of balanced growth is that different parts of the economy should grow in a harmonious manner so that there occurs neither a surplus nor a shortage in any sector. The balanced growth requires balance on the supply side and balance on the demand side. For instance, industry and agriculture should go hand in hand: industry should not get too far ahead of agriculture; basic overhead facilities such as transportation, power etc. must be adequate to support and stimulate the growth of industry. To cite Lewis, "...measures to increase the productivity of manufacturing industry (whether cottage or factory) must be paralleled by measures to increase the demand for manufactured products. This demand comes only to a small extent from industrial producers themselves who are only a small proportion of the population of such countries. It comes to a great extent from all other classes, of whom the farmers are far away the target category. If capital is being put into developing manufacturing industry while a country's agriculture remains stagnant, the result is bound to be distress in the manufacturing sector as factory and cottage workers compete for limited demand. But if there is balanced development, with the productivity of farmers growing rapidly and the demand for manufactures correspondingly increasing there is ample scope for investment in industry. Moreover, in overpopulated countries, industrialisation to some extent depends upon developing international trade in manufactures. The secret of most development problems is to maintain a proper balance between sectors."[1] "A balance is also necessary between domestic trade and foreign trade. Export revenue is an important source of financing development; imports rise as production and employment expands; and domestic trade itself requires increasing imports of necessary materials and equipment. To pay for these rising imports, and to allow exports to finance development as much as possible, the country cannot expand its domestic trade at the expense of its foreign trade. The domestic sector must grow in balance with the foreign sector."[2] To sum up in the words of Prof. Lewis, "In development programmes all sectors of the economy should grow simultaneously, so as to keep a proper balance between industry and agriculture, and between production for home consumption and production for export... the truth is that all sectors should be expanded simultaneously, but the logic of this proposition is unassailable as its simplicity."[3]

3. Vicious Circle of Poverty

According to Nurkse, vicious circles of poverty are at work in a poor country which retard economic development. If they are broken, economic development will follow. The vicious circle operates both on the supply side and the demand side.

On the supply side, the capacity to save is low because of low real income. The real income is low because of low productivity which in turn is due to deficiency of capital. The deficiency of

1. Lewis, *Theory of Economic Growth*, p. 141.
2. Meier and Baldwin, *Economic Development*.
3. Lewis, *op. cit.*, p. 283.

capital is the result of low capacity to save. On the demand side, inducement to invest is low because of low demand which is on account of low level of real income of the people. The inducement to invest is, therefore, limited by the size of the market which in turn depends upon productivity, because the capacity to buy is in fact the capacity to produce. And productivity depends on the amount of capital used in production. But for an individual entrepreneur the use of capital is inhibited by the small size of the market which in turn is limited by low productivity. Thus the vicious circle is complete.

The question is how to break this circle. Individual investment decisions cannot solve this problem. The output of any single industry newly set up with capital equipment cannot create its own demand. Human wants being of diverse nature, the people employed in the new industry will not spend all their income on their own product. As a result, there would not be adequate demand for the product of the new industry. The supply of the product is likely to exceed the demand for it and thus the industry is likely to meet a failure.

What is the way out of this impasse? According to Prof. Nurkse, "The difficulty caused by the small size of the market relates to individual investment incentives in any single line of production taken by itself. At least, in principle, the difficulty vanishes in the case of more or less synchronized application of capital to wide range of different industries. Here is an escape from the deadlock; here the result is an overall enlargement of the market. People working with more and better tools in a number of complementary projects become each other's customers. Most industries catering for mass consumption are complementary in the sense that they provide a market for and thus support each other. This basic complementarity stems in the last analysis from the diversity of human wants. The case for balanced growth rests on the need for a balanced diet."[4]

Incidentally, two subsidiary points may be noted in Nurkse's thesis. In the first place, Nurkse contends that the choice between public and private enterprise for attaining the required bundle of

---

4. Ragnar Nurkse, *Problems of Capital Formation in Underdeveloped Countries,* p. 11.

investment is mainly a matter of administrative expediency. Secondly, Nurkse joins the growing list of 'development economists' who deny that international trade provides an automatic escape from the limitations of the domestic market. "To push exports of primary commodities in the face of an inelastic and more or less stationary demand would not be a promising line of long-run development." He makes a case for building up import-replacing industries behind a tariff wall and points out that the ultimate result need not be a reduction in imports—even of goods first receiving protection. He cites the example of Canada where "textile manufacturing was one of the first industries to develop, with the aid of tariff protection from 1879 on; yet Canada today is one of the world's biggest importers of textile manufactures".

4. Case for Balanced Growth

The case for balanced growth rests upon the relation of complementarity between wants, between factors, and between factors and products at various stages of production.[5] Complementarity gives rise to a number of external economies.[6] Nurkse sums up the case for balanced growth as below:

> Human wants being various, the people engaged in the new industry will not wish to spend all their income on their own products. Suppose it is a shoes industry...People in the rest of the economy will not give up other things in order to buy, say, a pair of shoes every year, if they do not have enough food, clothing, and shelter.... As it is the new industry is likely to be a failure.
>
> The difficulty is not present, however, in the case of a more or less synchronized application of capital to a wide range of different industries.... People working with more and better tools in a number of complementary projects become

5. Paul Streeten, "Unbalanced Growth," *Oxford Economic Papers* (June, 1959), p. 170.

6. The term external economies is used here in a sense different from that in which Marshall used it. Marshall, generally, referred to external economies arising from the establishment of a new firm or from the expansion of an existing firm and accruing to other firms in the same industry. Here, we refer to external economies which arise from the establishment of a new industry or from the expansion of an existing industry and accruing to other industries.

> each other's customers. Most industries catering for mass consumption are complementary in the sense that they provide a market for, and thus support, each other. This basic complementarity stems, of course, from the diversity of human wants. The case for "balanced growth" rests ultimately on the need for a "balanced diet."[7]

Nurkse builds his case for balanced growth on the basis of only one of the several economies associated with the installation of a new industry or the expansion of an old one, *viz.*, the creation of market for other industries. Further, Nurkse has mentioned only one way in which the establishment of a new or the expansion of an existing industry enlarges market for the products of other industries, *i.e.*, through the expenditure of income earned by the newly employed labour. Establishment of a new industry enlarges the market for the products of other industries in several other ways, too. For illustration, let us suppose that a new industry is established. It will employ not only labour but also capital and land. Increase in the demand for capital and land will increase the remuneration of the owners of capital and land and thereby increase their demand for the products of other industries. The larger will be the increase in demand for the products of other industries, the lower is the income elasticity of demand for the products of industry X. Further industry X will employ not only factors of production but also the products of other industries, *viz.*, machinery, raw materials, semi-manufactured goods etc. Investment in a consumer-goods industry directly increases demand for the producer-goods industries which constitute the inputs of the consumer-goods industry.

Economies arising from the installation of an industry accruing to other industries engaged in production at the same stage are known as horizontal external economies, *e.g.*, economies arising from the installation of a consumer-goods industry and accruing to other consumer-goods industries, or economies arising from the installation of a producer-goods industry and accruing to other producer-goods industries. Economies arising from the installation of a new industry or from the expansion of an existing industry and accruing to other industries engaged in production at a different

7. R. Nurkse, "Some International Aspects of the Problem of Economic Development" *American Economic Review* (May, 1952), p. 572.

stage are known as vertical external economies, *e.g.* economies arising from the installation of a consumer-goods industry and accruing to producer-goods industries, or economies arising from the installation of a producer-goods industry and accruing to consumer-goods industries. If producer-goods industries are subject to the law of increasing returns, installation of a consumer-goods industry will lower the cost of production in these industries by increasing the demand for their products. Decline in the cost of production in these industries will benefit, all consumer-goods industries using their products as inputs. Profitability of those industries will also be increased whose products are consumed in conjunction with the products of the industry in which investment is made. Industries at different stages of production are more complementary and less competitive than the industries at the same stage of production. Vertical economies, therefore, are likely to be more important than the horizontal economies. Consequently, the case for a simultaneous investment in industries at different stages of the same 'line' of production is stronger than that for a simultaneous investment in industries at the final stage of different lines.[8] External economies from the establishment of a new industry or from the expansion of the existing industry also arise in the form of improvements in the general facilities, *viz.* transportation and communications, credit and finance, skilled labour, trade journals, etc.

Installation of a new industry or the expansion of an existing industry creates not only external economies but also external diseconomies. Establishment of a new industry decreases demand for products which can be directly or indirectly substituted for the products of the newly established industry and thereby decreases the profitability of industries producing these products. Further, it increases the demand for the factors of production. Unless the supply of the factors of production is perfectly elastic this will raise their prices and thereby increase the cost of production in all industries.

---

8. J. Marcus Fleming, "External Economies and Doctrine of Balanced Growth," A.N. Aggarwal and S.P. Singh (eds.) *The Economics of Underdevelopment* (Bombay, 1958), p. 285.

> ....Whereas the balanced growth doctrine assumes that the relationship between industries is for the most part complementary, the limitation of factor supply ensures that the relationship is for the most part competitive.[9]

Balanced growth is possible only if the supply of the factors of production is sufficiently elastic. Let us briefly examine the degree of elasticity of different factors of production by taking these one by one.

Labour: In underdeveloped countries, there exists considerable unemployment and underemployment. From this it appears that the supply of labour will be completely elastic. Actually, because of the nature of the unemployment and the organisation of society, the supply of labour is not so elastic. A considerable portion of the unemployment in the agricultural sector is of a seasonal nature. Under the present techniques and equipment in agriculture, labour can be transferred from agriculture to industry only during the slack season and not permanently. During the busy season (which, of course, is very short) whole of the labour is fully employed. Rather there is a shortage of labour in some regions. Labour can be permanently released from agriculture only after such improved techniques and equipment have been introduced as reduce the pressure of demand for labour during the busy season. Another important characteristic of unemployment in agriculture is that the workers are only partially unemployed. The common phenomenon is that of an excessive number of workers attached with a piece of land or the workers possessing land which is insufficient for providing full-time employment. Before surplus manpower can be released from agriculture, the available land will have to be pooled and regrouped into standard holdings, *i.e.*, holdings of a size which is sufficient to provide full-time employment to an average sized family. After allocating these holdings to some families, the others can be released from agriculture. A better way of releasing the surplus labour will be the introduction of cooperative farming. A very difficult problem involved in releasing labour from agriculture is of deciding as to which workers are to live on land and which are to leave land for taking employment in industry. At wage rates equal in agriculture and industry, every worker would prefer to

9. *Ibid.*, p. 279.

work on land rather than moving to industry. This problem can be solved, by keeping the wage rates higher in industry than in agriculture. The wage differential should be sufficient to overcome the resistance of workers to unfamiliar surroundings, discipline of a factory life and other such unpleasant factors associated with industrial life. This means that the expanding industries can draw upon agricultural labour only at wages higher than those prevailing in agriculture. Thus the degree of elasticity of supply of labour depends upon the speed at which agricultural reforms are carried out which release labour from agriculture. Unemployed or underemployed labour on which expanding industries can draw is, however, mostly unskilled. The supply of skilled labour is comparatively inelastic. If capital is available, however, labour can be trained without much difficulty.

Capital: Supply of capital is comparatively inelastic in an underdeveloped country. Supply of domestic capital is limited by the capacity to save. No doubt, simultaneous investment in several industries will raise incomes and thereby the capacity to save but this effect will occur after a long period. Under the prevailing conditions, there seems to be no possibility of a large scale movement of funds from developed to underdeveloped countries. In addition, if investments are financed from abroad, a part of the purchasing power created by the new investments will be transferred in the form of profits and interest payments and to this extent domestic market won't be enlarged. Development process imposed or financed from abroad cannot be self-generating. If the supply of capital is not sufficiently elastic, simultaneous investment in a number of industries will raise the cost of capital (*i.e.,* interest rates) and offset external economies to some extent. This will retard balanced growth. More important is the question not of the cost of capital but that of its availability. When the stock of the available capital is limited, a choice has to be made between the external and internal economies. By spreading it over a large number of industries of a small scale, we reap external economies and foreign internal economies which depend on the scale of the industry. If it is concentrated on a limited number of industries of a fairly large scale, we avail of the internal economies and forego external economies. Available capital should be allocated in such a way that the combined gain from the internal and external economies is maximised.

Entrepreneurship: The supply of entrepreneurship is also very inelastic in underdeveloped countries. It is not possible to considerably increase the number of entrepreneurs over a short period.

Different industries use various factors of production in different ratios. The elasticity of different factors of production being different, a simultaneous expansion in the production of all industries will raise costs of production to varying degrees. When the structure of relative costs changes with an expansion in production, with a view to maximising the rate of growth, the production should be concentrated along lines of falling or less steeply rising costs.[10] On the whole, the external economies resulting from the establishment of a new industry or from the expansion of an existing industry are likely to be larger than the external diseconomies resulting from the same.

Balanced growth avoids bottlenecks, shortages and excess capacities. Bottlenecks and shortages, often, lead to inflation which is very injurious to the process of economic development. If manufacturing industry develops more rapidly than agriculture, for instance, there will occur a shortage of foodstuffs and agricultural raw materials. Rise in the prices of foodstuffs and agricultural raw materials will retard the development of manufacturing industry.

5. Achievement of Balanced Growth

Balanced growth can be achieved only in a centrally planned economy. In an unregulated free enterprise economy, each enterprise is not aware of the production plans of other enterprises on which depends the demand for its product and the supply of its inputs. The utmost that it can do is to predict the rate of general growth or the rate of growth of particular industries from past trends. The plans predicted from past trends, generally, considerably vary from the actual plans of various enterprises. In a centrally planned economy, the available resources are allocated between different industries and between sectors of each industry by the central planning authority. At the time of deciding the allocation of resources for any sector, it possesses a comprehensive view of the plans of growth for all other sectors. In order to correspond the development of different sectors of the economy to the pattern of consumers'

10. Johan Sheahan, "International Specialisation and the Concept of Balanced Growth," *Quarterly Journal of Economics* (May, 1958), p. 190.

demand, a detailed study has got to be made of the pattern of consumers' preferences from statistics of family budgets. Even when a comprehensive plan of balanced growth has been formulated, actual rate of development of certain sectors may deviate from the planned rate because of a number of reasons. This requires continuous adjustments in the plan of balanced growth in the light of actual movements.

State has to play an important role in planning, directing and coordinating the development process in a poor country. Three important reasons may be mentioned to show the need for central planning and direction of the economy to attain balanced growth.

(*i*) In a free enterprise economy where the individual entrepreneur has to take the initiative on his own calculations of profit and loss, there is always an unavoidable element of irrationality because of the impossibility of making reliable predictions about the possible turn of a market. In such an economy, the productive process always assumes the form of correcting the imbalances which have already occurred owing to wrong calculations of the past. Errors are made and rectified but never totally avoided and the economy grows through a series of faltering steps which find expression in the ups and downs of business. Whatever balance is attained is always a precarious balance and there is the threat of some imbalance hovering round the corner. In a private enterprise economy, it is very difficult to inspire a set of entrepreneurs to start simultaneously a complement of mutually dependent activities. Unregulated private enterprise grows through the release of a series of disequilibrating forces between demand and supply. In an underdeveloped country private enterprise is incapable of taking benefit of external economies, *i.e.*, vertical and horizontal integration of industries, a better division of labour, a common source of raw materials and technical skill, an expansion of the size of the market and better utilization of social and economic overhead capital because of its incapacity to start a wave of capital investments on a wide range of projects. Since in a free enterprise economy, it is not possible to start simultaneously a complement of mutually dependent industries, state intervention is necessary to plan, direct and coordinate growth.

(*ii*) Under the system of free enterprise, entrepreneurs in an underdeveloped economy have a tendency to invest far less than is profitable from the social point of view. This is so because the profit to private entrepreneurs will be less than the benefit to the community owing to the existence of external economies. The growth of the economy gives rise to external economies, like the advantages of transportation, of expansion in markets, the availability of technical labour, of subsidiary industries, of specialised banking, insurance and other financial institutions. The private entrepreneurs do not take into account such benefits while estimating their profits and as such they considerably underestimate actual social benefits. It is essential, therefore, that production is centrally planned and integrated as if it were taking place in a single trust. In such a case all the external economies become part of one system one trust; this is known as internalising the benefits of external economies.

(*iii*) Balanced growth is a good foundation for international trade. International trade is promoted by improving transport facilities, reducing transport costs, abolishing tariff barriers and creating customs unions thereby enlarging the market in the economic and geographic sense. This all can be done by state interventions.

Nurkse, however, differs with the above view and maintains that as a means of creating inducements to investment, balanced growth is relevant primarily to a private enterprise system.[11] State investment does not require any market incentives. The planning authorities can invest the available capital in any line they choose. Private investment, in contrast, depends on market and, therefore, requires inducement of growing markets. It appears that Nurkse confuses the desirability and feasibility of achieving balanced growth. Balanced growth is desirable under both private enterprise and planned system but can be achieved only under a planned system and not under an unplanned system based on a freely working price mechanism.

The doctrine of balanced growth is more applicable to a depressed developed country with vast unemployed productive resources of all kinds than to an underdeveloped country characterised by a serious shortage of productive resources other than the unskilled labour. In a depressed economy, simultaneous

11. Ragnar Nurkse, "The Conflict between 'Balanced Growth' and International Specialisation", *Lectures in Economic Development* (Istanbul, 1958), pp. 172-73.

investment in a number of mutually supporting sectors expands markets, builds business confidence, creates a wave of optimism, raises the expected marginal efficiency of capital and thus helps in lifting the economy out of the depression. But simultaneous investment in a number of sectors is not possible in an underdeveloped country characterised by a shortage of productive resources; it will lead to inflation that may endanger the stability of the whole economy which is very essential for smooth development.

6. Balanced Growth and International Specialisation

Is the doctrine of balanced growth compatible with international specialisation? Apparently balanced growth and international specialisation seem to be incompatible. Balanced growth requires a simultaneous expansion of mutually supporting industries while the doctrine of comparative advantage states that the available resources should be concentrated on a limited number of industries in which the country possesses a comparative advantage. In fact, balanced growth is compatible with international specialisation and the two are not mutually exclusive. A country having no foreign trade can increase its total output by participating in world trade. Once a country has specialised in accordance with the dictates of the doctrine of comparative costs, is there no way of achieving further development if the external demand conditions do not induce it? Certainly, there is. The possibilities of economic development are not exhausted with international specialisation according to the dictates of the principle of comparative costs. If certain unemployed productive resources are available, without interfering with foreign trade, a country can develop by expanding home market through a simultaneous expansion of mutually supporting industries. Underdeveloped countries possess vast amounts of unemployed and underemployed labour. It can be used for producing domestic goods without interfering with foreign trade.

> Balanced growth is the best friend that international trade can have. Filling the vacuum in the domestic economy is the best foundation for foreign trade, since it means increasing the level of productivity and real purchasing power. After all, that is why the advanced nations are each other's best customers.[12]

12. *Ibid.*, p. 180.

Unless appropriate measures are taken, however, expansion of domestic market may lead to balance of payments difficulties.

7. Criticism of Balanced Growth

According to Hirschman the doctrine of balanced growth fails as a theory of development. Development implies the process of change of one type of economy into another more advanced type. But the doctrine of balanced growth involves the superimposition of an entirely self-contained modern industrial sector upon the stagnant and equally self-contained traditional sector. To cite Hirschman, "this is not growth, it is not even the grafting of something new on to something old; it is a perfectly dualistic pattern of development."

Hirschman feels that the doctrine "combines a defeatist attitude towards the capabilities of underdeveloped economies with completely unrealistic expectations about their creative abilities."[13] On the one hand, officials in underdeveloped countries complain of a shortage of skills and other resources for development. On the other hand, the advocates of the balanced growth doctrine assume that persons lacking in skill and entrepreneurial ability become omniscient overnight and are in a position to start a chain of new industries. The whole doctrine thus appears to be a contradiction in itself. It appears strange that what cannot be done piecemeal, can be done in a big way and is considered to be within the physical and intellectual competence of an underdeveloped country. It is as if a builder not in a position to construct the ground floor, were advised to build the next two floors, instead. To cite Singer, "The advantages of multiple development may make interesting reading for economists but they are gloomy news indeed for the underdeveloped countries. The initial resources for simultaneous developments on many fronts are generally lacking. Had the country possessed enough skill and resources, it would not have remained underdeveloped."[14]

Disproportionality in the factors of production is a great problem in underdeveloped countries. Some countries have abundant supplies, of labour but are short in capital and entrepreneurial skill. Others are short in labour and capital but have plenty of other resources. This is a great obstacle to the practical application of the concept of balanced growth.

---

13. A.H. Hirschman, *The Strategy of Economic Development,* p. 53.
14. H.W. Singer, *Economic Progress in Underdeveloped Countries,* pp. 7-8.

Professor Kurihara feels that "Balanced growth is not, as Nurkse supposes, to be desired to induce private investment but to be desired for its own sake, as far as an underdeveloped country is concerned. Nurkse's complaints about an underdeveloped economy's restricted markets and low real income tending to inhibit the private inducement to invest would be unnecessary if autonomous public investment of a capacity increasing as well as income generating nature was allowed to play a greater role."

Paul Streeten points out that, historically, it was not balanced growth but scarcities and bottlenecks which provided the stimulus to the inventions that revolutionized England's and the world's economic system, and that inventions in turn created new scarcities and bottlenecks. Had the world depended on balanced development, it would have reduced or even eliminated the incentives for discoveries, or at any rate for their application. Thus it is on unbalanced growth that the history of technological progress rests.

We may conclude in Singer's words: "The doctrine of balanced growth is premature rather than wrong in the sense that it is applicable to a subsequent stage of sustained growth rather than to the breaking of a deadlock."[15]

8. Unbalanced Growth

Recently many economists have sharply criticised balanced growth and proposed unbalanced growth as an instrument of accelerating economic development. They maintain that under certain circumstances, imbalances instead of hindering, stimulate economic growth. Hirschman states:

> In general, development policy...must keep alive rather than eliminate the disequilibria of which profits and losses are symptoms in a competitive economy. If the economy is to be kept moving ahead, the task of development policy is to maintain tensions, disproportions, and disequilibria. The nightmare of equilibrium economics, the endlessly spinning cobweb, is the kind of mechanism we must assiduously look for as an invaluable help in the development process.[16]

---

15. Hans W. Singer, *International Development, Growth and Change,* 1964.
16. A.O. Hirschman, *The Strategy of Economic Development* (New Haven, 1958), p. 66.

To cite Hirschman, again:

> An ideal situation obtains when...one disequilibrium calls forth a development move which in turn leads to a similar disequilibrium and so on *ad infinitum*. If such a chain of unbalanced growth sequences could be set up, the economic policy makers could just watch the proceeding from the sidelines.[17]

Historically, growth has been highly unbalanced. In Western countries, the development was not characterised by a simultaneous expansion of all sectors of the economy in accordance with the dictates of the doctrine of balanced growth. Balance between different sectors was the net result of a series of imbalances which were constantly created and adjusted.

> ...balanced growth was an end result produced and maintained by the ceaseless ebb and flow of innovations and changing factor combinations. It was not a phenomenon created by the simultaneous expansion of mutually supporting sectors. The mutually supporting sectors were in fact the survivors of a persistent war of attrition, the intensity of which was made possible by continued response to new profit possibilities.[18]

The fact that growth in the past has been unbalanced, however, does not support the case for unbalanced growth. It is quite possible that the rate of growth would have been much higher, had the growth been planned in a balanced manner. The growth in the past was unbalanced because the technique of planning growth in a balanced manner was not known or was not possible under the then prevailing organisation of society. The process of growth was left to the market forces. The growth in the past has been characterised by repeated booms and depressions which could have been avoided if the growth were planned in a balanced manner and not left to market forces. The rate of growth would have been much higher if the wastes involved in booms and depressions could be avoided.

---

17. *Ibid.*, pp. 71-72.
18. J.R.T. Hughes, "Balanced Economic Growth in History: A Critique," *American Economic Review, Papers and Proceedings*, 49 (May, 1959), p. 334.

Balanced growth can be a process as well as an end. Nurkse pleads balanced growth as a process or as a method of accelerating economic development. On the other hand, the supporters of unbalanced growth consider balanced growth to be the goal which may be achieved through a constant creation and adjustment of imbalances; they aim at achieving balance over a period of time.

Nurkse bases his case for balanced growth on the complementarity of wants. But the same complementarity of wants can also be used to make a case for unbalanced growth.[19] In a growing economy the non-availability of certain complementary goods provides a strong incentive for investment which would be absent under balanced growth, in conformity with the pattern of consumers' preferences. Complementarity exists not only between different consumer goods but also between factors of production, between factors and products, between savings and investment, between domestic and traded goods, between exports and imports, between present and future consumption, between present and future production, between productive capacity and consumption and between so many other economic variables.

Shortages and bottlenecks created by the unbalanced growth offer considerable incentives for inventions and innovations. Not only necessity is the mother of invention but also invention is the mother of necessity. Most of the historical studies of the great inventions of the 18th and 19th centuries show that inventions were not accidental and came in response to an economic need.

Large scale production brings in certain economies which reduce the cost of production and increase the profitability of investment. In case the total effective demand or the amount of productive resources is not adequate for constructing optimum sized plants in all industries whose construction is necessary for balanced growth, it may be profitable to concentrate resources on a few industries. A judicious compromise has got to be made between the benefits from balanced growth and economies of scale resulting from unbalanced growth.

In a dynamic society where demand is constantly rising, over a period of time, construction of a large-sized plant may turn out to be more profitable even if temporary excess capacity has to be

19. Streeten, n. 5, p. 172.

maintained during the transitional period during which demand was not sufficient for the utilisation of the full productive capacity. The ultimate benefit from the economies of scale may be much more than the loss involved in temporary underutilisation of the plant. Avoidance of temporary excess capacity may require constant adjustments in the size of the plant the cost of which may far exceed the loss involved in the temporary underutilisation of the plant.

In a dynamic world increases in productivity and reductions in costs owing to technological progress are not uniformly spread over all industries. Technological progress is far rapid in some industries than in others. Under such circumstances, a larger total physical output can be obtained by concentrating the available productive resources on the most efficient industries instead of spreading these over all industries—efficient or inefficient; value of output will increase only if the relative prices do not change considerably. In a closed economy, concentration of available resources in a few efficient industries will result in a considerable change in relative prices. Foreign trade is an important method of preventing considerable changes in the relative prices that may result from a concentration of resources in a few industries. In an open economy, prices of products are determined by the world demand for and supply of these, and, therefore, changes in the volume of production in any one country (particularly, when the country concerned is not very large) do not affect the prices considerably. A country can convert unbalanced growth (resulting from a concentration of resources in the most efficient industries) into balanced growth by participating in world trade. By exporting the products of its few industries, it can import goods conforming to the pattern of consumers' preferences and producers' needs. Thus unbalanced pattern of output can be converted through foreign trade into balanced pattern of product availabilities. In case, concentration of resources in a few industries unfavourably changes the relative prices of imports and exports (*i.e.*, deteriorates the terms of trade), the advantage of unbalanced over balanced growth may be offset, the extent of the offset depending upon the extent of change in the terms of trade.

Unbalanced growth involves a cost in the form of uncertainty that results from dependence on foreign trade. Benefit in the form of higher income has to be weighed against the cost in the form of uncertainty resulting from concentrated growth. Concentration should not be pushed beyond the point at which benefit and cost are equal on the margin.

Unbalanced growth involves considerable wastage in the form of maintenance of excess capacity. If sector A grows at a higher rate than other complementary sectors, equipment in this sector will stand idle or will be underutilised till other sectors are able to catch it. Let us take a hypothetical case to illustrate this. Suppose that, in the beginning, the investment is concentrated on roads and railways. Roads and railways will not be fully utilised till other industries develop which use them. On the other hand, if growth is balanced, every sector finds a ready market for its products and there is no wastage from the underutilisation of equipment.

Another weakness of the doctrine of unbalanced growth is that it concentrates on stimuli to expansion and has a tendency to neglect or minimise resistance caused by it.[20] The unbalanced growth argues that the active sectors pull the others with them whereas balanced growth emphasises that the passive sectors drag the active ones back. In fact, it would be better if all the sectors were active. The measures to activate them may take the form both of positive inducement and of resistance to resistances.

9. Hirschman on Unbalanced Growth

The concept of unbalanced growth has been popularised by Prof. Hirschman in his book *Strategy of Economic Development.* He is of the view that the best strategy of development is the creation of imbalances in the economy since it is observed that the efforts to correct the existing disequilibria constitute a major step for the progress of economy as is shown by the historical examples found in the currently developed countries of the world. In no country the Industrial Revolution has been achieved at one stroke in a balanced manner in the sense that mutually supporting industries were established on a planned footing. Development has taken place through a series of disequilibria through ups and downs of the trade cycles. Smooth and continuous progress without the disturbances of the disequilibria is a rare phenomenon. Hirschman,

20. Paul Streeten, "Balanced versus Unbalanced Growth", *The Economic Weekly* (Bombay, April 2, 1963), reprinted in Gerald M. Meier, *Leading Issues in Development Economics* (New York, 1964), p. 262.

therefore, appears to draw the conclusion that disequilibrium is a necessary condition to generate the forces that make for equilibrium and in the process create additional productive capacity, leading the economy on to a higher stage of growth. It amounts to saying that a durable balance is nothing but stagnation. Once balance is reached, no incentive is left for intense economic activity because the existence of the balance means a perfect adjustment to the situation that prevails at a certain point of time. The best strategy for economic development, therefore, is the creation of imbalances in the economy. Hirschman says that investments in strategically selected industries or sectors of the economy will lead to new investment opportunities and thus pave the way to further economic development. He maintains "development has of course proceeded in this way, with growth being communicated from the leading sectors of the economy to the followers, from one industry to another, from one firm to another." He considers development as a "chain of disequilibria" that must keep alive rather than eliminate the disequilibria, of which profits and losses are symptoms in a competitive economy. If the progress of the economy is to be maintained, the task of development policy is to maintain tensions, disproportions and disequilibria. This 'see-saw advance' is induced by one disequilibrium which in turn leads to a new disequilibrium and so on *ad infinitum*.

According to Hirschman when new projects are started they *appropriate* external economies created by previous projects and *create* new external economies which can be exploited by subsequent ones. There are some projects which appropriate more external economies than they create which he calls *convergent series* of investments. Hirschman also calls them induced investments for they are not beneficiaries of external economies. There are other projects which create more external economies than they appropriate which he calls *divergent series* of investments. From the point of view of the economy, the latter may have a greater social desirability than private profitability while induced investments may be less desirable from the social point of view. To cite Hirschman, "An ideal situation obtains when one disequilibrium calls forth a development move which in turn leads to a similar disequilibrium and so on *ad infinitum*. In the situation private profitability and social desirability are likely to coincide, not because of the absence of the external economies, but because 'input' and 'output' of external economies are the same for each successive venture."

In practice, the objectives of the development policy should be (*i*) to prevent convergent series of investments which appropriate more external economies than they create and (*ii*) to promote divergent series in which more economies are created than are appropriated. Development can occur only by unbalancing the economy. This can be attained by investing either in social overhead capital or in directly productive activities. The former generate external economies while the latter appropriate external economies.

Unbalancing the Economy with SOC: Social Overhead Capital is defined "as comprising those basic services without which primary, secondary and tertiary productive activities cannot function." SOC includes investments on education, public health, communications, transportation, and conventional public utilities like light, water, power, irrigation and drainage schemes, etc. A large investment in SOC later encourages private investment in Directly Productive Activities (DPA). Cheaper supply of electric power, for instance, may encourage the setting up of small industries. SOC investments indirectly subsidise agriculture, industry or trade by lowering the costs of various inputs which they use. In the absence of SOC investments which provide cheap or improved services, private investments in DPA will not be encouraged. Thus the SOC approach to economic development requires unbalancing the economy in a way that subsequently encourages investments in DPC. To cite Hirschman, "Investment in SOC is advocated not because of its direct effect on final output, but because it permits and in fact invites DPA to come in.... Some SOC investment is required as a prerequisite to DPA investment."

Unbalancing the Economy with DPA: An imbalance can also be created through DPA. The government might directly or indirectly invest in Directly Productive Activities instead of investing in SOC. In case DPA investment is undertaken first, the shortage of SOC facilities would considerably raise cost of production. In course of time political pressures might stimulate investment in SOC also. Investment sequences are generated by profit expectations and by political pressures; profit expectations generate the sequence from SOC to DPA and political pressures from DPA to SOC.

Path to Development: Hirschman calls the first sequence (from SOC to DPA) "development via excess capacity of SOC" and the second sequence (from DPA to SOC) "development via shortage of SOC." As to which of the two sequences should be followed for economic development, Hirschman prefers that sequence which is "vigorously self-propelling." This is explained with the help of Hirschman's slightly modified diagram.

Units of new investment in SOC are measured on the horizontal axis and units of new investment in DPA on the vertical axis. The

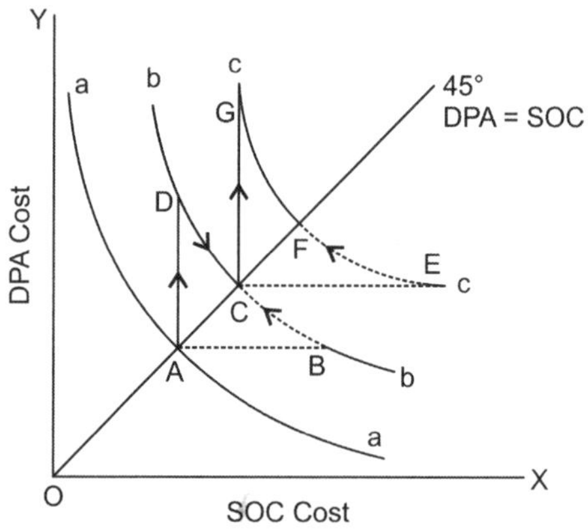

Diagram 28.1

curves are 'isopods' showing various quantities of SOC and DPA which will yield the same gross national product at any point of time. Each curve represents a higher gross national product as we move away from the origin. For convenience the curves are drawn in a way that the 45 degree line through the origin connects the optimal points on the curves. Thus "this line expresses the ideal of balanced growth of DPA and SOC: a bit of each at each step no doubt would result in the greatest economy of the country's resources."

The difficulty is that "poor countries cannot always afford to be economical." According to Hirschman the real scarcity is not the resources themselves "but the ability to bring them into play." Because of this limited ability to utilize resources, SOC and DPA cannot be expanded simultaneously. Thus the planning problem is to determine the *sequence* of expansion that will maximise *induced* decision-making.

We might start either by expanding SOC or by expanding DPA. If the path to development is followed via excess capacity of SOC, the economy will follow the dotted line ABCEF when the economy increases SOC from A to B the induced DPA increases to D until balance is restored at C where the whole economy is on a higher level of output. The higher gross national product thus attained induces governments to increase SOC further to E; DPA also follows suit to point F via point G.

If the other path to development via shortage of SOC is followed, the economy moves along the thick line ADCGF. When DPA is increased to D, SOC has to move to B and then to C. And when DPA is increased further to G, balance requires SOC to increase to F via E.

Either method of unbalanced growth yields an "extra dividend" of "induced, easy-to-take, or compelled decisions resulting in additional investment and output." But the development path via excess SOC capacity is more continuous and smooth than the other path. It is in a way what Hirschman calls "self-propelling". The other path via SOC shortage capacity is not like that because if there is a delayed adjustment of SOC, as is likely, owing to the absence of political pressures in the beginning, the DPA cost of producing a given output rises. To cite Hirschman, "Development via shortage is an instance of the 'disorderly', 'compulsive' sequence while via "excess SOC capacity is essentially permissive."

Having studied the virtues of specific imbalance, the problem is one of finding the kind of imbalance that is likely to be most effective. Any investment may have both "forward linkage" and "backward linkage" effects. Forward linkage effects encourage investment in *subsequent* stage of production and backward linkage effects in the *earlier* stage of production. The objective should be to discover projects with the largest total linkage. Such projects vary from time to time and country to country and can be discovered only by empirical studies of their input-output tables.

In determining the sequence of projects, planning authorities should also give attention to the alteration of "pressure relieving" investment. In countries with vigorously expanding private enterprise sectors the government's function can be largely restricted to pressure relieving. As private investment takes place, shortages and bottlenecks will appear in transport, public utilities, education and other activities traditionally assigned (in whole or in part) to public enterprise in such societies. Government should not feel "restless and slighted" when confined to this "induced role."

When expansion through private investment is not assured, the government must play a more active role. For instance, it might build an iron and steel plant. To cite Hirschman, "It is interesting to note that the industry with the highest combined linkage score is iron and steel. Perhaps the underdeveloped countries are not so foolish and so exclusively prestige motivated in attributing prime importance to this industry." But "the industrial development clearly cannot be started everywhere with an iron and steel industry just because the industry maximises linkage," the reason being the lack of interdependence and linkage in underdeveloped countries. For instance, agriculture including primary production and mining are weak in both backward and forward linkage effects. The primary production activities mostly of the "enclave" type leading to exports have hardly any development effects on the economy in adding either to employment or to gross national product in underdeveloped countries.

Last Industries First: Hirschman, therefore, advocates the establishment of "last industries first." In manufacturing industrial products, a developing country need not undertake all the stages of production simultaneously; it can import many 'converting assembling and mixing plants' for 'final touches' to almost finished products. Last stage industries are also called 'import enclave industries'. But they are quite different from export enclave industries. Export enclave industries have to face great difficulty in breaking out of the enclave situation and in producing forward linkage effects within the economy. In contrast, the import enclave industries produce backward linkage effects of wide range and depth. "Backward linkage effects are important not only from secondary back to primary production, but also from tertiary back to both secondary and primary production." Backward linkage effects which are the combined result of several "last stage industries' in a country are of great importance. A backward linkage is generated by increases in demand. Therefore the demand for commodities that could most economically be imported once may, in due course of time, increase to such an extent that it justifies domestic 'last stage production.' In other words, in case of some products, when demand reaches a certain 'threshold', it is beneficial to manufacture the product at home; while that 'threshold' is being reached, it is advantageous to import the product. When the 'threshold' is reached, Hirschman recommends subsidies or protection to import-replacing industries. In the 'parental stage', it is not desirable to give infant industry protection till the industry has been established. Granting of tax concessions is a good way for this type of conditional protection. Hirschman feels that in underdeveloped countries adequate importance is not given to the role played by exports in their economic development. They often treat exports like a stepchild. But "there is no real alternative between export promotion and import substitution. The former may often be the only practical way of achieving the latter."

Hirschman sums up his strategy of economic development as follows: "Economic development typically follows a path of uneven growth; that balance is restored as a result of pressures, incentives and compulsions; that the efficient path towards economic development is to be somewhat disorderly and that it will be strewn "with bottlenecks and shortages of skills, facilities, services, and products; that industrial development will proceed largely through backward linkage, *i.e.,* will work its way from the 'last touches' to intermediate and basic industry."

Critical Appraisal: The doctrine of unbalanced growth as formulated by Hirschman is a great attempt at showing the way to accelerated economic development for underdeveloped countries. It takes into consideration major aspects of development planning. It studies the various incentives, obstacles and resistances to development. The discussion of forward and backward linkage effects together with last stage production is very helpful. Hirschman's emphasis on export promotion and import substitution gives a realistic touch. He does not favour over all state planning of the Soviet type, nor does he advocate leaving everything to private enterprise. Unless the SOC path of economic development is followed by the State, private investment in DPA will not be encouraged. He, therefore, appears to be in favour of a mixed economy.

The doctrine, however, has its own limitations. The pressures and tensions created by imbalances are bound to be serious in underdeveloped countries; they may hamper the process of development.

Working of inducement mechanism pre-supposes a high degree of internal flexibility of resources. But in underdeveloped countries resources lack mobility from one sector to another.

The strains, pressures and shortages created by imbalances are likely to cause serious inflationary pressures in underdeveloped countries. It becomes difficult to control prices in underdeveloped countries because the monetary and fiscal measures are not very effective in these countries.

Hirschman's analysis of the linkage effect is not based on data relating to underdeveloped countries where social overhead capital is not fully developed for a long time.

Neither the criterion of social marginal productivity of different sectors nor the criterion of capital-output ratio is useful in bringing about development following the doctrine of unbalanced growth.

10. Conclusion

The case for unbalanced growth rests primarily on the impracticability of balanced growth because of limitation of productive resources. If productive resources of all kinds are available in plenty, balanced growth would be superior to unbalanced growth because it avoids waste involved in shortages and surpluses. The importance of unbalanced growth is still less in a socialist economy in which investment decisions are taken by the state and the market incentives created by unbalanced growth are not very important.

Insofaras the unbalance does create favourable attitudes, the crucial question is not whether to create unbalance, but what is the optimum degree of unbalance, where to unbalance and how much in order to accelerate growth; which are the 'growing points,' where should the spearheads be thrust, on which slope should snowballs grow into avalanches.[21] In the current literature, unfortunately, sufficient attention has not been paid to the precise composition, direction and timing of the unbalance.

21. *Ibid.*, p. 262.

Theory of 'Big Push'

29

The theory of 'big push' stresses the view that, because of inevitable indivisibilities in demand, supply, and saving, there is a certain minimum level of investment in most poor countries below which outlays for development will be largely wasted. In the words of Meier and Baldwin,

> According to this theory, a development programme must be at least of a certain size, a 'critical minimum', to reduce indivisibilities and discontinuities in the economy, overcome the diseconomies of scale, have an impact on values, and offset certain other forces that arise to depress development once development begins.[1]

Rosenstein-Rodan sums up the theory as below:

> "There is a minimum level of resources that must be devoted to... a development programme if it is to have any chance of success. Launching a country into self-sustaining growth is like getting an airplane off the ground. There is a critical ground speed which must be passed before the craft can become airborne...." Proceeding "bit by bit" will not add up in its effects to the sum total of the single bits. A minimum quantum of investment is a necessary (though not sufficient) condition of success. This is in a nutshell the contention of the theory of the big push.[2]

---

1. Gerald M. Meier and Robert E. Baldwin, *Economic Development Theory, History, and Policy* (New York, 1957), p. 9.
2. P. N. Rosentein-Rodan, "Notes on the Theory of the Big Push" (Cambridge Massachusetts, 1957), p. 1. The author quotes from Massachusetts Institute of Technology, Centre for International Studies, *The Objectives of United States Economic Assistance Programs* (Washington, 1957), p. 70.

The economic growth is considered to be a discontinuous affair, rather than a gradual one, with any effort below some minimum being comparatively ineffective if not absolutely useless.

The basis of the economic argument depends on three kinds of indivisibilities and external economies, *viz.*, (1) indivisibility of demand (complementarity of demand), (2) indivisibility in the production function (capital lumpiness), and (3) indivisibility (kink) in the supply of savings.

1. Complementarity of Demand

This point has already been discussed under the doctrine of balanced growth and we shall not repeat the whole thing here.

2. Capital 'Lumpiness'

Another justification put forward in support of the 'big push' is that the production is very often subject to the law of increasing returns. Increase in production leads to important internal and external economies. This point has also been already discussed in detail under the doctrine of balanced growth.

3. Kinked Supply of Domestic Savings

The third 'indivisibility', often put forward as an argument for the 'big push', is that in underdeveloped countries there is a discontinuous, relationship between national income and domestic savings. Below a certain national income level there may be practically no domestic saving. Above this critical level, the marginal propensity to save may involve a fairly substantial proportion of extra income. Professor Rosenstein-Rodan states:

> A high minimum quantum of investment requires a high volume of savings, which is difficult to achieve in low income underdeveloped countries. The way out of the vicious circle is to have first an increase in income (due to an increase in investment which mobilizes additional latent resources) and to provide mechanisms which assure that at the second stage the marginal rate of savings be very much higher than the average rate of savings.[3]

The above argument has also been used as a justification for the large minimum foreign aid for the underdeveloped countries. It is

3. *Ibid.*, p. 13.

argued that the investment provided from abroad may so raise the income in underdeveloped countries that they begin to save.

Critical Appraisal

Professor Rosenstein-Rodan considers his theory of development superior to the traditional static equilibrium theory because it appears to contradict the latter's motto that nature does make jumps. His theory is based on more realistic assumptions of indivisibilities and 'non-appropriabilities' in the production functions. It analyses the path towards equilibrium and not merely the conditions at a point of equilibrium. Thus it is mainly a theory of investment concerned with imperfect markets in underdeveloped countries. It is a high minimum quantum of investment rather than price mechanism in such imperfect markets that takes an underdeveloped economy towards an optimum position.

The 'big push' theory is, however, not without its limitations. The main argument for a 'big push' in investment on social overhead capital is the realisation of extensive external economies. But Professor Jacob Viner points out that underdeveloped economies realise greater economies from world trade independently of home investment. Rodan has recognised this fact but keeps silent over another fact that in the newly developing countries investment for exports and for marginal import substitutes accounts for a large chunk of total investment. The external economies argument for a 'big push' does not remain much valid because external economies are not important in the above types of investments.

Even in the production of local consumer goods and most public utilities, potential economies can be realised in a limited way. Investments in the case of fairly inelastic demand are cost reducing rather than output expanding. Since external economies accrue from the output-expansion in the initial industry, they are not significant in the case of cost-reducing investment.

An important shortcoming of the 'big push' theory is that it stresses the importance of a high level of investment in all kinds of industries—capital goods, consumer goods and social overhead capital—except the agricultural and other primary industries. In agriculture-oriented underdeveloped countries, a 'big push' of large investment in irrigation, transport facilities, land reforms, and in improving agricultural practices through better tools, implements, fertilisers, etc., are as important as investment in other industries.

The neglect of the agricultural sector in such economies will hinder rather than accelerate their development.

The launching of a high minimum amount of investment on social overheads is very expensive. Further, overhead capital has a high capital-output ratio and a long gestation period. This makes the job of developing countries more difficult and longer. This is because such countries do not have adequate financial resources to provide overhead capital required for the 'big push.' The period during which overhead capital is being built will also be one of inflationary pressures because of shortage of consumer goods. The inflationary pressures in turn would prolong the process of building overhead capital and thus make it very difficult for an underdeveloped country to attain rapid economic development.

Professor John Adler's statistical analysis of the economic development of the world shows that "a relatively low level of investment 'pays off' well in the form of additional output."[4] This conclusion is based on his study of low capital-output ratios in India, Pakistan and in many other Asian and Latin American countries. Thus there appears to be little conclusive evidence that a 'big push' of investment is a pre-requisite for economic development of underdeveloped countries.

The 'big push' theory is based upon a burst of state-engineered investment. Prof. Rosenstein himself says that the price mechanism is a very poor signalling system because of the imperfectly developed markets in underdeveloped countries. The dependence on state investment, however, poses a number of problems. The administrative and institutional machinery in such countries is highly inefficient and corrupt. Difficulties arise not only in formulating the plans for various projects but also in their execution.

Lastly, Prof. Rodan's thesis is a sort of 'prescription' for launching underdeveloped countries on the path to progress rapidly in the present. It is not an historical explanation of how development occurs. According to Professor Hagen, historically, nowhere the presence or absence of a 'big push' has been a distinguishing feature of growth.

4. "World Economic Growth—Retrospect and Prospect," *Review of Economic Studies*, August, 1956.

Deficit Financing

30

1. Definition

In the United States, the term 'deficit spending' or 'deficit financing' is generally used to mean any expenditure by the Government in excess of its current revenues. As such expenditure that is financed by borrowing from the public would be included in the measure of deficit in the budget. In India, however, expenditure financed by borrowing from the public does not constitute deficit financing. Thus only expenditure in excess of current revenues and non-bank borrowings is included in deficit spending. According to this definition, the term deficit is applied to expenditure financed only by those means which have a tendency to increase the total outlay in the community.

If a deficit is defined this way, expenditure financed by borrowing from the public can be excluded from the deficit only on the assumption that such expenditure, since it is financed out of genuine savings, has no tendency to increase aggregate outlay. This assumption, however, is not completely valid. In addition, it is difficult to classify government borrowing according to the type of lender. To cite the Planning Commmission, "While the monetary impact of government's borrowing will differ according to the type of subscriber, it would clearly be impracticable to record government's borrowing operations on this basis. Nor does the ownership of public debt remain with the same persons or institutions that bought it to begin with."[1] As such this definition of deficit is only "a convenient convention which under prevailing practices gives as near an approximation to the purpose in hand as possible."[2]

A deficit thus defined can be financed in one or more of the following ways: (1) borrowing from the central bank; (2) withdrawal

1. Government of India, *Second Five-Year Plan* (New Delhi, 1956), p. 84.
2. *Ibid.*, p. 84.

of cash balances; (3) borrowing from the commercial banks; (4) issue of new currency by the government. In governmental accounting practice, borrowing from the public and from the banks are combined together as 'market borrowings'. The figures of annual deficits released by the government or the Reserve Bank of India include only withdrawal of cash balances and net borrowing from the Reserve Bank.

2. Financing of Budget Deficit

It is very essential that an appropriate policy is adopted for financing the deficit budget. Such a policy should keep the interest rates low and stable. If the government borrowing to finance the deficit raises interest rates, it will have unfavourable results. The interest charges on public debt will rise. The investors will suffer heavy losses through capital depreciation. Private investment will tend to be discouraged. Unstable interest rates will disrupt the security markets and have unfavourable effects on private investment.

The financial technique followed in the United Kingdom and in other countries during the World War Second appears to be quite suitable for a budget deficit aimed at creating additional demand. Under this technique, long-term and short-term papers are offered on 'tap'. The excess of the budget deficit over subscriptions to the tap issues is covered by borrowing from the Central Bank. In this way, the deficit is met partly by borrowing the genuine saving of the public and partly through monetary expansion while keeping the rate of interest low and stable. If the government could convince the public of its determination to prevent a further rise in the rate of interest, there will be a decline in the assets-demand for money, and hence in the rate of interest, unless it is already very low.

3. Adverse Effects of Deficit Budgeting

The commonly mentioned limitations of deficit financing are increase in public debt, possible adverse effects on private enterprise, the fear that increased public expenditure may prevent desired cost reductions from being effected and its inflationary impact. These are briefly discussed below.

Increase in Public Debt: Since the public securities are held mostly by the richer classes either directly or indirectly (*i.e.*, by holding deposits with banks or owning stocks and shares of companies which hold public securities as one of their assets), it leads to an increase in inequalities in the distribution of income before tax. And since an increase in inequalities in the distribution of income raises the propensity to save, the offset to private saving currently provided by a deficit budget is at the expense of raising the propensity to save in future.

Since public securities are likely to be held by the older generation in the community, public debt would lead to a transfer of wealth from the younger to the older generation. And since the younger generation has greater capacity to enjoy wealth than the older generation, it would diminish aggregate economic welfare of the country. But to the extent, family and other liabilities of the older generation are larger than those of the younger generation, the transfer of wealth from the latter to the former is justified.

Adverse Effects on Private Enterprise: Deficit budgeting creates adverse effects on private enterprise in a number of ways. In the first place, the government's desire to direct increased public expenditure into socially useful investment may lead it to encroach upon fields which normally fall within the province of private enterprise. Secondly, the growing public debt, and the prospect of larger amounts required to service it, may lead to fears of higher taxation in future. Such fears, whether imagined or real, tend to discourage investment. To the extent, for one reason or other, increase in public expenditure discourages private investment, the deficit budgeting will prove self-defeating.

Obstruction of Desirable Cost Reduction: In case particular cost—say wages of a particular type of labour or prices of particular raw materials—are out of line with the general cost-price structure and as such excercise a depressive influence on the industry concerned, they must be lowered so as to help the revival of the industry. If the increased public spending obstructs such adjustment, it would tend to retard self-sustained recovery.

4. Deficit Financing and Inflation

Does deficit financing inevitably lead to inflation? No, it may be used without inflationary pressures if it is kept within the limits permitted by the following factors:

Growth of Production: Increased supply of money is essential to match the increased production if deflation is to be avoided.

Increase in Population: Increase in population increases the demand for money for holding cash balances. To the extent, the increased supply of money meets the increased demand for it, there will be no tendency towards inflation.

Replacement of Subsistence Economy by Exchange Economy: Underdeveloped countries are characterised by a marked degree of self-sufficiency. Workers consume a considerable part of their produce at home and sell very little in the market. With the development process, subsistence economy gives place to exchange economy. To the extent exchange requires money, demand for money is increased.

Extension of the Monetary Sector to the Barter Economy: In underdeveloped countries, a considerable portion of the transactions is carried out without the intervention of money. With the development process, barter economy gives place to monetary economy and thus the demand for money is increased.

Excess of Savings over Investment: Habit of hoarding money is very common in underdeveloped countries. To the extent the deficit financing offsets hoarded money, there will be no tendency towards inflation. It may, however, be mentioned that with economic progress, the people may realise the loss from hoarding and actually there may occur dishoarding instead of hoarding. Savings may remain unutilised, also because of lack of profitable investment opportunities or because of the underdevelopment of the monetary organisation through which small savings are transformed into investment.

Excess of Imports over Exports: Excess of imports over exports may be made possible by the use of old foreign exchange balances (e.g., sterling balances in case of several Commonwealth countries) or foreign loans. To the extent the additional supply of money is matched by the additional imported goods, there will be no inflationary pressure.

The extent to which deficit may lead to inflation depends upon a number of factors:

Elasticity of Production: The greater the elasticity of production, the greater will be the increase in production and smaller the rise in prices as a result of deficit financing. Production in underdeveloped countries, however, is comparatively inelastic because of the lack of excess capacity, shortage of complementary factors and other bottlenecks.

Nature of Investment: If the newly created money is used to finance projects which would soon start producing consumable goods, there won't be much inflationary pressure. Generally, there is a time-lag between the employment of additional labour and the increased demand for goods resulting from additional income. Firstly, there is a time-lag between the employment of labour and the payment of wages. Secondly, there is a time-lag between the receipt of wages and the incurring of expenditure. If the projects financed with the newly created money start producing goods during this time-lag, there may occur no inflation. On the other hand, if the newly created money is used to finance the production of capital goods, there may occur strong inflationary pressures. The extent to which additional labour can be employed for the production of consumption goods, however, is strictly limited because of the dearth of capital goods which are essential for the production of consumption goods. Cottage industries employing a small amount of capital and producing goods for which there exists a ready demand offer some scope for creating additional employment through deficit financing.

Credit Creation: Generally, a certain amount of deficit financing results into a much larger increase in the supply of money through credit creation. The larger the degree of credit creation, the larger will be the increase in the supply of money resulting from a certain amount of deficit financing.

Strength of Trade Unions: Increase in prices leads the labour to demand higher wages. The stronger the trade unions, the larger will be the increase in wages that labour can obtain. The larger the increase in wages, the larger will be the inflationary pressure.

Deficit Financing and Economic Development

Deficit financing to a certain extent is justified for rapid economic development. The danger of deficit financing leading to inflation is more in underdeveloped countries than in developed countries. In underdeveloped countries, the marginal propensity to consume is very high. On the other hand, supply is comparatively inelastic because of lack of excess capacity, shortage of complementary factors and other bottlenecks. Inflation has been described as a maiden who devours her own lover. It discourages voluntary savings. No doubt it forces people to save, but over a long period of time, it becomes increasingly difficult for them to maintain their saving rate against rising prices. Inflation may even lead to a decrease in the total supply. With the rise in prices and incomes, the agriculturists may consume more at home or they prefer leisure to additional income leading to a decrease in total production. Rising prices offer an incentive for hoarding leading to a reduction in the volume of goods brought to the market.

Inflation distorts the profitability of different investments. It induces people to invest in gold, foreign exchange, real estate, hoarding and speculation which offer prospects of fabulous profits rather than in fields which constitute a strong foundation for rapid and balanced economic development. Continuous inflation may endanger the stability of the currency with all its disastrous consequences.

No doubt, a rise in money incomes raises the revenue and still more revenue can be obtained by certain changes in the tax structure. But the cost of development projects may rise much more because of a rise in wages and in prices of equipment and materials and the government may not be able to carry out the planned programme.

It encourages imports and discourages exports and thus causes balance of payments difficulties. Continuous adverse balance of payments weakens the domestic currency in the world market and thus discourages the inflow of foreign capital.

No doubt, for political and administrative reasons, capital formation on the required scale cannot be undertaken by orthodox financial measures, it should not be forgotten that the very simplicity and convenience of deficit financing may lead to extravagance and inefficiency and to neglect of the possibilities for tapping savings and collecting high taxes that exist even in underdeveloped countries.

It is argued that as the projects financed by deficit financing are completed, they would have the effect of increasing production and thereby of increasing savings and tax yields which would provide finance for development in the next period. In underdeveloped countries, increased production, however, may not necessarily lead to a significant increase in savings. It is primarily the entrepreneurial class which gains from inflation. This class in predominantly agrarian societies consists largely of poor peasants and merchants with high marginal propensity to consume. Any increase in their income, therefore, is more likely to be consumed than invested. Moreover, the merchants rarely invest in productive enterprises.

The tax system in most of the underdeveloped countries is very inelastic. Many taxes, like land revenue, are difficult to revise upwards in money terms with the rise in prices. In fact the rise in prices caused by deficit financing may decrease government's command over real resources through taxation.

In the ultimate analysis, inflationary financing requires some groups to suffer a decline in their standard of living. But there is no surety that it will elicit the sacrifices from the required groups. In primarily agricultural countries, the classes, which have to bear the brunt of inflationary financing, are not many. The peasants, merchants and the few rich entrepreneurs do not suffer much loss in real income through rising prices. The only classes, which have to make sacrifice, are the small class of professional men, government employees, and the industrial proletariat. It is difficult to justify a method of enforcing savings which elicits sacrifices from only a few people.

Apart from this, the classes that are adversely affected by inflationary financing—professional men, government employees and industrial proletariat—play an important role in the process of economic development. Their co-operation and support for any programme of development is very essential. For this reason, to neutralise the effect of rise in prices, the governments often introduce measures like price control, rationing, cost of living allowances etc. The result is that almost everybody's income increases *pari passu* with rising prices, and there is very little forced savings, but a maze of administrative problems.

'Created money,' if injected into the economy in moderate doses at intermittent intervals, can certainly induce resources into the productive system and generate more capital even in the underdeveloped countries. Much depends upon the timing and quantity of doses of 'created money' and the watch kept over the reactions they produce on the economic system.

Inflation

31

1. Definition of Inflation

Different economists have defined the term 'inflation' in different ways. According to Chamber's Twentieth Century dictionary inflation means a "disproportionate and as relatively sharp and sudden increase in the quantity or money of credit or both, relative to goods available for purchase. Inflation always produces a rise in the price levels." Crowther defines inflation as "a state in which the value of money is falling, *i.e.*, prices are rising."[1] According to Kemmerer, "inflation is a state in which the value of money is falling, *i.e.*, prices are rising."[2] In Pigou's opinion inflation takes place "when money income is expanding relative to the output of work done by the productive agents for which it is the payment."[3] At another place Pigou says that "inflation exists when money income is expanding more than in proportion to income earning activity."[4] R.G. Hawtrey associates inflation, with "the issue of too much currency"[5] and T.E. Gregory calls it a state of "abnormal increase in the quantity of purchasing power."[6] Coulborn says, it is a phenomenon where, "too much money chases too few goods."

All these definitions show that the basic phenomenon is that of quantity of money in circulation exceeding the total amount of goods and services which leads to an extraordinary increase in prices. Inflation is a situation in which the general level of prices keeps on rising primarily due to stimulus that is continuously being

1. G. Crowther, *An Outline of Money* (1955 ed.), p. 197.
2. E.W. Kemmerer, *ABC of Inflation,* p. 6.
3. A.C. Pigou, *Veil of Money,* p. 34.
4. A.C. Pigou, "Types of Inflation," *Economic Journal,* December 1941, p. 439.
5. R.G. Hawtrey, *Currency and Credit* (1928).
6. T.E. Gregory, "Inflation", *Encylopaedia Britannica.*

administered by the ever-rising demand in the face of inadequate physical supplies. Thus inflation refers to a persistent rise in the general level of prices over a certain period owing to the continuous growth of demand very much in excess of the supply of goods and services.

No doubt a rise in prices is an important characteristic of inflation, every rise in prices may not be inflationary. A rise in prices resulting from a rise in production costs, for instance, cannot be regarded as inflation. Further, as some writers have pointed out, inflation may exist without a rise in prices. When costs are falling but prices are kept stable (as in United States during 1924-29), or when the decline in prices is less than that in costs, the country may develop all symptoms of inflation. Such a phenomenon is described by Keynes as "profit inflation" to distinguish it from "commodity inflation" (meaning a rise in prices). In a state of repressed inflation prices are prevented from rising by an efficient system of controls and rationing. The inflationary pressure is held strictly under control and hidden from public view but the pressure is still there, dormant, but ready to manifest itself in the form of high prices the moment controls are relaxed or removed. Nevertheless, a rise in the general price level is a common characteristic of inflation and any definition of the term inflation must explain this phenomenon.

On this basis, inflation can be defined in two ways. Earlier writers based their definition on the well-known Quantity Theory of Money and explained inflationary trends in prices in terms of an increase in the supply of money. Irving Fisher is of the view that the prices are affected much more by the supply of money than by the supply of goods. After an examination of the price trends in Europe and the United States in the nineteenth and the earlier part of the twentieth century, he concludes that "price level almost invariably shifts with monetary factors—gold, silver, paper, credit—and very little with, commodity factors. The latter control only the deviations of individual prices from average price movement. In a word, supply and demand dictate each individual price level itself."[7]

But this definition, according to which expansion of money is the cause and rise in prices the effect is open to question. It is commonly known that during the inflation of early 1920's in

---

7. Irving Fisher, *Inflation,* 1933, p. 45.

Germany, prices, far from being pushed up by the volume of money, actually constituted the active factor drawing out into circulation an ever increasing volume of money. The prices were increasing at such a fast rate that the rate of expansion of money supply could not keep pace with the demand for it. As such the relationship between the money supply and prices was reversed. The writers at that time did not hold increase in money supply to be responsible for inflation. On the contrary, they emphasized the relative deficiency in the supply of money and attributed the rise in prices to the unfavourable balance of payments position of Germany and the consequent depreciation of Mark in terms of foreign currencies. Thus this definition of inflation is not very appropriate in a situation of hyper-inflation. This led Paul Einzig to distinguish between money inflation and price inflation, the first relates to that stage as it were, in which over-expansion of money beyond normal requirement for it pushes up prices; the second relates to the next stage in which prices get out of control and rise so rapidly that money supply lags behind. Paul Einzig defines inflation "as a state of disequilibrium in which an expansion of purchasing power tends to cause, or is the effect of, an increase of the price level."[8] This definition of inflation covers not only the familiar phenomenon of too much money chasing too few goods but also the other and the more vicious aspect of the problem of a wage, cost of production and price spiral in which each becomes at the same time the cause and effect.

A definition which attempts to explain inflation in terms of a relationship between money supply and price is at best a statement of one aspect of the problem. While mentioning the factors which help in an inflationary price movement, it does not explain the root cause of the trouble. A proper definition of inflation should indicate not only the factors responsible for an exceptional rise in the price level but also show how these factors work themselves out and produce an inflationary situation. In other words, it should cover not only the static but also the dynamic aspect of the problem.

This definition has another drawback. During the depression period if the government undertakes monetary and fiscal measures which lead to an expansion of money supply and a recovery in the

8. Paul Einzig, *Inflation*, 1952, p. 22.

price level, it would obviously be wrong to call such a situation as an inflationary one.

The second approach to the problem of inflation has been put forward by economists, like Wicksell, Bent Hansen and J.M. Keynes. According to this approach, "general price level is determined by the total demand for and total supply of the group of goods concerned, the prices of which determine the general price level."[9] And the inflation is defined as that situation in which the total demand for goods, indicated by the volume of money offered, is in excess of the supply of goods at prevailing prices. Excess of demand over supply is a common factor to both repressed and open inflation. In the former case it is concealed by devices like controls and rationing while in the latter it appears naked in the form of excessive money prices.

It can easily be seen that there is not much difference in the basic premises of the two approaches mentioned above in so far as excess demand, which forms the cornerstone of the analysis of the latter approach, can become effective only by means of increased money supply. The basic difference between the two approaches is that while the earlier quantity theory approach explains the position as it is, it fails to point out the origin of the trouble; the latter supply and demand approach not only indicates the source of the problem but also helps in visualizing the means by which the causal factors work themselves out in an inflationary process.

Keynes makes a distinction between semi-inflation and full or true inflation. According to him an expansion of the supply of money in circulation before the state of full employment is reached will exhaust itself partly in increasing employment and partly in increasing prices through an increase in production costs. He calls it the state of semi-inflation. Theoretically speaking, so long as full employment is not reached, any increase in the quantity of money should wholly exhaust itself in raising the level of employment and output and not in price level. Because of the existence of various frictions and bottlenecks in the economic system, however, a part of the increased supply of money exhausts itself in raising prices while the remaining part finds its way into productive channels raising the volume of employment and production in the country. It is only

9. Bent Hansen, *A Study in the Theory of Inflation*, 1951, p. 2.

after full employment is reached through a series of inflationary waves occasioned by an increase in the quantity of money that there is established a direct nexus between the increments in the quantity of money and the price level such that an increase in the quantity of money causes a direct and proportionate increase in the price levels. It is here that the true or full inflation comes into operation. Before the full employment is reached prices rise on account of rising costs associated with higher wages and diminishing returns as the scale of output increases in the short period.

2. Types of Inflation

Inflation is of different types. These different types may be looked at by dividing them into different categories on different considerations. In the first place, we may distinguish between different types of inflation on the basis of degree or speed with which the prices rise. Secondly, the distinction may be based on the processes through which inflation is induced. Thirdly, different types of inflation may be distinguished on the basis of time. Fourthly, inflation may be either sporadic or comprehensive. Fifthly, inflation may be open or suppressed. On the basis of rapidity with which prices increase, inflation may be divided into four types: (1) creeping inflation, (2) walking inflation, (3) running inflation, and (4) jumping or galloping or hyperinflation. The speed at which prices rise is significant from the point of view of the dangerous effects on the economy. Creeping inflation is the most mild form of inflation and some economists do not consider it to be dangerous for the economy. In fact, some economists consider it to be an important instrument of economic development. It is argued that it keeps the national economy free from the cankering effects of stagnation. Creeping inflation in which prices rise imperceptibly over a long period has been attracting a good deal of attention in Germany and the United States since 1956.

There is another school of thought which considers creeping inflation to be dangerous for the economy. According to this school inflation is like conception which when once takes place goes on increasing till the baby is delivered. In course of time the baby ceases to creep. It learns to walk, run and finally gallop. It should, therefore, be nipped in the bud.

In case of walking inflation, the rise in prices becomes more marked as compared with the situation obtaining under creeping inflation; in fact, it is danger signal of the occurrence of running and jumping inflation under which the rise in prices takes place by fits and starts. In hyper or galloping inflation prices rise every moment and there is no limit of the height to which the prices might rise. The post-war inflation in Germany and Austria, when the quantity of money increased many hundred quintillion times over the pre-war quantity and the prices increased many trillions over the pre-war prices, is a classic example of the runaway or hyperinflation.

Hyperinflation is an indication of the highest degree of abnormality in the monetary system of a country. After the First World War (1914-18), prices in Germany rose at one time by one million times the pre-war level.[10] Under the conditions of such an inflation all assets having a fixed income lose their real value. The best examples of such assets and incomes are provided by salaries, savings, mortgages, insurance policies, bonds, etc. Hyperinflation ruined millions of German families; it more or less wiped out the German middle class. Hyperinflation was also experienced in Hungary, Poland, Greece, Austria, Russia etc. The question may be raised as to why the government issued such a large quantity of currency that led to hyperinflation. The answer is that the large issue of currency served as a major source of funds for government expenditure. Statistical data has revealed beyond any doubt that in the final stage of hyperinflation (1923) the half-yearly index of output in Germany declined by one-third in less than 6 months.[11]

On the basis of different processes through which it is induced, inflation is of three types:

(*i*) Deficit-induced inflation, which is caused by the adoption of deficit financing or by government spending in excess of its revenue receipts.

(*ii*) Wage-induced inflation, which results from an increase in money wages.

(*iii*) Profit-induced inflation, which occurs on account of an increase in the profits of the manufacturers.

---

10. Crowther, *An Outline of Money*, p. 103.
11. Philip Cagan, *Studies in the Quantity Theory of Money* (ed. Friedman) p. 53.

Coming to the third category, we may have war-time inflation which emerges from the exigencies of war during the war period and the post-war inflation which exists in immediate post-war period and more often is the legacy of war. The hyperinflation of Germany during the 'twenties' provides the classical examples of war and post-war inflation. There is also peace time inflation which refers to the rise in prices during periods of peace resulting from increased government outlays.

Inflation is comprehensive or economy-wide when the price of every commodity rises throughout the economy. Sporadic inflation is of ephemeral and sectional nature. It occurs when a group of prices rises as a result of sporadic increases in individual prices owing to abnormal shortage of specific goods. The condition of sporadic inflation does not mean more market shortages of goods caused by distortions of price structure such as might take place when the prices of raw materials or wages increase but the prices of finished products are not adjusted in upward direction. It results in situations where supply is restricted by physical conditions and cannot be expanded quickly. The shortages of current production are further accentuated by the backlog of deferred demand. Under such conditions, a rise in prices does not help in restoring supply in a high level of demand. A typical case of sporadic inflation would be an increase in prices of manufactured goods resulting from the formation of a successful monopoly which aims at the curtailment of output, or rise in the prices of those goods whose production has been interrupted and capacity curtailed by war.

Inflation may be open or suppressed. It is open when prices rise without any interruption. The hyperinflation during the 'twenties' in Germany, Austria, Russia, etc., and in China in the 'forties' provides an example of such an inflation. Suppressed inflation, in contrast, refers to conditions in which, as a result of adoption of certain policies (*e.g.*, price control and rationing) by the government, prices are prevented from rising. When price control and rationing or other physical controls are removed, suppressed inflation bursts into an open inflation with vengeance. War-time controls are an example of suppressed inflation developed into an open inflation. The word suppression here means: (*i*) the postponement of the present demand to some future date; and (*ii*) the diversion of demand from one kind of goods to another—from those goods which are subject to price-control and rationing to those whose prices are uncontrolled and which are not rationed.

Suppressed inflation suffers from a number of evils. It gives rise to administrative problems. It leads to a hierarchy of price controllers and rationing officers whose duty is to administer rationing and controls. Efficient administration of rationing and controls requires that the administrative machinery should be competent, experienced and honest. War-time experience of actual working of controls and rationing even in advanced countries, however, shows that the administrative machinery is inefficient and easily corruptible. Under such conditions, there grows the most unpleasant phenomenon of black market through which the rationed and price-controlled goods are sold. The administrative machinery being a party to the activities of black marketeers, there soon develops hidden price inflation which is worse than open inflation. To site Halm, "Excess purchasing power then causes a violent price inflation in the black markets, while the legal markets are drained of merchandise. Once the population finds that it cannot even buy its modest rations, black-market operations become the preoccupation of everybody. Where one such black-market transaction earns more money than a week's or a month's hard work, productivity will decline enormously."[12] Black-market demoralises national character.

Apart from all this, suppressed inflation causes uneconomic diversion of productive resources from essential goods industries whose prices are statutorily fixed to those industries which produce relatively less essential goods but whose prices, being not subject to price control, are free to rise. Thus the scarce resources of the community have a tendency to move from more productive fields to less productive but monetarily more profitable channels. Such a deviation from the optimum utilisation of resources is very harmful for the community.

Sometimes economists talk of the demand-pull, demand-shift and cost-push inflation.

3. Demand-Pull Inflation

It emerges when the aggregate demand exceeds the level of full employment output. Consumers and investors seek to buy more than the total amount of output that can be produced. This type of

12. G.N. Halm, *Economics of Money and Banking*, p. 417.

inflation is also known as excess demand inflation. Excess demand may arise either in the public or private sector. The demand-pull inflation may be caused by an increase in the quantity of money. An increase in the quantity of money would lower the rate of interest which would stimulate investment. This will also lead to an increase in consumption expenditure through the multiplier. The demand-pull inflation can also occur without an increase in money supply. This would occur when aggregate demand increases either because of a rise in the marginal efficiency of capital or a rise in the propensity to consume.

The diagram given below illustrates the demand-pull inflation. In this digram *D* curves show aggregate demand function and *S*

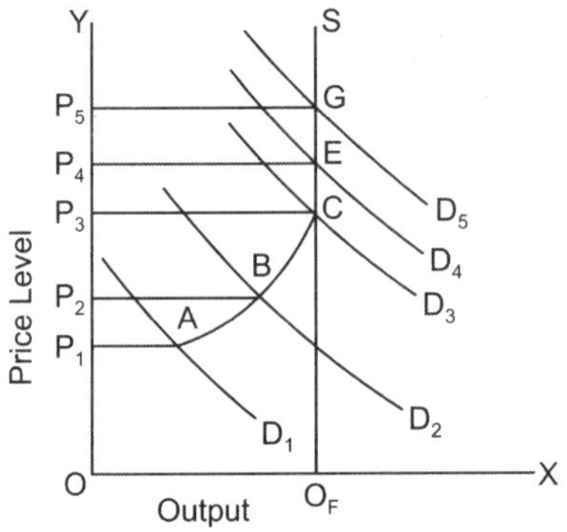

Diagram 31.1

curve shows the given supply function. As *D* curve rises higher and higher from D_1 to D_5 the price level rises higher and higher from P_1 to P_5. When the aggregate demand function rises from D_1 up to D_3, there takes place an increase both in the price level and the aggregate output because the full-employment level is not yet reached. This is known as bottleneck inflation. Full employment is reached at point *C* and, therefore, beyond *C* or above D_3, rise takes place only in the price level. This is known as true inflation.

4. Cost-Push Inflation

For a long time before the fifties, inflation theory ran mainly in terms of the generalised excess demand, explained either by quantity theory or Keynesian theory. During the fifties there occurred a revival of supply, or cost, theories of inflation. The general notion that price inflation can arise on the supply, or cost, side is not new. To cite M. Bronfenbrenner and F.D. Holzman, "Cost inflation has been the layman's instinctive explanation of general price increases since the dawn of the monetary system. We know of no inflationary movement that has not been blamed by some people on "profiteers", "speculators", "hoarders" or workers and peasants 'living beyond their station'."[13]

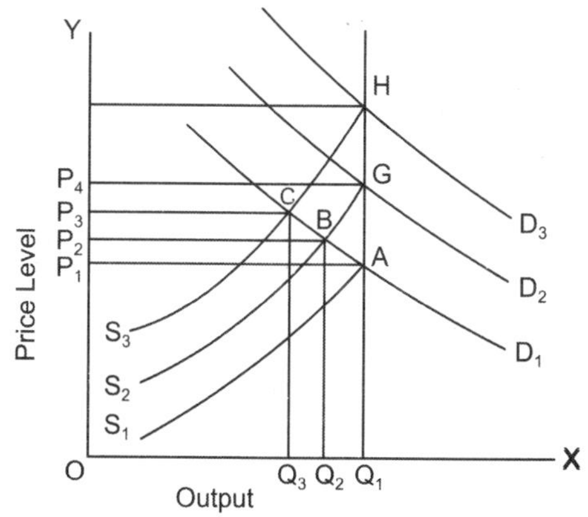

Diagram 31.2

The diagram given above illustrates the cost-push inflation. The full employment output equilibrium is determined at the point where the demand curve D_1 and the supply curve S_1 intersect each other. This is point A at which output is OQ_1 and price is OP_1. When the aggregate supply function shifts to S_2, output declines to OQ_2 and the price level rises to OP_2. Similarly, when the supply function further rises to S_3, output declines to OQ_3 and price level rises to OP_3. The process will continue for still further upward shifts in the supply function.

There are two main causes of inflationary shifts in the aggregate supply function, *viz.*, (*i*) higher money wages secured by labour unions and (*ii*) higher prices secured by business firms in monopolistic or oligopolistic industries. The inflation caused by the first factor is known as *wage-push inflation* while that caused by the second factor is known as *profit-push inflation.*

13. M. Bronfenbrenner and F.D. Holzman, "Survey of Inflation Theory," *American Economic Review* (September, 1963), p. 613.

Wage-push Inflation: If the increase in wage-rate is faster than the increase in productivity, there will occur an upward shift in the aggregate supply function. One cause of a rise in wage rates is an excess demand for labour. Once the economy has reached full employment, any increase in the level of money income will reflect only in a rise in prices and no rise in output. Higher prices mean greater profits, and greater profits induce employers to expand output. For this purpose they seek more labour which is not available. Competition among employers leads to a rise in the wage rate. Thus there occurs a rise in wage rates without any rise in the productivity of labour. But it may be pointed out that this rise in the labour cost per unit of output is not the *cause* of the rise in the price level but the result. Wage rates rose because of an excessive demand for labour; this would have happened whether labour was organised or not.

The concept of wage-push inflation is restricted to increases in 'labour costs which are the *cause* and not the *result* of higher prices. Wage-push inflation is the result of "spontaneous" or "autonomous" upward shifts in the supply function as against those which are "induced" by excess demand for labour. Induced shifts may occur with or without the existence of strong labour unions but spontaneous shifts assume strong labour unions which are able to push up wage rates in the absence of any excess demand for labour. Wage-push inflation cannot occur in an economy in which wage-rates are determined by purely competitive market forces. In such an economy wage rates rise or fall only in response to variations in the demand for and supply of labour, which in turn depend on variations in aggregate demand for final output.

Profit-push Inflation: This is another form of supply inflation. Just as labour unions may exercise their market power by forcing wage increases, so oligopolists and monopolists may, in order to increase their profits, raise prices more than needed to offset any increase in costs. Again just as labour unions are a pre-requisite to a generalised wage-push inflation, so the existences of imperfectly competitive markets in the sale of goods and services is a prerequisite to profit-push inflation. Where prices are determined by the competition among buyers and sellers, as is the case with agricultural commodities and raw materials, the seller cannot influence the price significantly. But many goods are not sold through such markets and the sellers of these goods "administer" prices. In an economy where so-called administered prices abound, there is at least the possibility that these prices may be administered upward faster than costs in an effort to increase profits.

The cost-push hypothesis, however, rarely considers autonomous attempts to increase profits as an important inflationary element. In the first place, since profits are generally a small fraction of the total price, an increase in profits would not have much impact on prices. Secondly, monopolists and oligopolists generally hesitate to raise prices in the absence of obvious demand-pull elements. Finally, the motivation for a profit push is weak since, at least in corporations, those who make the decision to raise prices are not the direct beneficiaries of increase in price. The cost-push is, therefore, generally conceived as being synonymous with wage-push.

5. Demand-Shift Inflation

A rise in the price level may occur without an increase in aggregate demand if the structure of demand changes so rapidly that the resources cannot be shifted equally fast. The year 1946 provides a typical example of demand-shift inflation in the United States. With the close of the War there developed a simultaneous reduction in government expenditure and an increase in private consumption and private investment. Further, during the year, real net national product declined below the 1945 level, although money national product continued to rise. Thus, while the real output declined, the price level rose up. In this way, it is possible for changes in the structure of demand to affect the general price level even though there is no increase in aggregate demand. The basic idea behind demand shift inflation is that a shift in demand would raise wages and prices in fields in which demand has increased. But since wages and prices are inflexible in the downward direction, the rising wages and prices in some sectors are not matched by corresponding reductions in wages and prices in the sectors in which demand has declined. As such the general level of prices rises in spite of the fact that no increase in the overall aggregate demand has taken place.

6. Demand-pull versus Cost-push Inflation

According to some economists inflation is neither demand-pull alone nor cost-push alone and, in actual practice, it possesses elements of both. They point out that there cannot be such a thing as cost-push inflation because, without an increase in the purchasing power and demand, cost increases would lead to unemployment and depression and not to inflation. Similarly, there are assumptions for which it would be appropriate to say that demand-pull cannot cause inflation unless it is produced by cost-push. In other words, it is contended that there are conditions under which 'effective demand' is not effective and would not pull up prices unless cost-push produces inflation. But this position ignores an important distinction, namely, whether the cost-push is 'equilibrating' in the sense that it 'absorbs' a previously excess demand or whether it is 'disequilibrating' in the sense that it creates an excess supply (of labour and productive capacity) which would have to be prevented or removed by an increase in effective demand. To cite Prof. Harry G. Johnson, "The issue of cost-push versus demand-pull was...a spurious one.... Neither cost-push nor demand-pull inflation models can generate a sustained inflation unless it is assumed either that the demand for money can be compressed indefinitely without adverse effects on demand and employment, which runs contrary to the theory and fact of monetary behaviour, or that the monetary authority permissively provides the additional money required to circulate the national income at ever increasing prices, in which case the behaviour of the monetary authority becomes the crucial factor in inflation (and, in addition, the question arises for the cost-push theory as to what determines the pace of inflation). The two theories are therefore not independent and self-contained theories of inflation, but rather theories concerning the mechanism of inflation in a monetary environment that permits it."[14] Further, in actual practice, it is very difficult to devise a test capable of determining whether a particular inflation is of the demand-pull or cost-push variety.

No doubt the distinction between demand-pull and cost-push inflation is not very scientific, it cannot be denied that it does help in separating two forces which might be in simultaneous and interdependent operation in any actual inflation. The distinction is also important for its policy implications. To cite Harry G. Johnson, "The importance of the debate stems largely from the difference

---

14. Harry G. Johnson, *Essays in Monetary Economics* (London, 1967), p. 128.

between the recommendations for anti-inflationary policy to which the two views of the cause of inflation lead, the demand-pull explanation leading to the recommendation of monetary restraint and fiscal orthodoxy and the cost-push explanation leading to the rejection of macroeconomic measures of this sort in favour of policies directed at the processes of price formation and wage determination."[15]

7. Inflationary Gap

Inflationary gap was defined by the Chancellor of the Exchequer in England in his budget speech of April, 1941 as "the amount of the government's expenditure against which there is no corresponding release of real resources of manpower or material by some other member of the community." As such it indicates an excess of total demand for goods over their total supply measured at constant prices. The concept of inflationary gap may be viewed in relationship to full employment level of real income and defined as the excess of the amount of aggregate spending over the amount of aggregate output at full employment level at the existing prices. Prof. Kurihara defines the inflationary gap as "an excess of anticipated expenditure over available output at base prices." According to Klein, this gap "is the difference between what the population will try to consume out of income (which is determined by the interaction of consumption function and the level of the government expenditure) and the amount available for consumption at pre-inflation prices."

Even if it is assumed that there exist some unemployed resources, which can be commissioned to raise the level of income above the present level, an excess of demand over supply will lead to a rise in prices because production cannot be increased instantaneously. It takes time to build new factories and to commission new plants. Increased raw materials have to be obtained by increasing agricultural and mineral production. Workers have to be trained in new skills. All this requires time. Thus even when production can be increased, such an increase would take place with a time-lag. As such when expenditure increases, prices would rise and inflationary gap would exist till the supply of goods is expanded.

To illustrate how the inflationary gap arises and how it is measured, we may consider the example of a war economy which is

15. *Ibid.*, p. 127.

more or less a full-employment economy. The aggregate real national income would be equal to the sum of government and private expenditures incurred on investment and consumption. Let us suppose this amounts to Rs. 1200 crores in money terms calculated at the existing price level. Now if, out of this total output, the government takes away output worth Rs. 300 crores for war purposes, output only worth Rs. 900 crores would be available for civilian consumption. This output worth Rs. 900 crores constitutes the supply side. Let us suppose that the money income paid to the community during the same period is Rs. 1200 crores, out of which the government takes away Rs. 100 crores in the form of taxes. This leaves a disposable income of Rs. 1100 crores with the community. Obviously, the community "would not spend the entire disposable money income on the purchase of goods and save a part of it. If people were in the habit of saving 10 per cent of their disposable income, the money income that would actually be spent on goods would amount to Rs. 990 crores (*e.g.*, Rs. 1100 crores—Rs. 110 crores saved). As such, the inflationary gap at the current level of prices would be Rs. 90 crores, *i.e.*, Rs. 990 crores— Rs. 900 crores. Thus when disposable income of Rs. 990 crores chases goods available for civilian consumption worth Rs. 900 crores, there arises an inflationary gap to the tune of Rs. 90 crores. The process may be summarised as below:

Table 31.1: Inflationary Gap

Demand Side	*Rs. crores*	*Supply Side*	*Rs. crores*
Money income paid to community	1200	Gross national product (GNP) at existing prices (or at preinflation prices)	1200
Taxes	100		
Total disposable	1100	War expenditure, *i.e.*, value of GNP appropriated for war purposes	300
Savings by community at the rate of 10 per cent	110		
Net disposable income (which represents total amount of anticipated expenditure)	990	Value available for civilian consumption at pre-inflation prices	900

A similar inflationary gap can arise during a period of development planning. The amount of money expenditure (and as such money income) may be high because of expenditure on development projects but there may not be a corresponding increase in the production of consumption goods because of the time-lag between the investment on development projects and flow of goods from them. Thus, the basic fact is that so long as the amount of disposable income in the community and the amount of goods available are equal, price level would remain stable; but if the former exceeds the latter, an inflationary gap would appear. If, in contrast, the amount of goods were in excess of the disposable money incomes, a deflationary gap would appear.

The diagram given below illustrates the concept of inflationary gap.

In this diagram, total anticipated expenditure is measured along the vertical axis while the real income (gross national product) is measured along the horizontal axis. *C* represents consumption expenditure, *I* private investment expenditure and *G* government expenditure, so that the total expenditure of the economy is shown by the *C+I+G* function. The 45° line *OE* is the equilibrium line

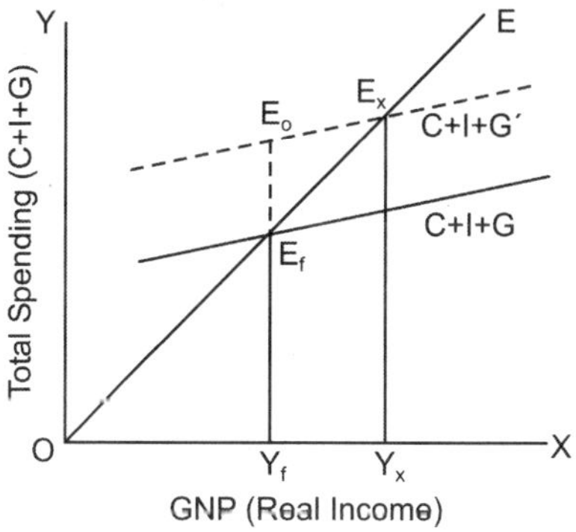

Diagram 31.3

showing that the economy is in equilibrium when the supply of goods and services (as reflected in real income) equals the demand for them (as reflected in the total spending function). The *C+I+G* curve intersects the curve *OE* (equilibrium line) at point E_f which gives the equilibrium income Y_f, which may be assumed as the full employment income at current prices. At this point the aggregate monetary demand reflected by the $C+I+G$ function amounts to E_fY_f which is equal to the total amount of goods available, that is, OY_f. As such, there is no excess demand and no question of inflationary gap.

Now, suppose, for some reasons, the government expenditure increases by E_fE_0 which gives the economy new function $C+I+G$. Since Y_f is the real income at full employment level, it does not increase with the increase in government expenditure by E_fE_0. Thus E_fE_0 represents an excess of monetary demand over the available quantity of goods (OY_f). In this case E_fE_0 is the extent of inflationary gap which forces up prices. Thus inflationary gap occurs when, with the economy at full employment, the money income rises faster than the output of goods and services. When the expenditures are rising faster than the output of goods and services, prices will necessarily rise to equate expenditures with the money value of output at a higher price level. The inflationary gap is, therefore, defined as the amount by which full employment exceeds the value of current output at existing prices. This implies that if the prices are to be prevented from rising, the output of goods must increase by an amount which would be sufficient to absorb the excess demand generated by an increased expenditure. In the above diagram, the prices can be prevented from rising only if the real income is increased from Y_f to Y_x.

In case it is not possible to increase real income (or the volume of goods and services), the inflationary gap can be bridged up by any one or more of the following three measures: (*i*) inducing the public to save more, (*ii*) mopping up the surplus purchasing power with the public through additional taxation, and (*iii*) raising the value of the available output to the level of disposable income by permitting the prices to rise. Among these three alternative measures, a good government tries to bridge up the inflationary gap by the first two measures, *viz.*, by inducing the public to save more and by increasing taxes. But a bad government may allow the prices to rise and thus expose the economy to inflation.

Significance of Inflationary Gap: The concept of inflationary gap is a highly useful analytical device because it indicates the direction and extent to which the various anti-inflationary measures should be carried out by the monetary and fiscal authorities. To cite Kurihara, "Analysis of the inflationary gap in terms of such aggregates as national income, investment outlays, and consumption expenditures, clearly reveals what determines public policy with respect to taxes, public expenditures, savings campaigns, credit control, wage adjustments—in short, all the conceivable anti-inflation measures affecting the propensities to consume, to save, and to invest, which together determine the general price level. It is by influencing those propensities, directly or indirectly, that the monetary-fiscal authorities hope to wipe out the inflationary gap and therefore prevent further price increase."[16]

8. Unemployment-Inflation Dilemma (Phillips Curve)

With remarkable prescience, both Keynes and Mrs. Robinson foresaw in the pre-war period the dilemma which most of the western countries face today; the possibility of attaining simultaneously, and without price or wage controls, the twin goals of full employment and price stability. The experience of many countries with strong producer pressure groups shows that as unemployment is reduced below a certain critical level, prices begin to rise; and that, when prices are stable, unemployment is above the level that is considered "socially tolerable" by countries committed in principle to a full employment goal.

Thus we cannot have price stability and full employment at one and the same time. If we want stable prices, we have to forgo a high level of employment. And if we want a high level of employment, we have to sacrifice stable prices. Thus we have to trade between unemployment and inflation.

A.W. Phillips has made an empirical study of the relationship between unemployment and the rate of change of money wage rates, which is known as "the Phillips Curve." The objective of his study is to investigate whether statistical evidence supports the hypothesis that the rate of change of money wage rates in the United Kingdom can be explained by the level of unemployment and the rate of change of unemployment and if so to form some quantitative estimate of the relation between unemployment and the rate of change of money wage rates. The empirical study appears in general to support the hypothesis that the rate of change of money wage rates can be explained by the *level* of unemployment and the

16. Kenneth K. Kurihara, *Monetary Theory and Public Policy* (London, 1956), p. 45.

rate of change of unemployment. The relation between unemployment and the rate of change of wage rates is likely to be curvilinear and not linear. Phillips has used this curve to determine

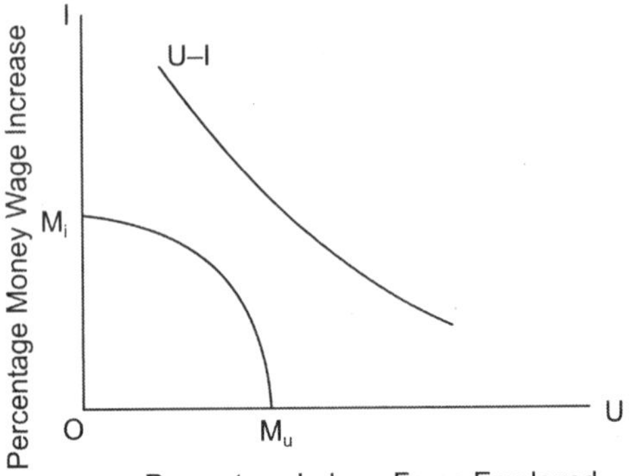

Diagram 31.4

that for the United Kingdom a rate of 5½ per cent unemployment is needed if wages are to be held steady, and a rate of 2½ per cent unemployment is needed if prices are to be held steady; this means that wages would rise by the same percentage as the increase in productivity, which is estimated to be 2 per cent per annum. Samuelson and Solow have estimated a similar curve for the United States and have found a more pessimistic figure of 5½ per cent unemployment necessary for price stability, assuming that productivity increases at 2½ per cent per annum.[17]

In the above diagram, the curve *U-I* represents the Phillips relationship. The curve can be derived from an economy's data for a period of years by plotting for each year the percentage money wage increase (vertical axis) against the percentage labour force that is unemployed (horizontal axis). The curve M_i—M_u represents the acceptable *trade off* between inflation and unemployment. This curve is concave indicating that as unemployment reaches low levels, more inflation is acceptable only if a relatively large decrease in unemployment can be traded for it and as the rate of inflation reaches low levels higher unemployment is acceptable only if increasingly large cuts in the rate of inflation can be traded for it. M_i is assumed to be the maximum rate of inflation which would be

17. Samuelson and Solow, "Analytical Aspects of Anti-Inflation Policy", *American Economic Review*, May, 1960, pp. 177-94.

tolerated by the authorities concerned; this rate is associated with zero unemployment. Similarly, M_u represents the maximum tolerable rate of unemployment and is associated with complete price stability. The curve M_iM_u represents the maximum tolerable rate of inflation for every rate of unemployment up to M_u and conversely. All the *U-I* points located on or within the M_iM_u curve are acceptable, each point representing a combination of an acceptable rate of inflation and an acceptable rate of unemployment. All points inside the curve, however, are not equally desirable.

If the *U-I* limit curve neither touches nor intersects M_iM_u curve, the goals of full employment and price stability would be in effective conflict. A tolerable rate of unemployment would have to be paid for by an unacceptable rate of inflation and conversely. In contrast, if the macro boundary intersects the M_iM_u curve, an acceptable rate of unemployment can be combined with an acceptable rate of inflation. Although a trade off must still be made between a lower rate of inflation and a lower rate of unemployment, there is no effective conflict in the sense that one of the choices in the trade off must be unacceptable. Actual experience in most of the Western countries shows that high employment and price stability are in effective conflict.

Critical Evaluation: The Phillips Curve has not been accepted by all economists and the empirical evidence is still a matter of great controversy. Many economists do not approve of an explanation of inflation which does not pay adequate consideration to the monetary conditions. Even if Phillips relation does exist, it does not necessarily imply that it will usefully lend itself to macroeconomic decision-making. They feel that changes in prices are at least as important as unemployment in determining changes in the wage rate. That is ignored in the Phillips Curve. The 'money illusion' among workers as suggested by Keynes is largely absent in today's bargaining because wage-earners would make every effort to retain their share of national income, if this has been eroded by rising prices. To cite Harry G. Johnson, "...there are some serious doubts about the applicability of the Phillips Curve to the formulation of economic policy. On the one hand, the curve represents only a statistical description of the mechanics of adjustment in the labour market, resting on a simple model of economic dynamics with little general and well-tested monetary and value theory behind it. On the other hand, it describes the behaviour of the labour market in a combination of periods of economic fluctuation and varying rate of inflation, conditions which presumably influenced the behaviour of the labour market itself, so that it may reasonably be doubled whether the curve would continue to hold its shape if an attempt was made by economic policy to pin the economy down to a point on it."[18]

Friedman holds the view that a function relating the volume of employment to the rate of change in money prices is fallacious because it implies a relationship between real and nominal magnitudes.[19] Since the former is determined by real forces in the economy, and only temporarily influenced by the monetary variable, while the latter is determined entirely by monetary forces, it is obvious that there is no reason to assume any relationship between the two.

It has been pointed out that the degree of non-linearity between changes in the wage rate and unemployment is an empirical question which needs further examination. Profits have often been suggested as another important determinant of the change in wage rates. This point needs serious consideration.

Phillips Curve and Control of Inflation: If we succeed in achieving full employment, we must find some way other than the use of monetary and fiscal policy to prevent the inflation which Phillips Curve suggests may well result. One of the ways is to link increases in wages to increases in productivity of the workers. Other measures include various forms of anti-union legislation, which at the extreme would abolish collective bargaining or prohibit industry-wide bargaining. Although all such measures have implications which go far beyond their possible anti-inflationary applicability, it may be emphasized that some such measures would be absolutely necessary if we want to attain full employment and rapid economic growth and at the same time avoid inflation.

---

18. Harry G. Johnson, *Essays in Monetary Economics* (London, 1967), pp. 132-33.
19. Milton Friedman, "The Role of Monetary Policy," *American Economic Review* (March, 1969).

9. Causes of Inflation

As seen above, basically speaking, the inflationary pressures arise when money income and corresponding expenditure or demand increase without being accompanied by a corresponding increase in the supply of goods and services. In other words, inflation results from factors which give rise to 'excess demand'. Broadly speaking, excess demand may be caused by two sets of factors, *viz.*, (*i*) those which shift the demand upwards and (*ii*) those which shift the supply downwards. These two sets of factors are briefly described below.

10. Factors Causing an Upward Shift in Demand

Deficit Financing: In recent years, there has been a tendency, particularly in developing countries, to heavily resort to deficit financing to obtain funds for executing development plans. Deficit financing increases money in the hands of people and thereby increases demand for goods and services.

Increase in the Velocity of Money: This factor is particularly important during boom periods. The velocity of circulation of money increases on account of an increase in the marginal efficiency of capital or reduction in liquidity preference, or an increase in the propensity to consume.

Credit Expansion: The credit structure of a country is determined by the policy of the government as well as that of the commercial banks. The Central Bank of the country can cause an expansion of credit by lowering the bank rate or by purchasing government securities. Similarly, the commercial banks can expand credit by lowering their cash reserves; but they can do so only when there is demand for loans from borrowers. It may be pointed out that once the credit expands, as a result of either the policy of the government or the initiative of the commercial banks, it continues for a sufficiently long period of time.

Rapidly Increasing Public Expenditure: In recent years public expenditure has been growing fast, particularly because of increasing defence expenditure and expanding role of the state in economic activities; this considerably increases the demand for goods and services.

Expansion of Exports: An increase in exports would mean less available for domestic consumption. This would make the existing unchanged domestic demand excessive for the commodities whose exports increase and thus cause a rise in their prices.

Rapid Growth of Population: A rapidly growing population increases the demand for goods and services and thus pushes up their prices. To cite Prof. Coulborn, "If population increases rapidly, while the aggregate of money remains stable, the consequent rise in the velocity of circulation is likely to outweigh the countervailing decrease in the volume of money per head; further, a rapid increase of population may increase output less than proportionately—another factor tending to raise prices."[20]

War: This has been one of the most common causes of inflation. Financing of war leads to a considerable expansion in the supply of money. Further, it leads to a diversion of productive resources from the production of consumer goods to that of war materials and thus causes a shortage of consumer goods.

Trade Union Activities: The trade unions continuously agitate for higher wages, shorter hours of work, more holidays with pay and other amenities. In a democratic country, the government is often compelled to accept even unreasonable demands of the labourers. The increase in wages of the labourers and other amenities provided to them beyond the increase in their productivity raises the cost of production and hence prices. Further, increase in wage increases purchasing power in the hands of labourers and reduction in working hours leads to a decline in the volume of production. This adds to the rise in prices.

Excise and Sales Taxes: Increased taxation is generally disinflationary because it mops up the purchasing power of the public. But if taxes are levied on the production and sale of goods which can be shifted to consumers, the prices of such goods will rise and add to inflationary pressures.

International Factors: Inflation in one country may be transmitted to other countries through trade. When prices are rising abroad, the importing country has to pay higher and higher prices for its imports. The rise in the prices of imported goods leads to a sympathetic rise in the prices of goods produced within the country.

---

20. W.A.L. Coulborn, *A Discussion of Money*, p. 159.

Devaluation: Devaluation of the domestic currency increases the prices of imported goods. It stimulates foreign demand for export goods which raises their prices. Rise in the prices of imported goods and exported goods cause a rise in the prices of non-traded goods also.

11. Factors Causing a Downward Shift in Supply

Natural Calamities: They can take a number of forms like floods, earthquakes, epidemics etc. They decrease production and thereby lead to a rise in prices.

Stage of Production: If the production has reached a stage where the law of diminishing returns begins to operate, the cost of production and hence the prices would start rising.

Hoarding: During periods of rising prices, dealers as well as consumers have a tendency to hoard commodities which aggravates shortages.

Shortage of Factors of Production: Non-availability of certain factors like capital equipment, land, skilled labour, raw materials etc., make it difficult to expand production in response to an increase in demand and thus leads to shortages.

12. Inflation in an Underdeveloped Economy

Basically speaking, inflation arises owing to a gap between effective demand and output. Inflation is normally considered to be a post-full-employment phenomenon because so long as unemployed resources exist, increase in effective demand is expected to lead to an increase in output and employment rather than to a rise in the prices. Theoretically, inflation starts only after the full-employment stage is reached. But in actual practice, prices may start rising much before the full-employment is reached because of lack of perfect elasticity of supply of goods and services and because of other factors which assist in raising the cost of production. Keynes mentions the following factors which cause an inflationary situation before full-employment is reached.[21]

(*i*) Effective demand will not change in exact proportion to the money supply.

---

21. J.M. Keynes, *The General Theory of Employment, Interest and Money* (London, 1936), p. 296.

(*ii*) Since the resources are not homogeneous and as such not perfectly substitutable, the law of diminishing returns starts operating as the employment of resources gradually increases.

(*iii*) Since various factors are not perfect substitutes for each other, some commodities will reach a condition of inelastic supply, while there are still unemployed resources available for the production or other commodities.

(*iv*) The wage-unit will tend to rise before the full employment has been reached.

(*v*) The remunerations of the factors entering into marginal cost will not all change in the same proportion.

Because of the bottlenecks mentioned above at various levels in the structure of the economy, an increase in the supply of money and hence in demand has a tendency to lead to a rise in the price level before the full-employment stage is reached. In addition to these general bottlenecks, an underdeveloped economy is characterised by various other forms of bottlenecks which cause a relative rigidity in the supply of goods and thus lead to a sharper rise in prices. Important of these are briefly mentioned below:

(*i*) There exist several market imperfections which present an optimum allocation of resources and thereby extension of actual production frontier to the maximum possible frontier. The important market imperfections include imperfect knowledge, imperfect mobility, specificity of factors and imperfect divisibility of factors.

(*ii*) In advanced countries the existence of unemployment leads to increased output as a result of increased demand. In underdeveloped countries what exists is not unemployment but disguised unemployment or underemployment which does not lead to increased production with an increase in effective demand. To the extent supply does not respond to an increase in effective demand caused by monetary expansion, the prices would tend to rise.

Apart from the bottlenecks mentioned above, there are other factors which cause inflationary pressures in underdeveloped countries. Because of lack of other sources of financing development plans, resort has to be made to deficit financing. High priorities given to the production of capital goods in development plans lead to a shortage of consumer goods. Thus while money incomes increase leading to a rise in demand, the consumer goods become inadequate, which results in a general rise in the price level.

13. Inflation and Economic Development

There exists great controversy as to whether inflation promotes or retards economic development. Some economists, including Keynes, hold the opinion that inflation, in one form or the other, helps economic development. It is held that inflation helps mobilisation of resources by redistributing income and wealth away from wage recipients towards the profit-recipients. Since the marginal propensity to save of the profit-earners is much higher than that of the wage-earners, transfer of income from the latter to the former class increases the volume of savings which can profitably be invested by the entrepreneurial class in productive channels, thereby raising the rate of economic development. Keynes favours mild inflation on the ground that slowly rising prices create an optimistic atmosphere resulting in high profit expectation which stimulates investment. Maurice Dobb remarks, "Inducements are necessary for large-scale movements of labour and for increased supplies of foodstuffs and raw materials to be made available by the village for the town."[22] Prof. Kaldor also remarks, "a slow and steady rate of inflation provides a most powerful aid to the attainment of a steady rate of economic progress."[23] Prof. Robertson also favours a mild inflation for economic growth. Such a policy is particularly important in underdeveloped economies where a great part of the labour force is self-employed and price incentives (through mild inflation) assume greater importance than wage incentives (at least in the initial stages of breakthrough). Prof. Rostow believes that several 'take-off' processes have been assisted by inflation. Hamilton holds the view that inflation has been a powerful stimulant in a large number of historical instances and can perform a similar function in underdeveloped countries.

Many economists believe that a mild inflation is not necessarily an undesirable thing because the alternative to this would be unemployment and impaired economic growth. The argument is that since prices are flexible only in the upward direction in our

22. Maurice Dobb, *Some Aspects of Economic Development,* p. 48.
23. Nicholas Kaldor, "Economic Growth and Problem of Inflation," *Economica,* 1959.

present institutional set-up, resource allocation through the price system must operate through price increases in the sectors of the economy which are growing rather than through price decreases in the sectors which are stagnating. It is argued that since the monopoly power of unions and enterprises is such that price increases are inevitable, it is better for authorities not to adopt deflationary policies which might cause unemployment rather than a decline in the price level. Prof. Lewis believes that inflation for the purpose of creating useful capital is often ultimately self-terminating because sooner or later it would increase the supply of goods in the market.[24]

Some economists believe that inflation is a product of economic growth. Some inflation is considered to be unavoidable in the process of economic development. At least in the initial stages of development process, there is bound to be a time-lag between the increases in money incomes and the availability of consumption goods in the country and hence a rise in the price level. The inflationary pressures are considered to be almost certain if the planned investment exceeds the volume of real savings.

Another group of economists hold the view that inflation does not facilitate economic growth and, on the contrary, hinders the process of economic growth. Milton Friedman, for instance, completely disagrees with the policy of 'development through inflation.' He also holds the view that "inflation is not inevitable in the course of development."[25] He does not find much substance in the argument that inflation tends to stimulate development through its redistributive effects. No doubt, there were some circumstances in the past in which redistributive effects were favourable to development; but there is no guarantee that these favourable effects would operate in all cases.[26] The reason inflation had favourable effects in the past was that it was unexpected. The process of inflation was unanticipated because it was not planned by anybody. Friedman believes that favourable effects cannot be obtained by a deliberate expansion in the supply of money without its degenerating

---

24. W.A. Lewis, *The Theory of Economic Growth.*
25. Milton Friedman, *Inflation—Causes and Consequences* (Bombay, 1963), p. 17.
26. *Ibid.*, p. 13.

into hyperinflation. When the process of inflation is deliberate, many people would know about it and act in a way which prevents the occurrence of redistributive effects. Prof. Nurkse also observes that "the success of inflation as an instrument of capital formation depends largely on the degree to which rise in prices is unforeseen and unexpected. When a further rise in price is expected and seems certain, the velocity of circulation of money increases, saving gives place to dissaving and inflation loses its capital forming power."[27] Further, inflation "invites development, if any, only through manipulation of markets rather than efficient production." This is obvious from the deterrent effects of inflation on productive enterprise, increasing cost of development, depreciating real value of cash holdings, accumulation of investment in real estates, decreasing investment in the export sector, speculation and hoarding resulting from rising prices.[28]

The decline in the real value of money resulting from inflation destroys the saving habits of the people and places a premium on improvidence and careless spending. Inflation may not only obstruct the process of capital formation but may drive the available capital out of the country. During inflationary periods business skill and efficiency tends to be used for speculative purposes rather than for productive purposes. Rising prices lead to a decline in the demand for export-goods resulting in unemployment in the export industries and balance of payments difficulties.[29]

14. Effects of Inflation

Though inflation implies a general rise in the price level, this rise is not uniform throughout the economy. If the rate of increase in the prices of goods and services were uniform in all sectors of the economy, the relative position of the various earning groups would remain unchanged and as such the economic effects of inflation would be neutral. But in reality, during the inflationary process, the prices of different goods and services rise at different rates. This

27. Ragnar Nurkse, *League of Nations: Course and Control of Inflation*, p. 13.
28. Indian Merchants' Chamber, *Inflation in a Developing Economy*, 1961, p. 82.
29. Also see section on *Deficit Financing and Economic Development* in the chapter on Deficit Financing.

results in a change in the pattern of income distribution in the community which is the source of many evil effects normally attributed to inflation.

Inflation resulting from excess demand of the government in a state of national emergency, as during a war, amounts to a forced levy on the community and helps in the mobilisation of resources to meet the emergency by restricting civilian consumptions. From this special point of view, inflation is useful. In addition to this, it is claimed that inflation benefits two important classes of people in the community who form the backbone of the nation's economy, *viz.*, (*i*) farmers and (*ii*) entrepreneurs. It can easily be observed that both these classes of people gain from a rise in prices because they are primarily a debtor class. In an inflationary period, repayment of debt becomes easier because the real burden of debt falls with the rise in prices of goods and services. Farmers gain partly because the products which they sell are highly inflation-sensitive and partly because the costs which they incur in connection with their productive operations, such as interest charges, taxes, wages, etc. rise only to a small extent, at least in the early stages of inflation, in comparison with the prices of the product which they offer for sale. Businessmen gain from a similar lagging of costs behind prices. They also gain from an appreciation in the value of their inventories. It is claimed that an increase in the profits of the entrepreneurial class stimulates capital formation, helps in the drawing up of idle resources for economic utilisation and in expanding production to the maximum capacity of the economy.

Though the advantages mentioned above have some validity in the short period, but it cannot be disputed that ultimately inflation has harmful effects on the economy. The very forces which are helpful in stimulating capital formation start retarding investment after a stage is reached. A study[30] conducted by an economist of the International Monetary Fund points out that while no definite conclusions can be drawn, the evidence available broadly indicates that among the underdeveloped countries the rate of growth of the economy was higher when the rate of inflation was lower. In his

---

30. U. Tun Wai, "The Relation between Inflation and Economic Development," *International Monetary Fund Staff Papers,* October, 1959, p. 302.

study of the course of inflation in Europe in the nineteen twenties, professor Nurkse points out that the "success of inflation as an instrument of capital formation depends largely on the degree to which rise in prices is unforeseen and unexpected."[31] When a further rise in prices is expected and seems certain, velocity of circulation of money rises, saving gives place to dissaving and inflation loses its power of stimulating investment. Thereafter there is cumulative process of inflation.

The declining value of the money and the failure of the wage-level to adjust itself to the price level leaves the workers with a sense of frustration which impairs their incentives to work more with a view to earn more. Declining value of money also impairs the incentives to save and places a premium on improvidence and careless spending. Continued inflation or the knowledge that the government budgetary or monetary policy would maintain inflationary forces for long drives out capital from the country as happened in France and Germany at the close of the First World War. Thus, beyond a certain stage, inflation not only obstructs domestic capital accumulation but also drives available capital out of the country. Nor is the attitude and behaviour of the entrepreneurial class in an inflationary period favourable to increased production. Cost accounting which is an important instrument of measuring efficiency, loses its meaning when the value of money changes very frequently. There is a tendency to employ business skill and efficiency for speculative purposes rather than for productive purposes. The chances of earning windfall profit out of the rapidly rising prices of existing supplies encourage business community to indulge in hoarding and helps in the growth of black markets. When producers do not find much difficulty in transferring higher costs on to consumers, they have a tendency to be wasteful and lethargic. The transfer of income from the middle and lower income groups to higher income groups resulting from inflation leads to a decline in the aggregate consumption and thus generates instability.

During an inflationary period, the revenues of government fail to respond to the growing responsibilities of the state. The result is the starvation of developmental services like public works, education and public health, on which depends largely the growth and prosperity of the national economy.

---

31. League of Nations, *Course and Control of Inflation,* 1947, p. 6.

Inflation affects different classes of society against the sound maxims of social justice. Comparing inflation to robbery, C.N. Vakil states, "Both deprive the victim of some possession with the difference that the robber is visible, inflation is invisible: the robber's victim may be one or a few at a time, the victims of inflation are the whole nation; the robber may be dragged to a court of law, inflation is legal."[32]

The people worst hit by inflation are those who are least able to protect themselves. Inflation causes hardship to all who live on fixed incomes, *e.g.*, pensioners, widows, teachers, civil servants, factory workers etc. Among the workers, the worst sufferers are those who are ill-organised. Long and sustained inflation corrupts the foundation of society. It erodes saving and undermines the provision for sickness, education and old age. It undermines the incentive for hard work and thrift. The investors in equities gain while those who invest in fixed interest yielding bonds are adversely affected. Since most of the middle class investors choose fixed interest bearing securities, insurance and saving accounts, inflation adversely affects the small investors. Angell describes the sufferings of the middle class during the postwar German inflation as follows: "The group which suffered most from the inflation, however, was the group which was also least able to defend itself; the middle classes among the town-dwellers...composed largely of people with small fixed incomes, such as salaried officials and clerks, recipients of pensions, and little investors living on interest and rent of whom the latter group were hit especially hard by the government control of city rentals—they were precisely the group most exposed to the evil consequences of currency depreciation, while they lacked both the knowledge and the opportunity to combat it."[33] Kemmerer makes similar observations about the impact of inflation on the middle class. "The middle class, however, which by hard work and thrift has built up a fund of savings to educate its children and to provide a livelihood for times of sickness and for old age, finds itself in a desperate situation in a time of serious inflation. The cost of living rises disproportionately to income, savings are wiped out, and hard work, independence, and thrift seem to be false goods. Under

32. C.N. Vakil, *Financial Burden of War on India*.

33. J.W. Angell, *The Recovery of Germany* (New Haven, 1929), p. 38.

such conditions the middle class is all too often overwhelmed by a sense of futility and desperation."[34] Thus the people worst hit by inflation are those belonging to the middle class who forms the backbone of modern democracy. The hyperinflation in Germany, Austria, Poland and France after the First World War completely ruined the middle class.

Though businessman, debtors and producer gain from continuously rising prices, creditors are hit hard. The creditors are affected adversely because the purchasing power of the money which is returned to them is much lower than that of the money which they had lent.

Although slowly rising prices simulate economic activity and increase the volume of employment, but if they start rising fast, they may lead to depression and cause widespread unemployment. To cite William McChesney Martin Jr., "If inflation is allowed to pursue its course it feeds upon itself in such a way that, when the inevitable correction finally comes, unemployment will be that much worse. It should not be difficult to see how inflation leads to unemployment. The danger becomes manifest when, as costs go up, it becomes increasingly hard to pass those costs along to the customer in the form of price increases, and it becomes increasingly easy to misjudge or miscalculate the market. Then for the first time volume dips, there is price-profit squeeze, and, at some point the profit-squeeze leads to a cutback in investment, income and production. The cutback in production leads to a cutback in employment."

Inflation makes business planning and long-term investment risky. It upsets calculations about depreciation costs and profits and thereby poses a threat to the solvency and sound growth of business. It deprives the economy of the benefits of a stable unit of account and store of value. It raises interest rates and creates a chaos in the money market. It causes disequilibrium in the balance of payments.

Inflation lowers the moral standards of the people, particularly of business community and government officials. Black market, bribery and corruption become rampant. When people are robbed of their savings accumulated through hard work, they lose all

34. Edwin Walter Kemmerer, *The ABC of Inflation*, p. 94.

confidence in the government. Andrew D. While depicts the impact of inflation on public moral at the time of fiat money inflation in France during the French Revolution as follows: "...with such masses of money and with such uncertainty as to its future value, the ordinary motives for saving and care are diminished, and a loose luxury spreads throughout the country. A still worse out-growth was the increase of speculation and gambling. In the leading French cities now arose a luxury and licence which was a greater evil than the plundering that ministered to it. In the country the gambling spirit spread more and more.... Nor was this reckless and corrupt spirit confined to businessmen; it began to break out in official circles, and public men who a few years before, had been thought above all possibility of taint became luxurious, reckless, cynical and finally corrupt."[35]

A severe inflation not only disrupts the economy of the country but also sometimes leads to social and political upheavals. The hyperinflation in Germany was one of the important factors which led to the fall of Dr. Cuno's liberal government and coming into power of Hitler. Constantino Bresciani Turroni beautifully describes the social and political consequences of inflation as follows: "The depreciation of the mark of 1914-23, which is the subject of this work, is one of the outstanding episodes in the history of the twentieth century. It was the most colossal thing of its kind in history; and next probably to the Great War itself, it must bear responsibility for many of the political and economic difficulties of our generation. It destroyed the wealth of the more solid elements in German society; and it left behind a moral and economic disequilibrium, apt breeding ground for the disasters which have followed. Hitler is the foster-child of the inflation. The financial convulsions of the great depression were, in part at least, the product of the distortions of the system of international borrowing and lending to which its ravages had given rise.

If we are to understand correctly the present position of Europe, we must not neglect the study of the great German inflation. If we are to plan for greater stability in the future, we must learn to avoid the mistakes from which it sprang."[36]

---

35. Andrew D. While, *Fiat Inflation in France,* pp. 27-28.
36. Constantino Bresciani, *The Economics of Inflation,* p. 5.

15. Anti-inflationary Measures

The measures for controlling inflation can be divided into three broad categories: (*i*) monetary measures, (*ii*) fiscal measures, (*iii*) direct controls and other measures.

Monetary Measures: The central bank of the country can curb inflation by restricting the supply of money and credit with the help of three important weapons available to it, *viz.*, (*i*) bank rate policy, (*ii*) open market operations, and (*iii*) varying the reserve requirements of the member banks. Monetary measures, however, are not very effective in underdeveloped countries lacking a well-developed and integrated money market. In underdeveloped countries, selective credit control is preferable to the general credit control. Care should be taken that the credit control measures do not restrict the supply of credit for development projects.

Not to talk of underdeveloped countries, monetary policy has not been very effective in curbing inflation even in advanced countries. Prof. Hansen assigns monetary policy only a secondary role in controlling inflation. It cannot be the primary measure. No doubt, a sufficiently sharp reduction in the supply of the money may quickly end an inflation. But stopping an inflationary development simply by reducing the quantity of money may involve dangerous consequences. To cite Hansen, "moderately used, monetary policy courts the failure of ineffectiveness; pushed to the needed fanatical extremes, it courts disaster."[37]

Fiscal Measures: The limitations of monetary measures make it important to make use of fiscal measures to curb inflation. Fiscal measures refer to taxation, government spending and public borrowing. Government should try to mop up through taxation as much purchasing power as possible without adverse effects on incentives to enterprise and invest. In underdeveloped countries, there exists considerable evasion of taxes. Measures should be taken to check this evasion.

Today, the government accounts for a considerable portion of the total expenditure. It should cut down all its unnecessary and wasteful expenditure and try to work in the most economical manner.

---

37. A.H. Hansen, *Monetary Theory and Fiscal Policy* (New York, 1949), p. 163.

Private savings have a strong disinflationary effect. The government should take measures to promote private savings. A strong savings drive reduces the spendable incomes of the people without involving harmful effects of the type associated with higher taxation.

Further, public debt should be managed in such a manner that the supply of money in the country is controlled. The government should avoid paying back any of its past loans during inflationary periods so as to prevent an increase in the circulation of money.

Voluntary saving schemes may, however, be of limited success, particularly among poor classes who may not be able to avoid the temptation of spending their increased incomes on goods which they could not afford to buy for long. Keynes, therefore, suggested a programme of compulsory saving like "deferred pay" or "forced savings" to control inflation. "Deferred pay" implies that a part of the pay of the workers is credited to their savings account and would not be available for spending so long as the inflation lasts. Such compulsory saving schemes are expedient during war-time, or during post-war hyper-inflation, but are not practicable in peace time, particularly in democratic societies.

Direct Controls and Other Measures: Many countries have resorted to price control and rationing for checking a rise in prices, particularly, in case of essential commodities. Rationing and price control, however, have not been very effective in underdeveloped countries because of a lack of competent and honest machinery to administer these. These have often led to the disappearance of goods from the market, black market, bribery and corruption. Keynes objects to price control on the ground that it fails to bring about equilibrium between purchasing power and available output.[38] Further, it is also detrimental to the consumer's sovereignty, freedom and welfare. Prof. Kurihara observes that when administrative difficulties in enforcing price control and legal restrictions against black marketing are considered, price control becomes dim by the side of monetary-fiscal policy.[39] Keynes also objects to rationing because it "involves a great deal of waste, both

38. J.M. Keynes, *How to Pay for the War*, p. 57.

39. Kenneth K. Kurihara, *Monetary Theory and Public Policy* (London, 1956), p. 100.

of resources and of enjoyment."[40] Kurihara, however, suggests that "a sensible progress of rationing should aim at diverting consumption from particular articles whose supply is below normal rather than at controlling aggregate consumption."[41]

Measures should be taken to expand the production of necessary goods at the expense of luxury goods because a shortage of the former type of goods raises the prices much more rapidly than a shortage of the latter type of goods.

Control of wages has often been suggested to check a wage-price spiral. During galloping inflation it may be necessary to apply a wage-profit freeze. Control of wages and profits keeps down disposable income and, hence, the level of effective demand for goods and services.

Efforts should be made to obtain as much foreign capital as possible. Investment financed by foreign capital is less inflationary.

In some cases, relaxation of restrictions on imports may lighten inflationary pressures by increasing the supply of essential goods available in the country. Similar effects may be obtained by a curtailment of exports. But increase in imports and curtailment of exports are possible only if the country is having a very easy balance of payments position.

Every effort should be made to increase production. Preference should be given to investment in those projects which start yielding production earlier.

It is now widely believed that inflation can easily be controlled in the initial stages but when it goes beyond a certain stage, it assumes such dimensions that it becomes very difficult to control it. A hyper-inflation, for instance, can be removed only by replacing the old currency by a new currency.

Inflation is a hydra-headed monster and should be fought with many weapons. Dependence on a single measure may not help much in curbing inflation.

---

40. Keynes, *op. cit.*, pp. 51-54.

41. Kurihara, *op. cit.*, p. 101.

Monetary Policy

32

1. Meaning and Importance

Monetary policy refers to measures designed to influence the cost and availability of money with a view to influence the working of the economy. In other words, monetary policy consists of all those measures which help the central banking authority of a country to manipulate the various instruments of credit control. In developing economies monetary policy plays an important role in accelerating development by influencing the cost and availability of credit, by controlling inflation and by maintaining balance of payments equilibrium. As development gains momentum, an appropriate monetary policy becomes all the more important to provide an elastic credit supply to meet the requirements of growing volume of transactions, a rapidly increasing population and an expanding monetized sector.

2. Institutional Setting of Monetary Policy in Underdeveloped Countries

Underdeveloped countries have some institutional characteristics which influence the potential role, scope, and effectiveness of monetary policy. Money does not play the same pervasive role that it does in economically advanced countries. A substantial portion of the agricultural production, which forms a large bulk of the aggregate output of most underdeveloped countries, is generally of a subsistence rather than market character. In many rural areas in these countries, barter transactions rather than purchase and sale predominate. Thus an important part of the aggregate economic activity of underdeveloped countries is often outside the scope of monetary policy.

In view of their heavy dependence on exports, externally-generated fluctuations play an important role in the economic life of the majority of underdeveloped countries. Since their exports consist mainly of primary products subject to wide fluctuations in world demand and prices, underdeveloped countries have a tendency to experience wide externally-generated fluctuations in their external reserves, money supply and money incomes. The primary changes in money supply associated with such fluctuations are not easily subject to the direct control of the central bank nor can they easily be offset by central bank action on that part of the money supply which is so subject.

In view of strong development drives, inadequate tax systems and narrow markets in government securities, changes in the volume of central bank credit to the government and its agencies are often another important cause of changes in the money supply. The central bank may not be able to control such credit if the government insists on undue recourse to the central bank to finance its expenditures.

The central bank can exert its most direct influence mainly on that portion of the money supply which is generated by the commercial bank's credit operations with the private sector of the economy, which is normally a relatively small portion of the money supply in most underdeveloped countries. Thus if the money supply tends to rise unduly as a result of large externally induced acquisitions of exchange reserves of large central bank-financed budget deficits, it would perhaps be too much to expect the central bank to be able to contract commercial bank credit to the private sector, which will be actually increasing to demand for accommodations at a time when the commercial banks have a large amount of reserves with which to lend. The maximum the central bank may be able to do may be no more than preventing the commercial bank from adding further to the money supply on the basis of these additional reserves, *i.e.*, prevent a secondary expansion of the money supply. But when an inflationary expansion of the money supply originates from an undue increase in commercial bank credit to the private sector, the central bank should be in a position to restrict such expansion.

Similar difficulties would arise when there is an externally-induced decline in exchange reserves, the money supply and money incomes as a result of a decline in world demand for the country's exports. The maximum the central bank may be able to do is to prevent the commercial banks from bringing about a secondary contraction in the money supply and additional deflationary pressures. If it were possible in such a situation to induce same credit expansion to the private sector, the drain on foreign exchange reserves would tend to be increased, particularly because of a high marginal propensity to import characteristic of most underdeveloped countries. The extent to which such counter-cyclical action could be pursued would depend upon the amount of exchange reserves that had previously been accumulated and upon whether or not and how far imports and other payments abroad were officially restricted.

In most underdeveloped countries, the banking habit is not widespread. Banking covers only a small portion of the total population. Bank services are used mainly by traders, businessmen and government entities. Some 50 per cent or more of the money supply normally consists of currency in circulation. An important result of this high degree of preference for currency is to restrict the deposit-creating capacity of the commercial banks on the basis of any given accretion of reserves, because any given increase in bank loans and investments leads to a significant drain of currency into circulation thereby depleting bank reserves and tending to reduce the ability of the banks further to expand their credit operations. This factor may be of some help to monetary authorities at times when bank reserves are changing rapidly and cannot easily be controlled.

In underdeveloped countries, money markets and particularly capital markets are either virtually non-existent or are of limited scope. There are hardly any organised markets in bills or commercial paper. Since commercial loans are normally made on over-draft basis, there is often lack of discountable paper. The markets in short and long-term government securities as well as in corporate stocks are generally narrow. These factors limit the scope and effectiveness of central bank open-market operations and also to some extent of discount operations.

Since developed money and capital markets are absent, the interest rate structure in underdeveloped countries is largely unintegrated and over a major portion of the economy interest rates are relatively insensitive to the actions of the monetary authorities. Even within given sectors or localities of the market there is often a wide variety of interest rates because of wide differences in the type and quality of risk or because of the forces of custom and tradition. The gap betbeen interest rates is particularly wide in the so-called organised and unorganised sectors of the money market. Interest rates play a lesser role than they do in more developed countries in influencing the volume and direction of investment. The availability of credit factor is likely to be more important, relative to the cost factor, than it is in more developed countries.

In most underdeveloped countries there is a marked lack of balance in the allocation of commercial bank credit. Commercial banks, largely because of their traditional concern for a very high degree of liquidity, tend to concentrate heavily on short-term loans to finance foreign trade, domestic commerce, inventory holdings and related short-term transactions. Such loans are generally more profitable than other types of lending. Loans for productive purposes to industry and agriculture, and particularly medium and long term loans, normally form only a very small part of bank portfolios. Commercial banking facilities are concentrated mainly in urban centres. There is a tendency to favour established concerns over new ones, and large concerns over small ones. Branches of foreign banks, which play an important role in the banking structure of underdeveloped countries, concentrate their activities mainly on servicing the foreign-trade sector of the economy.

As a consequence of these banking habits and of a lack of "credit-worthiness," large sections of the population, particularly farmers and small businessmen, cannot obtain credit through normal banking channels and have to depend largely on moneylenders, merchants, and lenders cannot create money, they can affect the income-velocity of money by influencing its rate of turnover and by providing money-substitutes, *e.g.*, open-book credits. They can thus influence to some extent the aggregate volume of spending and the level of economic activity but by and large they are outside the reach of the monetary authorities.

Commercial banks in most underdeveloped countries have a tendency to maintain the ratios of their reserves to deposit liabilities well in excess of the legal minima, where such are imposed. A substantial portion of any increment of reserves, over and above that needed for legal requirements, tends to be held idle. This is another factor, along with the large internal and external drains mentioned earlier, tending to keep down the coefficient of multiple credit expansion. This tendency to maintain relatively large excess reserves reflects factors like the lack of an adequate supply of short-term liquid assets which would serve as suitable secondary reserves, the volatility of externally dependent underdeveloped countries, the susceptibility of the banks to large and sudden withdrawals of currency and the absence in many cases of a long-standing tradition of discounting at or borrowing from the central bank.

Since the commercial banks in many of the underdeveloped countries do not discount at or borrow from the central bank to any great extent or on a frequent or regular basis, the discount mechanism as an instrument of credit control is weakened. Further, as the commercial banks tend to allow their holdings of excess reserves to undergo substantial fluctuations, the precise extent of their response to any given change in their reserves tends to be less predictable than in the more developed countries where banks normally keep relatively small excess reserves. Thus additional limitations are imposed on the effective use of the traditional instruments of credit control.

The foregoing discussion shows that the monetary policy is confronted with special problems and limitations in underdeveloped countries which lie deep in the institutional structures of such countries.

3. Objectives of Monetary Policy

The fundamental objectives of monetary policy in underdeveloped countries are the same as in developed countries, *viz.*, internal financial stability, high and rising levels of per capita income, and external payments balance. But there is a marked difference in emphasis on these objectives in the two sets of countries. In developed countries primary emphasis is laid on the avoidance of inflation and deflation. In contrast, in underdeveloped countries the promotion of economic growth tends to overshadow all other objectives of national economic policy. In fact, in their attempts to attain a higher rate of economic growth, many times underdeveloped countries have tended to sacrifice the goals of internal and external stability.

The central bank should try to ensure that development takes place within a framework of reasonable financial stability, *i.e.*, the aggregate spending does not exceed the available real resources at current prices.

Internal financial stability would help, though cannot guarantee maintenance of external payments stability. External payments stability would in turn facilitate the process of economic development.

4. Instruments of Credit Control

The principal instruments of credit control are: (*i*) open market operations, (*ii*) discount or bank rate, (*iii*) maximum legal reserve ratio, and (*iv*) selective credit controls. We have seen earlier that in view of the institutional setting in underdeveloped countries, open market operations and discount operations are not very effective instruments of credit control.

Changes in reserve requirements may often involve serious inequities since they uniformaly strike at banks with large and with small excess reserves and at banks which are expanding credit rapidly and at those which are not. An alternative method would be the imposition in periods of rapidly rising bank reserves of very high supplementary reserve requirements against deposits, while leaving the regular requirements unaffected. This would avoid the inequities mentioned above and also strike more directly at the root of the problem.

Selective credit controls are distinguishable from the general instruments of credit control in that they are directed towards particular *uses* of credit and not towards the total volume of credit. A general restriction of the volume of credit is sometimes unnecessary, or may be even harmful for the economy. The selective system restricts, credit for activities which are not useful for the economy. At the same time it ensures that adequate credit is made available for essential and useful activities. Selective credit controls, which have a more direct influence on the credit situation, often show better results when they are applied at the appropriate time and in the appropriate manner. Experience shows that their effectiveness is substantially increased when they are used together with other more general methods.

5. Monetary Policy and Economic Development

In an underdeveloped country cheap money policy would lower the rate of interest and thereby stimulate investment. In case it leads to misdirection of investment, the central bank can apply selective credit controls so as to direct investment into desirable channels. In an underdeveloped economy, private investment may not be forthcoming in adequate amounts and as such public investment on a large scale may become necessary. Cheap money policy would promote public investment by keeping the burden of interest on public borrowing low.

Some economists have suggested that the underdeveloped countries should follow a policy of high interest rates. According to them, a high rate of interest would limit the allocation of scarce capital only to the most productive uses and avoid wasteful use of resources. It would also serve as an effective anti-inflationary measure by restricting undesirable investment and stimulating saving. A policy of high interest rates, however, does not appear to be in the interest of the underdeveloped countries. No doubt high interest rates may check inflation by curtailing investment, it is not desirable for an underdeveloped country to resort to a general restriction of investment just for controlling inflation. On the contrary, a mild doze of inflation generates forced savings which can be utilised for purposes of investment. A better and more effective method of checking investments in undesirable directions would be to resort to direct controls and control over capital issues. Further qualitative methods of credit control can be so handled as to ensure reasonable control over investment without producing any adverse effect on investment in desirable directions. As regards the argument of stimulating saving, it may be mentioned that the volume of saving depends more on the capacity to save and the facilities for savings than on the rate of interest. Further, as already seen, an increase in the rate of interest will lead to a decline in the volume of savings in case of people who save with the objective of having a certain specified amount of income in years to come. A high rate of interest can, of course, be used as a shock tactic. When speculation in goods and securities becomes ripe and gets beyond control by other means, the rate of interest may be employed for pricking the bubble.

The monetary policy can influence economic growth by helping to create favourable environments for saving and investment. Past history tells us that rising prices have a tendency to discourage saving. When the money is expected to depreciate in value, people have a tendency to spend it rather than saving it. This is particularly the case when the prices are rising very fast. Inflation is a tax on cash balances. Stable prices, in contrast, promote savings which are the principal source of investible funds.

The monetary policy can perhaps be most useful in shaping the character of investment. This will, of course, depend on the range of credit institutions that exist and the forms of credit controls that are adopted. In most of the underdeveloped countries the commercial banks provide only short-term credit which is primarily used for carrying inventories, purchasing land and real estate, or financing the production of export crops. The banks are reluctant to provide medium-term and long-term finance on the required scale and as such there is a shortage of finance for public utilities, for purchase of raw materials, and for manufacturing in general. To induce banks to provide more medium-term and long-term loans of a productive nature, the government may make appropriate guarantees or provide rediscounting facilities. Joint loans by commercial banks and state-managed development finance institutions can be another method.

Selective credit controls can be used to influence the pattern of investment and production. By differentiating between the cost and availability of credit to different sectors, selective credit controls can influence the allocation of credit and thereby the pattern of development. This selectivity can be introduced in credit policy by directly stipulating the loans that can be made, the amounts, the rates of interest, the duration, the type that is not desirable, the amount of collateral, and other provisions. Alternatively, if the central bank has adequate power of controls over the commercial banks, such controls may be exercised selectively so as to indirectly influence the behaviour of the banks; rediscount rates, for instance, may vary according to the type of loan, or some selective exceptions may be made on reserve requirements.[1]

A developing country has a tendency to get into balance of payments difficulties. In such a situation, in addition to exercising direct controls on foreign exchange, the monetary authority should help in improving the balance of payments position by using traditional methods of control like raising the bank rate, etc.

---

1. I.G. Patel, "Selective Credit Controls in Underdeveloped Economies," *International Monetary Fund Staff Papers* (September, 1954) pp. 76-77.

The role of monetary policy should not, however, be overestimated. As an instrument of promoting capital formation, monetary policy is not as effective as the fiscal policy. An easy money policy makes credit more readily available but this credit will not be utilised unless profit expectations are sufficiently high. Moreover, such a policy will lead to inflationary pressures which may harm the process of economic development.

To permit the use of monetary policy, the underdeveloped countries must first improve their currency and credit system. There is the need for banks and financial institutions which will increase credit facilities and channel actual and potential voluntary savings into productive uses. At present the credit system is limited to providing credit for large estates, plantations and foreign traders. Adequate credit facilities are not available for peasants, small industry and small traders. There is the need to extend commercial banks and to introduce savings banks, co-operative savings societies and mutual societies. The need is particularly urgent in rural areas.